AMONG THE INDIANS OF GUIANA

Plate 1.

A Macusi Indian in full dancing dress.

AMONG THE INDIANS OF GUIANA

BEING

SKETCHES CHIEFLY ANTHROPOLOGIC

FROM THE INTERIOR OF

BRITISH GUIANA

By

EVERARD F. IM THURN, M.A. OXON.

WITH 53 ILLUSTRATIONS
AND A MAP

DOVER PUBLICATIONS, INC.
NEW YORK

This Dover edition, first published in 1967, is an
unabridged and unaltered republication of the work
originally published by Kegan Paul, Trench and
Co., in 1883.

The frontispiece and Plates V and VIII, which
appeared in full color in the original edition, are
here reproduced in black and white.

Library of Congress Catalog Card Number: 66-30384

Manufactured in the United States of America
Dover Publications, Inc.
180 Varick Street
New York, N. Y. 10014

TO

TOM COTTINGHAM EDWARDS-MOSS

FAMOUS AS AN OARSMAN BUT DESERVING
OF FAR GREATER FAME AS THE POSSESSOR, IN MOST
UNUSUAL DEGREE, OF THOSE RARE AND EXCELLENT QUALITIES
WHICH MAKE A MAN AN ENTIRELY HELPFUL AND
PLEASANT TRAVELLING COMPANION

THESE RESULTS OF TRAVEL ARE DEDICATED

BY HIS FRIEND

EVERARD F. IM THURN

POMEROON RIVER
  BRITISH GUIANA

PREFACE.

In July 1877 I first landed in British Guiana, and on Christmas Day, 1879, the intermediate two and a half years having been spent, in about equal proportion, in wandering among the Indians and in the chief town of the colony, I left the country, as I then thought, for ever.

During the following two years, spent in England, whenever there came a perfectly fine day, whether in spring, summer, autumn, or in winter, and whenever I was able to spend those too rare opportunities of perfect life in wandering over down-country, or through English lanes and woods, or by that ever pleasant river which runs past Oxford town, then I felt that the unspeakable pleasure of such a day surpassed by far all that the days, and all that the years, however pleasant, which a man may spend in the tropics can afford. But when, very much more often, gloomy days had to be endured, then my thoughts invariably turned westward, and I longed to be once more among the deep shadows and broken lights of the gigantic tropical forests, on the sunlit waters of the broad rivers, or on the rolling, limitless savannahs, among which I had learned to know the larger and more free ways of Nature. And so it happened that, two days before the Christmas of 1881, I once more came to Guiana.

During, and immediately after, my first visit to the colony, I had at various times and in various newspapers published disconnected sketches of my travels and, especially, of experiences among the Red men. These sketches very soon passing out of print, and there being among my papers much similar but unpublished matter, I, when finally settled, as I thought, in England, set to work to weave this material into a general description of the colony in all its aspects. Those who have tried a like task will understand how often I found myself in want of further information on almost every successive point. And so it happened that the work was not quite well enough patched together, was certainly not satisfactorily done, when I quite unexpectedly found myself about to return to the colony of which I was writing. Then I put away my papers and determined to wait for further experience.

But certain papers on anthropological subjects among those which had already been published had attracted some attention, more perhaps than they deserved; and it was exactly these which were in a most finished condition. I therefore re-wrote and added to them, and now publish them in this volume, together with a few chapters descriptive of the country where dwell the Red men of whom my story more especially tells.

I ought to add that the substance of the chapter on

Indian religion, and of that part of another chapter which deals with stone-implements, has already appeared in the 'Journal of the Anthropological Institute'; that the two first chapters in the present volume are re-written from a paper read by me before the Royal Geographical Society; and that the chapter on plant life appeared almost in its present form in the 'Gardener's Chronicle.'

Most men like to record in their prefaces the names of those who have helped them in their work; but were I to allow myself this pleasure with any freedom I should far exceed all reasonable limits. I must, however, make mention, among the friends who have helped me in England, of Mr. E. B. Tylor and Mr. A. W. Franks, and also of the authorities at Kew Gardens; nor can I pass without mention, among those, dwellers in Guiana, to whom I am indebted for services directed toward the same end, Mr. W. H. Campbell, who, but that the accuracy of his scientific knowledge and the deficiency of his years deny, might, in all other respects, be regarded as the proverbial 'oldest inhabitant' of the colony; or Mr. N. Darnell Davis, a true West Indian *bibliophile*; or Mr. James Thomson, whose kindness, both as editor successively of the two newspapers in which most of my sketches appeared, and as my informant on many points; or Mr. G. S. Jenman, the official botanist, whose botanical knowledge of Guiana is in exceeding proportion to the comparative shortness of his experience there. Lastly, but by no means least, I here record my gratitude to the lady friend who drew for this book two of the coloured plates as well as two of the smaller uncoloured illustrations.

As regards the other illustrations, the coloured figure of a new bird (*Agelœus imthurni*, Sclater) was prepared for me under the kind superintendence of Mr. P. L. Sclater ; the Royal Geographical Society has been good enough to supply the map ; the Anthropological Institute, with equal kindness, has lent a plate of stone-implements and one small cut which were engraved in illustration of my papers published in its Journal ; the engravings of scenery and figures were prepared from photographs taken for me ; and the figures of Indian implements, etc., and of rock engravings, are from my own sketches.

EVERARD F. IM THURN.

POMEROON RIVER, BRITISH GUIANA.

CONTENTS.

CHAPTER I.

A JOURNEY IN THE INTERIOR.

PAGE

CHAPTER II.

A JOURNEY IN THE INTERIOR (*continued*).

CHAPTER III.

THE KAIETEUR FALL AND RORAIMA.

CHAPTER XVIII.

FOLK-LORE.

CHAPTER XIX.

INDIAN ANTIQUITIES.

LIST OF ILLUSTRATIONS.

———◆◇◆———

PLATES.

WOODCUTS.

AMONG THE INDIANS OF GUIANA

CHAPTER I.

A JOURNEY IN THE INTERIOR.

Outline Sketch of the Interior—Methods of Travelling—Bartica Grove—
Moraballi—A Creek—Hauling the Canoes up the Rapids—Moë—Night
in the Forest—Scenery—Half-bred Brazilians—Paiwarikaira—A Peai-
man's Vengeance—Healthiness of the Interior—Aretaka—A Burning
Mora-tree—Magic Sticks—Apooterie—Up the Roopoonooni—Scenery—
Kaboori-flies — Stopped by Sand-banks — A New Crew—Quartama—A
Pretty Pond—Pirara Landing.

HE who would see the beauty and the great, though unde-
veloped capabilities of the only English part of the continent
of South America, must leave behind him the flat and swampy
coastland of Guiana, and, passing up wide rivers and through
vast forests, reach the magnificent and wide savannahs, inter-
sected by the rugged mountain ridges which lie on the furthest
limits of the colony, and stretch away into the interior of the
continent.   In so doing, the traveller will have to encounter
many difficulties and some hardships ; but, on the other hand,
his travels will be through a land the marvellous beauty of
which will more than recompense his pains, and where new objects will occur at every turn to draw his thoughts away from all
discomforts.   Nor have many travellers yet been before him ;
so that, though he will have the labour of making his own
path, this will be counterbalanced by the pleasure of visiting
untrodden ground.

   The country may be said to consist of four tracts, lying
one beyond the other, parallel to the coast-line.   Of these
only the outermost or sugar tract, which lies nearest to the

sea-coast, is at present cultivated and inhabited to any considerable extent. Next to this is the timber tract, from which alone timber has as yet been remuneratively brought to market. This extends toward the interior as far as the lowest cataracts on the various rivers. It is at present impossible to cut timber profitably beyond these cataracts, owing to the difficulty which there would be in carrying any cut beyond that to market; so that an imaginary line, roughly parallel to the sea-coast, and cutting each of the great rivers at their lowest cataracts, marks the further limit from the coast of this tract. This part of the country is only very sparingly inhabited by a few wood-cutters, white men and black, and by a few Indians.

The two remaining tracts are entirely uninhabited except by widely scattered Indians of four or five different tribes. The forest tract immediately succeeds the timber tract; and lastly, furthest from the coast, lies the savannah tract. The former of these is everywhere covered by dense forests, as yet untouched by the woodcutter, and consisting largely of the two most valuable trees of the colony—greenheart (*Nectandra rodiœi*) and mora (*Mora excelsa*). The land in all these three tracts is generally low, flat and swampy, though in the forest tract the level is occasionally broken by sloping hills, by solitary mountains, and even by low and unimportant ranges.

The last of the tracts is formed by the savannah of the interior. This must be distinguished from the meadows, also called savannahs, of the coast and forest tracts. Nearly all the small tributary streams of those regions rise in treeless marshes, which are under water during a large part of the year; and these are called savannahs. Again, along the banks of the Berbice and Corentyn rivers, often not far from the sea, there are considerable patches of open grass-land; and these, too, are called savannahs. But the chief savannah, that which forms the savannah tract, is of all the land of British Guiana farthest from the sea; it borders on the Brazils, from which it is only separated by the Cotinga and Takootoo rivers; and it is continued without any significant interruption into the great grass-plain which occupies so much of the interior of South America. Our share of this large meadow is about 14,000 square miles in extent. On it stand the only considerable mountains of British Guiana.

There are no roads in the colony except that which runs along the coast. But four great rivers, the Essequibo, the Demerara, the Berbice, and the Corentyn, run, nearly parallel to each other, from the interior to the sea; and into these pass many tributary streams, often of considerable size. The four main rivers are the high roads, and their tributaries, together with a few Indian tracks through the forest, perhaps hardly discernible to an unpractised eye, are the cross roads, along which all travelling within the forest region must be done by canoe or on foot. When once the savannahs are reached, it becomes possible to travel either, as before, along the rivers or by walking. It was up the largest of the rivers—the Essequibo—that I made my way in 1878 on to the savannah, over which I passed to the remote edge of the colony and on into Brazilian territory.

To give some account of the interior of Guiana is a necessary preliminary of my task. On each of my journeys I wrote down day by day the story of my travels. These diaries might, therefore, be transcribed with hardly any alteration. But such a diary, however interesting to the traveller himself and to his friends, and however many interesting facts it may contain, must always be tedious to the general reader. On the other hand, it is very difficult to give a description of a comparatively unknown land without using some such thread, on which to string the facts, as is afforded by a journal. And this is in a special degree true of the interior of British Guiana; for all that is known about it amounts but to a very considerable number of disconnected facts. I shall, therefore, use the diary of one of my journeys as a thread on which will be strung all pertinent facts derived either from my own experiences or from those of previous travellers in the same region.

A line of steamers, largely subsidised by the Government,
runs from Georgetown to the Berbice on the one hand, and
to the Essequibo on the other; and smaller steamers run
twice in each week up the Essequibo, the Demerara, and the
Berbice. These steamers are almost the only means yet attempted of opening up the colony. The small steamer runs
up the Essequibo for a distance of about thirty-five miles from
the mouth, partly for the convenience of the few who travel
in that direction, but chiefly for Government purposes, the
penal settlement of the colony being situated on the Mazeruni,
a large tributary of the Essequibo. It was by this latter
steamer that I reached the outskirts of civilisation, at Bartica
Grove, which stands at the junction of the Mazeruni with the
Essequibo.

Leaving Georgetown early in the morning, we passed for
two hours along the coast, and then ran into the Essequibo.
On board was a most heterogeneous and picturesque crowd
of East Indians, Chinese, Indians, Negroes, together with
Portuguese and a few other white men. Nearly every individual of this crowd travelled with a strange assortment of lug-
gage, varying from a bedstead or waggon to a pair of live fowls
or a parrot. On either side of the river the banks were low
and swampy, densely covered with courida bushes (*Avicennia
nitida*), mangroves (*Rhizophora mangal*), and palm-trees.
In the evening, about four o'clock, we reached Bartica Grove.

Bartica Grove, once a flourishing mission station, is now
reduced to a few wooden huts, used as stores, a church recently half-restored from a most ruinous condition, a few
small living houses, and some timber-sheds. These latter are
picturesque buildings, consisting of a few upright posts supporting roofs of withered palm-leaves. Under their eaves
colonies of gigantic green spiders, as large as thrush's eggs,
watch their webs, undisturbed from year's end to year's end.
The whole sleepy, beautiful village lies under the shade of an
avenue of large mango-trees. From this avenue the view
riverward is of an enormous stretch of water; the view land-
ward is of a tangled shrubbery of flowering bushes, from

which rise groups of graceful palms, and is bounded in the distance by the edge of the forest. The ditches and paths in the village are choked by great masses of maidenhair ferns and silver-backed gymnograms.

The decaying village is now chiefly inhabited by so-called 'river-men.' These are idle negroes and half-castes who make a living on the timber-grants, or as best they can. There are also a few inhabitants of a better kind, chiefly store-keepers. As many of the river-men have had considerable practice in passing the falls which so greatly obstruct the rivers of the country, these men have generally been employed as boat-hands by travellers into the interior. They are, however, as I had found on a previous occasion, an unmanageable and disagreeable set, and it is, therefore, far pleasanter to employ only Indians, who are not only much more easily managed, but also—and this is a most important consideration to a traveller who must make companions of his crew—are far more pleasant in manner. Having already made the necessary arrangements, I was met at the Grove by a crew of Macusi Indians who were to accompany me into the interior.

The party consisted of my companions Messrs. Flint and Eddington, myself, and our Indians.

For some distance from Bartica Grove we passed through scenery which, if somewhat monotonous, is yet extremely beautiful, and is characteristic of this timber tract. The river in this part varies from about one and a half to two miles in width. A few islands of various sizes are scattered through the reaches. The banks on both sides of the river, as well as the islands, are everywhere clothed, down to the edge of the water, with rounded masses of foliage, generally laurel-like in character, and really, though not apparently, rising to a great height. The whole scene is on so gigantic a scale that these forests seem hardly more than low bush. There was but little flower to add to the colour ; but here and there, highest among the banked foliage, a mora-tree, breaking into new leaf of most varied shades, white, pale liver-coloured, a deeper red, and occasionally even a deep bright crimson, stood out in vivid contrast with the varied greens of the surrounding trees. Lower on the bank of foliage, the large white and crimson flowers and huge dark pods of the white chocolate-tree (*Pachira aquatica*, Aubl.) attracted the eye to where small flights of day-bats, startled by our passing boat, flitted about among the roots which rose from the water in the shadow of the overhanging trees.

Some fifteen miles above the Grove, the river suddenly contracts to a width of less than a quarter of a mile, forming a narrow reach called the ' Monkey Jump,' through which the current forces its way with great violence. Passing through this we came out in a very few minutes into a new reach of the river, wider than before.

With a careful pilot a small steamer might penetrate a little beyond the ' Monkey Jump,' to a point a few miles before the first falls on the river at Aretaka. A few years ago a path was cut through the forest from this highest point navigable for a steamer to the Kaieteur fall on the Potaro river, which in height, volume, and in the beauty of the surrounding scenery, must rank among the very finest falls in the world. Probably, however, it will be long before this path, which was cut under Government direction in the hope of attracting strangers, is made easy enough for the ordinary traveller. At present it has not been once used, and much of it is already obliterated by the rapid growth of tropical vegetation.

Opposite to the point from which this path starts stands Moraballi, a cluster of three houses, inhabited by a wood-cutter and his family, and interesting to us as the last civilised houses which we were to see for six months.

The scenery was characteristic. The sheet of water, some four miles in length and from two to three in width, was closed at either end by a curve in the course of the river. The smooth and lake-like water was broken in some half-dozen places by projecting rocks on which there was perhaps a bush or two, or at least some long waving grass. In one place a school of white river porpoises was splashing up the water. The banks framing the scene were everywhere clothed with a dense mass of trees, the foliage of which passed in varied and rounded curves down to the edge of the water. These trees, really of enormous height, seemed but a low, even-topped, far-extending 'bush.' In one place only were the banks cleared of trees; and there, under the shade of two enormous clumps of gracefully arching bamboos stood the wooden-galleried cottages of Moraballi. Among these houses were a few crimson-flowered hibiscus bushes, and behind was a tree, at that time white with flower, like an English cherry-tree in May. A wonderfully clear, yellowish light was over the whole picture.

Just beyond the houses, Moraballi creek runs into the Essequibo. These creeks, or tributary streams, some of which are of such considerable size that they might well be called rivers, are very numerous throughout the courses of most of the rivers of Guiana.

It was in passing up this very creek, on a previous occasion, that I first understood the beauty of a tropical forest. On the main rivers the scenery is too large to be well understood; but these smaller streams give more definite impressions. Moraballi creek is about the width of the Cherwell at Oxford. The bright, dark red, wine-coloured water runs, arched over by gigantic trees and palms and ferns, through dense shade. The swampy banks are thickly set with ferns and large lily-leaved aroids. At the water's edge a carpet of half-transparent filmy ferns and mosses is kept continually moist. From the trees which meet overhead, roots and leafless stems of wiry creeping plants hang down to the water; and on some of these humming-birds fix their tiny nests. There is no colour; the light is very dim; the air is very cool and almost chilly. But in one place, where a tree had fallen and left a space in the forest roof, the glorious and intensely blue sky appeared, its colour thrown into extraordinary vividness by a wreath of scarlet-blossomed passion-flower which had thrown itself across the open space from tree to tree. On the fallen tree, now lying leafless and branchless across the stream, almost touching the water, perched a great grey-blue kingfisher, which, frightened by the approach of our boat, flew screaming down the dark, arched streamway which lay beyond us.

But I should never end were I to try to describe all the beauties of this creek; so I must satisfy myself by adding that the peculiarly impressive effect of a tropical forest is never more apparent than in such creeks.

Leaving Moraballi, we soon reached the farthest point to which the tide runs. This is some sixty miles from the sea, at the first rapids, called Aretaka, which separate the timber from the forest tract. These rapids, which interrupt the course of the river for upwards of fifteen miles, are very similar, differing probably only in their greater or less length, to most of those which obstruct the rivers of Guiana and render navigation difficult; so that a description of these will serve to give a general idea of all.

In Aretaka rapids it is impossible to form an idea of the real width of the river. As far as the eye can see is a vast extent of water, from which rise many rocks and islands of all sizes. The rocks sometimes stand singly, sometimes in groups, sometimes piled in large numbers one over the other; some of these support a few water-guava bushes or even a few stunted and gnarled trees. The larger islands are generally covered with trees, and often, from their extent, are hardly distinguishable from the banks of the river. The water rushes, gurgling and foaming, in all directions among the boulders. A few banks of yellow sand crop out among the rocks. It was normally the dry season, and an abnormal drought had prevailed for a year and a half, so that the bed of the river was even more exposed than usual.

On the larger islands and on the banks of these rapids live a good many Indians, chiefly Caribs, and a few half-breeds between negroes and Indians, called ' Cobungrus.' These latter retain the many good qualities of the Indian, and to these they add the few good qualities, such as physique and strength, of the West Indian negro. We took up our quarters for a few days at the house of one of these Cobun-grus, a finely built man named Cephas, more than half Carib, who held by commission from the governor of the colony the oddly combined offices of rural constable and chief of the Indians of the Essequibo river. His curly hair gave indications of his black blood, but in all other respects he looked and lived a true Indian. As he limped down to meet us under the trees at the waterside, his naked red skin, relieved only by the usual dark blue lap or loin cloth, and by a splendid necklace of highly polished teeth of bush-hogs or peccaries, he was certainly a picturesque figure. The cause of his limp was evident in a horrible-looking wound con-spicuous on one shin. This had been produced twenty-seven months previously by the bite of a large snake. The wound kept him in his hammock for fifteen months, but since that he had been able to get about as freely as ever except for the odd hopping action in his walk.

Some little distance from the river, on top of a hill, the three or four huts which form the settlement stand, sur-rounded by charred trunks of trees, by cassava and other plants cultivated by the Indians, and by razor grass (*Scleria scindens*) and other weeds, in a clearing walled by tall forest trees.

The houses consisted only of four posts supporting a roof of palm leaves. The women were at the moment engaged in making cassava bread. The rich red colour of their skin, made yet more red by paint, the red waistcloths which formed their only dress, the red-dyed cotton bands which were fastened round their legs, below the knee and above the ankle, the vast quantities of red beads round their necks and waists, and the many red-stained cotton hammocks slung in the houses made up a striking picture—a harmony in red and brown.

As on every other occasion in which I have taken up my quarter in the houses of Indians of various tribes, the people were civil, hospitable, and pleasant. On this occasion hospi-tality was largely exercised in bringing us calabashes of casiri —a slightly alcoholic drink made of cassava, maize, and sweet-

potatoes, which tastes, not unpleasantly, like something between sour porter and thin claret.

As our object in staying at Aretaka was to fill up some
vacancies in our crews, and as after a stay of two days we
found it impossible to get men to man more than two
canoes, we had to leave the third behind, and on the morning
of the 22nd of February our expedition, as finally organised,
made its real start up the river.

One day passes very like another to the traveller as he
ascends the river in his canoe. During the first two days
we were slowly making our way up the Aretaka rapids.
The rocks, on account of the unusual dryness of the season,
were very much exposed, and the water-channels between
them, though numerous, were both narrow and shallow.
The canoes often had to be dragged by main force over the
rocky floor. Where the channels were deeper the water
rushed down more violently, and it was difficult to haul the
canoes against the current. But the Indians worked wonderfully. Some swam, and had hard work to keep their course in
the rushing water. Others, up to their waists or even up to
their necks in water, stood on half-submerged rocks hauling
by means of ropes attached to the canoes. All laughed and
shouted ; and the roar of the river half-drowned their noise.
The only woman of the party worked at least as energeti-
cally as the men. Once she suddenly lost her footing,
slipped, and was swept down the river, the current carrying
her right under the canoe. The half-terrified, half-amused
expression on her wholly hideous face, when it reappeared
from under the water, was most ludicrous. She swam like a
fish, and was soon running on the rocks and pulling again
as strongly as ever. All Indians, men and women alike,
swim splendidly, but with a peculiar action. The legs are
hardly spread, but are bent somewhat downward at an angle
to the trunk, and are then suddenly again straightened, thus
driving forward the body of the swimmer.

Here the confusion may be noted which is caused by the
fact that travellers in those parts make no distinction in their

use of the words 'rapid,' 'cataract,' and 'fall' respectively. The first word should, it seems to me, be confined to places where the water passes down a very slight, however long, incline, usually among many scattered rocks. A 'cataract' is a place where a great body of water falls suddenly down a ledge of rock, abrupt but not perpendicular. Lastly, the word 'fall' should only be used of such places where the water falls abruptly down an unbroken cliff-like face of perpendicular rock, usually from a more considerable height than in the former cases. If these terms were used only in this way a very considerable increase in clearness would be given to our maps, and travellers would know better what lies before them.

Among our crew was a Macusi boy called Moë, the son of the woman just mentioned. He was returning to his home on the savannah, after having spent two years in the service of a coloured man in Georgetown, where he had learned to speak English and to wear clothes. It was strange how quickly he now fell back into his old Indian habits. Even on the first day he threw off his clothes and resumed the ordinary Indian lap, a narrow strip of cloth passed between the legs, and suspended in front and at the back on a string tied round the waist. As he moved about among the other Indians, it was very evident that the clothes which he had worn for two years had made his skin become much fairer in tint. Strangely enough, he alone of all the Indians looked naked, and it was some months before the lighter tint of his skin, with the consequent effect of nakedness, disappeared. In other respects also he differed from the other Indians. He was even from the first lively and talkative, while they were for some time reserved and shy. He had learned some ugly tricks in town, such as swearing, though he did not know the meaning of the bad language he used. Once when I was teasing him, he calmly and with a pretty smile recommended me 'to go to hell, Baas.'

The banks of the Essequibo above Aretaka are almost

uninhabited, even by Indians; throughout the several hundred miles of country through which we passed between
Aretaka and the mouth of the Roopoonooni, we came across
but three or four settlements. Our camps, therefore, were
generally made in the forest. As, however, Indians are
continually passing up and down the river, there are certain recognised camping-places, from which the bush has been
cleared. Sometimes, however, when as night approached
we were not near one of those places, we had to clear ground
for ourselves in the bush. The nights spent in the open
air in the tropics are a pleasant memory. By the time
the camp was ready the daylight had faded, and our fires
alone threw round a circle of flickering light, contrasting
strangely with the darkness of the surrounding forest.
Where the firelight was strongest the Indians lay, smoking
and talking in their hammocks, close to each of which was a
fire, which occasionally flared up and seemed to lick the naked
skins of the Indians through the meshes of the hammock.
Not content with this, the Indians sometimes made the boys
take lighted palm-leaves and singe them as they lay in their
hammocks, this strange proceeding being intended to destroy savage insects.

One by one the Indians fell asleep. Various kinds of
frogs kept up an almost deafening concert of marvellously
varied croaks, some musical, some most unmusical. One
imitated the beat of paddles striking in regular time against
the sides of a canoe after the Indian custom; and the likeness was the more deceitful because the sound alternately
rose and fell gradually as though a canoe came up the river,
passed the camp, and was then paddled up the stream out
of ear-reach. Often and often I have lain long in doubt
whether the sound heard was caused by paddles or by frogs.
And while the frogs croaked, every now and then a nightjar flitted swiftly and most silently by, and then suddenly
shrieked out its loud cry of ' *Work-work-work-to-hell.*' Or
another and larger species began to moan out the four notes
of its most hideous and depressing cry of ' *Who-who-who-*

who,' each note sounded in rapid succession, the first shrill and high-pitched, each of the succeeding ones lower, and the last an almost inaudible moan. It is only comparable to the cry of a despairing and dying human being. At times was heard the noise —something between a snort and a bellow— of a cayman ; and at other times mysterious sounds, resembling the crack of pistol-shots, which I afterwards found were caused by caymans raising their tails into the air and bringing them down sharply on the surface of the water.

Toward morning the loudest and most appalling noise of all broke out. Beginning suddenly in a deep roar, it became louder and louder, till the whole forest rang with the din. It is hardly possible on first hearing this to believe that the terrific roar is produced only by the somewhat small red howling monkey (*Mycetes seniculus*), called baboon in the colony.

Before daylight the Indians were out of their hammocks, making preparation for the coming day's journey. A plunge into the river was the first thing. In the early morning the temperature near the river is comparatively low ; though the thermometer stands perhaps at 70°, the air feels as chilly as on an autumn day in England, and the water, having retained much of the warmth imparted by the sun of the previous day, seems by contrast like that of a warm bath.

And now the sound and sights of the day began. Some toucans, perched on the very highest boughs of a tall tree, were revelling in the morning sun, and greeting it with their usual yelping cries. Emphasis is given to each puppy-like yelp by an odd and comical antic; the head is jerked down, the tail lifted almost at right angles to the body. In the distance an Indian canoe appeared from behind a bend in the river. The naked skins of the Indians in it literally flashed red in the intense light. A scarlet ibis (*Ibis rubra*) —the only one, by the way, that I ever saw so high up on this river—flew by and settled upon a tree between us and the approaching canoe ; but it hardly looked more red than did the Indians. Flights of parrots, crying shrilly, began to pass over the river to their feeding grounds, flying so high that their colours were not to be discerned. From the forest the 'pĭ-pī-yŏ,' or greenheart bird (*Lipangus cineraceus*), began incessantly to cry its own Indian name ; this is, if not the commonest, yet certainly the most noticed bird in the forests of Guiana, for its shrill cry, heard nearly all day long, is the most characteristic sound of these forests.

Having no animal food, we stopped early in the day to hunt. Half the booty, a young tapir, was given to the Indians, who, as usual, immediately boiled and began to eat it ; for an Indian, when he gets flesh, is never satisfied until it is all eaten, after which he contentedly does without animal food until he has sufficient energy to go and procure a fresh supply. The other half of the tapir was put on a babracot to dry. A babracot is a small stage of green sticks, built some two feet above the fire, on which the flesh is placed and smoked. Flesh treated in this way, though it loses its distinctive flavour, keeps good for many days even in that climate.

Just opposite to us was Gluck Island, which I visited on another occasion to examine a pond long known as one of the native haunts of the *Victoria regia* lily. The pond was so closely surrounded by high and rankly luxuriant vegetation that it was impossible to see the water from the damp, swampy banks. But by climbing a tree which grew out over the water, and so getting above the thick growth of tall reeds and prickly palms, we got a view over the whole pond. Except one small plant at the further end, the lily had entirely disappeared; this was probably owing to the late times of dry weather, which had caused the pond to dry and so allowed the heat of the sun to kill the plants. The same fate had happened during the past season to the lily in several ponds in and near Georgetown, into which it had been introduced.

While climbing down from my post of observation on the tree, I heard the Indians shouting out that they had found a cayman's nest. Among the deep mass of rotting leaves on the bank of the pond, in a gloomily dark and damp place under trees and reeds, was a fitting spot for such a nest. On a large heap of decaying vegetable matter, evidently collected by the parent cayman, lay thirty-seven large, long-shaped eggs with thick, porcelain-like shells. The True Caribs greedily seized them as a delicacy. Afterwards, at dinner, I eat part of one of the eggs, boiled hard, and found it very like a duck's egg in texture and taste, but with a faintly perceptible flavour of musk.

Just as we were going to sleep that night, the Indians insisted on loading the guns and placing them near our hammocks, saying that there were Ackawoi kenaimas, or murderers, about. We had seen men of that tribe passing and repassing during the afternoon ; but I need hardly say that the assertion that these had murderous intentions towards us was unfounded. It is, however, very common for one tribe to make this accusation against the members of another tribe. There is, as will presently be explained, some occasional foundation for it. The Ackawois bear a particularly bad character in this respect.

Far into the night the Indians, sitting in a circle round the camp fires, continued to gorge their food ; and at last, when weary of sitting up to eat, they threw themselves into their hammocks, over which they had suspended certain dainty morsels of meat so as to hang close by their mouths, that no time might be lost whenever they happened to wake. Their power of gorging is really wonderful ; I once was able to calculate the amount consumed in thirty-six hours by ten men, and found it to be 252 lbs. of smoked fish, 62 lbs. of fresh fish, a whole wild hog, and an indefinite quantity of cassava bread.

Before full dawn the next morning I was roused by the sound of a monotonous chant, varied occasionally by a couple of most distressing grunts—

> La, la, caviana, ana, ani,
> La, la, caviana, ana, ani,
> La, la, caviana, ana, ani,
> Ugh, ugh.

The singer was Moë, and he explained, pointing to a heron, flying high over the river, that the honuré, *i.e.* the heron, is a peaiman (a medicine man), who was singing this song as he flew. The heron at any rate gains one advantage by being a peaiman ; for no Macusi will eat its flesh.

The Indians, having finished all their meat, now announced their intention of waiting while the best huntsman amongst them went to try to get the mother tapir. To my great satisfaction this hunter came back emptyhanded ; for if he had been successful we should have probably have had to wait till this new supply of meat had been consumed.

That day was spent in travelling along smooth reaches of the river, which are more monotonous, though even there the scenery is beautiful. The banks of the river are everywhere covered by dense forests, which sometimes grow on low flat land, sometimes on rocky and undulating slopes, and sometimes clothe a solitary mountain or small range of mountains up to the very highest rock. But most wonderful of all are the views which may be obtained by climbing to the top of some of the hills, and looking down on the great and wide sea of tree-tops ending only at the circle of the horizon, and unbroken except where here and there a long narrow thread of white mist, lying along the tree-tops, marks the winding course of some small stream.

As among the falls, innumerable islands, some of considerable extent, stud the river and hide its real width from the eye. The beauty of the scenery is in great measure due to the effect of the distant views as seen between the approaching headlands of each two of these islands. The traveller from his canoe in the centre of a lake-like expanse of still water, in the midst of a group of these islands, sees the water flowing toward and from him, through many channels, each of which is framed by the trees overhanging from two neighbouring islands. In the more open reaches of the river, in the dry season, when the water is low, banks of bright yellow sand swell up from the water, and either form islands, often of very considerable extent, or fill the bays in the curves of the river-banks. Twice in each year, when at the end of each wet season these sandbanks show above water, the river turtles, which are very numerous, lay their eggs in the sand; and gull-like razor-bills (*Rhynchops nigra*) make their uncovered nests on the sand, and wheel about them incessantly uttering their harsh cry.

One evening we reached a hut on the Paripie creek belonging to some half-bred Brazilian Indians. These people, called Nikari-karus, are hybrids between Brazilians and Indians of various tribes. Their proper home is on the frontier of British and Brazilian territory; and the few settled on the Essequibo are deserters from the frontier forts and cattle farms, where, at any rate till recently, the labour done was forced. Except in two respects the habits of these people scarcely differ from those of the native Indians of the English territory. They make their cassava into farine, instead of into bread; and in making their hammocks they use coloured cotton, generally blue or yellow, instead of white, and the web is more close, and somewhat different from that of the ordinary Indian. At Yucarisi, a mile or two beyond Paripie, is another of these Brazilian settlements; higher up the river, at Arinda, is a third; and there is another on the Roopoonooni river near Anahee. These, I believe, are all.

While sleeping in a house at Paripie several of our party were sucked by bats. I never could succeed in inducing a bat to taste my blood, though men sleeping round and close to me have frequently been attacked. These animals are a serious trouble to some travellers; for they seem to have a special liking for some people, an abhorrence of others. An Indian boy who served me for a short time was nearly bled to death by their nightly attacks. No amount of care seemed to prevail against them. To keep a light burning, which is often said to prevent their attacks, proved useless in his case. His parents used to sit up night after night to watch, and while they watched the bats never made an attack; but as soon as they fell asleep the bats bit and blood began to flow.

The bite seems to cause not the slightest pain ; and the danger lies, not so much in the quantity of blood sucked by the animals, as in that which afterwards flows from the unnoticed wound.

One morning about this time the Indians noticed my sponge, and expressed much wonder about it. Moë, as usual, put himself forward as spokesman. First he guessed that it was a hat; then a bird's-nest; then a shoe. When its use was practically illustrated, the whole company were overcome with laughter.

After passing the mouth of the Potaro river, on which is the Kaieteur fall, the men began to hunt for turtles' eggs in the sand-banks ; and just before reaching Warrapoota they found a considerable number. The Brazilians at Yucarisi had given us some of these eggs smoked and dried. But in this state, though they keep good a considerable time, they cannot be recommended for delicacy of flavour. Now, however, that we got them fresh from the nest it was a very different matter. Those which we first found were about the shape and size of pigeons' eggs, with roughish and very elastic shells, or, rather, skins. Another species of turtle, equally common in these rivers, lays a much larger and rounder egg. Both kinds are boiled; the albumen is expressed, and the yelk, which is then of a buttery consistency, is eaten. These eggs are certainly very delicious food. The Indians fully appreciate them, and, though they will not touch the egg of a fowl, consume these turtle eggs greedily. I have occasionally seen large canoes literally filled with the eggs which Indians have collected. The egg of the iguana lizard (*Iguana tuberculata*) is very similar, and is equally sought after.

At Warrapoota cataracts I for the first time saw the rock-pictures which form so strange an addition to some of the landscapes of this part of South America. A large number of somewhat conspicuous figures are engraved on the surfaces of a group of granite boulders in the very midst of the cataract.

Camping that evening just above Warrapoota, I was once more disturbed by a freak of the Indians in the middle of the night. Roused by a moving light, I saw a procession of our Indians moving round the camp; foremost was one apparently taking aim with his gun; behind were others of whom each held a blazing palm-branch high over his head. To my sleepy remonstrances they replied that they had heard an omar (an evil being) and that they were looking for it; but, as the tracks showed in the morning, the noise had been made by a poor little labba (*Cœlogenys paca*).

The next day was memorable. We passed Paiwarikaira, a large granite boulder which rests on a slender columnar base. It is commonly reported that a certain Dutchman, when his countrymen possessed the land, brought a hundred slaves to overturn the rock; but he failed, and the rock remains to this day in position, to interest the traveller and to awe the passing Indian. No Indian, unless he be a peaiman, willingly looks at Paiwarikaira; for the sight of it is followed by misfortune. Heedless of this, and regardless of the entreaties of the Indians, I approached, and even touched the rock. When, shortly afterwards, it began to rain the Indians attributed this solely to my disrespectful treatment of Paiwarikaira; nor, as will presently be shown, was this the only evil that befel us, as my men said, in consequence.

Only about two hundred yards higher up the river is another rock in which, according to the half-civilised Indians, God has shut up a negro, who is not to be let out until for one whole year he ceases to swear. His chance of freedom, if he is like most of his race, must be small indeed. The Indians' hatred of black men is noticeable in this and many other circumstances.

That evening we were stopped for the first time by a fall, up which it was impossible to take the loaded canoes; but in the morning they were unloaded, hauled up empty, and then reloaded.

Among our men was a peaiman, or medicine man, who about this time gave me some trouble. He used to tie his hammock to the same tree to which mine was tied; and being, like all Indians, very restless at night, he frequently shook and disturbed me. On telling him to move his hammock he did so with a very bad grace, and when I laughed at him, he angrily and somewhat inconsequently told Moë that 'he was not afraid of us.' Some fresh offence being again given to this man, he, once more using Moë as an interpreter, remarked that he would kill us all, and even mentioned the order in which he would do this. We shortly had good reason to remember this remark.

Misfortunes now began to fall thickly upon us. First, our bread was exhausted, and it was with great difficulty that we obtained a small fresh supply from one of the few Indian settlements on the river. Then sickness appeared among us. Moë, owing, not improbably, to his sudden rejection of clothes, had been ill for some days. He and another boy, named Woijeau, were our cooks. The peaiman, who was usually unwilling to do work of any sort, of his own accord now undertook to prepare our meals. Soon after, one by one, we all became ill, in exactly the order in which the peaiman had threatened to kill us. I cannot prove the case against the man, but I have little doubt that he intentionally caused our illness; the Indians, on the other hand, were convinced that the misfortune was due to our disrespectful treatment of Paiwarikaira.

This illness greatly impeded our progress. Fever was especially prevalent. As a similar misfortune is very likely to attack all travellers in that land, where the days are always burningly hot, the nights, by comparison, bitterly cold, and the atmosphere is always saturated with moisture, it may not be out of place to say that these attacks, though frequent and very troublesome, are but rarely dangerous. The traveller of ordinarily good constitution, who leads a temperate life, need not fear anything more than great discomfort. If, on the other hand, his system has been saturated with alcohol, or broken by other excesses, there is considerable danger. To this cause must be attributed the fatal consequences which have overtaken more than one of those who have travelled in the interior of Guiana, and which have given a reputation for unhealthiness to that country. Having carefully examined the history of various unfortunate expeditions into the interior, I could, were it not an ungrateful thing to many still living, show that most of the misfortunes have been due to some form of intemperance. Once or twice also, men have gone into the bush when no longer young and, unaccustomed to the hardship often unavoidable in such a life, these men have been knocked up for life.

In addition to fever, two other forms of illness—dysentery and ophthalmia—both of which at a later time attacked members of our party, must be carefully guarded against. Ophthalmia is very common indeed among the Indians, nearly every individual of whom has weak eyes in consequence. The disease seems very readily to affect travellers, its germs being probably conveyed from the eyes of some Indians to those of the new comer by the countless tiny flies which settle constantly on the eyeball and thus form one of the most serious plagues of that country. The form in which ophthalmia occurs is extremely severe, and, as I saw in two distinct and entirely unconnected cases, affects the brain, in the case of white men at least, and produces delirium. But on the whole these interior lands are not unhealthy.

Owing to the illness of so many of our party, and to the now complete failure in our supply of provisions, it was with great pleasure that, on the fourteenth day after our start from Aretaka, we reached the site of an old Dutch settlement at Arinda, where a family of half-bred Brazilians have now established themselves.

Some groups of fine coffee-trees, long left untended, alone mark the site of the old Dutch settlement entered in the map published by Hartzinc in 1770 as 'Post Arinda.' It was the highest on this river, with the exception of a small plantation, probably a branch establishment, of which there are still some traces at Ouropocari, some few miles further up the river.

The Dutch had pushed so far up most of the rivers, that it seems probable that if the country had been left in their hands it would now have been fully utilised. But when their rule was confined to the comparatively small district of Surinam, their interest in the whole of Guiana cooled, and the development of the colony received a check from which it has not yet begun to recover. Arinda now lies a twelve days' journey beyond civilisation, and a group of four Indian huts, occupied by Nikari-karus and by some Portuguese now alone occupy the place.

After a three days' stay at Arinda, having got rest and provisions, we once more started on our way. After a few hours we passed the mouth of a creek, called Haimara-kuroo by the Indians, from which a path leads across to the Demerara river. Neither the path nor the creek are marked in any of the maps of Guiana. The courses of the two rivers are almost parallel, and not far apart, and there are several of these connecting paths between the two. They are made and used by the Indians of the savannah, who go by that way to work for short periods on the wood-cutting grants of the Demerara river.

At noon on the second day after leaving Arinda we reached the falls at Ouropocari. On the rocks at the side of one of the channels of this are some more rock-drawings, very similar in character to those at Warrapoota. The channels at Ouropocari being often impracticable for loaded canoes, there is a portage, or path, along which the Indians carry their canoes and their goods separately from the bottom to the top of the fall, where they reload their canoes. These portages exist at the side of nearly all the larger falls on this river, and are frequently used; but on the less-frequented rivers of Guiana it is often necessary for each traveller to make such a portage for himself. This is no easy work. The trees have to be felled and the ground cleared; and skids have to be laid at very short distances from each other along the whole path. When this has been done, the travellers harness themselves by a rope attached to the bows of the boat, like a team of horses, and the boat is very quickly drawn over.

At the highest point of this portage-path there is a huge boulder, one side of which is most curiously marked by regular and deep natural flutings.

One morning, soon after passing Ouropocari, I was lying in high fever under the tent of the canoe, which was passing steadily through a wide reach of shallow water in the middle of which was a small wooded island. Suddenly the Indians began to shout loudly. One who was nearest to me seized me by the feet and pulled me out of the tent. We were close by the island. From its banks a large jaguar was quietly examining us. Almost immediately it left the island, and, fording the shallow river, passed across our bows to the mainland. Unfortunately the other two canoes were out of sight, and I was too miserable and weak to care to use my gun. Most unexpectedly one of the Indians found courage to face the beast, and, running close up, shot an arrow into it. A shake made the arrow fall out, and with a roar the animal sprang into the forest on the mainland and disappeared.

That night fever raged yet more strongly in some of our party, and it was necessary to rest next day from wearisome canoe-travelling.

In the morning, to amuse themselves, the Indians set fire to the trunk of a dead tree which had fallen and leaned from the top of the bank, there somewhat high, down to the edge of the water. The flames crept along the log and in time seized upon the bush on the top of the bank. In this way it continued to advance until it was close to our camp. Two or three times during the day the Indians were sent to beat it down ; which they did with a very bad grace, seeming to expect us to stop the mischief which they themselves had caused. In the afternoon the fire caught the brushwood round the stem of a huge, half-dead mora-tree, and by dusk it had cleared a considerable space round this and left the mora standing in the centre of a circle of other trees, the tops of which all met overhead. Just after dusk a loud roar told that the central tree had at last also burst into flame, and before long its trunk formed a pillar of fire. This was not pleasant, for the tree was some hundred feet high, and was not sixty feet from our camp. But we were very loth to move ; and so, knowing that a tree generally falls towards the nearest space—in this case the river—we took our chance. The darkness round the circle of the fire, intense as it usually is under those gigantic trees, seemed by contrast unusually great. The fire burned within a huge green dome, formed by the leafage above and around the flaming trunk. Each leaf stood out distinctly in the fierce glow of the fire. Sparks soon began to fall from the blazing centre, and then presently fell in a continuous shower. Birds and butterflies, startled from their rest, together with moths and bats, darted here and there among the burning masses, and sometimes fell into the fire. As the flame crept higher and higher up the tree, the roar became louder and louder, till suddenly the fire leaped up with a deafening noise into the masses of dried leaves overhead. Presently a creaking sound was heard, warning that the trunk would not stand much longer. But at last the end came with terrible suddenness, and the creaking sound was lost in a loud crash.

The noise made by a great tree, as it falls in the silence of those forests, is at all times wonderful. It is like the crash of thunder followed by the prolonged, hurrying din of a landslip ; but in it there is another awful and indescribable element. And when the sound at last suddenly ceases, it is followed by a strangely contrasting silence. But in this case the fire added yet more to the grandeur of the effect. No silence came after the tree had fallen ; for the fire blazed with renewed fierceness, and almost bellowed, as in triumph, among the tops of the surrounding trees.

The suddenness of the fall startled me, ill and weak as I was, out of my hammock more quickly than I ever got out of it on any other occasion. But the tree had fallen toward the river, and all danger was over. Yet throughout the night blazing fragments continued to fall at intervals.

On the next day we reached the cataracts of Akramukra, and, on the day following, those at Rappoo. These latter take their name from a kind of bamboo which grows on the islands among them, and which is much used by the savannah Indians for making arrow-heads, which are, we were told, as poisonous as those tipped with ourali. I afterwards tried one of these rappoo arrows; but the fowl which was shot showed no symptoms of poison; and an Indian who was standing by ingenuously remarked that a rappoo arrow is only poisonous when it enters far enough into the body. This recalls another Indian story. A plant is said to grow somewhere, a stick from which proves fatal to any living thing at which it is pointed. The virtues of this are supposed to have been discovered by an Indian woman, who, when suddenly attacked by a jaguar, seized the nearest stick to defend herself, and pointed it at the animal, which immediately fell dead.

These rapids of Rappoo are the last up which we had to pass during this particular canoe-journey. The course of the Essequibo is smooth from here to some distance beyond the junction of the Roopoonooni river, up which we were going. The falls above this junction, near the source of the Essequibo, are of very great height and difficulty, and present a barrier as yet insuperable to travellers who have attempted to pass up the higher Essequibo. The Roopoonooni also is free from falls from its mouth to beyond the point at which we were to leave the river and begin our life on the savannah, at Pirara landing.

From Rappoo, driven as usual by want of bread, we pressed on, and reached Apooterie, a Carib settlement at the junction of the Roopoonooni with the Essequibo, the same evening. The head man of the place received us hospitably into his house. But within an hour of our arrival his wife gave birth to twins; so that, much to the surprise of the Indians, we preferred to remove our hammocks to an unfinished house which stood in the same clearing. It was used as a storehouse for a large quantity of badly dried fish ; and the evil smell from this mingled strangely with the sweet scent which came in from some blossoming coffee-trees outside.

During our two days' stay here the chief amusement was afforded by the tame animals which, as usual in an Indian settlement, thronged the place. Among these were more than a dozen parrots of different kinds, two macaws, two trumpet-birds, two troupials, three monkeys, some powis or curassow birds, and a sunbird.

After two days' stay at Apooterie, we started again, and, leaving the Essequibo, passed up the Roopoonooni river. The water of the latter, unlike the clear, dark-red water of the Essequibo, is opaque, and of yellowish-white colour. The river is about five hundred yards wide. Its banks are wooded, though far less luxuriantly than those of the main river. The water, being at that time excessively low, in places left much exposed the high, cliff-like banks of white clay, crowned by weather-beaten trees, shrubs, and palms; in other places, long even stretches of water-guava bushes (*Psidium aromaticum* and *P. aquaticum*), looking like English osier-beds, edged the river. The palms, here much more numerous than on the Essequibo, gave character to the scenery.

The withered, scrub-like appearance of the vegetation was no doubt partly due to the neighbourhood of the savannah, to which we were now coming near ; but it was also doubtless partly due to the abnormal dryness of the previous seasons, for when I afterwards passed down this river in the high rainy season, the plant growth, at least near the mouth, was far more luxuriant, though even then greatly inferior to that on the Essequibo.

During the rainy season the Roopoonooni presents a very different scene. The banks, instead of appearing as clay cliffs, are then almost everywhere under water ; so that it is often hard to find sufficient dry ground on which to camp. Instead of an almost dry river-bed obstructed by many sand ridges, with high tree-capped banks, the sand ridges then lie thirty feet under water, and the trees, rising directly from the flood water, alone mark where the river-banks once were.

On the first day of our journey up this river, we travelled long, and at a fairly rapid rate. But on the second day the sandbanks began to cause delay ; and from that point these increased so greatly in size and number, often covered only by an inch or two of water, and sometimes extending right across the river, as to offer a most serious obstacle to our progress. It was impossible to float the large and heavily loaded canoes over them. Sometimes it was just possible to drag them over by main force, as over dry land ; but more often it was necessary to dig a channel with the paddles. Once we had to wait for six hours to dig a channel through a sandbank of not more than three hundred yards in width ; and so on some occasions we did not advance a thousand yards in the day. These times of waiting were rendered almost unendurable by the great abundance of the small black *kaboori* fly, called in the Brazils *pium* (*Simulium*). From the Atlantic to the mouth of the Roopoonooni the country is quite free from these terrible little blood-suckers ; but on this river they abound, as they do generally westward, especially on the rivers of the Amazon system. Wherever they settle on the flesh a small round patch of raised skin, distended by blood, is formed, and is very sore and trouble-some. The naked bodies of the Indians, whose hands were occupied with the paddles, and who, therefore, could not pro-tect themselves, were so wounded by these insects that it was sometimes difficult to detect any sound skin. Where these insects occur they are far more annoying than mosquitoes, which, abundant and almost universally distributed as they are on the coast-land, are only very locally distributed in the interior.

We slowly crept on for some time, but gradually made less and less progress each day. The labour of digging through the sandbanks and of dragging the canoes over by main force began to tell on the Indians, who grew weary and disheartened. Cassava bread, which is almost essential to their health and comfort, had again failed us; and some of them who, like most Indians, had been sleek and fat, suddenly and in the course of but a day or two, became so thin that they looked hardly more than skin and bone.

One after another—ill, weary, or lazy—our men gave up working. One afternoon, when with infinite pains the canoes had been got halfway across a sandbank in a wide reach of river, the Indians declared they could not and would not move further that day; so we had to wade up the river for about a mile until we found camping ground. Then the men spoke of a small settlement called Morai, not far from where we were. We sent there to get bread, but the messengers returned empty-handed. They had found the huts, but the people were almost famishing, and gave most ominous accounts of the famine which the long-continued drought had caused in the savannah.

The next day the crisis came. We had been creeping on, even more slowly than usual, for about two hours, when we again stuck on a sandbank, from which it was declared utterly impossible without assistance to move the canoes forward or backward. There was nothing to be done but to form a camp in the bush and consult as to the next move.

We were then about a day's walk—the distance by land being considerably less than by water—from a considerable Macusi settlement called Quartama. Eddington, who was at the time the strongest of the party, undertook to go on to this settlement, and there, if possible, to procure fresh crews, as well as a supply of provisions.

Four tedious days we waited. One night, just as dusk fell, a tremendous thunderstorm broke over us, and lasted some hours. The waterproof sheet which I was using as a protection against the weather was not long enough to cover the scale-lines of my cotton hammock; and these lines getting soaked, acted as conductors for the water till the whole hammock was saturated. Taught by experience, I afterwards found it better to remove the scale-lines from the hammock, so as to reduce its length as much as possible and make the work of sheltering it more easy. There can be no doubt that the hammock is the greatest possible luxury to a traveller camping out; so that any expedient that may add to its importance is worthy of notice. Another night a labba came and lapped the soup out of a pan which stood actually under my hammock and within a foot of my body. These animals are often very bold at night, when they occasionally even venture into inhabited Indian houses, in quest of any scraps of food that may be within their reach. These were literally the only events that broke the monotony of that dreary time. In the middle of the fifth night Eddington returned with a set of merry, shouting Macusis, very different from the disheartened set who had brought us so far. He also brought back an abundant supply of cassava, and the welcome news that a further supply would be waiting for us at Quartama.

We started very hopefully the next day. The new men worked splendidly. The character of the country also began to change. For some time past a comparatively narrow belt of forest on each side of the river had alone separated us from the savannah; but now even this belt failed in places, and the open savannah came down to the river. After having been shut up for nearly two months in a dense, damp forest, to reach open country, to see a really wide plain, and to feel a real breeze, seemed to give new life. So we soon reached the 'waterside' of Quartama.

The settlement itself, as usual in the savannah region, is several miles from the river. But crowds of Macusis soon began to come down to us. Luckily the clearing in which was our camp was large, for all our visitors brought their hammocks and evidently meant to make a night of it.

The spot was rather pretty. A piece of high ground, in the angle formed by the junction of a small creek with the Roopoonooni, had been partially cleared, a few scattered trees only being left, to which hammocks might be tied. Up these single trees multitudes of climbing palms (*Desmoncus*) had crept, and, reaching the top, had there woven their

tendrils into a dense tangle, so that the place was completely roofed over by fretted green palm-leaves and grape-
like clusters of scarlet palm-fruit.

The place soon became densely crowded by men, women,
children, dogs, and poultry; for many of the Indians had
brought their whole live stock with them. Under each
hammock was a fire. The men—a few of them good-looking
—were loaded with necklaces of the teeth of various animals
and with beads, tassels of birds' skins, and wore brilliant
feather crowns. They were generally finely built, and were,
in short, a fine-looking set. Of the women, two or three of
the younger were really pretty; others had spoiled their appearance by painting broad streaks of black, moustache-like,
over their mouths and from ear to ear. But the old women,
as always among Indians, were really hideous. Almost every
woman had brought a baby, as well as one or more older
children. Some mothers carried their babies by placing one
arm round the child's neck, so that the poor little wretch
hung suspended against the mother's body; others, more
careful, carried their babies in tiny hammocks suspended
from their shoulders. Babies and children were all perfectly
naked but for a necklace, which each wore, and a piece of
twine tied round the body above the hips. Taking a fancy
to one or two of these necklaces, I began to bargain with the
mothers for them. One, made of deers' teeth, was really very
pretty, and another consisted of three magnificent jaguar
teeth. The mothers, stripping their children of these, their
only garments, gave them in exchange for red beads; the poor
children screamed and bawled till, ashamed of my barbarity,
I made peace by giving them some beads for themselves.
In the meantime more Indians continued to arrive, until the
whole available space was occupied. Each newcomer insisted
upon shaking hands, a practice which they were told by
our own men was customary among white men.

After this the rest of our canoe journey passed quickly
and pleasantly. The only drawback was the growing report
of famine which met us at the settlements, which now

became more numerous. At Quartama we had certainly found abundance, but everywhere else there seemed to be great scarcity. Whole settlements were deserted, and in others, where a few old or infirm people remained, nothing but the seeds of palms and other plants were eaten.

The change in the scenery continued and increased. The places where the savannah came down to the river became more numerous; and in no place were the two separated by more than a very narrow line of trees. In one spot a mountain, bare of trees up to its very top and with rocks cropping up here and there from the scanty herbage on its sides, afforded an entirely new feature in the scenery. A mountain, or even a hill, is most interesting in Guiana.

One evening, landing at a creek called Mopai, we camped near a pond full of the splendid flowers and gigantic leaves of the royal water-lily (*Victoria regia*). Such a scene, in the soft and yet intense evening light of the tropics, is exquisite beyond description. Round the pond was a wall of dark forest. Water-fowl abounded, dainty spur-wings (*Parra jacana*) ran about on the lily leaves, and one of these birds had a nest on a leaf; high over head a flight of large white cranes (*Mycteria americana*) passed in Indian file to their night's rest. Flocks of vicissi-ducks (*A. autumnalis*) rose, flew by, whistling out their name, 'vicissi—vicissi—vicissi'; and, a more practical matter, several fine musk-ducks (*A. moschatus*) rose, and fell to the guns.

At last, on the 22nd of March, about midday, we reached our destination at Pirara landing, and so came to the limit of our canoe journey, having taken forty-nine days to traverse a distance that, under ordinarily favourable circumstances, ought to be passed in about twenty.

CHAPTER II.

A JOURNEY IN THE INTERIOR (*continued*).

The Savannah—Indian Settlement at Quatata—Indian Visitors—A Buck-
gun—The city of El Dorado—Rain after Drought—Start for the Brazils
—Down the Takootoo—Fort St. Joaquim—Cattle Farms—Homeward—
Fording Lake Amoocoo—The Rivers in the Rainy Season—A Notorious
Murderer—Shooting the Falls.

THAT night the Indians kept up a great firing of guns to
attract the people from Quatata and Karanakru, two settlements respectively nine and fifteen miles distant, across the
savannah.   They were wanted to carry our goods; for our
own men, when they reached the landing-place, considered
their duties at an end.   At earliest dawn, the shrill sounds
of Indian music were heard from a distance, and grew louder
and louder.   Then Macusis began to arrive in family parties,
walking in single file, many of them playing on flutes
made of the bones of jaguar or deer.   In each party the
men and boys came first, carrying only their bows and
arrows ; after these came the women, burdened with the
hammocks and other chattels of the whole party.   As they
came up to our hut, which was some distance from the water-
side, the men came in and talked to us, while the women
stood outside in a shy, laughing group.   Presently the whole
party moved on down to the river, where our baggage was ;
and when it passed back again, the women were always more
heavily loaded than the men.   This went on at intervals
throughout the day, and again early the next morning ;
so that eventually there were probably about sixty Macusis
in all.

When the last of the goods had been carried off, we
ourselves started to walk to Quatata, which was to be our

head-quarters for some months. The undulating savannah is chiefly arranged in parallel ridges, hills, and valleys, sometimes large and sometimes small, rapidly succeeding each other. The soil changes often and abruptly; sometimes it is peaty (pegass), sometimes hard and impregnated with iron, sometimes gravelly, sometimes sandy. But whatever its nature, the soil, on the hills, is somewhat scantily covered by harsh grass, from which rise a few wind-blown, sunburnt shrubs. But in the moist valleys, of which some are mere strips, lying between the ridges of higher ground, while others are vast, perfectly level plains, many miles in extent, the grass is high and luxuriant; and these level plains are made beautiful by groups and forests of æta palms (*Mauritia flexuosa*), each with its exquisite crown of green fan leaves standing erect above the hanging fringe of older, withered leaves. The rising ground is everywhere dotted over with the huge nests of ants or termites, from two to ten feet high, built of yellow clay, and looking like very pointed haycocks. Sometimes, again, but at long intervals, stand palm-thatched, domed Indian houses, looking like haystacks. As a background to all this, in the far distance, on the right, is the Parcaraima range, and on the left are the Canakoo mountains.

At the end of our walk to Quatata, it was not pleasant to find that not only food, but water also, was fearfully scarce. In ordinary times there is a sufficient supply of the latter in a small river which runs past the foot of the hill on which Quatata stands. But in this extraordinary season, in one pool only was there a little water, thick and milk-white with clay, and unpleasantly tainted with iron.

Quatata stands on high ground, within half a mile of the now extinct settlement of Pirara, which forty years ago was the scene of a dispute between the English and Brazilian Governments. A year or two before that event, a Mr. Youd, a clergyman of the Episcopalian Church, had established himself as missionary at Pirara. But the Brazilians, who had at times made vague claims to that district, were stirred up by a Brazilian priest, Frater José dos Santos Innocentes, to enforce their claim and at the same time to destroy the Protestant mission. A Brazilian force was sent from the frontier fort of St. Joaquim, and the priest accompanied the soldiers. The English missionary retired for a time to another station, but a company of English troops being sent from Georgetown to reinstate him, he returned to Pirara. The English on their arrival threw up an earthwork which yet remains to mark the site of Pirara, and, entrenching themselves in this, waited for some days. The Brazilians, in the meantime, looked on. At last, without coming to blows, both parties agreed to retire, leaving the question of the ownership of the savannah to be settled by diplomacy. The quarrel yet remains at that point.

Meanwhile, Mr. Youd returned to Pirara, but was once more forced to retire, by ill health, caused, say the Indians, by poison ; and before long he died. The Indians of Pirara, disliking the disturbance to which they had been subjected by both Brazilians and English, moved away, and no trace now remains of the place, except the parts of the mission church and the earthwork already mentioned. In its place, after a time, Quatata rose.

This, which is one of the largest settlements on the savannah, consists of ten houses, all oval or round. These, as always on the savannah, are not mere open sheds, as in the forest, but have very thick walls of wattle and mud, surmounted by high conical roofs of palm thatch. The very cold winds which at night blow across the savannah, have probably induced the building of these walls. Another distinctive feature of the Indian houses on the savannah, is that there are no signs of cultivation round them.

At first, constant attacks of fever, and the difficulty of moving about in a famine-stricken country, prevented our undertaking any distant expeditions; but there was very much to interest even in the immediate neighbourhood.

The houses of the Indians were always interesting, and the Indians themselves, after a time, and when their reserve had somewhat decreased, were sufficiently communicative, and sometimes even too hospitable. When we entered a house, one of the women generally filled a calabash with pai-wari, a liquor, the horrid preparation of which will presently be described, from a jar standing somewhere in the dark background, and offered it to us. Etiquette demands the offer, and etiquette demands that the visitor should finish the horrid draught to the last dregs. Intent on establishing friendly relations with the people, I often found myself obliged to undergo this disagreeable ordeal; for, after it, I was allowed to walk about the house, handle all things, and ask any number of questions.

At other times the Indians used to return our visits, coming for the purpose not only from Quatata, but also from very distant places. Some came merely from curiosity, others came to barter. These levées were often very curious. Our goods were spread out on the floor; the Indians, on their part, brought provisions, hammocks, tame birds and animals, or specimens of their manufactures, dress, and ornaments. Often, however, they merely sat for hours, speechless, but observing our slightest movements. One of the most remarkable visitors came from a part of the Canakoo mountains about fifteen miles distant. Our house was built on piles, and a rough ladder gave access to it. One morning this man, springing suddenly up the ladder, stood bolt upright, with his gun in his hand, much in the position of a soldier standing at ease. He was short, sturdy, and well-built; his hair, which, unlike that of his fellow-tribesmen, was shaggy, was bound round with a cotton fillet. He was also the only Macusi I ever saw with a defined moustache. For nearly an hour he stood without altering his position, without moving a muscle, or speaking a word. He merely stood and gazed. Then he turned, bolted down the steps, and immediately went home.

Such of our visitors as came often grew accustomed to us, and not unfrequently ventured upon jokes. Once especially, a party of them being much struck by the hairiness

of the calves of my legs—their own being entirely hairless—
one went away and returned with a baby a few weeks old,
and this child's head was then held down close to my leg,
and there were many jeers about the resemblance between
its scalp and my skin.

Often the Indians brought their guns to be mended.
These are mostly cheap weapons, of a most trumpery kind,
manufactured in England for the trade with savages. But
that the Indian, careful of such scarce commodities, uses but
three or four shots and a very small modicum of powder
to the charge, explosions and consequent injuries to the
Indians would be the frequent result from the use of these
guns. How tenderly an Indian uses his gun is well illustrated by the fact that I have known one such weapon used
for some time after its nipple had been lost and replaced by
a piece of bent tin cut from a sardine box.

Just after sunrise sometimes, before the sun was hot,
I strolled to the brow of the hill on which Quatata stands,
and there sat down. Below, at my feet, lay a vast and level
plain covered by just such luxuriant grass and other plants
of low growth as clothe the small moist patches of higher
ground. In the far distance the plain was bounded by the
ridges of the Pacaraima mountains, which were at that
moment much hidden by dense white clouds. Gradually
the masses of these clouds rose, and only a long, rugged, and
broken line of opaque white mist remained, marking where
the mountains rose from the plain. Presently the sun began
to shine with power, and lighted up each jutting fantastic
point of this low-lying mist, until the whole seemed a city of
temples and towers, crowned with gilded spires and minarets.

The level plain at my feet was the so-called Lake Amoocoo
or Parima, and the glittering cloud city was on the supposed
site of the fabled golden city of El Dorado or Manoa.
'Manoa,' as Raleigh wrote of it, 'the imperial citie of Guiana,
which the Spanyardes call El Dorado, that for the greatness
of its riches, and for the excellent seate, it farre exceedeth
any of the world; at least of so much of the world as is

knowen to the Spanish nation; it is founded upon a lake of salt water of 200 leagues long, like unto Mare Caspium.'

The so-called lake is almost throughout the year a dry plain, on which lines of æta palms mark the courses of streams, the overflowing of which in very wet seasons makes the 'lake.' Even as I looked at it that morning, the last of the mist melted, and the city once more went out from my sight, as it has from the belief of the world.

Many other things seen during that time occur to me; and especially the glorious beauty of the mountains on either side of us, as they appeared nightly emphasised and coloured in the intensely clear evening light. But space sufficient to tell more of these matters fails.

It was also at this time that I put myself in the hands of an Indian peaiman, or medicine man, and had experience of the method of cure employed by these people; but of this I shall have to give an account at another time.

For some time after our arrival the famine increased. Wherever we went, either the houses were deserted, or the people were living on palm-seeds, caterpillars, and ants, and we ourselves were often without even a morsel of bread or any vegetable food. But just when matters were at the worst, and it was almost impossible to get food to support life, rain came at last. The effect on the savannah was wonderful; for the very next day it began to look bright and green and gay. The grass grew as if by magic, and flowers grew among it; especially a beautiful and large pea-flower (*Clitoria guianensis.* Benth)—lilac-coloured, with a strong scent like clove-carnations; a tiny yellow crocus-like lily (*Hyposcis breviscapa*?) flowering close to the ground; and where the grass grew higher, tall white twin lilies (*Hippeastrum solandræflorum*) lifted their heads. Even the stony and more bare places were brightened by large numbers of yellow mullein-like flowers (*Byrsonima verbascifolia*). The greater abundance and pleasanter conditions brought back our strength and made it possible to extend our excursions.

Early in May Eddington and I started to visit the

frontier fort of St. Joaquim, in Brazilian territory. In that neighbourhood there are large cattle-farms, belonging to the Brazilian Government, and I was very anxious to see these. We had some little difficulty in getting men to go with us as guides and porters; for the Indians of the English savannah, remembering that not so many years ago the Brazilians were in the habit of capturing and enslaving them, do not much care to venture across the frontier. The difficulty was, however, at last overcome and we started.

Three days' walking across an almost uninhabited savannah—sometimes undulating, sometimes a huge, perfectly level plain—brought us, after crossing various small rivers, and among others the Nappi near its source, to Euwari-mana-kuroo, a settlement of Nikari-karu Indians, not far from the Takootoo river, which for some distance separates the British and Brazilian territories. Here we hoped to get the head man of the place, a Nikari-karu nicknamed 'Chirura,' or 'old breeches'—on account of his wearing clothes—to go with us as guide and interpreter. We also wanted to borrow a canoe from him in which to descend the Takootoo. In both these matters we succeeded; but we had, as usual, to wait some days before we could get Chirura to move.

Our stay was, however, not unpleasant. The settlement of three very large houses, each of which shelters several families, stands on the open savannah, on high ground, within a mile of the western end of the Canakoo mountains, the rugged sides of which are densely clothed with wood. Down from the mountains there is a waterfall of considerable size, the sound of which reached us in the houses. The people of the place are a mixed lot; for among the Nikari-karus there were several Macusis, as well as one Piriana, a woman indescribably fat, and consequently, especially in her un-clothed state, inexpressibly ugly.

Very little is known about the Nikari-karus, who are an ill-defined group of hybrids between Brazilian Portuguese on the one hand, and Indians, possibly Wapianas, on the other. Their language is a much corrupted form of Portuguese, which, as we found, when we took Chirura with us as interpreter into the Brazils, was almost unintelligible to speakers of pure Portuguese. Perhaps the most striking thing about them is the habit, which some of them have adopted from various Brazilian tribes of Indians, of filing each tooth to a sharp point, thus giving to their faces a most savage and hideous expression. Various other peculiarities of these people I have already mentioned ; but I may here add that they also differ from most other Indians of Guiana in their habit of living in large houses, several families together.

The children at Euwari-manakuroo, perhaps because of the European blood in their veins, played and sang in child-like ways very unusual among pure-blooded Indians; and the women even joined in the games, which is a still more unusual custom. In the evening the women and children sometimes caught hold of each other, and holding on one behind the other, marched round the house singing and dancing. I was especially attracted by one merry little fellow of about five years old, whom I first saw squatting, as on the top of a hill, on top of a turtle-shell twice as big as himself, with his knees drawn up to his chin, and solemnly smoking a long bark cigarette.

One point of interest in this neighbourhood was the comparatively frequent occurrence of stone hatchets and other similar instruments. Stone implements, though no longer used in Guiana, are to be found in greater or less abundance throughout the district.

At last, after four days' stay, we got off. The two or three people from Euwari-manakuroo who came with us gave their wives knotted strings or quippus, each knot representing one of the days they expected to be away, and the whole string thus forming a calendar to be used by the wives until the return of their husbands.

On going down to Yarewah on the Takootoo, we found the two canoes which we had engaged, and from there we once more started on a river journey. But now, instead of being on a river of the Essequibo system, we were descending the

water-shed of the Amazon. The Takootoo runs into the
Rio Branco, that into the Rio Negro, and that into the Amazon at Manaos. From Yarewah the boundary between the
Brazilian and British territories passes along the Takootoo,
until that river is joined by the Cotinga, which flows in from
the north, and up which the boundary line passes. This is
the line laid down by the boundary commission under Sir
Richard Schomburgk about 1840, and is really accepted by
both nations, in spite of the vague claims which, as I have
said, have been advanced by the Brazilians to the land between the Takootoo and the Roopoonooni. The commandant of St. Joaquim, an educated Brazilian gentleman, and the
chief resident official on that frontier, in his conversation fully
recognised the boundary line thus described. I have been
led to say so much on this subject because this part of the
boundary is generally wrongly laid down in even the standard English atlases ; and it is much to be desired that this,
as well as the boundary line between British Guiana and
Venezuela, should be more correctly represented.

We paddled gently down the Takootoo, which is a river of
considerable size, getting an occasional shot at one of the
many turtles which lay, basking in the sun, on the logs at the
river-side, or at an ibis as it fed on one of the innumerable
ridges of sand. The journey led us, for two days, past the
mouth of the Ireng and Cotinga rivers ; past many flocks of
beautiful rosy spoonbills ; past porpoises, which our men said
were omars, or water-women, and 'had frocks ;' past manatees,
which venture up the Amazon rivers even as far as this ; past
ugly green iguanas climbing on the trees on shore ; past high
cliff-like banks capped with long lines of white lilies (*Hippeastrum*), well defined against the sky ; and past long reaches
of bush-covered banks densely matted with wreaths of passion-flowers, at that time heavily loaded with large purple
blooms. By the third day the river had become considerably wider, and the Rio Branco appeared before us, the
Takootoo running into it almost at right angles. On the left,
in the angle formed by the junction of the two rivers, the

high bank was crowned by a little stone fort. It was
St. Joaquim, and our destination.

This fort was built more than a century ago by the
Portuguese. It consists merely of a two-roomed house, under
which is a lock-up, while a rampart surrounds the whole.
When Schomburgk visited the place about 1840, he found a
Jesuit mission with a chapel and a few houses. But these
have now disappeared, and the fort and the range of low huts
serving as soldiers' quarters alone remain. For many years
past it has barely been kept in repair, and, as it is now perfectly useless as a military station, the Brazilian authorities
are said to intend abandoning it. It is certainly quite time ;
the gates are never shut—indeed only one of them is left ;
no sentinel paces the ramparts, no bugle ever sounds.

The commandant received us most hospitably. He had
volunteered to serve in this lonely place in the hope of
seeing something of the Indians, in whom he feels great
interest ; but his nearest white neighbour—for the men
forming the garrison are all negroes—is many days' journey
away, and his only communication with the outside world
is by a steamer which comes up the Rio Negro at very rare
intervals, or by Indian canoes. He had only been at the fort
some six months, but was, not unnaturally, already somewhat
tired of the place.

After spending a very pleasant day and night with the
commandant, who gave a most interesting account of the
farms, supporting many thousand head of cattle, which lie
round the fort, we turned homeward, intending to visit some
of these farms on our way.

The cattle on these farms are left almost entirely to
nature. The farms were established about the end of the
last century, but were again destroyed, the cattle being dis-
persed over the savannah during the revolutionary times.
When order was restored, the cattle, which had in the
meantime greatly multiplied, were not all again gathered
together ; the greater number were allowed to roam and
breed where they pleased. Once a year a certain number

of the younger of these wild cattle are driven into the strongly stockaded pen which forms the central point of each of the gigantic farms into which these savannahs are divided.   These impounded cattle, after being branded, are let out every day, but are driven back into the pen at night.   Every now and then a large number of them are taken down the Rio Branco to Manaos, the nearest Brazilian town, and are from there distributed along the Amazon. Much of the cattle is also slaughtered on the farms; the meat, after being cut into thin slices, is slightly salted and dried in the sun, and is then carried down to the Amazon and there sold.

At the central farm of the district resides a Government official, who is responsible for all the cattle in his district. His only assistants are a very few cowherds, a few of whom are Brazilians of a low class, a few are half-bred between Brazilians and Indians, but by far the greater number are the Indians of the district.   Most of the work of these herdsmen is done from the back of small but strong horses, which, when not in use, roam all but free on the savannah. All the food required is produced on the spot.   For meat, the men are allowed to kill a certain number of cattle for their own use, and the milk, which, however, as always in the case of any but thoroughly domesticated cattle, is very small in quantity, is at their disposal.   Game, especially deer, is abundant.   Cassava is grown at the principal farms, where it is made into farine, a coarse but most excellent and nutritive flour, which is distributed twice a month to the men of all the farms.   Vegetables, such as yams, potatoes, and plantains, and fruits are but little grown, except in the fields of the Indians, where, however, they flourish so well that they might evidently be cultivated with advantage elsewhere.

Some statistics published by the Brazilian Government in an account of the country, printed in connection with the Philadelphia Exhibition of 1876, afford some idea of the profit derived from this industry.

' Of all the branches of industry, the most profitable, and that which has acquired most importance, is the breeding of horned cattle. . . . . Cattle-raising is confided entirely to nature ; the breeder does nothing, but receives the profits ; the whole labour consists in collecting the cattle now and then in proper places, called *rodeios*, in order to mark the calves; in this work half-bred Indians are generally employed at the low wages of ten dollars a month.

' An idea may be formed of the importance of this industry from official statistics which show that in the year 1873–74, the province of S. Pedro do Rio Grande do Sul alone exported 23,860,636 kilograms of jerked beef, of the approximate value of 6,000 dollars.

' The natural breeding of horned cattle in Brazil yields considerable profits, not only because the outlay is limited, but because the current expenses are small, as will be seen by the following demonstration.

' A meadow of 9,000,000 square metres can easily graze 1,000 head of cattle, for which two men are sufficient ; these are generally known by the name of *campeiros* (field men), or *vaqueiros* (cowherds). This number of cattle produces generally fifty oxen and as many cows yearly.

' The . . . . average value of an ox is 20 dollars, and that of a cow is 10 dollars ; the result therefore of the work of two herdsmen will be 1,500 dollars a year, which is equal to, if not more than, the same number of labourers can gain in the best plantations. If, however, it be considered that prairies most suited to this industry, situated in the interior of the provinces, are generally of much less value than the lands in the coffee districts, or those fit for the sugar-cane; that the price of cattle in the breeding districts is very low ; that stock-raising does not require many labourers; and that the expense of carrying the produce to market is but small, as they are driven there and not carried,—it will be seen that in Brazil no industry can be compared to this.' [1]

[1] *The Empire of Brazil at the Universal Exhibition of* 1876 *in Philadelphia,* pp. 264 *et seq.*

Now, as has been said, some 14,000 square miles of these savannahs on this side of the upper Takootoo and the Cotinga rivers lie within our territory. Probably the only difference between the English and the Brazilian plains is that on the former high ground and single detached hills are more common than on the latter.

The life of a cattle-farmer on these savannahs would surely be not unpleasant to many who can find no work nearer home. Food for the cattle is there in abundance ; and food for man might at small pains be made equally abundant. Cassava, yams, plantains, and fruits flourish. Game, such as deer, wild hog, birds, and fish, is plentiful. A certain number of the cattle kept would also supply more food. Sufficient labour might also be had. There are plenty of Indians living in the district, at present idly, but who, as they are of the same, or at any rate of kindred, tribes to those Indians who do the work on the Brazilian farms, might with care and kindness be turned into useful cowherds ; and horses, which would be required to drive the half-wild cattle, might readily be procured from the Brazilian side of the boundary.

The one real difficulty in the way of the establishment of such cattle-farms is that of getting produce to town. The distance between Georgetown and the English savannahs is probably about equal to that between Manoas and the most remote Brazilian farm on the Rio Branco and Takootoo ; but the rivers on our side of the water-shed, which here practically divides the English and Brazilian territories, are more rocky and difficult of navigation than those on the other side appear to be. This would of course offer but little obstacle to the conveyance of jerked or otherwise dried or salted meat ; but there would be considerable difficulty in getting living cattle to town, except during the height of the wet season, until either a river-road for large flat-bottomed boats, such as those used for cattle-carrying on the Brazilian rivers, has been cleared by blasting the rocks in the worst of the falls, or until a road has been cut through the bush.

To make such a road would probably be beyond private enterprise, unless on a large scale; but if evert he work of 'opening up the country' is seriously undertaken by the Government, one of its first acts must be to make one or other of these highways.

Our first halt after leaving St. Joaquim was at the farm attached to the fort. It was under the joint charge of a rough-looking Venezuelan, and the most highly civilised Macusi I ever saw; and these two were assisted by the son of the latter, who, in that he spoke both Macusi and Portuguese fluently, seemed to share the intelligence of his father, but, in that his teeth were filed and painted after the Indian manner, seemed not entirely to have rejected barbarism.

We were in great want both of meat and farine, both of which we had hoped to procure at this place, so that it was not pleasant to hear that neither were at the moment to be had. However, our offer of gunpowder, shot, and caps induced the Macusi to bring a small quantity of farine, and shortly afterwards the Venezuelan offered to sell us one or more head of cattle. This offer was at once accepted, and the price for a young bull was fixed at three-quarters of a pound of gunpowder.

Both the farm-keepers at once made preparations to drive the cattle into one of the two huge wooden pens or corrals which were before us. Each slung his whip, the whole of which, handle and lash, was formed of one long piece of plaited raw hide, round his right hand, and mounting on his horse, which stood by, ready equipped with a high wooden Spanish saddle, rode off; and we were left to smoke and look at the scene. But for the hut against which we leaned, and the two corrals, on the rails of which were perched many expectant vultures, the scene might have been on any uninhabited part of the savannah. There was the same scanty grass growing from a pebbly soil, among which many small boulders were scattered here and there; there were the same scattered, wiry-looking bushes; and in the distance there was the not unusual background of mountains. It was, by the way, from a place called by the Indians Toucana, somewhere among these mountains, that I got many specimens of stone axe-heads, and I was assured by the Indians that they abound there.

When we were tired of this scene we went into the hut, which we found occupied by two Macusi women. One of these was a girl of the usual type, but the other was the oldest-looking Indian I ever saw. Her very scanty hair was of the dirty grey colour to which, instead of to white, the hair of an Indian turns in old age. Her only clothing was the usual queyu, a small bead-apron. When the girl offered me some farine boiled in milk, the old lady got angry, and, managing to get out of her hammock, tottered towards us with the help of a large stick. But the milk and farine were very good to one who had fared but poorly for some time, and I ate it in spite of the protest.

The sound of the stamping of many feet now told that the cattle were near, and this grew louder and louder until, at last, herds of cattle, varying only in colour from dun to black, came awkwardly galloping from several points, tumbling and bellowing out from among the bushes. The animals were cleverly kept together by the mounted drivers, and in a very few minutes four hundred head of cattle were penned in one corral, only just large enough to hold the number. The ungainly movements of a crowd of our own domestic cattle, even when these are driven or are otherwise frightened, can give no idea of the frantic convulsions moving this mass of half-wild animals. The noise, too, was deafening.

The drivers now dismounted, and the Venezuelan, apparently without the slightest trouble, threw his plaited lasso of raw hide over the horns of a fine young black bull, which had been selected, and which was then drawn out of the surging mass of its companions. The poor beast was very quickly pole-axed and then stabbed to the heart. This quick manner of inflicting death is, I am afraid, not always practised on these farms, where they say the meat cannot be tender unless the animal has been bled to death.

By the time this was over it was too late to go farther
that day, so we slung our hammocks in an empty house by
the side of the river. All through that night fires, above
which were babracots loaded with beef, burned, but, as never
happened on any other occasion when there was meat in
prospect, I had hard work to make the Indians keep up the
fires ; for these people will not eat beef.

The next day we started at a late hour, and the current
running very strongly against us, it was not till noon on the
following day that we reached Anaikim or, as the Portuguese
call it, St. Anton, the highest farm on the Takootoo, occupying the angle formed by the junction of that river and the
Cotinga. The farm is very similar to the one already described but that the house, of wattle-work and with a gallery,
is of a much better kind and is situated a long distance from
the river. There is, however, an abundant supply of water at
hand in a curious series of long ponds, which look like traces
of a former course of the Cotinga river. The farm is kept
by three young Brazilians, of a very superior class to the men
of the Fort Farm ; even one of these, however, had his teeth
filed to points.

I am inclined to think that it was on this farm that an
earlier traveller[1] saw, as he thought, herds of wild cattle. It
was certainly in this neighbourhood that these cattle were
seen; and as that writer does not mention the farm of
Anaikim it is probable that he did not know of its existence.
The cattle roam far and, as has been said, almost free, and
even, when the water is low, they wade across the Cotinga
and have to be reclaimed by their Brazilian owners from
English territory. That a traveller, who chanced to see such
cattle in a neighbourhood where he knew of no farm, should
think that the beasts were wild was not an unnatural mistake.

For many days it had rained incessantly, and as we were
generally without shelter by day or night, we were most
anxious to get back to Quatata as quickly as possible.

[1] C. B. Brown, *Canoe and Camp Life in British Guiana.* London, 1870.

Travelling once more up the Takootoo we reached the mouth of the Ireng or Mahoo river, and turned up this, purposing to force our way home up the Pirara, a small river, then much swollen by rains, which rises not far from Quatata, and runs into the Ireng about one day's journey above the point at which that river joins the Takootoo. The Pirara, therefore, if its waters were high enough to allow the passage of our canoe, would afford a much nearer road to Quatata than that by which we had come.

The rain gave occasion to some amusing conduct on the part of the Indians. Some of them had become the proud possessors of some old clothes, such as shirts and trousers. Whenever rain began to fall they carefully took them off to put them under shelter. But in the crowded state of our canoe it was somewhat difficult to find a dry place for them. The matter was finally arranged by one of the Indians keeping on his shirt and allowing the tail to hang loose from the bench on which he sat paddling, while the other clothes were put under the shelter of this tail.

The Ireng as we turned into it was in high flood, and the current which met us was so strong that we made but slow progress. Every now and then the branch of a tree or a log swept by us, hurried along by the swift, steady flow of the water. Once the whole trunk of a dead tree, torn away from the bank, met us; two or three of the main branches remained standing straight up from the water; a turtle lay on the trunk. As it sailed quickly past us it looked like a wrecked ship; the branches seemed masts madly zigzagging in all directions, and the turtle represented the last survivor of the crew.

That night we camped, in mosquito-haunted ground, just below the mouth of the Pirara; and early the next morning we entered that river. The water in the Pirara had risen above the low banks, and the narrow belt of trees which generally separates the river from the savannah now rose from the flood. As there was, therefore, little current, we advanced rapidly. At noon on the day on which we entered the river we reached a point which, according to the Indians, was the highest to which a canoe could at the time pass. It afterwards appeared that we might have kept to the river much longer; but, believing the Indians, we disembarked, and walked the rest of the journey. Our way led across the bed of Lake Amoocoo. This, as I have said, is usually dry; but now we found that the water was out, and that for once the lake was a lake. For long distances we had to wade through water up to our waists, and often up to our necks. Had anyone been there to see we must have presented an odd appearance; as regards myself, all that was visible above water was my face and two arms, holding up some Indian featherwork which I had bought, tobacco and a pipe, and some papers which it was important to keep dry. I was much struck by the way in which the Indians managed to follow the path, which, even when there is no water, is hardly discernible to an unpractised eye, and which now was completely hidden under a sheet of water; yet we emerged from the flood exactly where the track led out. But before this, when we came to the deepest part of the flood, the Indians became frightened, as they generally are in water, though they can swim like fishes, and it was hard work to persuade them to advance. At last we came to higher and therefore dry ground, and after a twelve miles' walk came to Quatata.

Only those who have had a like experience can imagine the comfort of that first night spent under a dry roof, with a comparative sufficiency of food, after a fortnight of almost constant exposure to heavy rain, with an empty stomach. Rain fell all night, and there was much thunder; the sounds of these added greatly, if on somewhat imaginative grounds, to our comfort.

June came, and it was quite time to be thinking of returning to Georgetown; but at first it seemed almost impossible to get Indians or to get possession of our canoes. The Indians were very unwilling to go with us, partly because food was still so scarce that we could expect only scanty rations on the journey, and partly, as they said, because a

party of English soldiers were on their way up from Georgetown to capture and press Indians as soldiers.   The same
rumour has been heard by nearly every traveller in the
interior; it is probably due to a half-remembered tradition
of the slave-hunting expeditions which the Brazilians, as
lately as forty years ago, used frequently to make among
these people, mingled with other traditions of the visit of English soldiers to Pirara in 1840.   Whatever the origin of the
rumour, it is a constant excuse used by the Indians when they
are unwilling to undertake the fatigue of a journey.   The
other difficulty which delayed our immediate return to the
coast, was that some strange Indians had carried off my
canoe from the waterside.   Indians have a large, but occasionally inconvenient, code of hospitality.   An Indian thinks
nothing of walking into the house of any other Indian of the
same tribe and appropriating the food which may be in it;
nor do the owners in any way resent this.   In the same way,
when an Indian, in his frequent wanderings, finds a canoe in
a convenient spot he takes it and leaves it wherever his own
journey happens to end; rumour, passed from Indian to
Indian, at last tells the owner of the craft as to the where-
abouts of his property, and if he wants it he must fetch it
back himself, or must wait till some other chance Indian,
travelling, brings it back into the neighbourhood from which
it was taken.   In this way my canoe was out of reach just
when I most wanted it, and the Indians who had removed it
were surprised by my objecting to this conduct.   However,
at last we were ready to start; and very severe ophthalmia
having broken out among the Indians and even attacked
my two companions, everything urged speedy departure.

The Indians of Quatata carried all our goods down to the
river-side, and though this work occupied two days, they
wanted no payment.   At Pirara landing all but those of our
own crew said good-bye to us.

It was in the very middle of the long rainy season, so
that the currents in the river swept us down very rapidly.
At night it was often very difficult to find dry ground on

which to camp, and even when in the evening we slung our hammocks over dry land we sometimes found ourselves over water when we awoke in the morning, so rapidly was the water still rising. The creepers which festooned the trees on the banks were in most brilliant and full flower. It was one of the rare occasions on which I saw anything of that splendour of flower which dwellers in colder climates sometimes suppose to be characteristic of and universal in the tropics.

At Apooterie, at the junction of the Roopoonooni with the Essequibo we were delayed some days while bread was being made. Joseph, our old Carib friend and host, had removed his settlement to a point some hundred yards lower down the river. The two houses stood, as usual, in a small circular clearing in the forest. One evening during our stay here there was a most magnificent storm. Just before dusk the sky over the clearing was bright and cloudless ; suddenly the sound of a storm sweeping over the forest from far away was heard, travelling quickly toward us. The parrots began to scream and the Indians busied themselves in fetching in their bread, which had been out all day in the sun. A long thread of white cloud began to appear over the tops of the trees to the north, and then swept on with terrific speed over the whole round tract of sky, drawing up behind it an intensely ink-black cloud-curtain; in hardly more than a moment this blackness had spread over the whole sky, and night was upon us. These sudden storms were always accompanied by one unbroken, mighty blast of wind, followed by much thunder and lightning. The effect was marvellous.

Hearing that there was a chance of getting some cassava from an Indian living in the forest some two miles from Apooterie, I, with one Indian, started in a woodskin or bark canoe to find this man. He was a notorious Wapiana, who, having killed his father and mother and some other people, had found it advisable to settle in a remote place and difficult of access. Certainly he had found such a place. Going for a short distance down the Essequibo we passed into a creek which, instead of running into the main river, receives a tremendous rush of water from that river. Our poor little piece of bark was whirled by the water into this place with terrific force, and in a moment we were some distance down the creek, which is very narrow and winding, and is choked by many trees. It was very difficult to keep our canoe from being dashed to pieces. Then, pushing aside some bushes at the side of the creek, we passed on to a swamp covered with shallow water and thickly set with trees; and, after winding in and out among these in the most surprising way, we suddenly emerged on to a large and still lake in the centre of a palm forest. Following this for about a mile we reached a landing place, where we disembarked. The lake is very long and, as I believe, receives at its upper end the creek through which we had passed from the Essequibo, and discharges water at its lower end through another creek into the main river. Such side-streams, or itaboos, as they are called by the Indians, are not uncommon in Guiana. After walking from the lake for some distance through the forest we at last reached a field where we found the assassin living in a tiny hut alone with a young and pretty wife and a baby. The assassin was gentle enough in appearance, and the only thing remarkable about him was the enormous size of the plate of silver which he wore, as other Indians do similar but smaller plates, suspended from his nose. This ornament was so large as entirely to overhang his mouth, so that when he drank he had to lift it with one hand while he tilted the drinking vessel with the other. He supplied me with so much cassava that, returning to Apooterie that day, we were able to continue our journey on the next.

On the high flood we passed for a time between banks thickly festooned with creepers, which were then in most brilliant and full flower; for at the beginning of the rainy season these plants all bloom.

We soon reached Rappoo, and below that had to maintain an almost constant struggle with falls. Every morning the Indians rubbed red peppers or lime-juice into their eyes, after which they were ready to shoot the falls.

During the high rains the falls are very difficult to pass, and long reaches of the river are transformed into vast rapids, through which the Indians steer their canoes with perfectly marvellous skill. Shooting a big fall, or running down a rapid of any size, is certainly exciting work. The canoe floats in smooth water at the top, and from there the bow-man and steersman examine the fall and agree as to the particular course to be taken; this once decided, the rush begins. Suddenly the canoe, guided into the eddying, rushing water, bounds forward; it perhaps rushes straight towards some threatening sunken rock, but one strong, swift turn of the bowman's paddle saves it from that danger; it rushes on again, turned here and there by waves and contrary currents, the bowman and steersman contriving to guide it, until in its headlong rush it in some way reaches smooth water at the bottom.

It is difficult to find words to convey a picture of such a rapid or flood to one who has never seen any of the great rivers of South America. It is no ordinary river falling down a step of rocks, but a great and wide sea of contending waves and currents, surging and breaking in most chaotic confusion in, over, and round countless rocks and obstructions.

Sometimes, however, as happened to us on this occasion at Etannime, the main fall is too high and too rough to make it safe to shoot it. There are generally side channels (itaboos) to all these falls, and Etannime was no exception, so we made up our minds to lower the canoes down one of these. A rope was fastened to the bow of the canoe, and some of the men, standing on the bank, firmly held the other end of this. Then the canoe was allowed to glide stern foremost down into the narrow, rushing channel. This is a rapid of some two miles in length but hardly ten yards in width, down which the water rushes fast and foaming, in and out among thick, overhanging trees, and round corners, and down low, but abrupt falls. As soon as, by slow paying out of the bow line, the canoe had been safely lowered down the first of the short reaches, those who were on board kept her in position by holding fast to the overhanging tree-trunks and branches, while those on shore dropped the rope, and then hurried through the bush to a point commanding the next reach, down which, as soon as they had again grasped the rope, the canoe was allowed to drift. In this way most of the reaches were passed; but sometimes the course of the channel was so crooked and rocky that it was impossible to pay out the rope from the shore. In these latter cases all got into the canoe, which was then allowed to hurry down the turning rapid, and was fended from the rocky banks as well as might be, with poles and much grasping of overhanging trees. So we got to the bottom of Etannime falls. It was very tedious work, but far safer than shooting the main fall.

Shooting the falls was a frequent and most exciting event during our downward journey, but once we had a different excitement. Early one morning, having started before dawn we reached the place where the Potaro river joins the Essequibo in a large lake-like expanse, which looked even more than usually beautiful in the wonderfully clear morning light. Suddenly my bowman got excited, and standing up, shading his eyes with his hand, gazed steadily at a line of white foam in the far distance. Presently he uttered the word ' whinga,' and the next moment, he and the other Indians, bending to their paddles as I never saw them do before, the canoe shot rapidly over the perfectly smooth water towards the line of foam. Whinga is the Macusi name for that sort of bush-hog, or peccary, which lives in large herds (*Dicotyles labiatus*); and one of these herds was now swimming the river. While the men worked with a will at the paddles, I looked to all the guns, and then stood up and watched the herd as it neared the shore. The race was for more than two miles, and the hogs won. No sooner, however, had the bow of our canoe touched the shore at the point where the beasts had disappeared, than everyone was out and after them, with gun or bow and arrows. The forest was alive with the sound of men crushing through the brush-wood, and with the grunts and squeals of the pigs. Pre-sently, finding the bush too dense for a man with clothes, I turned back to the canoe, and after a time the men dropped in one by one bringing their prey. I can safely affirm that sucking 'whinga,' roasted, is as good meat as can be had anywhere.

Such herds as these not unfrequently cross the rivers in their journeys. If they come to the river-side at night they wait grunting on the bank till dawn. As soon as it is light the whole herd plunges into the water and makes for the opposite shore. They are very easily killed when in the water, and their crossing offers a splendid opportunity to one whose larder wants replenishing. In one case, I heard of one single man killing fifty hogs out of a herd which was crossing the Mazeruni just below the Penal Settlement. On another occasion some negroes were taking a timber punt up towards the Monkey Jump on the Essequibo, when, just be-fore they reached that point, a herd of bush-hogs crossed in front of them. There was no gun in the punt, nor was there a small boat from which to attack the animals; but one of the men, a splendid swimmer named Sassington, plunged into the water, carrying with him one end of a rope of which the other end was attached to the punt. He managed to tie the rope to the legs of six of the hogs, and then, scrambling back into the punt, hauled in his prey.

At last all the adventures of the expedition were over, and we reached Georgetown after an absence of six months from the civilised world.

CHAPTER III.

THE KAIETEUR FALL AND RORAIMA.

The Kaieteur Fall—First Visit—The Potaro River—Amootoo Cataract—
The Kaieteur Ravine—To the Foot of the Fall—The Kaieteur, in Dry
Weather, from above—The Kaieteur Savannah—A New Plant (*Brocchi-
nia cordylinoides*, Baker?)—A new bird (*Agelæus imthurni*, Sclater)—A
Second Visit to the Kaieteur—Beautiful Flowers—Portaging the Boat
—The Kaieteur Fall, from above, in the Rainy Season—The Best Way
to Visit the Fall—Roraima.

THE two most interesting natural features in the interior of
Guiana, those which have attracted most attention from the
outside world, are the Kaieteur fall and the mountain called
Roraima. Some account of these is therefore necessary.
Unfortunately I can write only of the former from personal
experience, and, as regards Roraima, must trust to the accounts of the three or four travellers who, unlike myself,
have had the good fortune to visit it.

The existence of the Kaieteur fall was unknown till 1871,
when it was discovered and described by Mr. C. Barrington
Brown, who was at the time engaged in making a geological
survey of the colony. It is formed by the fall of the river
Potaro, a tributary of the Essequibo, over an abrupt cliff of
741 feet. The width of the fall at times of high water, is
370 feet; while at low water it decreases to rather less than
half that width.

Compared with some other falls the Kaieteur is
small; for while it ranks far below the Yosemite both in
height and width, it falls far short of Niagara in width
though it exceeds it in height. But as regards the surrounding scenery it is impossible to believe that even the
scenery of the Yosemite can exceed that of the Kaieteur;

PLATE II.

and that round Niagara is, now at least, notoriously commonplace. It is, in fact, the marvellous surroundings combined with the magnitude, which should make the magnificence of the Kaieteur.

In the ten years since its existence was first made known, the Kaieteur has but seldom been visited. The discoverer, accompanied by some other travellers, paid a second visit to it within a few months. But between that time and 1878 it was seen by white men only on four occasions. In the last-mentioned year, and again in the following year, I was able to visit it twice, seeing it on the first of these occasions during a very dry season, and on the second during a very wet season.

Leaving Georgetown on the 13th of October 1878, we passed up the Essequibo—a journey up which I have already described, as far as the mouth of the Potaro river. On the sixth day we reached Toomatoomari cataract, some eight miles up the Potaro. This place is indescribably lovely. A large land-locked bay is filled with groups of trees, with bright yellow sand in smooth stretches and in sloping banks, with rocks, with pools of still water; and at the upper end is a low but broad foaming cataract. It was Saturday evening, and we determined to spend the whole of the next day there, for the large canoe could go no further, and we had to select from our stores what seemed absolutely necessary for our further journey, which would have to be in the boat and a woodskin purchased from some passing Ackawoi.

The next morning when I awoke I found that the tree, of a genus (*Eugenia*) new to me, to which one end of my hammock was tied, had burst into a marvellous sheet of pure white blossom. The branches touched the ground. Dense masses of its tiny feathery flowers, nestling along each branch and branchlet, made the whole look as if weighed down with snow. Its scent filled the air, and had attracted a host of humming-birds, butterflies, and bees, filling the air with their murmur. Sight, scent, and sound were equally grateful.

Early next morning, having hauled our boat up the cataract on the previous evening, and leaving four men in charge of the canoe and the surplus stores, we walked along the portage path past the cataract; and thirteen of us embarked for our further journey.

Toomatoomari cataract is one of the gates of Fairyland. Beyond it the scenery of the Potaro, at least when the river is low, is one constantly changing beautiful picture, and far surpasses that of any other river I have seen in Guiana. It is in times of low water, when the rocks are uncovered, that the rivers of this country are seen to best advantage. This river of wonderfully clear wine-red water is about three hundred yards wide, and flows among single rocks and islands of rocks, confusedly piled, some large, some small, some water-worn into flutings so regular that it is difficult to remember that they are not fragments of huge masonry; some so regularly square that they look as if cut by a Norman builder; some rounded like the boulders of our English downs; some of every conceivable shape and fracture; all heaped on each other in most chaotic confusion. The gaps between the jutting points of the rock-islands are filled by banks of clean bright sand sloping gently into the water. Wherever the sand met the water on the edges of these banks, great troops of yellow, white, or blue butterflies were clustering to suck the moisture. The river-banks, thickly wooded as on every other river of Guiana, are here rounded into many hills and slopes, between each two of which one of innumerable small streams runs down into the main stream.

The first day from Toomatoomari, spent in an untented boat, on level water, and under a hot sun, was somewhat trying, and was the one hardship which we had to endure during the whole expedition. In the afternoon we passed the mouth of the Cooriebrong river, then very low. Opposite to the mouth of this river, on the left bank of the Potaro, was a newly built Ackawoi settlement, then temporarily deserted. This was the first of many new settlements which we passed; for it seemed that the Ackawoi were beginning to

populate the banks of the Potaro thickly. We were surprised
to find that all the settlements we passed were deserted.

Towards night we reached the first rapids at Chowrah;
and from that point up to the Kaieteur, the reaches of
smooth water between the rapids, cataracts, or falls were but
short. By the side of Chowrah rapid we settled down for
the night, that our men might have a chance of shooting
some of the blood-red pacu (*Pacu myletes*) which flitted
about in the clear shallow water.

Next day, after passing a few other small rapids, we came
to Mowraseema cataract. Here we had to unload the boat,
and carry it and the goods along a rocky island which
divides the river. This portage was short.

A short reach of smooth water, broken here and there by
rapids, now small, but past one of which it is necessary to
portage in times of high water, led to the bottom of a series
of three cataracts and one fall at Pacoutout.

This is the only really difficult portage on the river. It
is generally necessary to drag the boats and goods up, over,
and down a very steep hill covered with thick forest, for
a distance of over two-thirds of a mile. Our Arawaks
wished to do the same now, though they admitted that, as
rollers would have to be cut and laid along the whole path,
the work would take a day and a half. Moreover the difficulty of the portage had recently been much increased,
owing to the fact that some Ackawoi Indians, having lately
made a settlement in these parts, had chosen to make their
cassava field over a considerable part of the path, which was,
consequently, almost entirely blocked up by the trunks of
felled trees. Dreading the difficulty and delay, and considering the somewhat low state of the water, we determined to
haul the boat up the river, and carry only the goods across.
The more adventurous Caribs agreeing in our plan, the
Arawaks were at last persuaded to help; and both boat
and woodskin were without very much difficulty dragged up
the falls to the higher end of the portage-path that same
evening, thus avoiding a delay of two days. Above the

portage the first beautiful view of the sandstone range of the
Kaieteur appeared, framed in trees, and with the river, thickly
blocked with tangled masses of a peculiar sedge (*Carex*,
nov. sp.), as a foreground.

Early next morning we passed another newly formed
Ackawoi settlement, about a quarter of a mile above Pacoutout fall. It also was deserted. A few hours later we came
to yet another new settlement, this time a very large one, at
the mouth of the Aykooroo creek. As we drew near this, a
most unusually large crowd of Indians came down to the
water-side to meet us. Some were almost covered up in
long loose folds of coloured calico; some were dressed from
head to foot in palm-leaves; some, naked but for the usual lap,
had painted their whole bodies with most elaborate patterns;
others had all sorts of quaint ornaments in most marvellous
variety. All were somewhat the worse for paiwari. A great
paiwari feast had been begun here on the previous day and
was to continue for several days more. There were at least
two hundred men, women, and children present, each one of
whom, down to the youngest babies, instigated by their
mothers, insisted on shaking our hands. The deserted state
of the settlements lower down the river was now fully
accounted for.

On reaching the captain's house we found the centre of
it occupied by three or four large troughs of paiwari, round
which a long procession of Indians, men and women, each
provided with some variety of drum or rattle, was moving.
Each individual was stamping in monotonous time with his
feet; each was keeping up the usual fearfully monotonous
chant, Hia-Hia-Hia-Hia.

That same afternoon we came to Amootoo fall and
cataract. It seemed as if the beauty of the scenery increased as we advanced. As we paddled up a straight river-
reach, a dome-shaped, wooded island lay before us in the
centre of the foreground, dividing the river into two channels. On one side of this island a large cataract, some
twelve feet in height, fell foaming down the violet-brown

PLATE III.

PORTAGING THE BOAT.

sandstone rocks to where, in the water below, the feathery leaves of a water-weed (*Lacis*), dotted with its small, pink flowers, formed green and pink cushions ; on the other side, a magnificent perpendicular wall about fifteen feet in height of the same sandstone ledges, then dry, marked where in the time of high rains the water falls down into the black pool of the second channel. The wooded undulating banks curved towards us from the cataract on the left and from the fall on the right, forming a complete amphitheatre, behind which, in the distance, towered precipitous sandstone mountains, most quaint in outline, and tree-covered except on the most abrupt faces of the gray-brown rocks. Behind us lay the granite formation ; in front was all sandstone.

We were obliged to carry our boat across the portage, which is about a quarter of a mile long, up and then down a very considerable hill. Our men laid rollers all along the path, then harnessed themselves, by a rope attached to the bows of the boat, like a team of horses, and drew the boat merrily over in a very short time.

Here, at Amootoo, we passed between two high hills into the ravine of the Kaieteur. From Toomatoomari to this point the valley of the Potaro passes through undulating, but comparatively level, forest-covered country. At Amootoo this plain is crossed at right angles to the bed of the river by an abrupt sandstone cliff, 700 or 800 feet in height, from the top of which a plateau runs back. Through this high plateau the Potaro has cut for itself a ravine, which extends from the Kaieteur to Amootoo, where it bursts through the cliff into the general plain of the lower region. In journeying up this river, therefore, one passes first through forest country but little above the level of the sea, then, at Amootoo, into the Kaieteur ravine, having the high, mountainous cliffs of the upper plateau on either hand ; this ravine ends in a complete amphitheatre at the great fall itself. Into this amphitheatre the column of water drops down from the plateau, which still further from the sea is shut in by distant hills.

It was at Amootoo—that is, on first entering the Kaieteur ravine—that we reached the most beautiful scenery of that beautiful river. If the whole valley of the Potaro is Fairyland, then the Kaieteur ravine is the penetralia of Fairyland. Here, owing to the moisture-collecting nature of the sandstone rock, the green of the plant-world seemed yet greener and more varied. Under the thick shade countless streamlets trickled over little ledges of rock among pigmy forests of filmy ferns and mosses. The small plume-like tufts of these ferns, each formed of many half-transparent fronds of a dark cool-looking green colour, were exquisite. Larger ferns, with a crowd of aroids, orchids and other plants, covered the rocks between these streams in new and marvellous luxuriance. Several curious forms of leafless, white-stalked parasitic gentians (*Voyria*), one yellow, others white, and one violet, were especially noticeable.

On either side rose the tall, grand cliffs which form the sides of the ravine. The sandstone plateau of which they are the edge, extends from this to Roraima. The appearance of the perpendicular tree-crowned cliffs, broken here and there by gaps, recalled the pictures of that mountain ; indeed, one of my Indian companions, who had been to Roraima, ejaculated, as he pointed to one of these rocks, ' little Roraima.' Far up on the faces of the cliff were ledges on which grew what appeared to be a few green plants ; some idea of the size of these cliffs may be drawn from the fact that the field-glasses showed these plants to be tall forest trees.

Among this scenery animal life was nowhere abundant. Bright orange-coloured ' cocks of the rock' (*Rupicola crocea*, Vieill) flitting like flashes of light from tree to tree, were perhaps the most abundant form ; a hawk occasionally rose screaming from some high ledge of rock ; now and then a maroodi (*Penelope*) cried shrilly from among the trees ; and a few kingfishers darted across and along the water. On one tree a pair of bright green toucans (*Aulacoramphus sulcatus*), the only examples of the genus I ever saw, were feeding.

On the same day on which we left Amootoo we reached the last small cataract at Waratoo. The portage is short, but we were not even obliged to use it; for by carrying the goods past the cataract, we were able to drag the boat up in the water. Half-an-hour after leaving this place, I experienced a most strange and memorable sensation.

A partial view of the distant fall should be obtained from this point. Before us, in the distance, the ravine ended in a bare cliff face. Over that the Kaieteur should fall. But now there was no trace of water; only dense clouds of white mist, undefined from the cloudy sky above, rose from towards the foot of the cliff and slowly passed upward along its face. Our two Indians who had visited the place before gasped out ' Kaieteur, he dry.' We looked at each other with solemn faces and then laughed nervously. We seemed the victims of a great practical joke, of which Mr. Brown and nature were the perpetrators; the former by over-estimating the fall, which according to him had 'foamed for ages past,' the latter by drying up ' one of the grandest falls in the world' in this not particularly dry season. All our long and difficult way had been passed, all our pains expended, all our hopes nourished, to see a fall where no fall was. It was the old story of ' the play of Hamlet with the part of the Prince of Denmark omitted.'

Almost as soon as we had caught the first glimpse of the Kaieteur cliff a turn in the river hid it, and we had time to realise our feelings. The great white clouds which we had seen were my only hope as we paddled gloomily on to the landing place at Tookooie cataract.

Beyond this point it is impossible to take boats; for from here up to the great fall is no smooth water, but only a long succession of rapids, falls, and cataracts. We had to camp at a spot some fifty yards beyond the real landing-place, which was entirely occupied by a large party of Ackawoi who were on their way down from their homes above the fall to the Essequibo, or ' Scapi' as they call it, to eat fish and turtles' eggs. There are a few fish in the

Potaro below the Kaieteur, but none above; turtles are altogether wanting in the river. We hoped to induce some of these Indians to guide us to the foot of the fall; but, like all the Indians of the district, they were far too fearful of its supposed supernatural character to approach either the bottom or the top. Even in carrying their woodskins down past the fall, they make an immense detour of five or six miles, rather than go near the place.

We had reached this place only eleven days after leaving Bartica Grove. Two of these days had been spent without travelling. So that Tookooie was actually reached in nine days.

The next morning we started to make our way to the foot of the fall, taking our hammocks and a small supply of provisions with us. There is no track of any sort. Each traveller must cut and climb his own way: and the journey is of a most arduous kind. Starting at about eleven o'clock in the morning we followed the track leading to the top of the fall for a few hundred yards, and then struck off, as it afterwards turned out, too soon, to the river on our left. Before long we climbed down the face of a considerable fall on a creek running into the Potaro. On the dry ledges of this was a splendid growth of large filmy ferns (*Trichomanes Prieurii*, Kunze) with fronds a foot long. Following the course of this creek we reached the boulders on the edge of the main river, and climbed for some time along these. Presently, by an unlucky thought, we left the river-bank and again ascended high up into the hill forest. Then the way became absolutely terrific. The whole floor of the ravine, as well as the hill-side for some distance up, is covered, apparently to the depth of several hundred feet, by a litter of huge boulders varying in size from that of a large house to a few feet square, piled in the wildest confusion. Those by the water-side are smaller, and, being quite bare, are easily passed. But within the forest, trees, shrubs, creepers, aroids, begonias, all growing in the most eccentric places and directions, formed, from rock to rock, a covering treacherously hiding the crevasses and ravines. Among, over, and under these boulders we had to creep, climb, or slide as best we could; we had to walk across fallen, often rotten, trees bridging over ugly-looking crevasses; we had to pass over places where the ground, seeming firm, really consisted of a network of small roots, over which was a deceitful covering of dead leaves and growing ferns and mosses; again and again when trusting ourselves in such places we found ourselves buried up to the waist; once I disappeared entirely. On the whole it was a very ugly climb; and yet it was just in the worst places that the wonderful beauty of the plants, especially the ferns and begonias, most repaid the toil. My only regret was that under the circumstances I was only able to snatch a plant here and there, leaving many and many a wished-for specimen ungathered. As a collecting place for a naturalist no better spot could be found.

By about three in the afternoon we came out of the forest to the river-edge, at a point about a quarter of a mile from the fall and just at the mouth of the Kaieteur amphitheatre. Before, and close to us, was the fall, about two-thirds of its upper part visible. The Kaieteur was not dry; but it was less than half the width proper to it in the rainy season. Still it was very splendid, and the beauty of the surrounding scenery made great amends for the deficiency of water.

The reason that no descending water had been visible from Waratoo was now obvious. At the fall, the Kaieteur ravine ends in a complete amphitheatre with cliff-like walls 800 feet in height. It is into this amphitheatre that the Potaro falls from the plateau above. Supposing the amphitheatre were divided into quarters by drawing one straight line from the entrance to the opposite cliff and another straight line cutting the former in the middle and ending on either side at the cliff, then the space over which the water falls is included within the left-hand quarter farthest from the entrance. Therefore, when looking into the amphitheatre from a point directly opposite its entrance we could only see the bare cliff at the side of the fall. When full the fall extends over the part of the cliff directly opposite the entrance of the amphitheatre, so that part of it is then visible from a long distance down the ravine.

The floor of the amphitheatre is occupied by a waste of fallen rocks, made black by constant moisture, but capped with short, intensely green grass, except round the dark stormy pool into which the water falls, where the rocks are entirely bare, slippery, and black. Immediately behind the fall a huge, dark cave is visible in the cliff. The upper edge of the cliff serves as a horizon to the whole scene when viewed from below.

After spending twenty-four hours at the foot of the fall, we started back to the landing-place. By keeping as much as possible to the rocks by the river-side and ascending into the bush only when absolutely necessary, we found a far easier route than that by which we went on the previous day, and the camp at Tookooie was reached in about two hours and a half.

The next day was spent at Tookooie, and on the day after we started for the top of the fall. The way lay along a beaten Indian track, which is only difficult because, in parts, very steep. After two hours' climb through the forest, we came out on to the savannah from which the Kaieteur falls. No more strange place than this was ever imagined. The ground is formed by an entirely bare layer of hard conglomerate rock. No soil exists except in the cracks and fissures. In these small deposits of earth innumerable gigantic Brome-liads, looking more like agaves,[1] have taken root, and form the

[1] The somewhat imperfect specimens of the flower of this plant, which were all that I could procure at that season, led Mr. J. G. Baker of Kew to suppose that the plant was a new species of Cordyline, and very interesting as being only the second species of the genus that had been discovered on the American continent. Mr. Baker accordingly described and figured the plant as *Cordyline micrantha*, nov. sp in the *Gardeners' Chronicle*. More perfect specimens, since obtained by my friend Mr. Jenman, have proved that the plant is really a gigantic Bromeliad, and of even far higher interest than had been supposed, as being by far the most

PLATE IV.

THE KAIETEUR FALL (*in dry weather*).

(FROM BELOW.)

most prominent feature in the scene. Thickets of splendid-flowered orchids (*Sobralia*), as tall as a man, and many other rare and quaint plants grow among the agave groups, each of which is laced together by a large fern (*Pteris aquilina*), almost, if not quite, identical with the delicately beautiful and graceful English bracken.

This plant-growth lends a most strange character to the scenery of the place. It is quite unlike anything I have seen elsewhere in the colony, and for once realises the common idea of tropical scenery. The savannah is of itself well worthy of a visit.[1]

Crossing the savannah we soon reached the Kaieteur cliff. Lying at full length on the ground, head over the edge of the cliff, I gazed down.

Then, and only then, the splendid and, in the most solemn sense of the word, awful beauty of the Kaieteur burst upon me. Seven hundred and fifty feet below, encircled by black boulders, lay a great pool into which the column of white water, graceful as a ceaseless flight of innumerable rockets, thundered from by my side. Behind the fall, through the thinnest parts of the veil of foam and mist, the great black cavern made the white of the water look yet more white.

My first sensations were of a terrible and undefined fear. Those who visit the fall will understand this. When some of the men hurled down one of the big Bromeliads, the act seemed to cause me unbearable pain ; I had as soon have hurled myself over as have allowed a repetition of the act just then. Gradually, however, these painful feelings gave way to others of intense wondering delight ; and the whole scene,

colossal Bromeliad ever discovered. Mr. Baker has now provisionally named it *Brocchinia cordylinoides*.

[1] Mr. Jenman, who has since had a prolonged opportunity of collecting plants on this savannah, procured and sent from there to Kew a herbarium collection, which is declared by the assistant-director of the Royal Gardens to be ' almost the most important collection ever received from South America.'

the gigantic weird fall, the dark and slippery places below, the grass-covered rocks at the gate of the amphitheatre, and beyond that the bright thickly wooded valley of the winding river, visible for many miles, were revealed, never to be forgotten.

As soon as we could force ourselves away from the cliff, we formed our camp in a clump of small trees which stands at the very edge of the fall. Here we spent two days, which were fully occupied in searching the whole strange place.

In the rock plateau, not far from the edge of the cliff, are certain long, narrow, and immeasurable deep fissures, lying parallel to the cliff, and therefore at right angles to the bed of the river. They exactly resemble the very narrowest crevasses in a glacier. These seem to throw some light on the process by which the ravine and amphitheatre of the Kaieteur have been formed. It must be remembered that the plateau consists of a layer of hard conglomerate overlying a bed of softer sandstone. The cave behind the column of water has been formed, as Mr. Brown has said, by the back splash from the fall, which has washed away the sandstone from under the conglomerate. The ordinary theory is that the constant passage of the water gradually wears away this conglomerate roof, and so the cave and fall continuously, but very gradually, retreat backward. But it seems to me that the process is not gradual, but by occasional, sudden catastrophes.

Though I was unable to find one of these narrow fissures crossing the actual bed of the stream, yet from their frequent occurrence on other parts of the plateau, and considering that the rock close by the top of the fall is extraordinarily uneven, looking as if much creased and folded ; and that the bed of the river just there is much choked by a dense mouth of sedges, it is probable that such fissures do occur across the bed of the river. If so, while the main body of the water would, by reason of its velocity, rush over them, yet some water would trickle down through these fissures, and would gradually

widen them. The result of this would be that the conglomerate would form, not a roof, but a bridge, over the cave.
This bridge would in time give way, its fragments falling to
the bottom of the amphitheatre. Only in this way, it seems
to me, can the enormous masses of boulders which fill the
whole bottom of the ravine be accounted for.

The water being very low at the time of our visit, we
were able to obtain a better view of the cave and pool than
has been obtained by others; and it certainly seemed that
there was a small flow of water outward from the cave and
from behind the fall. If this is so, it of course corroborates
the above theory.

The more I saw of the Bromeliads of the savannah the
more striking they appeared. Unlike most other succulent
plants they are of a bright light yellowish-green colour, and
seem at first sight very unfitted to find nourishment on this
parched plain of earth-bare rock. A second glance, however,
shows a special adaptation to the place of growth. The base
of each leaf of the rosette-shaped plant is so curved in at its
edges against the leaf immediately within it that it forms a
large reservoir for water. Each of these receptacles contains
from a half-pint to a pint; so that the whole plant is provided
with a store of several quarts of water. These receptacles
being fully exposed to the sun, the water within them must
evaporate quickly; but the heavy dew which falls here, and
the thick clouds of mist which continually rise by night and
during the early morning from the fall and drop back on
this plain in the form of rain must continually renew the
store.

Another perhaps yet more curious, though inconspicuous
plant was a small round-leafed sundew (*Drosera rotundi-
folia*), an insect-eating plant which grows plentifully among
the loose stones overlying the rocks in the very driest parts
of the savannah. Its small red leaves are covered with long
hairs, each. of which carries a drop of very sticky liquid.
Small insects, hovering round the plant, are caught by this
gummy substance, and are unable to get away from the

plant, which slowly absorbs their life-juices. How this plant, usually such a lover of watery places, manages to subsist on these rocks is mysterious.

Each evening, at dusk, the flocks of swifts (*Acanthyllis collaris*) spoken of by Mr. Brown arrived; but they were by no means as numerous as they seem to have been at the time of his visits. They fly high in the air above the fall, then so suddenly descend straight down into the amphitheatre, that their wings make a hissing noise which is not the least curious phenomenon of this wonderful place. After descending straight down, they settled for the night on the face of the cliff, by and behind the fall.

Here, too, we were lucky enough to obtain specimens of a new species of bird, which Mr. P. L. Sclater has done me the honour to name after me, *Agelæus imthurni*.

The nights were bitterly cold. The moon was big at the time, and as it shone on the fall seemed to make it grow more weird. The thunderous roar of its water sounded much louder than by day. Towards morning it became evident that masses of thick white clouds filled the whole valley below the fall; nor did these clear away till nine o'clock in the morning.

It was with regret that we turned, at last, to leave the Kaieteur, but after a six days' stay in the neighbourhood, it was time to start homeward.

No new or striking incident occurred during our return, and I may therefore bring my story to a close.

In the following February, at the end of a heavy rainy season, having a month's leave of absence, it seemed that the time could hardly be better employed than in again ascending the Potaro and seeing the fall of the river in flood. Mr. T. C. Edwards-Moss went with me; and with twenty Indians we started from Bartica Grove, in three boats, on Monday, the 10th of February, and, in spite of the large quantity of water both in the Essequibo and Potaro rivers, accomplished our journey comfortably, and so quickly that we were back

Pl. V.

AGELŒUS IMTHURNI

again at the Grove on the 3rd of March, after an absence, that is, of only twenty-two days.

The journey up the Essequibo to the mouth of the Potaro occupied five days. The river was high; but the heavy rains having just come to an end, somewhat later in the year than usual, the water was beginning to sink.

The falls in this part of the river were easily passed, and almost without adventure. On landing at the side of the rapids at Coomaka, which were almost completely smoothed over by the great quantity of water which was coming down the river, we found a great snake, a camoodi (*Eunectes murina*) asleep on rocks. My companion shot it; and it proved to be twenty feet in length and three feet in girth at the thickest.

On Friday night we camped just opposite the mouth of the Potaro river; and early on the next morning we turned up that river, and in a couple of hours reached the first cataract at Toomatoomari. Here we spent the afternoon in the bush in a vain attempt to hunt—unfortunately we saw nothing to hunt. At Toomatoomari the scene was very different from what it had been in the dry season. Now, below the cataract, instead of a plain of sandbanks and rocks with a few water-channels, all was one sheet of water, covered with masses of white foam from the tumbling water above. And now the cataract, instead of being small and narrow, rushed in through the whole upper end of the plain, and was at least three or four times as wide as it had been in October.

As it was at Toomatoomari, so it was throughout the whole river. The water in the Essequibo had been high, but in the Potaro it was yet higher. Within the few weeks before and during our expedition much more rain must have fallen on the sandstone region in which the Potaro rises than in the parts about the upper waters of the Essequibo. When we reached the latter river on our return we found it had sunk considerably, while the Potaro was then much higher than when we entered it. Hardly a day during our expedition was without rain, and while we were near the Kaieteur the rainfall was often very heavy.   Of the twenty-two days of our absence from Bartica only two were dry: during the same period very little rain fell on the coast region; and, judging from the state of the river, very little can have fallen towards the sources of the Essequibo.

The Potaro was, as has been said, in flood, and rose yet higher during the time we were on it.   Rapids, cataracts, and falls had widened, since I had seen them three months before, from a width of a few yards to many hundred feet. And in the reaches between the falls the innumerable sand-banks and rocks which I had seen were now quite covered by a strong, swift flow of dark water carrying long lines of masses of white foam, which looked like large flocks of white birds swimming with the current.   It is hard to say whether the scenery on the river was more, or less, beautiful than it had been when the river was low.   The cataracts now were un-doubtedly very far finer, and were in themselves quite worthy of a visit; but, on the other hand, the smooth reaches of the river had lost much of the fairy-like beauty which had charmed me before, and had acquired something of the monotonous character common to most of the rivers of Guiana.

But even in these smooth reaches there was one thing more beautiful than it had been before.   It was, as has been said, the chief flowering season of the year; and the flowers were more strikingly beautiful than I have ever seen them in the tropics.   For it is not in these warm regions, but in the temperate northern climates, that plants most profusely cover themselves with masses of flowers and produce their most gorgeous effects.   But for once, as we went up the Potaro, great masses of bright flowers gleamed in places on the banks. Three plants were most especially striking. One, the loveliest of all, the cakeralli (*Lecythis ollaria*), was in full flower.   In the forest it grows tall; but here on the banks of the river, where it was very abundant, it was a small gnarled and knotted tree. Some of its many small leaves were green, some of various shades of bright bronzy red.

Each of its flowers was like a beautiful pink orchid; but their clusters were in habit and colour like those on the branchlets of a standard peach at home. Indeed, no better idea of the general effect of these trees can be given than by saying that they vividly recalled these English peach-trees, or perhaps still more our pink, double-blossomed hawthorns. Often these cakeralli trees were half in, and overhanging the water; and then the reflection of the mass of its warm pink blossoms in the still dark water was supremely beautiful. Once we passed the mouth of a creek far down which, seen at the end of a shady passage formed by overarching trees, a cakeralli, half-fallen, reached nearly across the stream; and yet it lived, and was flowering and reddening all the water under it. At another time the eye would be attracted by a deep blue patch on the surface of the water, and looking up the bank to see what caused this new reflection, would rest on a cluster of many foot-long wreaths of the intensely blue star-flowers of the *Petræa martiana*, one of the most strikingly beautiful flowers of Guiana, and one which is not as common in gardens as it should be.

A third plant which was then in full bloom was a white waxy flower (*Posoqueria longiflora*) with clustered blossoms like long-tubed, hanging gardenias, with a strong sweet scent, and with pretty egg-shaped, orange-coloured fruits, ripe even on the flowering branches. And between these plants were many others equally beautiful though not so prominent.

The height of the river did not cause much extra difficulty. Our boat and one of the canoes were portaged past Toomatoomari cataract, instead of being hauled up as is possible in a lower state of the water. At Mowraseema the rapids had increased much in number, though not individually in difficulty. But when we came to the portage at Pacoutout, which we had avoided before by hauling up the bateau, we found that we could not this time shirk the work of clearing the path, laying it with skids, and carrying over the bateau. We therefore left the canoe at the lower end of

the portage, and took only the ' Adaba,' our built boat, together with three woodskins which the Indians living at
Pacoutout offered to lend us. A whole day was, however,
occupied in getting our one boat across. The path, along
which it had to be dragged, passes through a cassava field, so
that much extra labour was occasioned by the number of
felled trees which had to be cleared away. Some Indians
have, however, settled here since our last visit, so that the
path was in better order than it then was. A very severe
and unlucky illness of my companion, a memorable event to
both of us ever after, caused a day's delay here, and nearly
caused our return. Portaging again at Amootoo, and hauling the boat up past Waratoo, on the fifth day from Toomatoomari, we came in sight of the Kaieteur. It seemed
about four miles off. This was the point from which on the
occasion of my former visit the Kaieteur was not, as it ought
to have been, visible, so that when we came here, we thought
for an hour or two that the fall was quite dry. But now, far
off at the end of the valley, the white water was very visible
as it fell over the wall-like cliff which closes the end of the
ravine. The Kaieteur was now evidently very full.

One hour later we were at the landing-place at Tookooie,
which is within three hours' walk of the fall, and beyond
which it is impossible to take boats. We had taken twelve
days to reach this point from Bartica Grove ; but of these
nearly two whole days had been spent without travelling.

I have already described the steep, but not difficult, walk
through the forest, up the higher level of the fall. On
coming out on to the savannah we found that it had been
burned. The Bromeliads with which it is chiefly clad
were hardly more than charred stumps and leaves ; but the
low-growing vegetation round the roots of these had re-
covered and was more vigorous than in October. The
bracken (*Pteris aquilina*), pushing up its young woolly
heads, reminded one of spring at home ; a few ground orchids
were in flower, but unfortunately not the *Sobralia*, which I
had most hoped to see.

Crossing the savannah, and coming to the edge of the cliff over which the Potaro falls, we once more lay down, bodies along the top of the cliff, heads over its edge. It was a very different scene from the last time. Then it was beautiful and terrible; but now it was something which it is useless to try to describe. Then a narrow river, not a third of its present width, fell over the cliff in a column of white water, which was brought into startling prominence by the darkness of the great cave behind; and this column of water, before it reached the small, black pool below, had narrowed to a point. Now an indescribably, almost inconceivably, vast curtain of water—I can find no other phrase—some four hundred feet in width, rolled over the top of the cliff, retaining its full width until it crashed into the boiling water of the pool which filled the whole space below; and of the surface of this pool itself only the outer edge was visible, for the greater part was ceaselessly tossed and hurled up in a great and high mass of surf and foam and spray.

The fall, when the river was almost dry, had seemed as grand and beautiful a thing as it was possible to imagine; but now it was so infinitely more grand, so infinitely more beautiful, that it is painfully hopeless to try to express in words anything of its beauty and grandeur. Indeed the very words beauty and grandeur, and indeed all other words, seem absurdly weak when applied to such a scene as that. It is indeed possible to write down a few separate impressions that came to me as I looked at the fall, but it is impossible even to hint at the overpowering effect which the whole scene produced.

We made our camp at the old spot, at the actual edge of the fall. The river there had been choked by sedges (*Cyperus*)[1] among which the water used to creep hidden to its fall; but this plant-growth was now quite covered by the rushing river.

About an hour before sunset on the first evening of our stay rain began to fall in light showers. Low down at our

[1] The species is new to science.

feet, across the river below the fall, the sun and rain built
a coloured arch right across the ravine; and through this the
river, narrowed by a seemingly endless series of projecting
cliff buttresses, was seen winding through the forest-covered
country till it passed the far-away sugar-loaf mountain
at Amootoo, and then lost itself in the great wooded plain
beyond.

An hour later heavy low-lying clouds had gathered, and
almost shut us in in our camp on the edge of the cliff. Then
the mist and cloud and rain and wind made another wonderful
scene. The great rocky ravine at our feet was filled by huge
masses of rolling, driving cloud which hid everything, except
when, now and then, a cold blast of wind, separating two
clouds for a few seconds, showed in the gap some projecting cliff-ledge, or some tree-covered rock, apparently
hanging suspended in a cloud world. And all the while the
great river rushed swiftly at our side to the edge of the cliff
rolled over, and as it fell plunged through strange weird
pillars of white mist, which continually rose from it and
passed up into the low leaden-coloured sky overhead, down
into the denser, unbroken mass of clouds below, and there
hid itself. Night came on, and as it grew darker and
darker, the few swifts (*Acanthyllis collaris*) which were
about fell headlong down from the sky above; and they
too were gone into the cloud. And the noise of the fall—
the rustling sound of falling water and the deep boom rising
from the unseen pool below—added to the effect. The
whole world seemed unreal and grandly fantastic. In such a
scene as that one forgets one's self, forgets real life, and
seems carried into a new, hardly formed universe. It was
a picture which only Turner could, and would have delighted
to paint; nor could even he have shown more than a small
part of its strangeness.

Presently the rain, coming on more and more heavily,
drove us to our hammocks, in which we lay awake, cold
and wet, nearly all that night. Our hammock covers were
almost useless against such rain, and with such wind to

PLATE VI.

THE KAIETEUR FALL (*in wet weather*).

drive the rain. In the morning it was nearly nine o'clock
before we got a fire lighted. Then the rain ceased for a
while, and we managed to turn out to get a bathe in the
river. The water had risen much in the night and was
evidently still rising ; it was already within a few feet of the
point at which the rock-covering of dead and withered water-
weed (*Lacis*) showed high-water mark. As the clouds again
threatened rain, and as we meant to stay where we were for
at least another day, our men built a capital and substantial
house of posts and palm-leaves, which ought to be useful to
future visitors.

That day was passed in much walking about, and in
seeing the fall from many points. We had a stop-watch
with us; and by repeatedly fixing our attention on particular
rocket-like points of water, we timed the falling water from
the instant at which it passed over the upper edge of the
cliff to that at which it reached the pool below. The time
was almost exactly 6·5 seconds. Another thing noticed during
that day was that the swifts did not as usual leave the
place during the day to return at night, but hovered about
the face of the cliff all day. It was probably their breeding
season.

At night the shelter of our house was most welcome;
for the rain, which had only fallen at intervals during the
day, began to fall again heavily. But the next morning
was splendidly fine. On the whole, we were very lucky in
the weather. It had been tolerably dry while we were
walking up to the savannah, then came thirty-six hours of
almost incessant rain, which increased and entirely filled the
fall ; and then our last day there was gloriously fine, so that
we could fully enjoy the marvellous scene.

The river was now quite full, the water being up to the
bushes on either bank, and the fall was at its grandest. In
bathing that morning, we found that the current had become
so strong that we had to keep close in to the bushes, and
even then it was very difficult to stand ; a step too far might
have sent us down the Kaieteur.

All the time we had to spare we lay at the edge of the cliff wondering at the exceeding beauty of the fall, and all our talk was of its grandeur. Its edge and surface was no even line, but was thrown into many and varied curves by projections and inequalities in the cliff. And the water at each curve seemed different (in the mode in which it fell, and in colour) from each other part. In places the fall was of purest white; this was where a rise in the level of the cliff edge caused the water to break over it, and, shooting out into the air, to fall in a vast dense body of white drops. But the greater part of the curtain of the fall was formed of the beautiful overlapping rocket-like points, which constantly fell and were constantly succeeded by others; here the colour at each point varied according to the depth of the water, and was of many shades of a peculiar amber, lightening below into the colour best described as 'ecru.' It is impossible to tell more accurately the endless variety in the contour and colour of the fall.

The great curtain of water, entirely covering the whole front of the cave, seemed as a curtain in front of an entrance to an Inferno. Even were it possible, one would almost be afraid to penetrate behind it.

But perhaps the most beautiful effects that morning were produced by the rainbows down in the ravine below, caused by the sun shining on the ever-rising masses of mist and spray. One end of the bow passed over the lower part of the fall itself, and blending with the water and losing all regularity of outline, it seemed to become a part of each beautiful rocket of water and of each of the myriads of white water-drops, till the whole fell like a vast shower of jewels. Nor was the other end of the arch, lying along the flat black boulders, capped with grass of pale but most brilliant green, round the pool, less beautiful.

Some small white butterflies seemed in some way irresistibly attracted into the fall; they occasionally passed us and flew lower and lower, the sunlight glittering on their white wings, till they flitted about in the rainbow-tinted spray; and then they were sucked in by the water.

Time passed, and we had to turn homeward; and so on the afternoon of the third day of our visit, after a last long look at the fall, we went down to our boats and camp at Tookooie. We had determined not to attempt to make our way into the ravine at the foot of the fall; for on my previous visit I had found that the view obtained from there was not worth the great labour of the journey. But now, even if we had wished to go in, it would hardly have been possible; for the river was now so high over the rocks on which we had walked that we should at least have had to make an entirely new path.

So, after another wet night at Tookooie, we started down the Potaro the next morning. The short spell of fine weather was over, and rain fell almost incessantly. As we passed down, the ravine was grand in its clothing of clouds and mist; and the rains had made numberless fine cataracts down the cliffs, filling the valley with their roar.

Our homeward journey was unadventurous. At the settlement of Aykooroo they had collected a very large quantity of cassava bread, with a few yams and plantains for us. At the next settlement, called the Island, at the upper end of Pacoutout portage, they had more bread, some mai-purie meat (*Tapirus americanus*), and some delicious wild honey. The head man of this settlement said that he owned the deserted settlement at the mouth of the Cooriebrong river, that he meant to build a church there, and that he wished me to send him a 'domini' (parson). This is a common whim among Indians; they build a large house, which they are pleased to call a church, use it for holding paiwari feasts, and whenever a white man approaches are loud in their calls for a parson.

In shooting one of the rapids at Mowraseema, our boat came suddenly against a sharp rock, and a hole was knocked in her bottom. However, a little baling till we got to shore, and then a little caulking, made all right. The rest of the falls were easily passed.

In three days we reached Toomatoomari, where, on account of the rise in the river, there was considerable difficulty in getting the boats over. Coming to the Essequibo we found that it, unlike the Potaro, had sunk considerably during our absence. Four days later, on the 3rd of March, we reached Bartica Grove, and the pleasantest of all my journeys into the interior had come to an end.

A few words as to future expeditions may be useful.

Firstly, as to the means which might be taken by the Government to facilitate the whole journey ; I confess that money spent on cutting paths from any point on the Essequibo to the Kaieteur seems to me thrown away. A small amount of money and labour might much more advantageously be used in permanently improving the portage paths, and in making a moderately good path from Tookooie landing to the foot of the fall. An annual present might also be made to the Indians settled along the route, on condition that they keep open the portages, keep boats for travellers, and give all assistance in their power.

Secondly, as regards the travellers' own part in organising the expedition ; the first requisite is that none but Indians be taken in the crew. A large and comfortable boat may be taken from Bartica Grove as far as Toomatoomari ; but above that one or more small boats are necessary. It adds much to the travellers' comfort without entailing much trouble, if a few iron stanchions and a movable awning to cover these small boats are taken.

As to the time of year at which it is best to visit the Kaieteur, I think the dry season is to be preferred. The volume of the water is then undoubtedly much reduced, but on the other hand the ease and comfort of the journey is much increased, while the really exquisite scenery of the whole of the Potaro river is only then seen in its perfection.

The following directions as to the path from Tookooie landing-place may be given. I must first state that even if

the easiest way to the foot of the fall is found, the difficulty
of the walk is by no means slight, and should not be
attempted by any but a young and fairly active man. And
when the foot of the fall is reached, the view obtained does
not repay the toil expended. I should strongly advise all
but the most adventurous to be content with the far finer
view to be obtained from above.

Those, however, who are determined to see the fall from
below must follow the beaten track which leads to the top
for rather more than a quarter of a mile to a point where it
is crossed by a very considerable creek, the bed of which,
twenty to thirty yards wide, is formed of perfectly flat sandstone ledges. This is the creek on the ledges of which, on
crossing at a point lower down, I noticed the splendid luxuriance of the filmy ferns (*Trichomanes prieurii*). The way then
lies down the bed of this creek if the water is shallow, or
along its southern side if the stream is deep, till the main
river is reached. After that it is necessary to keep to the
bare boulders as close to the river's edge as possible. It is
only necessary to go into the forest when passing the head
of the last cataract, called Serikabaroo, before the Kaieteur.
Here the boulders are so huge and have such cliff-like sides
that it is absolutely necessary to go some distance up the
side of the ravine ; and this is the most fatiguing part of the
journey. It is very difficult to get within the actual amphitheatre of the fall, and the traveller must form his camp at
its mouth. But it may be entered by swimming from rock to
rock, and in this way the actual edge of the pool into which
the river falls may be gained.

The top of the fall is easily reached from Tookooie by following the beaten path, though this is occasionally very
steep.

The only good place to camp is reached by walking
straight across the savannah, on coming out from the forest,
to the opposite side, close to the edge of the fall. But the
best view is to be obtained by turning to the left immediately
on entering the savannah, instead of crossing to the camping

place, and by going in the most direct way to the edge of the cliff of the amphitheatre.

The mountain called Roraima, about which a few words must be said, lies on the extreme western edge of the colony on, or perhaps on the other side of, the Brazilian boundary. It has attracted much attention because of its peculiar form and circumstances. The first travellers who noticed it were the brothers Schomburgk, who were in that neighbourhood about the year 1840. Since then it has been thrice visited: by Mr. C. Barrington Brown in 1869, while surveying the geology of the colony; by my friends, Messrs. Eddington and Flint, in 1877; and lastly, by my friends, Messrs. McTurk and Boddam-Wetham, in 1878. Moreover, in 1881, Mr. David Burke, an orchid collector, and Mr. Whitely, a zoological collector, separately approached within sight of the mountain.

It is a table-land formed of sandstone, which rises in a perpendicular cliff from the general plain; or rather, the savannah slopes somewhat abruptly upward to a height of some 5,000 feet above the sea-level, and this swelling is crowned by a flat-topped mass of sandstone some 2,000 feet in height, the walls of which are perpendicular. The circumference of this mass is entirely unknown, for no traveller has yet been round it. Round the whole circumference the wall is said to be equally perpendicular; but this is a mere matter of conjecture and must remain so until some traveller makes his way round it. The flat top appears to be forest covered; and down its sides, at any rate at times, considerable masses of water fall at various points. On the supposition that the summit is really inaccessible, not only to men, but to all unwinged animals, there are those who hold that on this table land, cut off as this must thus be from all communication with the rest of the world, very possibly animal forms of a primitive type exist which have undergone no modification under the influence of new-coming forms since the plain was first isolated in mid-air. Whether the place be quite inaccessible to such modifying influences or not, it is at least certain that not only the fauna, but also the flora, must present features of great interest. At present there is, as I have already hinted, nothing to indicate that the mountain is really inaccessible on all sides. The first thing to be done is for a traveller to make his way all round it. The difficulty of doing this would be great. The task would take a very considerable and indefinite time, and as the distance of the mountain from any main and easily navigable river is great, it would be impossible for the traveller to carry with him sufficient provisions from the coast to support himself and the assistants necessary to him during this time. It would therefore be necessary to live almost entirely on such food as may be procured from the Indians of the district, or by hunting; but the Indians there are few and have but little land under cultivation, and game is said to be scarce. The explorer would, therefore, have to undergo considerable hardship.

To a botanist the time spent in such a preliminary walk round Roraima would be full of interest. For whether the plants on the top of the mountain are ever reached or not, the vegetation round the base is extraordinarily rich and interesting. The following description of the plant life in the Roraima district, by Richard Schomburgk,[1] who, though the only botanist who had been there, was only in the neighbourhood for a few days, ought to be sufficient in itself to attract an explorer :—

'From the crevices in the sandstone strata sprang various orchids; and besides these, the rosy-flowered *Marcetia taxifolia* (Dec) had established itself in the fissures—a plant which I had not before seen, and which from a distance I mistook for an *Erica*. On reaching the summit a wide and splendid plateau, broken by small hills and clumps of rich green trees and bushes, stretched towards the north-west, north, and north-east, and was bounded in the far distance by high ranges of mountains. Our way was across a soft

---

[1] Richard Schomburgk. *Reisen in Britisch Guiana* (Leipzig, 1848) vol. ii. p. 216.

velvety sward, still wet with dew, directly northward, till
I was attracted by a dense clump of tree-like plants. These
were indeed remarkable. Their naked stems, several feet
in circumference, at last branched in two, while at the ends
of these branches were long grass-like broad leaves. In the
absence of flowers and fruits it was impossible to determine
whether these remarkable plants belonged to the *Pandanaceæ*
or *Vellozieæ*. These strange plants rose straight up into the
air from the sandstone rubble, which was covered by an
Eriocaulon and a curious grey-black grass. My brother had
seen a group of these plants in 1838 when he first ascended
this sandstone range ; but on that occasion also they were
not in flower or fruit. On reaching the declivity, a breeze
from the north came loaded with a delicious scent, and our
astonished eyes were attracted by innumerable stems of
white, violet, and purple flowers which waved about the surrounding bush. These were groups of superb *Sobralias ;* and
amongst them *S. Elizabethæ* rose tallest of all. I found
flowering stems of from five to six feet high. But not only
these orchids, but the shrubs and the low trees, still dripping
with heavy dew, were unknown to me. Every shrub, herb,
and tree was new to me, if not as to its family, yet as to
species. I stood on the border of an unknown plant zone
full of wondrous forms, which lay, as if by magic, before me.
I once again felt the same delighted surprise which had
overpowered me when I first landed on the South American
continent ; but I now seemed to be transported to a new
quarter of the globe, amongst the *Proteaceæ* of Africa and
New Holland and the *Melaleuceæ* of the East Indies and
Australia. The leathery, stiff leaves, the curiously coiled
branches, the strange large flowers of various forms, the
dazzling colour of these—all were essentially different in
character from all vegetation that I had before seen. I did
not know whether to look first at the wax-like gay flowers of
certain species of *Thibaudia, Befaria,* and *Archytaea,* or at
the large, camellia-like flowers of a *Bonnetia,* or whether to
fasten my eyes on the flower-loaded plants of various kinds of

Melastoma, Abolboda, Vochysia, Ternstromia, Andromeda, Clusia, Kielmeyera, or on the various new forms of *Sobralia, Oncidium, Cattleya, Odontoglossum,* and *Epidendron,* which covered the blocks of soft sandstone—and there were very many plants not at the time in flower. . . . . Every step revealed something new.'

To the ethnologist also the district will prove interesting; for it is so remote and unexplored that the Arecuna Indians, who chiefly inhabit it, are in a very unusually primitive condition—for instance, they alone still sometimes use stone, instead of iron, girdles for baking purposes; and, moreover, the strangeness of Roraima seems to have made deep impressions on the minds of these Indians, and to have filled their thoughts with folk-lore to an unusual extent.

In short, there is a great reward in store for the traveller, whether he be botanist or ethnologist, who, having sufficient pecuniary means, will first gain experience of the ways of travelling in that part of the world, so that his knowledge of ordering an expedition may be as precise as possible, and will then go to Roraima prepared, at all costs, to spend as long a time in the district as may enable him to make his way slowly round the mountain; and his labours will possibly result, as no other means can, in the discovery of a way even to the top of Roraima.

A few words will not be out of place as to the best way of approaching the mountain. Schomburgk, Brown, and Eddington visited it by going up the Essequibo and Roopoonooni to the neighbourhood of Pirara, a route which I have already described, and then making their way northward to the mountain; McTurk and Boddam-Wetham went up the Mazeruni and then walked southward to the mountain. But there is a way, as yet untried, which I am convinced will prove far more practicable. This is up to Potaro and from there westward across the savannah. I have already described the journey up the Potaro as far as the Kaieteur fall; and it is evident that there need be no great difficulty in taking boats of considerable size up to that point.

There a depôt should be formed. Small boats might either be carried past the fall and launched on the Potaro above the Kaieteur, or these might be procured from the Ackawoi Indians who live above, but at some distance from, the fall; and thus the expedition might proceed by water yet further in the direction of Roraima. The walk across the savannah from the point where it may be necessary to leave the river would be shorter and almost certainly less laborious than the corresponding walk by either of the other routes.

But, as my last word on this subject, I must strongly warn any against approaching Roraima without first fully weighing the difficulty and the cost.

CHAPTER IV.

THE appearance of a country which has been little modified
by the hand of man, depends, in very great measure, upon
its vegetation. Much has lately been written on the real, as
opposed to the commonly conceived, appearance of tropical
vegetation. But men in temperate regions are still apt to
think that tropical plant-life blazes with gorgeous colour, and
is composed almost exclusively of quaint forms. Two fallacies,
as to colour and as to form, are involved in this conception.
The spread of the colour-fallacy is due to the fact that it is the
more gorgeous plants which, being selected from an infinitely
greater number of less brilliant hue, are grouped together
in our glass-houses. The form-fallacy has arisen partly from a
similar cause, but chiefly from the fancy sketches of tropical
scenery made by artists. This latter source of error may be
well studied, for example, in certain pictures of Guiana
scenery by a German named Carl Appun, a botanist and a
draughtsman of some merit, who lived for some years in the
interior, and who has furnished almost the only attainable
pictures, drawn on the spot, of that scenery. In these pictures palms and other plants of forms strange to temperate
regions, occupy the whole scene. Appun knew how to draw
plants, so that even in his most crowded compositions it is

possible to recognise the species of each individual plant ; but
his pictures are no true records of the scenery, because in
them, much as the gardener does in his hothouse, he grouped
only the most striking plants, and entirely omitted all such
as are but little distinguished in character or size of foliage
from the plants of temperate regions.   In correction of the
false views thus spread Mr. Wallace's careful analysis of
tropical scenery in general, in his admirable essay on Tropical
Nature, is of great value.   The purpose of the present
chapter is to supplement, as far as may be, that general account by representing the most characteristic aspects of the
special plant-life of Guiana.

The forests and woods of Guiana, which, it must always
be remembered, are situated at a very low level above the
sea, are mainly composed of trees and shrubs of much the
same general type, as regards both form of growth and of
foliage, as our own Spanish chestnuts, oaks, acacias, and
laurels.   Three things must, however, be remembered in
thus transferring in imagination our own forms of vegetation
to the tropics ; and these are, in the first place, that in the
tropics, the trees and plants of all sorts are generally on a
much more gigantic scale, and that this rank growth and,
especially at this low level, the absence of small neat-grow-
ing plants, such as elsewhere carpet the ground and fill up
the spaces, gives an impression of weediness ; secondly,
that the light being much more intense, the spaces within
the gigantic outlines of the scenery are seen in even exaggerated bareness and nakedness ; and thirdly, that scattered
among these familiar forms a large number of novel forms
occur.

Starting with this general idea of the vegetation, it will
be convenient, first, to consider the three special points, as to
the occurrence of colour, of novel and striking forms, and of
scents, and then to draw, as far as may be done in words, a
few typical scenes of vegetable life in the forest and on the
savannah.

The general colour of the forest is due rather to the

various shades of the leaves than to any wide scattering of flowers. Yet at no time is the Guiana leafage as splendid as in an ordinary English wood either in the early spring or in the glorious golden autumn time. But, on the other hand, the tropical forest throughout the year is more variously coloured in this respect than is the English wood at any other time than spring or autumn. This peculiarity of the tropical forest is due partly to the fact that, without special season either for the bursting or the fall of leaves, throughout the year it has trees both putting out new leaves, white, or brilliantly tinted with green, pink, or red, and others from which drop leaves with red, yellow, and bronze colours burned deeply into them by the blazing sun; and partly to the fact that in it trees of innumerable kinds, each with foliage at least slightly distinct in colour, grow intermingled, and not, as is usual in lands of beech or oak forests and fir coppices, in more or less distinct groups. The whole amount of colour afforded by flowers is probably not very different in tropical and temperate trees, but is differently distributed. With flowers, just and for the same reasons as with remarkable leaves, those in temperate climates are all gathered into the springtime and into particular spots, whereas in Guiana they are scattered throughout the year and on single trees through the forest; so that in the latter place, though no sheet of flower such as decorates an apple or cherry orchard or a hawthorn thicket in spring is ever seen, yet throughout the year, though more frequently in the wet than in the dry season, trees as fully covered with flowers as any individual apple, cherry, or hawthorn, may be remarked, like huge nosegays, in the leafy, otherwise unflowery forest. It must be added that this description of the flowers of Guiana refers only to those of the trees or shrubs, and that there is never there a growing carpet of flowers, such as is made in England by primroses and anemones, by wild hyacinths and dog violets in the woods, or by marsh marigolds and red fritillary bells in the water meadows, or by heather and gorse on the moors.

The splendour of colour of many single tropical trees,

heightened by contrast with the green of the surrounding forest, is most vividly present in my mind. No effect of colour could be more brilliant than a hackia tree (*Tecoma, sp.?*), the leafless branches of which, standing high above the surrounding forest, were covered and weighed down by dense masses of golden-yellow flowers, gleaming with a wonderful and almost dazzling brilliance against a pale, clear blue sky ; or than a male Long-John (*Triplaris surinamensis*) loaded with flowers, arranged in great plumes, like, but much larger than, bunches of lilac, at first creamy-white in colour, but afterward, as the florets grow old, taking a beautiful red tinge ; or than the same tree when each floret, shaped like a tiny parachute, falling with many twirls to the ground, fills even the air with flowers; or than the hipponai (*Parkia pendula*), perhaps the most beautiful plant I can remember, its branches arranged in tiers after the manner of the Cedar of Lebanon, its finely cut acacia-shaped foliage very dark in colour, while from the end of each branchlet hangs, at the end of a long pliant whip, three or four feet long, a globe of crimson flowers — these flowers, because of the regular strata-like arrangement of the branches, hanging in deep even fringes from the outer edge of each shady branch ; or than another tree, of a kind unknown to me, covered with a dense mass of pale mauve flowers, which I once saw in strangely harmonious contrast against a grey, rainy-looking sky ; or than a curiously coloured purple pea-flower (*Calopogium cœruleum*) which climbs and flowers so abundantly over certain small trees that it appears from a distance like an odd smoke-coloured light ; or than another creeper (*Norantea guianensis*) which runs, like fire, over the highest trees, throwing out many flame-like spikes of dense scarlet flowers, two or three feet long. Yet it must not be forgotten that these are only widely separated spots of colour in a huge forest generally green.

It will perhaps be noticed that this account of the distribution of flowers in Guiana hardly agrees with such statements of Mr. Wallace,[1] applied apparently to tropical forests

[1] *Tropical Nature* (by A. R. Wallace, 1878), p. 61.

in general, as that in which he says that 'conspicuous masses of showy flowers are so rare that weeks and months may be passed without observing a single flowering plant worthy of special admiration.' That a man, if he confined himself quite strictly to the shadiest parts of the forest, might pass weeks or months without seeing a single plant of striking beauty might be just possible ; yet, in Guiana at least, he must never during this period enter the many open spaces formed by rivers and streams, or by the fall of large trees, or he will be in danger of seeing on an average at least one beautiful mass of flowers in each twenty-four hours. In short, the old tropical fallacy was great; but the reaction against it, exemplified in Mr. Wallace's essay, has been slightly exaggerated.

The beauty of individual flowers, as distinct from masses, is more frequently noticeable in Guiana ; for not only are all those flowers which have been described above, and many others which might be added to the list, beautiful individually as well as in the mass, but there are others, and far more, which, though distributed too sparingly on their plants, or growing in too unfavourable a light, to make any great show, are individually as delicately beautiful or as splendid as any that are arranged in a florist's bouquet. The flowers are lost in the forest. For example, a man may, as I know, pass by a *posoqueria* shrub without noticing that it is in flower, because the white flowers and orange fruits are not very distinguishable among the many small flecks of intense light which make their way into the deep shade under the forest ; but if he does stop to examine this plant, he will find amongst its laurel-shaped leaves the most beautiful white flowers, of wax-like texture, like but larger than those of jasmine, each at the end of a very long white tube. This is only one out of innumerable instances that might be found even under the shade of the forest ; while at the sides of the river openings, in the forest glades, and especially on the savannahs, the number of individually beautiful flowers is very far greater.

We now pass from colour to form. In describing the

ordinary types of trees as akin to those of temperate lands,
it was stated that among these are scattered many striking
forms quite or almost peculiar to the tropics. In now describing these, the first to claim notice are the creepers,
which mat together the whole forest, and pass in inextric-
able confusion from trunk to trunk and over the tops of the
trees. Not only are these immensely more numerous, but
very many of them are very distinct in character, especially in the form of their stems, from the creepers of
temperate climates ; some have stems like broad ribands,
either tightly stretched, or with their edges fluted in a
most extraordinary way ; others are very regularly spiral,
and yet others are twisted round each other as evenly
as if by human art. Many kinds of palms occur in places,
some species singly, others in thickets, and others massed
in numbers even large enough to deserve the name of
forest ; so that while in some places none of these plants
are visible, in others many individuals of one species fill the
scene. Of the erect palms, the leaves of which spring from
a common centre, generally from the top of a more or less
lofty and stout stem, those with fan leaves are, with the exception of one very common species (*Mauritia flexuosa*)
extremely rare ; those with feather leaves form the bulk,
and one of these (*Maximiliana regia*) has its leaflets so
arranged almost spirally round the midrib that the whole leaf
is rather plume-like than feather-like ; another (*Manicaria
saccifera*) has an enormous oblong entire leaf, not split into
leaflets. But, beside these erect palms, there are others
which climb (*Desmoncus*), their feathered leaves branching off
along the whole stem. Another plant (*Carludovica plumieri*)
—not a palm, but very similar in appearance—creeps like ivy
up the trunks of trees. After the palms, the genera that
figure most largely in the ordinary fancy picture of tropical
scenery are those plants with large, very bold, simply oblong
leaves, the best known of which are the bananas and plantains, and of which certain very small forms, the cannas,
are now commonly seen in English gardens. These banana-

leaved plants do figure, in places, largely in Guiana scenery. The most striking among them is the so-called wild plantain (*Ravenala guianensis*), a second species of the far-famed ' Traveller's Tree of Madagascar,' the enormous leaves of which rise from near the ground to a height of ten to fifteen feet. The bases of their leaf-stalks sheath, the one over the other, and in the pockets formed by each of these sheathing parts much rain-water is retained even through the dry season, which water, having often served to quench the thirst of travellers, has gained for the Madagascar plant one of its English names. Another noticeable enough feature in these plants is that the seeds within the tough thin shell of the fruit are packed in a large quantity of short fibrous substance like clippings of wool, in the Guiana species of brightest scarlet colour, but in the Madagascar plant of blue. Much smaller, but similar plants are the *Heliconiæ*; and yet smaller are various species of *Maranta*, or rather *Ischnosiphon*, the tough, dark-green oval leaves of which are raised on a cane-like stem. The leaves of the latter plants serve the Indians in place of wrapping paper, for many purposes, and the stems are woven by the same people into baskets. Wild pine-apples (*Ananassa*, *Bromelia*, &c.), and other similar but much larger plants, each being but a great rosette of long, pointed, saw-edged leaves, grow singly or in small groups on the more sandy parts of the forest floor. Aloe-like plants are very rare ; a few occur scattered widely over the savannah, and one form, the largest Bromeliad in the world, grows in such dense masses on one particular plateau that it constitutes the whole prospect. Among ferns there is no need for much mention of the low-growing herb-like forms, such as are familiar in temperate lands. They are enormously abundant throughout Guiana, the chief forms being various species of *Adiantum*, *Lindsaya*, *Polypodium*, *Acrostichum*, and, above all, the lovely little filmy ferns, *Trichomanes* and *Hymenophyllum*. But three forms, occurring in Guiana, which belong more especially to the tropics, are the tree-ferns, the climbing

and the creeping ferns.   Tree-ferns occur abundantly in
certain higher sandstone tracts in the far interior, but far
more sparingly in the forest near the coast, where, however,
they are sometimes seen in thickets (*Alsophila aspera*),
sometimes singly (*Hemitelia macrocarpa* and others).   The
true climbing ferns, with delicately cut leaves, support
themselves after the manner of hops on the low shrubs
(*Lygodium*).   But there are others which, growing in
shrubless places and finding no support, allow their branches
to grow into a dense self-supporting bush, perhaps six feet
high (*Gleichenia*), which grows on rocky banks, exposed to
the full blaze of the sun, covering these places with a dense
mass of beautifully fretted foliage ; and another, but much
rarer, fern of similar habit is *Oleandra hirtella*, which has
a long, upright, and firm stem, so stiff as not to need support,
crowned with lance-shaped leaves.   Yet other ferns (*Polypodium* and others) creep like ivy up the tree-trunks ; and
even some filmy ferns have this habit.   Club mosses (*Selaginella* and *Lycopodium*) often carpet the ground under the
forest.   True mosses are scarce.   The striking heart-shaped
leaves of aroids, too, are frequently seen.   One of the commonest plants of Guiana, which is indeed hardly ever absent
from any shallow water, is the moco-moco, an aroid (*Caladium arborescens*) with leaves like that of the well-known
Calla, borne at the top of a long stick-like stem often from
ten to twelve feet high.   Here and there on the ground in
the more open parts of the forest the green, bright-red or
white-spotted leaves of *Caladiums*, so well known in English
hothouses, are seen ; and, growing epiphytically both on
standing and fallen trees, are large numbers of other aroids,
the leaves of some of them pierced with regular window-
like openings (*Monstera obliqua*).   Passing from these
to the masses of other epiphytes which load the trees,
the most striking of these are the *Tillandsias*, mostly like
wild pine-apples, but one curiously distinct form (*T. usne-
oides*), which hangs in large masses like long streamers of
grey wool, swaying in the wind from the outer branches of

the trees, produces a most weird effect; the *clusias*, with larger or smaller leathery leaves, like those of the well-known India-rubber plant (*Ficus elastica*), which first grow in some fork of the branches high up in the trees, and then send long, unbranched, rope-like roots straight down to the ground; and the orchids. The number of the latter plants in Guiana is enormous; some few grow on the ground, but the greater number are epiphytic. One, the vanilla plant, creeps like ivy. The quaint but unlovely general character of the plants is too well known to need description; their flowers, though many of them are individually of exceeding beauty, are in nature seldom sufficiently numerous to attract attention.

One class of plants which is generally conspicuous in tropical scenery is somewhat rarely noticeable in Guiana. These are the bamboos. The large, splendidly graceful clumps of bamboos—more graceful, as it appears to me, than any other form of vegetation—chiefly appear in Guiana near places now or once inhabited, and were therefore probably introduced. Other species—their feathery stems scattered instead of springing in definite clumps—are more widely scattered, but are seldom sufficiently numerous or remarkable to affect the character of the scenery.

The subject of the perfumes of plants in Guiana requires but few words. Strong sweet scent is a much more marked feature throughout the interior than is brilliant colour. Many of the trees, though carrying inconspicuous flowers, yet load the whole air with a perfume almost too powerful. The long white-flowered *Posoqueria*, already mentioned, is one of many plants as strongly scented as Stephanotis; and when the large yellow flowers are on the vanilla vines their scent may be distinguished from far off. Even the highest trees of the forest, which lift their flowers so far from the ground that their beauty is invisible, and their scent for a time imperceptible, yet afterwards, when they drop their flowers, make the odour in the forest at first really sweet, and then, as decay sets in, sickly sweet. Another source of perfume lies in the numberless resins which exude from the trees. Where the hyawa tree (*Icica heptaphylla*) grows, the whole air for some distance round is pleasant and wholesome with the incense-like odour of the white resin that drops from its stem, and falls in masses to the ground ; and a still more powerfully scented resin, which coats the trunk of another tree, the tauranero of the Indians (*Humirium floribundum*, Mart.), seems to imitate and surpass the odour of vanilla.

Having in these general considerations provided the necessary materials, as a painter provides colour, brushes, and canvas, I shall now attempt to describe a few special pictures of plant-life, some from the forest region, others from the savannah ; and thus try to give as true a notion as may be of the appearance of the land. In so doing it will hardly be necessary to notice the coast region, for the obvious reason that the greater part of this has been much modified by the hand of man, whereas we are now regarding only natural conditions ; and for the same reason the forest pictures will be taken, not from that part which has been described as the timber tract, most of which has at some time been deprived of its finest trees by the hand of man, but from the more remote virgin forest. It may, however, be noted that the most remarkable difference between the timber tract and the virgin forest is that the space under the forest roof is in the former place much filled with shrubs and lower trees, while in the latter place it is much more open.

Let us first suppose ourselves to stand far from any opening, somewhere in the deep shade under the unbroken forest roof. The eye is first attracted by the enormous girth and various character of the tree-trunks. Many of these for some distance from the ground are not columnar, but formed by many board-like natural buttresses, radiating from a common centre, between any two of which several men may often stand ; these buttresses run so far up the trunk that if the tree is to be felled, this being impossible near the ground, a platform, sometimes twenty or thirty feet

high, has first to be built round the tree, above the point
where the buttresses unite to form a trunk of the ordinary
pillar-like form ; and from this platform the woodcutters ply
their axes against the trunk, at that height circular and of
moderate dimensions. The largest of these buttressed trees
are the moras, the commonest tree of the colony. But
among the two or three moras which are in sight, there
are other trunks of every degree of circumference—some of
the familiar pillar-like form, others like the clustered shafts
of a stone pillar, apparently made up of a number of small
coalescent trunks ; most are smooth, but on some there are
curious prickles, each supported on a separate tumour on
the bark, and on others clusters of star-like or pea-shaped
flowers and pods (*Swartzia*), spring directly from the bark
of the trunk or branches. Up the trunks there are a few
isolated tendrils of various creeping plants, some with curiously spotted and marked leaves. There are no large palms
in sight, but on the right there is a tangled thicket of small
erect palms (*Geonoma bacculifera*) eight or nine feet high,
with a smooth, many-jointed, light-coloured stem, familiar
in the form of a walking-stick, and with a few simple or
slightly feathered leaves. Here and there there are also a
few other palms (*Bactris tricospatha*), hardly taller, growing
singly, each with a very slender and straight prickly stem
supporting a crown of a few delicately feathered leaves.
There are but very few shrubs visible, or anything but the tree-
trunks to impede the view at the level of the eye. Looking
up the tree-trunks the eye travels far, past many clumps of
epiphytal plants, past the forkings of the first branches,
and yet higher up to the dark, impenetrable roof of leaves,
before it perceives the enormous height of the trees. From
the roof hang down tangled masses of innumerable creepers,
here leafless, for their leafy parts lie above the tops of the
trees. On these hanging creeper-ropes one or two enormous
masses of epiphytes are perched. Then the eye, looking
down on to the floor, is struck by the scarcity of moss and
other small plants such as carpet temperate woods ; here the

ground in many places consists only of bare mud, or is covered only by a few dead leaves or fallen fruits and branches; only in a very few and small patches is it carpeted by dense masses of seedling trees a foot or two high, among which grow a few herbaceous ferns and club-mosses (*Selaginella*). On a heap of dead leaves grow one or two tiny parasitic gentians (*Voyria*), the flowers of which are to be described not so much as white, but rather as colourless, supported on short wiry stems, leafless, and of the same colourless aspect. Lastly, a huge prostrate tree-trunk is half-buried under epiphytal plants, orchids, wild pine-apples, and aroids.

It is difficult to obtain a view of the outside of the roof of the forest, but it may sometimes, as has been said in a former chapter, be seen from the top of some steep-sided hill rising above the forest. Standing on such a place as that one looks on to a level sea of tree-tops, a mass of very various foliage most closely woven together by innumerable creepers. Both of the trees and the creepers, some individuals may sometimes be seen made gorgeous with flowers, but these are better seen from the level ground in some opening in the forest. It is on these tree-tops, exposed to the full blaze of the sun, that many of the finest orchids grow; but their small size, and the distance from which it is alone possible to view them in their natural positions, prevent them forming a feature in the landscape.

Where many species of palms are gathered together in any one spot in the forest the scene has a very distinct character. The most common of these social palms is the æta (*Mauritia flexuosa*), which, though it occasionally grows singly at the river-side, its seed having probably been placed by the current, grows more generally in large numbers either in some swampy part of the forest, or entirely filling some moist valley on the savannah. A large æta swamp in the forest is a curious and somewhat gloomy place. There are hardly any other trees or plants. The simple massive trunks, free for some distance from the ground from all litter, but crowned with giant fan-leaves, of which some hang down, withered and brown, round the upper part of the trunk, rise at some distance from each other, each from a hillock of fallen leaves; and between the hillocks stretches the bare black mud, through which narrow streams of dark red water wind in places. The leaves of the palms interlock and make a roof and a thick shade hardly less dense than that elsewhere in the forest. Occasionally a fallen trunk lies like a bridge, from one hillock to another, and in other places there are a few young palms, stemless as yet, their leaves rising straight from the mud. As far as one can see, looking between the trunks, the scene is continued as it is in the foreground. A swamp filled by the troolie palm (*Manicaria saccifera*) is equally striking. In the north-western part of the colony, between the mouths of the Orinoco and Essequibo, large stretches of land are occupied almost exclusively by this palm, the immense leaves of which, uncut into leaflets, and sometimes from twenty to thirty feet long by five broad, meet overhead, and thus maintain a constant gloom and a damp and humid atmosphere round their stems, which is very favourable to the growth of small ferns. It is while standing in a troolie forest up to one's knees in the level floor of palm *débris*, and looking up at the almost monstrously gigantic leaves, that one most realises the effect of tropical vegetation.

The most graceful of all the palms of Guiana, the mani-cole (*Euterpe edulis*), grows in masses at the sides of most rivers; but in places it also occupies whole swamps. These differ principally from the æta swamps, in that the mani-cole grows, not singly but in groups, consisting of many gracefully bent slender stems of very various heights, each raised on a common dense mass of exposed roots. These groups arise in this way. A single seed takes root and sends up a single stem; after a time a new stem buds out from the base of the original stems, and this happens again and again until the whole group, or plant, perhaps, consists of a dozen stems of various ages. And as the number of the stems increases, more and more supporting roots are sent out, and these in time get welded into a great mass, which gradually pushes up the crown, and lifts the stems far into the air. Because of their most feathery foliage and the grouping of the slender stems, each clump of these palms is a thing of exquisite beauty; and the swamp in which many of these clumps stand as islands has none of the solemnity of the æta or troolie swamp, but rather is full of light and cheerfulness.

A much rarer palm, which also sometimes grows in considerable quantity in swamps within the forest, though hardly ever entirely occupying such places, is the booba (*Iriartea exorrhiza*). It grows so often scattered singly in manicole swamps that one or two may well be inserted in any picture of such a place. Each straight single stem of the booba, instead of rising directly from the ground, is supported high in air on many much and widely forked prickly roots, sometimes eight or nine feet high; each leaflet of its feathered leaves is triangular, like those of a maidenhair fern, and is set on to the midrib at a peculiar angle, which gives to the whole crown of leaves a most plume-like effect.

One other palm, rare in Guiana, but which grows within the forest in at least one place in considerable numbers, is an *Orbigignia*, of a species new to science, which Professor Trail of Aberdeen has named *O. Sagotii*. It grows among trees and shrubs of the ordinary type, but its huge feathered leaves, in that they are not raised as in other palms, on a trunk, but spring directly from the ground, have a peculiar effect.

Passing out of the forest into some open space, either a river-course or a glade, the edge of the forest as seen from here presents a very different aspect. We will suppose ourselves to look at it from some river.

The character of the river-side vegetation within reach of the tide differs somewhat from that which prevails in the higher parts. Generally in the former parts the true forest does not extend to the open river, but between the two a belt of mangrove trees (*Rhizophora mangal*) stands, raised high above the mud flat on aërial roots, except where in one or two places a projecting spur of the higher real bank runs out above the mud, through the mangroves, into the river, these banks being clothed by a dwarf palm (*Bactris palustris*) so densely packed that the bold feathered leaves completely hide the stems, and the whole look like high, swelling banks of ferns. In the shallow water of the bays between these banks and the lines of mangroves numbers of eucharis-like lilies raise over the water their grassy leaves and clusters of large delicate, sweet-scented flowers, sometimes pure white (*Crinum commelyna*), sometimes with the white relieved by red-stained anthers (*Hymenocallis guianensis*).

It is somewhat difficult to describe a piece of the bank along the higher parts of the river, for each stretch differs, yet differs but slightly, not so much in the plant-materials which compose it as in the way in which these materials are combined. In a typical stretch of river-bank three somewhat different phases of vegetation are chiefly discernible : one where the bank has not within any recent period either been increased or decreased by the action of the passing river ; another where it has been washed away ; and the third where it has had new soil added outside it. As the traveller faces the bank he may from one place be able to notice all these three phases : part of the bank is undisturbed ; part has recently been carried away, so that the river here has made its way into the forest, and runs immediately next to the forest wall ; and a little lower down the earth thus swept away has been again deposited, built up as it were in a spit of low land, which runs from the original, somewhat higher bank, out into the river.

Where the bank has been undisturbed the forest leafage slopes in beautifully rounded curves down to the water's edge, trees shrubs and creepers being all blended into one ; and the curve is continued and repeated without the slightest break in the almost perfectly faithful reflection in the water. No single plant is distinctly seen in the mass, and the general monotony is broken only by some isolated patch of colour. Yet, on the other hand, many individual

flowers and seeds attract the observant eye.   In one place,
for example, a number of large pods hang each at the end of
a whip-like stem some two feet in length, and again, a very
curious green flower, shaped like the spokes of a wheel, are
sure to attract notice; but so confused is the mass that it is
long before it is possible to determine that the former belong
to a tree (*Eperua falcata*), the latter to a creeper (*Marc-
gravia umbellata*).   In short, the whole is one confused
rounded mass of innumerable plant-forms.

Where the bank has been broken away, in place of
the rounded mass of the foliage, the trunks of the outermost
trees of the forest rise like a wall, straight from the surface
of the river.   The creepers, which before the bank gave way
ran among the tree-leaves up from the water and away over
the roof of the forest, have now already sent down tendrils
towards the water; and these, weaving themselves together,
hang exactly like a drawn curtain, straight down from the
outer edge of the tree-branches which project over the
water.   At certain seasons of the year this curtain of
creepers is dyed with the most brilliant colours by the various
flowers which it puts out.   In one place, the wall of trees
and creepers is broken by a magnificent palm, a cokerite
(*Maximiliana regia*).   This plant is a study in itself.
The word palm generally calls up before the mind a hardly
varied picture of a more or less tall, more or less straight
trunk from the top of which a few leaves branch off somewhat at right angles; as a matter of fact, though such a
description does roughly apply to the generality of palms,
yet differences, slight in themselves, in the nature of the
trunk, and in the set of the leaves and leaflets, give to each
genus and often to each species a very distinct aspect.   For
instance, this cokerite could never be mistaken from any
distance for any other palm occurring in Guiana.   It grows
singly, though occasionally there are a good many near together.   Sometimes, in old plants, the stem is clear and
columnar for some little distance from the ground, but upward
from this, or much more often from the ground itself, the

bases of the stalks of former leaves remain, encircling the stem, and these adherent remnants of stalks are longer and longer higher up the tree till the present green leaves are reached, and these, set not at any acute angle to the stem below them, but at a very obtuse angle, rise high into the air till at the very top, they curve very gradually and gracefully outward. The whole shape of the tree is, in fact, that of a cornucopia-shaped vase, which rises from a narrow base and curves outward. The leaves themselves are feathered, but the many long grassy leaflets are thickly set on the midrib at a peculiar angle; and these, straight for some distance, then hang their ends loosely down, so that the whole leaf has the aspect, not, as usual among feathered palms, of a flat feather, but rather of a curled plume. The plant is made yet more beautiful by the fact that among the remnants of leaves on its stem some ferns have taken root (chiefly *Nephrolepis acuta* and *Polypodium decumanum*), and these mingle their green leaves with the great hanging bunches of yellow palm flowers and fruits.

On the spit of new-forming land plants have already begun to grow, and the refuse from the first-coming plants is gradually building up soil for more enduring forms. Nearest the river, the spit is edged with a uniform belt of some particular bush growing in the water, either guavas (*Psidium aquaticum* and *P. aromaticum*), with white scented flowers and green-yellow, bitter-tasted fruits; or mahoes (*Hibiscus tiliaceus*), with leaves like those of English lime-trees, and large pale primrose-coloured mallow-flowers with chocolate throats; or inga (*I. meissneriana, et var. sp.*), along every branchlet of which white flowers, like downy feathers, nestle thickly. Over these bushes twine not a few creepers, their roots on land, some with bright-coloured flowers, such as purple-white *Bignonias*, *Allamandas* with huge yellow trumpet flowers, and a *Combretum* with scarlet bottle-brush flowers. Behind this outer hedge the spit is, for some distance back, covered by a tangled mass of dwarfer vegetation, apparently of shrubs, but so completely clothed

by convolvulus (*Ipomœa*) and other creepers that it
is impossible to discern their kind. From among these
shrubs rise a few single trumpet-wood trees (*Cecropia
peltata*), the straight or but slightly branched stems of
which, each crowned with a rosette of large maple-shaped
leaves, spring up to a great height in a few months, and
then, by their equally rapid decay, help largely in the formation of soil for more permanent trees. Accordingly, yet
further back, but still on the spit, a few Long-Johns
(*Triplaris surinamensis*) rise singly ; for these, less enduring than the true forest trees, but more so than the trumpet-
woods, grow on the soil deposited by the latter, and in their
turn prepare the soil for more noble products. Lastly,
where the original bank begins, the dense forest wall serves
as a background to all this ephemeral vegetation.

One other very characteristic river-side picture must be
given. In this, as far as the eye can see, the whole sandy bank
is occupied by a dense thicket of souari palms (*Astrocaryum
[vulgare ?],*) their long grey stems slightly curved in various
directions clear of hanging leaves, but horridly armed with
long spines arranged in broad bands round the tree, their
feathered greyish-green leaves also spiny, and the ground
round their roots made impassable to naked feet by an
unbroken carpet of heaped spines and spiny leafage.

Passing from the forest tract to the savannah the
characteristic scenery may easily be shown in a few pictures.
The first is taken from the great savannah of the interior.
The scene is bounded towards the right by a distant chain of
mountains, on the face of which bare cliffs and wooded slopes
mingle ; toward the left the plain rolls away until it meets
the horizon. The land is not unlike those wider parts of the
English downs where the rolling surface is broken by a few
stunted hawthorns or clumps of tall furze. But in the
hollows between the ridges of the savannah, instead of the
fir, beech, and hazel coppices of the English downs, there are
long, regular-looking groves of æta palms or belts of
other tropical trees. The æta forest is like that which has

already been described. The shrubs are windblown, but many of them bear bright flowers. Commonest of all among the shrubs are hard-leaved, yellow-flowered species of *Curatella*. Here and there the highest ground is so thickly covered by these shrubs that it looks almost well wooded. In parts the soil is somewhat exposed and stony; but even here there are numbers of a curious low-growing plant (*Scirpus paradoxus*), with a thick swollen trunk, like that of a tree fern, surmounted by a dense rosette of very fine grass-like leaves. In other places there is high and luxuriant grass, among which mix many bright flowers, chiefly white, red, blue, and yellow pea-flowers, and even a few ground orchids. One great stretch of ground is entirely covered with a cabbage-like plant, with great bunches of yellow flowers (*Byrsonima*). A second savannah picture shows more sandy ground, a coppice not far off forming a background. On the loose sand there are many scattered tufts of coarse grass, and amongst these stand a few tall straggling plants (*Jatropha urens*) with inconspicuous flowers and hemp-like leaves, which, when touched, sting more sharply than any nettle.

Of the scenery of the somewhat different and peculiar sandstone part of the savannah, lying between the Kaieteur fall and Roraima, I have told elsewhere.

Before leaving the subject it must be mentioned that there are certain water plants which are so striking and in places so abundant that in themselves they make scenes. Two of these (*Mouriera fluviatilis* and *Lacis alata*) grow on the half-submerged rocks in most of the falls. As the water decreases in the dry season, the tall spikes of bright pink flowers of the former plant rise from their large leaves, the edges of which are cut and curled into the likeness of moss, which lie flat on the rocks ; and at the same time and place innumerable tiny pink stars rise an inch or two over the equally moss-like leaves of the *Lacis*. A rapid, apparently encircled by the forest, and with its rocks all reddened by these flowers, is very beautiful and noticeable.

CHAPTER V.

ANIMAL LIFE.

General Considerations—Mammals—Warracaba Tigers—The Colours of Birds—Bird-notes—Chief Forms of Birds—Scenes of Bird-Life—Reptiles—Alligators—Iguanas—Snakes—Turtles—Fish—The Dangers of Bathing—Insect Plagues—Butterflies—Beetles—Ants—Wasps—Mosquitoes—Sandflies—The Mosquito Worm—Jiggers—Bush-Ticks—Spiders—Centipedes—Scorpions.

IN a tropical country so varied as regards physical features as British Guiana, and so sparingly inhabited by man, it will naturally be supposed that animal life, both in its beautiful and its baneful forms, is very abundant. This is indeed the case; but yet animal life is not in any marked degree prominent, nor, with the exception perhaps of insect ravages, is it in any way troublesome. It is not surprising that the ordinary colonist, who generally lives in the more inhabited parts of the coast land, should not see much wild animal life around him; but the traveller in the interior, even if he is in search of wild beasts, cannot avoid a feeling of surprise that so few of these present themselves unsought to his notice, and that he has to search so diligently before he finds others. The untravelled man, living in temperate climates, while he overcolours in his mind the picture of the brilliant birds, insects, and animals, thinks with horror, not only of the powerful savage animals—which are probably represented in his mind by beasts of prey and by gigantic or venomous serpents—but also of the thousand annoying insects and other such small cattle, which, as he imagines, everywhere lie in wait for the traveller, or even the dweller, in the tropics. If these imaginations were

anywhere near the truth, it would indeed be a surprising
thing that any man could long survive in the tropics.   And
if the man whom we have thus supposed to send his thoughts
from temperate to tropical regions is at last drawn by a fate
which appears to him unkind to travel for a short time to these
places detestable to him, he reaches home with a consciousness
that he has seen too little of the expected beauty, and felt little
of the expected evils; and then, by a not unnatural reaction
of thought, he is apt to regard all that he afterwards hears
of the abundance, the beauty, or the annoyance of animal
life in the tropics as merely the proverbial traveller's tale.
And, unconsciously, travellers of greater experience help to
confirm this erroneous view; for when they tell their experiences to those at home, they tell only of moments made
eventful to them by exciting or evil experiences, and leave
unnoticed the long periods intermediate between such
moments, in which nothing of any consequence occurred.
For example, not long ago, I found at the end of an evening
during which I had told adventures which had occurred to
me, in the course of several years, with many sorts of harm-
doing animals, from jaguars to mosquitoes, that the impression made on the minds of my hearers was that life in
Guiana, at any rate in the interior, is one long unending
conflict with such foes; and I had to correct this impression
by pointing out that the story told that evening was, as one
of my hearers expressed it, the concentrated misery of three
years.   In the same way it is dangerous to tell of the many
beautiful and interesting animal forms, unless stress is laid
on the fact that these are but picked out from a large
number of less interesting forms.   Thus the traveller's true
tale of his experiences, unless carefully guarded as I found
necessary on the occasion just mentioned, helps to spread
wrong impressions, both by helping to confirm those who
are no travellers in their belief of the everywhere present
beauty, and the incessant danger from animal life, in the
tropics, and by leading those who have travelled a little,
generally in the more inhabited parts, to regard these new

traveller's tales, and in consequence all other traveller's tales, as false, or at least as greatly exaggerated.

Therefore, in telling of animal, as I have already of vegetable, life in Guiana, I want not only to show its real abundance and beauty, but also and equally to show its slight prominence and general harmlessness. And as in this respect Guiana may fairly enough be said to be typical, not only of other parts of South America, but also (due allowance being made for the fact that the animal forms of the American continent are as a rule smaller and less powerful than those of the other continents) of other tropical regions, I should, if I could succeed in giving a correct impression of animal life as it affects man in Guiana, at the same time afford some idea of animal life in the tropics generally.

The number of mammals is somewhat large. It will be best to take them in the order of their abundance.

The most prominent animals in Guiana are three rodents —the labba (*Cælogenys paca*), the acouri (*Dasyprocta aguti*) and the water-haas (*Hydrochœrus capybara*).

The labba, an animal like a large guinea-pig, with brown skin spotted with white, is distributed throughout the country on the banks of rivers. Its flesh is more esteemed than that of any other animal, not only by Indians, but also by the colonists; indeed the latter have a proverb that ' the man who has eaten labba and drunk creek water will never die out of the colony.' The labba lives during the day chiefly in hollow, fallen trees, and goes out to forage at night. The acourie, elsewhere called the aguti, is in appearance like a rabbit on long legs, and with coarse, chestnut-coloured hair. It is as abundant everywhere as the labba, but lives more in the forest, only venturing to the water to drink. It feeds by day on fallen fruits. There is a second species very similar, but smaller, called adourie (*D. acuchy*) only less common than the acourie. The water-haas, or capybara, is a much larger animal, which, like the labba, resembles a guinea-pig in shape, but is much larger

even than the labba. It lives among the roots of trees
in the mud at the river-side. It is a good swimmer,
and it may not seldom be seen in the water. The skin
of this animal seems to be especially adapted only for
frequent immersion in water, for if exposed only for a
short time to the sun, the outer skin (*epidermis*), with the
coarse, scanty hair peels off in sheets, leaving the true skin
(*corium*) exposed. All these animals, common as they are,
are of retiring habits; and the traveller, until he learns
their ways and knows how to find them, may go for many
days without seeing a single individual of any kind.

Bush-hogs, or peccaries, of two kinds wander about in the
swampy parts of the forests. The smaller of these (*Dicotyles torquatus*), is called abouyah, the larger (*D. labiatus*)
kairooni[1] by the Arawaks. The former kind lives in parties
of five and six: the latter in large herds often of a hundred
head. In a previous chapter[2] the habit of these animals of
swimming across rivers has been mentioned. In the daytime they take to the water without hesitation; but if in
their travels they reach the edge of a river at night, the herd
settles down, after much commotion and grunting, to wait
for daylight before crossing. It is sometimes dangerous to
attack, single-handed, a herd of kairooni in the forest; for
they are apt to use their tusks with terrible effect—they are
even said to kill large jaguars in this way—and, if the
attacker takes refuge in a tree, the pigs squat patiently
round until sometimes he is either starved out or relieved by
other men.

Nor is the tapir (*Tapirus americanus*) a rare animal.
His tracks may often be seen at the side of the river, and I
once saw a pond in the forest, the mud round which had
been trodden by tapirs much as the edge of a pond in an
English farmyard is by cattle. The animal itself is seldom
seen, though it frequently ventures strangely near inhabited
places.

There are about a dozen species of monkeys, and some of

---

[1] This is the " whinga " of the Macusis.   [2] See p. 54.

these may frequently be seen. The pretty little bright-coloured sackawinki (*Chrysothrix sciureus*) lives in large herds which may often be seen on the trees by the river-side, the individuals generally following each other in single file, and, one after the other, hurling themselves for extraordinary distances from tree to tree. Very often they are quiet enough and would escape notice but for the rustling they make among the leaves. But if one is shot, the rest, instead of at once escaping, seem to the eyes of the astonished hunter suddenly to fill the tree with grinning faces, all chattering with more than the proverbial monkey garrulity. Next to these, the commonest monkey is that called in the colony the baboon, and elsewhere the red howling monkey (*Mycetes seniculus*), but which might much more aptly be called the red roarer; for, though not bigger than a setter, it roars like any jaguar, tiger, or lion. Many travellers have tried, but failed, to describe the sound produced by this extraordinary animal; and I do not pretend to find the required words, though it seems to me that the sound is more like that which is heard when the beasts of prey in the Zoological Gardens are fed than anything else I ever heard. Why this animal should make this most extraordinary noise, being specially provided for the purpose with a peculiar bony apparatus in its throat, has, as far as I know, never been satisfactorily explained. The effect produced in the stillness of the night, or in the early morning, is utterly astounding; and the noise is continued at intervals through the day.

Three species of ant-bear, differing very much in general appearance, are all equally common. The largest of these (*Myrmecophaga jubata*) is a strange-looking animal, about the size of a large bloodhound, with an enormously bushy tail which, when reversed over the body, shelters the whole animal. This is sometimes found in the forest, but more commonly on the savannah. It is said to be capable of successfully defending itself against a man, by hugging him with its fore-feet and pressing its powerful claws into his body. The second (*M. tamandua*), the size of a spaniel, with a smooth tail, is hardly ever seen except climbing on trees in the forest. And the third (*M. didactyla*), a very gentle and pretty little creature, with a body no bigger than that of a toy-terrier, covered all over with soft silky short hair, is also found on trees in the forest, and occasionally near human habitations on the coast.

All the cats, of which there are many species not fully determined in Guiana, are locally called 'tigers' or, in the case of the smaller species, 'tiger-cats.' Under these names are included the puma, and several species of jaguar and ocelots. The Indians assert that each kind hunts a different prey. Thus, *Felis jaguarundi* is called a hacka-tiger, because it is supposed to prey chiefly, if not exclusively, on the hacka (*Galictis barbara*); the puma is called the deer-tiger; *F. nigra* is called the maipuri (tapir) tiger; and *F. macrura* is called the abouyah (or peccary) tiger. All these are more or less common in Guiana, though they are seldom seen by man. It is hardly possible to find an Indian house in which there are not teeth or portions of the skin of one of these species; and on the cattle-farms on the Brazilian border, I was assured that hardly a night passes in which the cattle are not attacked by jaguars. Indians have a great dread of jaguars, and tell how these animals will sometimes even enter Indian houses and carry off a dog, or even an old woman or a child. Again and again when sleeping in the forest I have been waked by the Indians, who declared that there were jaguars about; and I have known these Indians, in places where they supposed jaguars to be, sling their hammocks high up in some tree, having first made a fire round its roots, and sleep aloft, leaving incredulous me to my fate below. On the other hand, though I have known a jaguar prowl round my hammock at night, I never knew them to attack a man.

Some special mention must be made of certain real or mythical animals called warracaba tigers—as some say, from the resemblance of the noise made by these cats to the note of the warracaba bird or trumpeter (*Psophia crepitans*); or, as others say, from the purplish shade on the skin of these tigers, which is like the breast feathers of the bird; or, as yet others say, from the fact that the tigers prey on the birds. Never having had any personal experience of warracaba tigers, I cannot present the common belief in them more graphically than by giving the following extract from the writings of a previous traveller in Guiana.[1] 'In the evening,' he writes, 'I was attracted by our two dogs, which were tied up, barking furiously, followed by a great stir in camp. Then some voices proclaimed loudly "The tigers are coming;" and one man called to me to come down as quickly as possible to the boats, and bring my gun. . . . Jumping down the low bank, to my surprise I found the beach deserted. Where some twenty Indians had been encamped, there was now not even a hammock left; all had suddenly and completely vanished. My men had all taken to the boat, and had it afloat, with its bow barely grounded, in readiness to shove off. They greeted me with cries of " Quick, sir, quick! the warracaba tigers are coming!" There was quite a flutter of relief amongst them when the boat was pushed off into mid-stream, when they all began to talk excitedly over our escape. The dogs still gave tongue, and were even more excited than the men, the hair on their backs standing erect as they sniffed the air in the direction of our camp. I eagerly inquired what were warracaba tigers, and was hastily informed that they were small and exceedingly ferocious tigers, that they hunted in packs, and were not frightened by camp fires, or anything except the barking of dogs. To water they have a special aversion, and will never cross a stream which is too wide for them to jump. . . . I believe that some terrible animals had nearly pounced upon us, otherwise the Indians would never have acted as they had done. As we stopped, a shrill scream rent the night air, proceeding from the opposite side of the river, not two hundred yards above our camp, and, waking up echoes through the forest, died away as suddenly as it rose. This was answered by another cry coming from

[1] C. B. Brown, *Canoe and Camp Life in British Guiana*, p. 71.

the depths of the forest, the interval between them being filled by low growls and trumpeting sounds. Gradually the cries became fainter and fainter, as the band retired from our vicinity, till they utterly died away. Seeing nothing of them, and only hearing their diabolical screams, I pictured them in my mind as a withering scourge sweeping through the forest. As many as a hundred are said to have been seen in one pack. They are said to frequent the mountains, but when pressed by hunger during the dry seasons they descend to the lowlands.'

I was naturally anxious to learn something of these cats hunting in packs; but I never myself met with them, and only found three men who professed to know anything about them. One of these three witnesses was my friend McTurk, a man thoroughly acquainted with the forest and its inhabitants, and incapable of telling what he did not believe. He told me that, while walking through the forest from the Essequibo to the Kaieteur fall, his Indian companions suddenly became terrified and declared that there were warracabas in the neighbourhood. Sounds were audible which McTurk thought were those of the warracaba bird. Shortly afterward, a single 'tiger,' a slim mouse-coloured beast, was seen; but nothing else happened. The same informant told me that he has on several occasions seen the tracks of the pack, which seemed to him to be composed of animals of all sizes, from that of a cat up to that of a full-grown jaguar. Another witness was an Indian on the Pomeroon river, who told me that the pack consists of two large and many small individuals, all grey-coloured except for a small mark over the eyes. The third witness was a Portuguese policeman, famous for many expeditions into the interior, who assured me that he had 'met up' with a 'flock' of warracaba tigers, and had been obliged to take refuge in a tree from them; but his further account was evidently much exaggerated.

I have put before the reader all the evidence I know as to the existence and nature of warracaba tigers. I cannot pretend to decide what these animals are, or even if they exist; but I may suggest that possibly all the stories may be founded on the fact that families of pumas (*F. concolor*), consisting of parents and cubs, occasionally move about together.

Various kinds of small deer occur, one species chiefly in and near the cane-fields on the coast; others are confined to the forest; and another species (*Cervus savannarum*) to the savannah. The distribution of this last species may be indicated in the fact that over great parts of the savannah it is hardly to be found at all, while in others it occurs so abundantly that one party of Indians sometimes kills as many as a dozen individuals in a day.

The more important of the other animals may be mentioned in a few words. Two kinds of racoons, called quashi by the negroes, kibihee by the Indians—the one living singly or in pairs (*Nasua solitaris*), the other in small droves (*N. socialis*)—are more often seen tame in Indian settlements than wild. Armadilloes of many kinds burrow in the forest and under the ant-hills on the savannah. Sloths are occasionally, and in some parts frequently, found clinging so tenaciously to the leafy branches that they often remain motionless while the trees on which they are are felled. Several kinds of opossum (*Didelphys*), the only pouched animals of Guiana, live, the larger species on palm-trees, the smaller chiefly among bamboos. A grey squirrel (*Sciurus æstuans*) runs like its English cousin among the trees. Occasionally a most offensive odour attracts attention to where a porcupine (*Sphingurus insidiosus*), despite the ground-keeping habits of most of its kindred, climbs among the branches. It is hardly possible to pass for many hours along any of the rivers without seeing small parties of otters swimming, while from the bank the hideous shriek of others may occasionally be heard. Porpoises (*Delphinus*) plunge in the waters of rivers which are not separated from the sea by large and rapid falls; and in the same places a huge lumbering manatee (*Manatus australis*) occasionally rises near the boat of the traveller or plunges in alarm into deep water from shallows where it had been browsing on the leaves of water plants.

After all, we have left to the last the set of mammals which is perhaps most prominent and most widely distributed. These are the bats. There is certainly a considerable number of species; and, as these have never been accurately determined, an interesting field for observation is thus offered to some future zoological specialist. It is here only possible to tell of bats as they appear to the ordinary spectator. Most prominent of all is a huge fruit-eating bat, with wings which occasionally measure three feet from tip to tip, and this, from its supposed blood-sucking propensities, is erroneously called the vampire. It is—bats generally, deservedly or not, having acquired a reputation for repulsiveness—an ugly animal, but innocent enough. Its strength must be great; for in certain houses in Georgetown about which these bats live, every night during the mango season these large and heavy fruits fall in considerable numbers, and with a loud noise, on to the slates of the roof, being dropped, as I found, by so-called vampires as they flew. The real blood-sucking bats, or vampires, are small, light-coloured animals, of probably several species, of the genus *Phyllostoma*; and they occur not in towns, but in large numbers almost everywhere else. Their habit of sucking the blood of men has already been mentioned in an earlier chapter;[1] their attacks on other animals are so serious that it is, for example, impossible to keep poultry where these bats are, except by shutting up the birds by night in some carefully closed building. Another very noticeable bat is a small dark-coloured kind which lives during the day in large flocks on the trunks of trees overhanging the rivers. If a boat approaches, the whole flock rises and flits along under the shadow of the overhanging trees until another convenient stump or trunk is reached, and there it once more settles. These animals are so abundant on most rivers that they form one of the most characteristic features of waterside life.

[1] See p. 17.

Probably no country of equal extent is richer than Guiana in birds. It is a common idea that great brilliance of colour is the almost universal characteristic of these. But this notion has arisen merely from the fact that the bright-coloured birds, of which there certainly are a good many, have been diligently collected and sent out of the country as curiosities, while those of less brilliant hue—the number of which is in nature very far greater—are, as the naturalist knows, but seldom exported.

Moreover, the traveller in Guiana sees in nature very little even of that brilliancy of colour which undoubtedly exists. Nothing can be more resplendent than the male cock-of-the-rock (*Rupicola crocea*), a bird about the size of a small bantam, which is everywhere clothed, except at the end of the tail, and on the larger wing feathers, in ruddy orange, so brilliant, while the bird is alive and in health, that it has a glow like that of fire. Then there is the bird (*Threnœdus militaris*), called in the colony 'baboon-bird,' from the resemblance of its deep note to that of the 'baboon' or red howling monkey, which is of the size of a pigeon and is almost entirely of a very rich deep crimson. Among the chatterers, the fire-bird (*Phœnicocircus carnifex*) has a rich deep brown back, with a tail, head-cap, and breast of most vivid crimson; the wallababa (*Ampelis pompadora*) is of a curious fine purple colour, very rare among birds, but like that of beautiful wine, with pure white wing-feathers; two other chatterers are of bright forget-me-not blue, somewhat gaudily varied with a patch of purple on the breast (*Ampelis cœrulea* and *cayana*). The curri-curri or scarlet ibis (*Ibis rubra*) is too well known to need description. Then there are parrots and parroquets of very many kinds, and of almost as many brilliant colours; and there are macaws entirely dyed with red, orange, and green, blue, and soft yellow. Lastly, there are humming-birds of very many species, whose colours are proverbial. All these, and a few others which there is no need to mention, could not possibly be surpassed in richness of colour. Yet, when in a state of nature, they show but little. It is true that in the remote parts of the colony the cock-of-the-rock is occasionally seen to pass like a flash of orange light, and that on the mud-flats on the coast the scarlet curri-curri may be seen from far off, the more markedly in that it feeds among pure white egrets. But the colours of the others are not apparent, or very seldom indeed, to the traveller. The chatterers, probably as a family the gayest of all the birds, keep to the tops of the tallest trees; even the parrots are so high up that their colours are not distinguishable from the ground; and when macaws fly over, or shriek from the top of some dead tree, it would generally be difficult, but for the difference in their harsh notes, to discern even whether they are of the red or of the blue species. One of the few mis-leading passages I know in Waterton's writings is that in which he says that 'it is a grand sight in ornithology to see thousands of aras (macaws) flying over your head low enough to let you have a full view of their flaming mantle.' It must be a very rare sight to see so many together; they are generally either in pairs, or at most five or six fly together, and even where they are most abundant I have never seen above a score together; nor has any man, either European or Indian, ever admitted to me that he has seen larger flocks. Moreover, their colours, as I have already said, are at best but barely discernible as they fly.

In this matter of the exhibition of colour the case of humming-birds is somewhat peculiar. No birds in the whole world are more gloriously coloured; but the texture of the feathers is so peculiar that these colours appear only in certain lights. Even with a humming-bird in one's hand, it is impossible to see at one glance more than a small portion of the beauty of its colour, and generally, though in some positions the whole bird looks dull, yet if it be slightly moved some point on its body flashes out with colour more brilliant than fire. This matter is well illus-trated by Mr. Gould's beautiful book of humming birds. For example, to take a Guiana species, the picture of the 'king humming-bird' (*Topaza pella*) is exquisite, and is

faithful in so far that each detail of colouring is correctly
given; but the drawing serves as a signal example of the difficulty of representing a humming-bird. Hardly more than
one of the points of colour is in reality ever visible in any
one humming-bird at one and the same time, for each point
only shows its peculiar and glittering colour when the light
falls upon it from a particular direction. A true representation of one of these birds would show it in somewhat
sober colours except just at the one point which, when the
bird is in the position chosen for representation, meets the
light at the requisite angle; and that point alone should
be shown in full brilliance of colour. A flowering shrub
is sometimes seen surrounded by a cloud of humming-birds,
all of the same species, and each, of course, in a different
position. If some one would draw such a scene as that,
showing a different detail of colouring in each bird, according to its position, then some idea of the actual appearance
of humming-birds might be given to one who had never
seen an example. And if so small a portion of the colouring,
however intense such a portion may be, is visible in a
bird held in the hand, it will easily be understood that in
nature, these birds flying with such exceeding rapidity, only
by a very rare chance is any colour flashed by a living
humming-bird on to the human eye.

It is natural to turn from the colour to the note of birds.
The almost entire absence of sweet bird-notes at once strikes
the traveller who comes from thrush and warbler-haunted
temperate lands. There is hardly a bird in Guiana with
sweet notes; perhaps the chief songsters are the tiny 'louis
d'or' (*Euphonia violacea* and *E. minuta*), birds with dark
steel-blue backs and yellow breasts, which chirp out a few
feeble notes sweetly enough, and the shik bird.

But if sweet notes are few, striking notes are abundant.
Most characteristic of all is the pĭ-pīyŏ (*Lipangus cine-
raceus*), a bird, somewhat like a song-thrush, which, crying
its own name all through the day, makes the sound echo and
re-echo through the forest. The toucans also, in the early

morning and in the evening, yelp, like excited puppies, from the high trees. The famous so-called bell-bird (*Chasmarhynchus carunculatus*) is often heard in the forest, and a second species (*C. variegatus*) as often on some parts of the savannah. I never could detect much resemblance in the note of these birds to the sound of a bell. The cry of the first species is more like the ring produced by two pieces of iron struck against each other; but the notes of the male and female birds differ considerably. The cry of the second species is like the sound made by the drill in blasting operations. Then, also in the forest, is heard an extraordinarily deep sound, like the lowing of an ox, and it is long before the traveller realises the fact that this is made by the ' quow,' or ' calf-bird' (*Gymnocephalus calvus*), a bird no bigger than a pigeon. Each of many kinds of parrots shrieks a different, but always discordant cry; and the cries of different species of hawks are almost equally discordant and yet more striking. In another chapter I have already spoken of the strange, weird notes in which various kind of goatsuckers moan at night. How striking and peculiar the cries of all these and of countless other birds is, is seen in the fact that the Indian uses each cry as the name of the bird that makes it, and thus has a perfectly good and distinct name for each of the innumerable birds of Guiana.

After a time the traveller begins to recognise what are the commonest forms among the birds. Among birds of prey he sees vultures, only of three species, but often in immense numbers; hawks in very great variety and number, and occasionally, though more seldom, owls. It is perhaps worth noting that the only English bird with which the traveller meets in Guiana is the barn-owl of our church towers. The perchers in Guiana, as elsewhere, form the common feathered flock. The climbers are well represented by many woodpeckers, by toucans, and by parrots, macaws, and parroquets. Among the game birds the most important are the powis or curassow bird (*Crax alector*), about the size of a turkey, black everywhere but on its bright yellow beak and legs; several species of partridge-like maams (*Tina-mus*), and the duraquara (*Odontophorus guianensis*), and a quail (*Ortyx cristatus*). There are various pigeons. Among the waders there are many species of heron, ibis, snipe, and rail. And lastly the swimmers are chiefly repre-sented by ducks, razor-bills, terns, the ducklar or diver (*Plotus anhinga*), and by a gull or two.

Probably the best way to give an idea of the distribution and habits of these birds will be by grouping them according to their haunts. We will take these in the order in which they occur from the sea inland. Sea-birds are not numerous, probably because of the flatness of the coast and absence of rocks. Only once have I noticed a scene in which sea-birds played an important part. This was just off the mouth of the Pomeroon river. The land there very recently ex-tended much further seaward, but it has been much washed away, and there is now a wide stretch of shallow water, from which in many places the dead trunks and branches of forest trees yet rise. It is a strangely desolate scene of sea passing imperceptibly into forest. When I saw it, some pelicans rested on the tree-trunks, or flew languidly from one to the other; flocks of gulls fished in the more open water; some ibis and egrets stood up to their knees on the mud-banks, which reached nearly to the surface; a few sandpipers hovered uneasily about, unable to find convenient resting place either on the water or in the forest; and a long line of a score of rosy spoonbills came flying along the edge of the forest.

In other places, between the forest and the sea, there is a more or less wide reach of rank grass and mud and sand. Such a place is nearly always gay with innumerable scarlet ibis and white-plumed egrets.

Directly inland from these mud-flats are the inhabited places. Here the most common bird of all is the keskedie (*Lanius sulphuratus*), a yellowish shrike, which there takes the place of the sparrow in England. It is exces-sively bold, and may often be seen high up in the air

chasing the vultures, while at other times it occupies itself
in darting after its insect prey, regardless of the presence of
man. Another bird which is here to be soon noticed is the
redbreasted *Leistes americana*—the ' robin ' of the colonists.
Handsome yellow and black starling-like plantain birds
(*Icterus xanthornus*) are also abundant. And on the way-
side bushes, or sitting on the backs of cattle, there are sure
to be some ' old witches' (*Crotaphagus ani* and *major*),
like small black magpies, but with curiously enlarged, keeled
beaks ; these birds are remarkable as socialists, for they not
only live in small flocks, but have one large nest common
to many individuals. These are all roadside birds. High
up in the sky a few black vultures or ' carrion crows'
(*Cartharista aura* and *urubitinga*) are visible, and if the
observer goes from roads and houses to some refuse heap or
foul mud-patch, he is sure to see some of these same birds
solemnly fishing in the filth for their food. In the gardens
there are now few birds to be seen—a humming-bird, generally of a somewhat dull green species (*Trochilus bicolor*),
perhaps hovers over a flowering shrub or creeper, and a
few blue sakis flit about in the trees. On the water-weeds
in the trenches, where these are not quite close to houses,
walk some spurwings (*Parra jacana*), like rails, but with
enormously long toes, which seem to support them on the
floating leaves, and armed with sharp, horny spurs on their
wings. Of course other birds, more properly belonging to
less peopled places, occasionally visit the towns, villages, and
plantations, but those which we have named are the most
prominent and constant in the latter places.

Leaving the coast and going up any one of the rivers,
birds at once become more numerous. Here the most universally distributed and abundant birds are kingfishers of
five species, varying in size from that of a jackdaw (*Alcedo
torquata*) to that of a sparrow (*A. superciliosa*). As the
traveller advances in his canoe, one of these birds starts at
every few yards from some tree, and, with a cry like a
hideous laugh, flies further along the bank. It is worth notice

that not one of these kingfishers is nearly as brilliant in colour as their English cousin. Probably the next bird to attract attention is a ducklar (*Plotus anhinga*). This is the creole name; but the bird is more usually known in England as a darter, or snake-bird—the former because of its extraordinarily direct method of diving after fish, the latter because of the great length of its snake-like neck as compared with the length of its body. Generally less abundant than kingfishers, at least one ducklar is yet almost sure to be flushed in each reach of the river; and in some places—as I noticed, for instance, on one occasion on the Takootoo river— hundreds of these birds may be seen at a time sitting on the trees. Before long the sharp cry of the ' mocking-bird ' (*Cassicus persicus*) calls attention to some tree, from the branches of which dozens of the long purse-like nests of these birds hang swaying in the wind ; for these birds build in colonies, and, it is said, always on trees on which there are nests of certain venomous wasps, these insects being useful in that they deter monkeys from attacking the nests of the birds. On some rivers far in the interior, especially on the Takootoo, a much handsomer relation of this ' mocking-bird,' the moramoroota or troupial (*Icterus jamacaii*) is more abundant. This bird is somewhat smaller than the *Cassicus*, and its chief colouring is a bright ruddy orange relieved by a few black feathers ; its nests are solitary, not in colonies, but are also purse-shaped. Indians attach a high value to the moramoroota (which, by the way, is the Carib name) and tame them frequently. Herons of various kinds are also seen; especially one (*Ardea cocoi*) very like the English heron, and a smaller bird like a bittern (*Tigrosoma brasiliense*), called from its brown spotted colouring the ' tiger-bird.' Occasionally a flock of warracabas or trumpet-birds (*Psophia crepitans*) comes flying by, and the birds, alighting, at once begin to run about as if very busy, uttering the oddly deep and sonorous note which has gained for these birds their popular name. When seen at close quarters nothing could well be more beautiful than these latter birds, sober as they are in colour; their softly shaded grey plumes, long, and hanging more gracefully than those of an old male heron, contrast most exquisitely with the metallic-looking, deep purple-black feathers of the throat and neck. And of much the same habit as the trumpet-birds, but more rare, is the sun-bird (*Eurypyga helias*), with small but graceful body, supported by splendidly large wings and tail, the feathers of which are minutely banded with brown and black and white and purple, so that, sober as the colours are in themselves, the whole effect is resplendent. In the morning and evening parrots and macaws fly high overhead, in parties of two or three. Lastly, on the top of some high tree, a hawk, one of many species, is often to be seen watching for prey. As a rule the traveller on any of the main rivers of Guiana will see these and but few other birds along the banks.

But the very extensive sand-banks which lie in midstream in some of the broader river-reaches have a peculiar avi-fauna of their own. Some of these banks are so low that they are entirely covered when the rivers are in flood; but on others there are higher parts, generally with a few scattered sand-loving shrubs, which are never covered, and which thus give a haven to all the birds of the banks during the rains. Chief among these birds of the sand-bank are the scissor-bills (*Rhynchops nigra*), gull-like black and white birds with very curiously twisted beaks, which through the day fly over the sand, screaming loudly. Among these fly also several species of sea-swallows, or terns (*Sterna*). And at the water's edge numbers of small sandpipers (*Tringa sp. var.*) race excitedly along the wet sand. One or two species of nightjar (*Caprimulgus*) especially affect these banks. All these birds become unusually active at the beginning of the dry season, for then much of the banks is exposed, and the birds lay their eggs on the bare dry sand. In some of these places it is hardly possible to walk many yards without coming across the nest, or rather the eggs, of one or other of these birds.

But if the traveller turns from the main river into any
of the small, little-visited creeks, he will see other birds ;
indeed, it is often in such places that the prettiest scenes of
bird life are to be found. I remember, especially, once,
turning from the Cabalebo, a tributary of the Corentyn, into
a small side stream, known from the hard sandstone rock
which abounds there and which is carried away by the
Indians to be used for sharpening knives, cutlasses, and
axes, as ' Grindstone creek.' Just above the mouth of the
creek the water tumbled over some rugged rocks into a pool
of black water. Round this the ground rose and was
covered partly by ordinary forest trees, partly by groves of
an especially beautiful but very prickly palm (*Astrocaryum
plicatum*, Drude.) Three white egrets of a species peculiar,
as regards Guiana, to the Corentyn, and a kingfisher or two
which were fishing in the pool, lightened the picture.

And it is in such places that humming-birds are chiefly
seen. On the open river or on the savannah they are sometimes to be seen buzzing round a flowering tree, and in the
depths of the forest they occasionally fly past the wanderer
with startling rapidity. But it is in the openings formed by
the creeks that they are chiefly at home, for there numbers
of them hang their nests to the swaying ends of creepers, or
fasten them to leaves, or in between some forking twigs. Most
abundant of all the species in such places is the gorgeous
king humming-bird (*Topaza pella*), with ruby and green
flamelets instead of feathers, and with enormously long
forked tail. The boldness of these birds is very remarkable ;
I have seen one hover angrily round and round the muzzle
of a gun aimed at it. The nest of this species is, I think,
always suspended to the stem of a creeper overhanging the
water. The material, like a thick felt formed of a yellow,
tinder-like substance, long puzzled me, till I recognised it as
the fluff which clothes the young flower-spathes of an abundant species of palm (*Maximiliana regia*). The eggs, two
in number, are white, but pink-tinted by the contents.
The young birds very soon grow ridiculously large for the nest,

on which they rather rest than lie inside.   After a time the deserted nest often affords hold to the spores of moss, which, growing rapidly in the close damp air, soon transform the whole into a ball of green attached to the creeper.

In the forest itself bird life seems even much rarer than elsewhere.   The cries of bell-birds, parrots, toucans, trogons, chatterers, pigeons, and hundreds more, tell the wanderer that the birds are there; but these live in the forest roof, unseen except by the man who, having found some tree with ripe fruit, will wait patiently till the birds come to this to feed.   Occasionally a curiously loud yet small whirr startles the traveller, first by its apparent closeness to his ears, then by its remoteness, and by the way in which it seems to be on all sides at once and yet consecutively, till he looks helplessly round but fails to see a bird—for it is a humming-bird, which at such times seems a very sprite in the rapidity of its movements and in the power which it thus has of making its presence invisible to the eye.   Before long the tapping of some woodpecker is sure to attract the eye to a more evident bird.   And then the cry of some game-bird, powis, maam, or maroodi, sounds, and perhaps—though this does not often happen—the bird itself afterwards comes into sight.   That these latter birds are really abundant is evident from the number which an Indian, if a good hunter, will kill in such places in an hour or two.   In short, birds, though abundant enough in the thick forest, are but seldom seen there.

But occasionally there is a clear space, either natural and due to the fall of the trees, or made and then deserted by Indians.   It is in such places that vultures, not only of the two species common on the coast, but also of a third and really most beautiful kind, love to congregate.   The two former kinds (*Catharista aura* and *C. urubitinga*) are in general colouring black, the bald head being in one case of an unwholesome red colour, and in the other black ; both these birds are of very ignoble appearance.   But the king vulture (*Sarcoramphus papa*) is a larger and more powerfully built bird; its body feathers are of beautifully blended shades of white, grey, and black; round its neck is a splendid ruff of softest grey feathers, and the naked head, instead of being repulsive as in the other species, is beautiful and gay with blended yellow and red colours. The ugly birds are much more numerous than the beautiful. With the former I once had a curious interview. Very early one morning I had taken my gun and wandered into the forest, and having about dawn reached a clearing evidently made by fire, which seemed likely to be visited by birds, I sat down on a fallen tree near the centre to wait. For some fifty yards on every side of me there was a dreary waste of fallen and half-burned trees, some blackened, others whitened by exposure to the weather; the soil was covered with ash, and only a rank herb grew here and there. At the outskirts of the clearing some trees, burned and dead, yet stood erect; a little further off the trees were only scorched, and beyond that again was the dense, living forest. Not a sound was yet heard. As the sun rose the little weird field of white in which I sat literally glowed with light and heat. Presently, almost at my feet, something moved, and then a black vulture rose slowly from the ground, leaving two eggs exposed, and flew to one of the dead standing trees. While I watched this bird there was a slight sound behind me, and, turning, I saw another vulture standing on another burned tree on the other side of me. Once more, and again and again, this happened. Surprised at the presence of these living things where all had seemed to me strangely lifeless, I began to count the birds; and I had to count quicker and quicker, for every moment a new vulture woke and attracted my attention by stretching its wings to dry them in the morning sun, in which position it remained awhile motionless. The only sound was the slight rustle caused by this wing-stretching. At last I found myself the centre of a circle of thirty-seven vultures, each with outstretched wings, standing motionless on a gaunt, fire-blackened, sun-whitened tree, and all gazing curiously at me. At last, to break the spell, I fired into the

air, and the birds rose and began their day's task of soaring
high up in the air. I found that this was a favourite roost-
ing-place. Every evening the birds collected near the place,
and for some time, instead of flying high and steadily as
they do through the day, rushed frantically about overhead,
frequently turning, and at each turn making an extraordinary noise by clapping their wings, like the sound of a
heavy sheet flapping in the wind. A negro who stood by
me as I watched this performance once remarked that they
came down like a whirlwind. Just before dark they settled
down in the clearing which I have described.

Not only at early morning, to dry the dew, but also after
a shower, vultures stand with outstretched wings, sometimes
motionless, sometimes alternately closing each wing. The
negroes say that when these ' crows ' collect on a tree during
rain, it is to consult about building a house for shelter ; but
when the rain leaves off, then they stretch out one wing and
then the other, and they cry in chorus, as one wing goes out,
' We want no house,' and as the other goes in turn, ' We
want no hall,'—and so on until all their feathers are dry.

Through the day the vultures are generally distributed
singly or in pairs high up in the air ; but wherever dead
meat is there many vultures collect. First come the small
black kinds, but before long the king vultures swoop down,
and driving off the first comers, who retire to wait on the
surrounding trees, gorge themselves and then sit languidly,
too heavy to fly, while the others take their turn.

One other bird of the forest region demands notice. This is
the brilliant-coloured ' cock-of-the-rock ' (*Rupicola crocea*),
which has already been mentioned. It never occurs in the
lowland forests, but is abundant in all places where trees and
rocks are mingled. Thus its home is both in the mountainous parts of the forest region, as on the Potaro and
Mazeruni rivers—and in the wooded mountains, such as the
Pacaraimas and Canakoos, of the savannah region. It is very
remarkable, not only for its brilliant colour and for its extraordinary crest, but also for its habit of dancing. It was

never my fortune to find the dancing-place of these birds; but the brothers Schomburgk were more fortunate, and one of the latter—Richard—thus describes the scene : ' A number of these splendid birds were taking part in their dance on a smooth slab of rock, ... some twenty birds, male and female, being perched on the bushes round the place, and uttering very peculiar cries, a cock-bird danced in proud self-consciousness on the ground—its tail, which it jerked up and down, and its wings extended ; the dancer scratched the ground and sprang vertically up into the air till, wearied with its steps, it took its place, with a peculiar cry, among the bystanders on the bushes ; then a new performer appeared.'[1]   By the way, Schomburgk is mistaken in supposing that the cock-of-the-rock always avoids the neighbourhood of other birds ; for on the Potaro and Mazeruni it lives among many others.   High up on the savannah mountains, where Schomburgk saw it, it is alone probably only because the elevation and other conditions are unsuitable for other birds.   The same writer is also mistaken in his belief that these birds are not successfully reared and tamed by Indians; I have seen them of all ages in Indian houses, and was once fortunate enough to see nearly two score of fully developed male birds in the hands of one party of travelling Indians.

On the savannah, except in the coppices and in the narrow band of forest which generally edges the rivers, bird life is somewhat different.   On the open grass lands a number of small insectivorous birds flit, much after the manner of larks, from tuft to tuft.   Tiny ground-pigeons are numerous ; and occasionally a covey of quail (*Ortyx cristatus*, Gray) is flushed.   A beautiful lapwing (*Vanellus guianensis*), not unlike the English bird, but mainly gray instead of green, and with curious horny spurs on its elbows, is not rare.   Among the low solitary trees the ' savannah starling ' (*Sturnella ludovicina*) is the commonest bird ; and round these trees, when in flower, one or two species of hum-

---

[1] Richard Schomburgk. *Reisen in Britisch Guiana,* vol. i. p. 442.

ming-birds may often be seen. Hawks and owls are unusually numerous, both in number of species and of individuals. When a fire passes over any part of the savannah, the creeping flame is always preceded by many birds of prey in pursuit of the lizards, snakes, and other small animals which are then forced to fly from their shelters. On the reedy ponds which occur in places on the savannah, ducks, especially the large musk-duck (*Anas moschatus*) and the whistling viccissi-duck (*A. autumnalis*) are often numerous; and on the high trees near these ponds, and on the banks of the rivers, the great stork-like 'negrocop,' so called because of its bald black head (*Mycteria americana*), builds its nest.

Probably the reader will find some difficulty in realising the certain fact that even the reptiles are, under ordinary circumstances, not dangerous, and are rarely ever annoying to man. For instance, it is a matter of common and sted-fast belief that snakes must be troublesome in the tropics; but as a matter of fact, though snakes are without doubt numerous in Guiana, they are very seldom seen, and even when seen are exceedingly seldom harmful to human beings, except perhaps to Indians, whose nakedness and habits of life expose them to such harm. Probably there is hardly one of the ordinary town-dwelling colonists of Guiana who could not count the number of snakes he has seen on the fingers of one hand. Those who live on the plantations and in country districts of course see more; but even these would in most cases probably be able to count the number seen in one year on two hands. And as regards the interior, I need only say that I once carefully noted the number of snakes seen during two months of travel in forests and on savannahs; and it was but eleven. It is not that snakes are few—though they are probably not so abundant in the western, as in the drier eastern tropics—but that they are shy and retire silently before the approach of man. And of reptiles other than snakes none need be regarded with much fear.

The reptiles which I shall have to mention are alligators, lizards, snakes, and turtles.

In the coast region alligators are very numerous wherever there is mud and water. They are often to be seen in the trenches of estates; and in one case, not long ago, one was found even in the streets of Georgetown. Because the larger they grow the more noticeable they are, only those of small size generally escape detection and survive in the inhabited districts; but in remote mud swamps they grow much larger. The largest that came under my notice measured twenty feet from snout to tail. They are rarely harmful to man, though one occasionally hears stories of how an arm or a leg has been snapped off by one of these reptiles.

In the interior alligators as well as caymans are numerous on some of the rivers. Elsewhere I have described the nest of one of the latter kind, as well as their curious habit of floating on the surface of the water and occasionally raising their tails to bring them down smartly on to the water. It has been said that the object of this latter trick is to attract fish, but this probably wants further confirmation. Generally when lying, basking, on the surface of the water the cayman is a sluggish animal, and it is not dangerous to bathe, in shallow water, close by them, if the bather only keeps his eye upon them and is prepared to run as soon as the cayman seems about to move. It is a well-known fact as regards lizards that, not only when the tail is by some accident torn off does a new tail bud and grow, but also that even if this appendage is only injured without being lost, a new secondary tail occasionally grows from the injured spot and, with the original tail, forms a fork. Knowing this, I was yet surprised one day by the sight of an alligator of considerable size with a double tail. This animal was on a sandbank in the Corentyn river, but it made its escape into the water when we attempted to approach it.

Of all lizards far the most prominent in Guiana is the iguana (*Iguana tuberculata*). This is a large tree-dwelling, herbivorous lizard, often four or four and a-half feet in

length, of a beautiful brilliant green when young, but afterwards of a dull ugly grey-green, made hideous, especially
in the case of the male, by a curiously jagged raised ridge
along its back, and by an enormous dewlap. They live about
the banks of rivers. The flesh of these lizards being like, but
more delicate than chicken, is much appreciated, not only by
Indians, but also by Europeans, and the animals are therefore
much sought after. In the more peopled districts iguanas are
now scarce, but along the rivers of the interior, and especially
on the Corentyn, long stretches of which are entirely uninhabited even by Indians, they are abundant.

But it was on the Cabalebo, which is entirely uninhabited, that I saw most of these animals. One or more
was lying on the upper branches of many of the creeper-
tangled bushes and low trees overhanging the water.
Often the first notice of the presence of these was
the loud splash which they made when, as we came up,
they threw themselves headlong from the top of the trees
into the water. Sometimes, however, we got near enough to
shoot them, when, if not killed outright, they sank into
the water and were never seen again. Others were basking
among the dead leaves on the river-bank; and these, as we
came up, raised their tails and scampered off with a clatter
loud enough for an animal of four or five times the size.
We began to find their eggs, too, buried in holes in the
sand-bank; and the men often dug out hundreds of eggs in
the course of a few hours. There are generally from thirty
to forty eggs, all laid by one lizard, in each nest;[1] but from
the larger number in some of the holes, I imagine that
occasionally more than one lays in the same place. The
holes are often very deep, so that the Indians have to dig
four or five feet, or even more, before reaching the eggs.

The iguanas wait to lay till the dry season, when the sand-

[1] Schomburgk (*Reisen in Britisch Guiana,* vol. i. p. 303) states the
number of eggs as seldom more than fourteen; but I have always found
the larger number which I have stated, and have on several occasions taken
about forty eggs from out of the female lizard when just about to lay.

banks are uncovered.   Then they either go to the banks at
the side of the river or swim—they are capital swimmers—
to those in mid-stream.   They dig a tunnel, only just wide
enough for their bodies, down into the sand.   After laying
their eggs, which are oval, about the size of a pigeon's egg,
and are enclosed in a white elastic skin instead of shell,
they must wriggle backward out of the holes—no easy task.
The eggs are left to hatch untended.   When the germ
begins to develop the egg becomes irregular in shape.   How
long a time passes before the young emerge from the egg
I have never been able to find out.   That their instinct
should lead them to find their way up through the great
mass of overlying sand is wonderful.

The Indians find the nests by following the tracks made
by the parent on the sand, and by noting the very slight disturbance of the sand which exists at the mouth of the hole.
They then push a pointed stick into the sand in various
directions, and where the sand is soft and yielding they
know that the tunnel of the iguana must have been.   With
their hands they dig down, but cautiously, for they say a
particular kind of poisonous snake which shares their liking
for the eggs is occasionally met with in the holes, and
that Indians have often been bitten in this way and
have died in consequence.   Moreover, the iguana itself
is often found in the hole, having just deposited its eggs,
and not yet having had time to come up, and it is apt to
bite sharply.   When the lizard is thus caught 'in the act'
the chase is exciting: as the Indian digs down, the iguana
digs deeper and deeper to get away from him.   In this race
the man of course finally wins.   The lizard is caught by the
tail, but still holds fast and refuses to be drawn out.   The
Indian pulls, and often the tail snaps.   This gives the lizard
a fresh start, of which it takes advantage by digging on
vigorously ; but it is finally caught and drawn out.

The Indians assert that jaguars are in the habit of
digging out the eggs for themselves.   Certainly jaguar
tracks very commonly occur intermingled on the sand with

those of the iguana.   But it is more probable that the jaguars, knowing that these lizards are frequenting the sand-banks, prowl about during the breeding to catch the old lizards than that they dig for the eggs.

Other enemies that the iguana has to fear, especially at breeding time, are the perai, or houma as they are called on the Berbice and Corentyn, (*Seralsalmo niger*). These most sharp-toothed and voracious fish so frequently bite off the end of the tail of the iguana as it swims from sand-bank to sand-bank, that I could hardly find one with a perfect tail among the large number which we got.

Other lizards of smaller kinds are very abundant, and are universally distributed throughout all the regions.

Of the real abundance, but retiring habits of snakes, I have already spoken. The most dreaded of the common kinds are the two species of *boa,* called respectively the land-camoodi (*B. constricta*), and the water-camoodi or cul-nacanaro (*Eunectes murina*), the labarria (*Trigonocephalus atrox*), and the rattlesnake (*Crotalus horridus*). The last-mentioned kind is seen, if at all, on the dry savannahs; the others occur equally commonly in suitable localities in all regions.

The land-camoodi is seldom seen and does but little harm to man. The only one I ever saw in a state of nature glided away at my approach. The water-camoodi is more often noticed. The largest I have ever seen alive was the one killed, as I have mentioned in an earlier chapter, by my friend Edwards-Moss; it was twenty feet long and three feet in circumference at the thickest. But they occasionally grow much larger—one, the skin of which I measured and found to be thirty feet, was found in a curious place. A friend of mine, living in a somewhat remote place surrounded by forest, was somewhat particular about having his morning coffee brought to him just at dawn. His cook, when she went in the dark into the shed which served as a kitchen, was in the habit of striking the match to light the fire on a particular corner post; but one morning she was surprised to find that one match after another broke instead of catching fire. At last she struck a light in a new place, and having done so, she found to her great horror that a thirty feet long camoodi was coiled round the corner post, and on this she had been rubbing her matches. Young camoodies of small size are not unfrequently found in houses near the forest, and when in that stage they are much more beautifully coloured than when adult. They frequent the neighbourhood of water and often swim, for which reason they are much dreaded by Indian bathers. The Chinese, I believe alone of the various inhabitants of the colony, eat and relish the flesh of these snakes. It was probably a water-camoodi that first taught me that snakes snore. Once, as I was wandering according to my habit from my hammock in the middle of the night to smoke a pipe in the surrounding forest, my companion, who had just retired to his own hammock, called to me to beware of a particular tree, for he had heard a snake snore there. Curiosity, of course, drove me to the tree, where the sound of snoring was plainly audible, and where, after some time, I succeeded in detecting a moderate-sized snake curled round a branch. Alone and in the dark I did not care to attack it, and in the morning, when I wanted to find the animal once more, it had disappeared.

The labarria is a much more terrible snake. It is small, being from three to five feet in length, but most venomous, and is of a dull colour, so like a dead stick that it is often not noticed until it strikes. Once when passing along a forest path, the hindmost of a single file of nine men, I drew back my foot just as I was about to put it down on a labarria coiled in the middle of the path, its head raised to strike. Eight men, seven of them barefooted Indians, had passed safely and without notice over this animal. It is a curious fact that, this snake having been beaten to death with large sticks and removed to some distance from the spot where we discovered it, on repassing the place some hours after, we found another labarria in the same place. This and other cases which came under my notice tend to confirm the statement of the Indians that where one snake is there is sure to be another. Even the labarria, however, probably never attacks human beings unless it is trodden on or otherwise disturbed. The bite of this snake may often result in the death of the sufferer, and, perhaps as often, in the loss of the particular limb or part of the body on which the wound is inflicted. A curious instance of the latter result came under my notice in the case of an Arawak Indian who had but one foot, the other, with the leg as far as the knee, having gradually withered and dropped off in consequence of the bite of a labarria ; yet, with the aid of a stick, the man still ran, worked, and even hunted, as actively as any of the other Indians.

The rattle-snake is too well known to need description. It is very rarely seen by Europeans. Only once did I nearly come into unpleasant contact with it, and that was when one had taken up its quarters in a basket in which our store of bread was kept; but it made its escape without doing any harm.

Of other venomous species of snakes there are doubtless plenty, but these are seldom seen. Negroes, and sometimes even Indians, will say that any snake they see is poisonous, but the accusation is in many cases quite unfounded.

On the other hand, there are some very beautiful snakes, such as the long whipsnake of brightest green, called in the colony the parrot-snake, and the very lovely coral snake with its bands of brilliant pink.

From what has been said in earlier chapters it will be evident that turtles are abundant in most of the rivers, but there are few in the sea or anywhere on the coast region. The two commonest species are the cashapan of the Indian (*Emys amazonica*, Martius)—which sometimes attains a length of four and a half feet, and a smaller species, probably identical with the *Emys tracaja* of Martius. Both these species are so numerous that I have sometimes seen large canoes heavily loaded with their eggs, in about equal pro-

portions.   Another species is the very curious mata-mata
of the Indians (*Chelys mata-mata*), which has an extraordinarily rugged, instead of a smooth shell, as in most species,
and is endowed with a peculiarly disgusting smell.   The
flesh of all these species is largely eaten by the Indians, who
have learned the fact that the smell of the mata-mata may
be entirely removed by careful washing.   There are other
species which have not yet been identified.

It is a curious fact that jaguars are very fond of the flesh
of turtles, and still more curious that they manage to extract the animal from its shell.   I am not aware that any
European has actually seen the jaguar performing this operation; but many, I among others, have seen the freshly
emptied shells scratched all over by the claws of jaguars, and
lying on the sand among recent jaguar tracks.

In the forest a species of tortoise (*Testudo tabulata*)
wanders about.   That it is frequent is shown by the fact
that an Indian hardly ever returns from hunting without
bringing home one or two, for its flesh is most excellent
food.   It lays two large round eggs—which, unlike those of
the other tortoises, have hard, porcelain-like shells—on
the forest floor.   The animal when irritated has a surprising habit of grunting—a power which some individual tortoises possess, at least use, more vigorously than
others.

Of the frogs and toads in Guiana it is impossible to
speak in detail.   They are enormously abundant, and their
varied and strange croaks combine in a chorus, which hardly
ever ceases, gains redoubled force at night, and forms the
characteristic sound both on the coast, in the forest, and on
the savannah.   So deeply does it impress the traveller that,
when it has once been heard, he never, walking by an English
ditch in spring, hears the feeble croak of one of our own frogs
without seeing gigantic tropical scenes rise instantaneously
before him.   The amphibian which most annoys the colonist
is a toad (*Bufo agua*), which swarms everywhere in muddy
places, and at night crawls from the trenches in Georgetown

out on to the streets in such numbers that it is often impossible to avoid treading on them.

Fish swarm in enormous numbers and immense variety both in the sea and in the rivers. Certain mud-loving kinds which abound in canals and trenches are caught in large numbers by the negroes and others in a similar position, and indeed form the chief animal food of these people ; but fishing for the better sorts of fish, either in the sea or in the rivers, is so little practised, that there is hardly any regular supply in the markets.

In the interior the number and the beauty of the species is very great, and many of these have been well described by Schomburgk in his 'Fishes of British Guiana.' But without special search the traveller will probably meet only with a few prominent forms—those which are especially caught for food —such as the pacu (*Pacu myletes*), which haunts the unquiet waters of the rapids, and feeds on the water-plants growing on the rocks in such localities; the haimara (*Erythrinus macrodon*, Agas.), which is found principally in the mouths of creeks ; the gigantic lowlow (*Silurus*, sp.?); and, in the more remote rivers, the arapaima (*Sudis gigas*), both of which attain a length of from eight to ten feet. But there are three fishes which every traveller is sure to notice, not because they are good for food—though by the way all these kinds are occasionally eaten—but as dangerous enemies. These are the perai (*Serasalmo niger*), the electric eel (*Gymnotus electricus*), and the sting-ray (*Trigon hystrix*).

The perai swarms in nearly all rivers, though not within twenty miles from the sea, and is probably as voracious an animal as exists. Where ducks are kept by the few people living on the banks of perai-haunted waters, the poor birds almost invariably soon have more or less of the webs of their feet bitten off by these fish. It has already been said that the tails of iguanas are almost invariably docked in the same way, and it may be added that even alligators do not always escape with whole tails. A perai itself, if wounded by any chance, is at once attacked and devoured by its fellows. If a monkey or bird, when shot, falls in the water, perai rush together from all quarters and carry off the prey before the sportsman can reach it ; and more than once, when fishing in clear water, the bait having been taken by some other fish, I have seen the captive as it was pulled through the water towards the boat, pursued and snatched by rushing perai.   Again, the Indians having a habit of setting night lines for haimara and other big fish, it not unfrequently happens that when these are drawn up in the morning, only the head and shoulders of a fish are found on the line, the rest of the body having been carried off by perai.   On more than one occasion I have known instances in which, men being drowned in the rivers, their skeletons have been found not many days after, almost stripped of flesh by perai. It is, therefore, a source of danger to bathe in smooth reaches, in which places perai are principally found.   One of my boatmen, a mulatto, once, when wading by the side of the canoe, suddenly began to scream out certain strong expressions, and being reproved, successfully justified himself by showing his foot, from one of the toes of which a perai had suddenly stripped all the flesh ; and on another occasion, when I sprang from the canoe to bathe, a sharp pain almost at the instant I reached the water told me that I had been bitten by one of these fish.   Yet these terrible fish are small enough, being rarely more than two pounds in weight, but their teeth are so sharp that a jaw is carried by Indians and used to sever the poisoned point from the darts to be blown from their blow-pipes.

The electric eel is another fish to be avoided.   Its power of inflicting an electric shock is well known, and this shock is really very severe.   My first experience of this was in this way : Some Indians, having built a dam across the mouth of a small creek, were, after their manner, poisoning the water to get fish, and I was standing on the dam to prevent any of the larger fish from struggling over and thus escaping, when I saw a black form in violent agitation in the water close by my feet; having in my eagerness seized this, I found to my great pain that it was an electric eel. These fish are specially abundant in certain places; and one of these being in the Mazeruni river by the Penal Settlement, the convicts there, though, because it is the only time in the day during which they are allowed to talk, they generally look forward to the bathing hours, yet occasionally receiving an unexpected shock, are frightened and try to avoid the bath for some time after. The eels, if they are long kept in confinement lose their electric powers; one very large one which had been in possession of a gentleman on the west coast of Demerara for some fifteen years, was, I found, entirely harmless.

The third fish to be dreaded is the sting-ray. This large flat fish, with a long whip-like tail, armed with a much-barbed spine, three inches long, which it can erect at pleasure, lies on the sand in shallow waters, where because of its colour it generally escapes notice till, when trodden on or otherwise disturbed, it strikes its spine into the adversary, and thus inflicts a terrible wound, which, for some not very obvious reason, occasionally causes even death. The spine seems to possess some poisonous and unwholesome quality. An Indian in my service being struck in his foot by one of these fish, the wound remained open and in a most horrible condition for some months, and having daily to dress this wound, I gradually acquired so unreasonable a dread of the power of this ray, that when shortly afterwards I was wading in water too shallow to float the canoe, which lay about a quarter of a mile from me in one direction as the land did in the other, and the Indians shouted a warning that sting-rays abounded in the place, an utter inability to move in either direction kept me motionless for some time. The spine is used by the Indians in place of a lancet; and long after it has been removed for this purpose from the animal, it seems, when drawn across human flesh, to exhibit a curious irritating power not to be accounted for even by its minute barbs.

It will afford a good idea of the proportion which imaginary danger from animals in Guiana bears to the real evils inflicted by these if we try to realise the possible thoughts of a nervous man when bathing in one of the rivers of that country. The nervous bather remembers that from the moment when he throws off his clothes, every part of his body not covered by water is exposed to the attack of mosquitoes, sandflies, and many other sharply stinging insects; but, on the other hand, that every part of his body covered by water may at any moment be bitten by perai, may receive a violent shock from an electric eel, or may be horribly lacerated by the poisoned spine of a sting-ray, or a limb may be snapped off by a passing cayman or alligator, or his whole body may be crushed, and thus prepared for swallowing by a huge water serpent; or, even if none of these pains come upon him, he may remember that the egg of a certain worm, of which I shall presently have to speak, may be deposited unnoticed on his flesh, there to develop and become exceedingly painful. Now all these dangers are real enough, and any one of them may make itself felt at any moment. But on the other hand, of all the men who trust themselves in these waters day after day, and many times a day, for years together, not ten per cent. have ever felt even any of the smaller evils which have been described, except perhaps the bites of mosquitoes or sandflies; and not one in a thousand has suffered any serious or permanent harm. While therefore the nervous man feels all the pain of anticipation of evils, neither he nor the less timid man as a rule feel the actual evil.

From this digression we will turn to the consideration of insect life. Here many readers will probably make a final and determined stand against my plea for the acquittal of animals of all kinds from the charge usually brought against them of unceasing annoyance or harmfulness to man. Yet this plea may justly be extended to cover even insects. I should be more irritating than the mosquito itself were I to assert that that insect, and sandflies, and other such creatures, never annoy, that cockroaches are not repulsive, or that spiders are not ugly; but I do say that these and other insects are not sufficiently numerous or vicious to make life burdensome.

It may be as well to begin by taking the case of an ordinary householder, and see what the insect foes of such an one are. The test is somewhat formidable, for it must take count, though some of these are but rarely seen in well-kept houses, of mosquitoes, wood-ants (*termites*), real ants, cockroaches, certain beetles called 'hardbacks,' spiders, centipedes, and certain wasps called 'jack-spaniards.' These are arranged according to the degree of annoyance which they cause, the worst offenders being placed first.

Mosquitoes are by no means equally distributed in all places. In many parts of the interior they are rarely seen, but on the coast, especially in some places, they are more numerous. They are most abundant of all on the muddy banks of the Pomeroon river near the sea. There the few white settlers find it necessary to protect their hammocks with close-fitting curtains, not, as elsewhere, of muslin, but of stout calico; and the Indian, before venturing on the mud flats to catch crabs, covers his body with a complete armour of mud. Mosquitoes are also very abundant along the road from the Demerara to the Berbice river, and in a few other special places, chiefly where there is little drainage. Elsewhere they are few at most seasons of the year, and throughout the greater part of the day they appear not in swarms, but singly. It is chiefly during the rainy season, and especially at night, that they cause any trouble. Opinions probably vary as to the amount of annoyance caused by these insects, for they attack some people much more vehemently than others. Of two adjacent bedrooms—the conditions of which were exactly similar, except that one was occupied by a man subject to, the other by one free from, such attacks—I have, morning after morning, seen the one black with swarms of mosquitoes that had collected during the night, the other with hardly one of these insects. But even those who are happy enough to be seldom stung by mosquitoes suffer no little annoyance from the buzzing of these insects, which is of all sounds probably the most irritating. On the whole it must be admitted that in an ordinary house, more or less, but frequently considerable, annoyance is caused by mosquitoes.

A more harmful, because unsuspected, enemy of the householder, is the wood-ant. The houses are entirely built of wood, and too often the beams and boards, apparently sound, are mere shells, within which these insects, though hardly ever visible, swarm. Other substances besides wood are occasionally devoured by these insects, and in a large linendraper's store I was once assured that the only things safe from their ravages are woollen goods. Various species of real ants occasionally take possession of a house for a time ; and that others are nearly always present, though seldom seen, is sufficiently shown by the fact that if a piece of sugar-cane or other attractive food is put on the floor it is very soon surrounded by numbers of ants ; but all these do but little harm to human beings, and do much good, in that they devour large numbers of other insects, especially cockroaches. Even in well-kept houses probably few days pass in which two or three of the last-named insects, equally detestable in appearance and odour, are not seen ; and in houses which are not well kept they swarm. If therefore these insects are annoying, the remedy, by greater cleanliness, is easily applied. Another kind of insect visits houses only occasionally, and then under circumstances which are rather amusing than annoying. These are the so-called 'hardbacks'—small dark-coloured beetles of several species, but most often *Tomarus bituberculatus*, which, perhaps two or three times a year—always during rainy seasons—enter houses in perfectly astounding numbers. Attracted by the lights on a dining-table they literally cover the cloth, and being swept away again and again, they are as often replaced by others coming as thickly as ever. On such a night I have known it become quite impossible to play billiards, the table being strewn with hardbacks much as sea-beaches often are with pebbles. These beetles develop from the grub within certain plants, generally within the roots of such juicy plants as sugar-canes, plaintains and bananas, but sometimes, most curiously, in the unopened flower-buds of the *Victoria regia* and other water-lilies. When they enter houses they are often still encrusted with dry mud, collected while escaping from their vegetable homes. Their muscular power is enormous. It is a trick commonly enough done for the benefit of strangers to put an ordinary wineglass on the back of one hardback, when the insect crawls over the table at a fair pace, dragging the glass with it. After all, the annoyance caused by hardbacks is very slight ; their visits occur only at long intervals, and the morning after such a visit every one of the insects has disappeared.

Spiders, large and small, are of course occasionally seen in houses, but they do no harm, and the objection to them is founded merely on the universal and firmly established belief in their disgusting appearance. There are, of course, spiders in Guiana the bite of which is more or less painful, but such kinds rarely, if ever, enter houses. Centipedes, too, are rarely seen even in country houses and still more rarely in town houses ; of course, provided, in both cases, that the houses are ordinarily clean. Large wasps of a very harmless kind fly in and out of the rooms, and frequently build their clay nests, like pretty little clay vases, on the walls even of living rooms.

In short, mosquitoes and wood-ants are the only serious plagues in houses, and even these, except at times and in places, only now and then annoy.

Just outside the houses, in the short grass about inhabited places, a small red insect, called *bête rouge*, like the English harvest-bug, swarms, and, burying itself in the feet and ankles of passers-by, produces an irritation which is to some people almost unbearable, to others of slight consequence.

But it is in the interior that insects chiefly abound. It

will probably be best to discuss these as nearly as may be in the order in which each class is likely to attract attention. Accordingly, the first place must be given to the butterflies.

The splendid beauty and great variety of tropical butter-flies has been so often told that it is only necessary here to add that Guiana is surpassed by no country in such riches. The generally received and erroneous views of the appear-ance of tropical nature are perhaps more nearly true as regards butterflies than aught else. It is true that, just as most of the bright-coloured birds live in the forest roof and out of sight, so do many of the butterflies; but of the latter, though not of the former, there are many species that keep close to the ground, and therefore more frequently come under the eye of the traveller.

The most striking of all the butterflies are the huge *Morphos*, the large wings of which are entirely blue, and so gorgeous, brilliant, and shining, that the insect as it comes flaunting lazily down through the dark alleys between the tree-trunks, seems even from a considerable distance like a flash of blue light. They generally fly high, at the tops of the trees; but for a short time every morning, apparently when the sun is at a particular point in the horizon, they come down into the openings made in the forest by a fall of trees, and there flaunt—I use the word purposely—lazily in and out between the sunshine and the shade. They are so large that, as they passed high over such openings, I have traced their movements, as I sat below, by the shadows they cast on the ground. These forest openings, during that part of each day when the sunlight is in them, are haunted not only by these blue, but also by other kinds of high-flying butterflies. Other kinds—especially the curiously shaped and scented *Heliconias*, with black wings, spotted, accord-ing to the species, with blue, scarlet, or white—fly round the bushes and half-way up the tree-trunks, careless of whether they are in sun or in shade. Others again, with wings marked with red and brown, after the manner of English fritillaries, but differing in shape from these latter,

fly also at a height about half-way up the tree-trunks, but
always, as a rule, in shade. And actually on the ground,
especially when this is carpeted with the sickly-scented
fallen flowers of the kakaralli tree (*Lecythis ollaria*), other
butterflies shaped like fritillaries, and with wings veined
like fritillaries, but quite transparent and devoid of colour,
flit among other clear-winged butterflies. The thought is
irresistible that these, in the scented deep shade and the
solitude, with their colourless transparent wings, are but
pale ghosts of butterflies. Passing once more into the sunlight, tiny hawkmoths flash straight backward and forward
from bush to bush so rapidly that only colour, without form,
is seen. On the wet sand at the edges of rivers and streams
armies of yellow butterflies, very like the English sulphur
yellow, rest, as thickly as dead leaves in the forest, and
enjoy the moisture. And sometimes a constant and most
abundant stream of butterflies, of various kinds, passes for
hours together, always in one direction, across a river, coming
whence and going whither or with what purpose no man
knows.

At night the butterflies give place to moths; and even in
the daytime a considerable number of the latter may be
seen in the forest shade. Yet, as will be easily understood,
moths attract comparatively little attention. For the purpose of the present sketch it is more important to make
mention of the caterpillars. Some of the latter are of the
strangest forms, and I greatly regretted that time and the
opportunity only to be afforded by settled residence in one
place both so failed me that I was unable to rear some of
these caterpillars to determine their species. One form,
evidently occurring in many species, is a marvellously perfect
instance of mimicry. These caterpillars are covered with
processes which differ from ordinary hairs in that they are
much branched, and not only exactly resemble in form the
leafy stems of certain mosses, but also exactly resemble these
mosses in colour. Some are light green, of exactly the shade
assumed by moss when growing in damp places, others are of

the yellow and brown shades of moss long exposed to the sun. As the caterpillar rests on a tree-trunk or rock it so closely resembles a small rounded patch of moss, that I was at first often completely deceived. And these insects not only thus hide themselves from their enemies by pretending to be plants, but they also enjoy further protection in their power of stinging like a nettle with the hairs which have been described. Another caterpillar of about two inches in length is entirely covered with shaggy silky hair, more than an inch long, and of the bright yellow colour of the natural silk from the cocoon of the silkworm. This animal has a perfectly black head, and was not inaptly compared by the friend who brought it to me to a yellow Scotch terrier. It passed into the chrysalis stage after a time, but for some unknown reason the perfect insect never emerged.

Beetles will probably be principally remarkable to the traveller for their apparent absence. They are really plentiful, as becomes apparent when the bushes are swept with a net, but they generally live concealed. Near palm-trees the large black palm weevil (*Rhyncophorus*, var. sp.) may often be observed. This is the perfect insect of which the disgusting gru-gru worm, largely eaten by white men and red, is the grub, and it is also one of the most harmful of the so-called 'cane-borers;' for it has passed from the palms, which seem its proper home, into the sugar-canes, among which it works terrible havoc. Another smaller weevil (*Sphenophorus sacchari*) is equally abundant and destructive where canes are cultivated. Another beetle often seen is a *Buprestis* with purple and green shot wings, which are much valued by the Indians as body ornaments. And occasionally a monstrous elephant beetle (*Dynaster hercules*) may be caught, and if so, it will probably begin to hiss like a cat spitting. A curious long-shaped beetle (*Elator*), with wings that look as if powdered with fine flour, is common enough ; and this, more like a child's toy than a real insect, if caught and placed on its back, suddenly bends a hinge in its body, with a loud clicking noise, with such force that the insect is hurled to some distance through the air, and then flies away.

The number, variety, and ubiquity of the ants is perhaps more striking than anything else in the forest. No foot of ground, no tree-trunk or creeper, hardly a stem or leaf, is without some of these insects. Some even pass the greater part of their lives in hollow, jointed plant-stems. They are of all sizes, of many colours, and of various degrees of viciousness. Some wander about singly or in pairs, others in bands so vast that only those who have seen will realise their multitude.

Of the solitary kinds, the one that, by its evil repute and conduct, most strongly presses itself on the notice of the traveller, is the large black manoorie ant (*Ponera clavata*), the sting of which is most painful and often produces fever. It sometimes goes up the stems of trees, but generally wanders about among the dead leaves on the floor of the forest. In such places, because of the fever-giving repute of this ant, I was at first always nervous about sitting down ; but after a time I found that they as a rule wander round, and even over, one without stinging, unless they are pressed or otherwise irritated. It was nearly two years before I felt the pain of their sting. Then, a tall palm-tree which I had cut in order to measure, having fallen, not to the ground, but with its crown resting on a neighbouring forest tree, and I having therefore climbed half-way up its sloping stem, measuring-tape in hand, a sudden pain made itself felt in the back of my neck, so intense that it can only be compared to that which would be caused by the sudden application of a red-hot iron ; and this pain lasted some time, though it was not, as is often the case, followed by fever.

Of the social ants, on the other hand, the most surprising is a species of *Eciton*, called by the creoles Yackman, the name being a corruption of the Dutch word *jagdmann*, or hunter. This insect is indeed a mighty hunter. Its hunting parties consist of countless individuals. Of one party that passed me one morning I had had warning some little time before it came in sight, in the rustle and stir which the ants and their prey made in the dead leaves. The line of march was twenty yards broad, and within that space the whole ground was a moving mass of black ants which continued to pass for nearly half an hour. Before them fled cockroaches, beetles, lizards, and so on ; but they fled in vain, for each was caught after an exciting chase and was almost immediately covered with ants and devoured. Some ants, as regularly as if told off for the purpose, climbed up each tree that was passed, and then, having driven down or devoured all hunted beasts that had fled up the tree for safety, instead of troubling themselves to climb down again, simply hurled themselves from the branches to the ground, and then once more joined the line of march. But the victims were not unavenged ; for, following in the train of the ants, a host of small ant-eating birds fluttered through the bushes, and there eat many of the hunters. On another occasion, springing out of my hammock before dawn, I was unfortunate enough to put down my bare feet into one of these herds of ants. These bands of ants sometimes pass through houses, and do good service by clearing out all other insects. Where they all come from and where they go to is a mystery, for I was never able to find their nests.

Another common, indeed much more common, species of social ant is the cooshie (*Ecodema cephalotis*). In many parts of the forest there are places where the yellow, sandy earth is piled up in an irregular heap, often many yards in diameter, and bare of all vegetation. These are the nests of the cooshie ant. From these, parties of cooshies start each night, and sometimes by day, to forage, especially for leaves. The foraging party starts from home along a well-defined narrow path, which before long is worn by the ants as bare as any fieldpath is trodden in England. Cultivated plants, especially cassava and orange-trees, are specially affected by these ants, whose destination as often as not is the field of some Indian, or, near the coast, some settler. When once cooshies have found out any cultivated ground, it seems impossible to keep them off until they have stripped the whole place. In one night a party of them will strip every leaf from many trees, cutting each into pieces about a quarter of an inch across, each of which is carried home to the nest by a single ant. It is a most comical and strange sight to see the long line marching home, each ant completely hidden by the huge portion of leaf which it carries. I once saw this scene under somewhat peculiar circumstances. Being engaged in digging in a shell-mound, and, while thus engaged, having caught a considerable number of a certain kind of red butterfly and put them into a zinc insect-box, I was surprised when I looked up to see a long row of small red objects moving slowly past me and down the mound; and it was only after some seconds that I realised that the cooshies had got into my insect-box, had cut my butterflies into small pieces and were marching off with them. These ants seemed to delight in robbing me ; for, on another occasion, they made their way into a tin canister which I had filled overnight with a number of orchids which were to be put between the drying papers in the morning, and they so completely emptied this that there was hardly a shred of green left.

Another kind of ant always makes its nest round the root of a certain showy mauve orchid (*Imatophyllum roseum*), which grows abundantly on some trees on the banks of most of the rivers. Or it is possible that the orchid only grows in such nests. At any rate, nests and orchids are so inseparable that the Indians when they saw us collecting the plants and, somewhat vainly, trying to free them from ants by long immersion in water, warned us that the plant could not grow without the insect.

But it is quite impossible to tell of all the different kinds of ants. Two methods of stopping an advancing column of ants—the only two known to me—must, however, be mentioned. One of these is to sprinkle corrosive sublimate in front of them ; the result of this being that the ants, on reaching the sublimate, attack each other so furiously that the column is soon transformed into a ball of struggling creatures, apparently fighting each against the others. The other method is simply to spit on the path over which the ants are about to move; and in this case they always turn aside and go by a new and roundabout path.

The so-called white or wood-ants (*Termites*) are in general appearance, and still more in habits, so like real ants that the common belief in their identity is very intelligible. In the interior of Guiana they are at least as ubiquitous as true ants. In the forest they build covered ways under which they walk in all directions over the ground and up the trunks and stems of all plants. The rapidity with which they build these tunnels is surprising; often the loose baggage and properties which the traveller, when camping in the forest, puts on the ground at night are in the morning found to have a wood-ants' tunnel over them. On the savannah another white ant, of course of a distinct species, builds huge clay nests, shaped like haycocks, often ten or twelve feet high, which form one of the most characteristic features in the landscape; and there, at certain seasons of the year, when the winged individuals leave the nests, the whole air is darkened with their numbers.

In the forest, among the ants' nests, which hang in apparently shapeless masses on nearly every tree, there are often other irregularly shaped nests of various species of bees, as well as the more shapely nests—like those of the corresponding insects in England—of many kinds of wasps. The bees are for the most part much smaller than our domesticated species. Some build their nests in hollow trees, but others hang from the tree-trunks black, leathery nests, which look very like much battered and brimless felt-hats, and in which the cells are very large and contain honey, very slightly viscid, but much more of the consistency of water than of English honey, with a most highly aromatic and acidulated taste. The wasps vary much more in general appearance and size, some of them being large and beautifully coloured insects. The forest-dwelling social species are indiscriminately called by the colonists marabuntas. Many of these have a habit of building their nests on the branches of low shrubs, or even on the under sides of large leaves; so that a man forcing his way through the bush is very apt to disturb one of these nests, and thus effectually to impress the presence of marabuntas on his recollection. Wherever there is loose sand there are sure to be sand-wasps. These beautifully banded creatures live in pairs, and buzz all day long over the sand in which they make their nests. I have often amused myself by proving the wonderful instinct for locality possessed by these insects, by trampling down, digging into, heaping up, and otherwise disturbing the sand in the neighbourhood of their nests; but, notwithstanding, the insects never failed to find their nests. If one failed to find the place when it first flew toward it, it retired to a little distance and flew once more; if it still failed it made a third attempt, and I never knew this third attempt fail.

The group of insects to which we now turn are the most troublesome of all to the traveller, for it includes mosquitoes, sandflies, jiggers, and ticks.

The various species of mosquito, for there are several, are distributed very unevenly in the interior, but are very rarely as troublesome there as they are on the coast. It is only in a few widely scattered places in the interior that mosquitoes are constantly troublesome, but in some other places they make their appearance in large numbers during the wet seasons. Thus, in travelling during the dry months up a river for ten days, perhaps only one of the camping places at night is haunted by mosquitoes; but, on the other hand, camps that are entirely free from these pests during the dry season are occasionally visited by them during the rains. It is somewhat curious that even in mosquito haunts the insects do not make their appearance every night, but only, as it sometimes appeared, perhaps every alternate night. Some of the worst mosquito-haunts are in districts entirely uninhabited even by Indians, and very seldom visited; and I often wondered how in such places mosquitoes provide themselves with sufficient blood for their meals. Animals of various kinds there are doubtless in such places, but not, as it appeared to me, in numbers large enough to solve this question. It seems, rather, as if the sucking of blood is not a normal habit of mosquitoes, but that they indulge themselves in this way when they have opportunity, not as being necessary to their existence, but rather as a treat.

Sandflies (*Simulium*, sp.?) of the kind to which the name is usually applied are confined to the coast, where they occur in very troublesome abundance in most waste, sandy ground. But on some of the rivers of the interior their place is supplied by another species which I have already described under the name of kaboora[1] in a previous chapter, as covering the whole bodies of the Indians and the exposed parts of travellers with innumerable small but very irritating sores. Away from rivers these insects are, however, unknown.

The so-called mosquito-worm, or, as it is elsewhere called, æstus-worm, is the larval form of a gadfly. It is found, though not very commonly in Guiana, in the flesh of men and of other animals. The first warning of its presence is a sensation as though caused by the pricking of a needle, which is felt not constantly, but at short intervals. As this increases in intensity, the part of the flesh affected rises as though in a tumour. The animal is a worm-like larva, about an inch long, clothed with curious stiff hairs or bristles. It must develop from an egg deposited, unnoticed—and, it is said, when the subject is bathing—in the flesh, and it grows rapidly. The pricking sensation is probably caused by the hairs as the animal turns in its position. It is often said that the extraction of the animal is a difficult matter; but this really may be easily enough done by completely excluding the air for some hours from the affected spot, by carefully coating it with sticking-plaister or, if that is not at hand, with any of the many natural resins of the forest, the result being that when the plaister is removed, the

[1] See p. 27.

insect, either dead or at least no longer firmly fixed in its position, is drawn away at the same time.

A far more troublesome animal, because very common, is the far-famed jigger or chigoe (*Pulex penetrans*). This flea lives in dust on the ground wherever human beings congregate. In the untidily kept huts of the negroes and others on the coast it is abundant; but it is in the interior, in the settlements of the Indians, which are very frequently built on loose sand, that it swarms. The females of these horrible little insects penetrate the skin and take up their position between that and the flesh of men and domestic animals. Their favourite position is under the soft skin between the nails and the fingers or toes, but any attainable part of the body is sometimes used; twice they have buried themselves in the flesh under the ring on my finger, and there is little doubt that the Indian habit of sitting on stools in their houses is due to a desire to raise their bodies out of the reach of these insects. When once under the skin, these insects, becoming full of eggs, increase to about the size, and assume somewhat the shape, of peas. If left undisturbed, the whole animal after a time drops off on to the ground, where the young presently hatch and add greatly to the number of individuals. The round patch of skin under which they are, is white surrounded by a dark rim. The sensation which they cause in the subject is of a somewhat curious kind, and has been described with odd variety by travellers either as a painful itching or as a rather pleasant tickling; to me it seems exactly like the pain caused by a severe chilblain. Where these animals abound boots are no real protection; though I was always careful to keep my feet covered by day and night in these haunts, I have been entered by as many as twenty-three insects in one day. Troublesome as they thus are to the stranger they are yet more troublesome to the natives. The children suffer especially by them, their feet, and, when they roll in the sand, their whole bodies, being appropriated by the insects. It is not really difficult to extract jiggers, for it is only necessary to raise the skin under which they lie

and pull them out with a needle, and any chance of inflam-
mation, owing to part of the animal remaining in the sore,
may be avoided by filling the cavity either with laudanum
or with tobacco ashes. If, as is sometimes though rarely,
the case with Indians, and is often the case with negroes
and others on the coast, jiggers are left undisturbed in the
foot the whole of the latter becomes seriously affected and
eventually drops away.

We now come to the last of the really troublesome
animals. In the forest the bushes are often inhabited by
bush-ticks (*Ixodes*), with flat, hard-looking bodies like tiny
disc-shaped seeds. These insects seize with their vice-like jaws
on men and animals as they brush by, and, being carried off,
bury their heads in the flesh of their victims, and there feed
till their bodies swell into sack-like bodies of four or five
times their former size. Probably these animals are very
locally distributed, for they seldom trouble the traveller, but
occasionally do so in enormous numbers. They may always
be made to drop off either from clothes or flesh by exposure,
as close as possible, to a fire.

The three insects which next claim notice are spiders,
scorpions, and centipedes, all of which may be found in
abundance by search, but very rarely attack human beings.

Spiders are certainly very abundant, of many forms,
some most quaint, of all sizes, from such as are as small as
our own ' money-spiders' to the great, black, hairy bird-eating
spider (*Mygale avicularia*), which is as big as a baby's fist,
and of many colours, some being in this respect most beautiful. The bite of some species, especially of the bird-eating
spider, is said to be dangerous and even sometimes fatal;
but though these spiders are common enough, I never knew
them bite on any occasion. Another very large spider,
(*Phrynus reniformis*) occurs on the ground in the mora
forests about the upper part of the Mazeruni river; it is said
that not only the bite of this is very poisonous, but also that
the insect unprovoked frequently attacks men. This insect,
being somewhat like a scorpion in appearance, is called by

the Indians by a name signifying 'mother-in-law of scor-pions.' Scorpions of two, and perhaps of three, species live under stones and fallen wood. It is chiefly the wood-cutters in their work of moving timber that come into con-tact with these animals. But one small and white species has an unpleasant habit of living about the beams of Indian houses, where, if it is accidentally touched, it stings: the wound is, however, as I have experienced, not serious and not even very painful. Centipedes, often attaining a length of four or five inches, are about as numerous as scorpions, and live in the same places. Both alike are, as a rule, only acci-dentally seen, but both can be easily found by search.

Four other insects, of most harmless kinds, are sure to attract the notice of the traveller. In describing the hunt-ing ants I have already mentioned the bush cockroaches. These, which live under every fallen leaf, are much smaller than the domestic kind, and seem to be without any offen-sive odour. Many large grasshoppers live both in the open country and in the forest. These are often of most brilliant colours, chiefly red or green, and some kinds attain a length of four inches. The green mantis, or praying-insect, may often be seen hunting other insects, but is harmless to man. And, lastly, certain curious insects, locally called razor-grinders (*Cicada*, sp. var.), from the extraordinary sounds that they make, or six-o'clocks, from the fact that these sounds are redoubled about that hour, are sure to be soon noticed. Occasionally in the forest, just before dusk, the whole place rings with the whirr of these insects, as though fifty pairs of scissors were being sharpened at once on half a hundred grindstones; and from the scattered trees on the savannah another kind sounds a loud prolonged whistle, so like that of a railway engine, that, hearing it, it is sometimes difficult for a moment to remember that one is on the deso-late South American savannah.

CHAPTER VI.

THE INDIAN TRIBES.

Indian Groups in Guiana—The Value of the Groups—Race, Branch, Tribe, and Family—Classification of Principal Tribes—Some unimportant or little-known Tribes—The term ' True Carib'—Tribal Differences in Language, Physical Characters, and Habits—Geographical Distribution of the Tribes—Forest Indians and Savannah Indians—Probable History of the Tribes—The Earlier Tribes : Warraus, Arawaks, and Wapianas—The later Immigration of Carib Tribes.

THE aboriginal population of the whole continent of America is made up of an extraordinarily large and disproportionate number of more or less well-defined small groups of so-called Red Indians, which are chiefly distinguishable in that each uses either a peculiar vocabulary, or, in the case of the minor groups, a peculiar dialect of a vocabulary common to several of the larger groups. It has been estimated that within the (in round numbers) 15,000,000 square miles of the whole continent, there are nearly 500 of these distinct vocabularies, and 2,000 dialects. Yet there is one great and important feature common to all these diverse languages, so immensely numerous in proportion to the extent of land occupied by them, and absent, with one possible and insignificant exception, from the language of the rest of the world : and this is, that though the vocabularies of the languages differ, their structure is the same and is peculiar. The structure of all, and only of these languages, is polysynthetic. This community of speech is a strong, though not absolutely certain, indication of community of race. When, however, the bodily structure, and to some extent the customs, of these groups of Americans are examined, it appears that in these points also, with considerable differences there are yet features which are on the one hand common to all these groups, and are on the other hand unrepresented elsewhere in the world. Therefore, tested by language and also by structural characters, the aboriginal American population proves to be one great race distinct from the people of the whole of the rest of the world.

The 70,000 square miles of American land which now bear the name of British Guiana contain a number of more or less distinct groups of Red Indians, which are probably as numerous as in any other district of equal size of the same continent. The number of individuals forming these groups can hardly be determined, for they live widely, more or less thickly scattered, in a country uninhabited, and only partially explored, by Europeans. An attempt was indeed made about the year 1840, and again in 1881, to estimate their number by counting those living along the banks of four rivers[1] supposed to be those most thickly inhabited by Indians, and from these results estimating the number elsewhere. The numbers returned from the four rivers were, on the first occasion, with somewhat suspicious detail, 4,265; and from this the Indian population of the whole district has been variously estimated as from 12,000 to 20,000; were I to add another to the guesses which have been made about the matter, I should suggest that 20,000 is probably slightly, but not much, below the real number.

These Indians are known by a very large number of different names. Even from the following alphabetical list, formidable as it appears, there are probably some omissions :—

Ackawoi.	Caribisi.
Amaripas.	Caribs.
Arawaks.	Carinya.
Arecuna.	Cobungrus.
Arecuma.	Daurais.
Atorais.	Engaricos.

[1] The four rivers were the Pomeroon, Moruca, Waini, and Barrama.

Kapohn.	Pshavaco.
Lokono.	Taruma.
Macusi.	Taurais.
Maiongkongs.	Waccawai.
Maopityans.	Wapiana.
Nikari-karus.	Warrau.
Paramona.	Woruma.
Partamona.	Woyowai.
Pianoghotto.	Zurumutas.
Piriana.	

Many of these names are, however, synonymous; others do not represent distinct groups; and yet others are names of tribes settled beyond the limits of British Guiana, individual members of which occasionally wander across the border. It will save trouble if we dispose of these unnecessary names at once. The Ackawoi, by a mere variation in pronunciation, are also known as Waccawais; and, using neither of these names, these people call themselves Kapohn, which in their language means simply 'the people.' We shall find that several tribes have both a name for themselves—that is, each calls itself in its own language 'the people'—and a name used by other Indians. The Arawaks, for instance, call themselves Lokono. Arecuna, it would hardly be necessary to say, but that the two forms are sometimes given in ethnological books as distinct, is the same as Arecuma. Atorais, Daurais, and Taurais are, I think, identical, though Schomburgk considered that the two latter words are synonyms of a tribe allied to but not the same as the Atorais. It is at least certain that people bearing these three names live intermingled in the same settlements. The Caribisi are the same as the so-called Caribs; and Carinya, or 'the people,' is their own name for themselves. We shall presently find it convenient to reject all these three names and to substitute the term True Carib. The last case of synonyms is that of Paramona and Partamona. Names which do not represent distinct groups are Cobrungru, *i.e.* hybrids between any Indian and negro; Nikari-karu, *i.e.* hybrids between Macusis and Indians of some Brazilian tribe, or perhaps between Macusis and Brazilians of Portuguese extraction; Engaricos, *i.e.* hybrids between Macusis and Arecunas. I believe that the Pshavacos and Worumas are also names for hybrids between some two of the better-known tribes. The Maiongkongs and the Piriana are tribes living beyond the British border, which they only occasionally cross. Thus we have already greatly simplified the list of tribes with which we are concerned. It now stands thus :—

Ackawoi.	Paramona.
Amaripas.	Pianoghotto.
Arawak.	Taruma.
Arecuna.	Wapiana.
Atorais.	Warrau.
True Caribs.	Woyowai.
Macusi.	Zurumutas.
Maopityans.	

Each of these groups has a name for itself, and a name by which it is known by Indians of other groups. Sometimes the esoteric name and the exoteric are the same, sometimes they are different. But, however this may be, the existence of such a name indicates a certain amount of distinctness in the group.

It is absolutely necessary, before proceeding to define certain terms, to express the value of the different groups with which we shall have to deal. The indiscriminate use of such terms as family, nation, branch, race, group, gens, phratry, can only lead to confusion. In the absence of any common standard usually accepted, I am obliged to explain the exact sense in which I shall use certain divisional terms. The four words which I shall require are race, branch, tribe, and family. By race I mean to express the whole group of red-skinned Americans, whose language varies greatly in vocabulary, but is absolutely uniform in structure. By a branch I mean such a portion of this race as is distinguished by the use of a vocabulary common and peculiar to that portion; for example, all members of the Carib branch use, with more or less dialectic variations, the Carib vocabulary. It must be noted that this mark of distinction of a branch is not absolutely exact, for there are occasionally a few single words common to the vocabularies of two or more different branches; for example, the word 'peaiman,' which means ' medicine-man,' appears to be common to the Carib, the Arawak, and other vocabularies. But the general distinctness of the vocabularies is sufficient to distinguish the branches using them respectively. By a tribe I mean to express such a portion of a branch as uses the vocabulary common to that branch, but with dialectic variations peculiar to itself; for instance, the Macusis and the True Caribs are different tribes of the Carib branch. This mark of distinction of the tribe is, again, not absolutely exact, for two tribes using two dialects of a vocabulary common to their branch occasionally use distinct, and not merely dialectically differing, words; for example, though both are of the Carib branch, the True Caribs call fire ' wotah,' while the Macusis call it ' apo.' A possible explanation of this is, that one or other of these divergent pairs of words has been borrowed from the language of some other branch with which the tribe using it has in past history come in contact.[1] But the difference, if any, between the mass of words used by two tribes of the same branch being merely dialectic, the distinctness of the tribes and the community of the branch may be assumed.

With the last divisional term, family, we shall not be concerned in this chapter; but for the sake of freeing ourselves once for all from such definitions, it may be as well to explain it briefly here. There are signs of a separation within the tribe into families, such as the families, or perhaps rather the clans, of our own society; and these families within Indian tribes are kept distinct by means of certain regulations, which will afterwards be described, concerning marriage, and by the fact that each has an inalienable name of its own. The somewhat obscure family-

[1] Such divergent words are, therefore, of great importance, since, if they can be traced to other vocabularies, they certainly indicate intercourse between the two tribes, of different branches, using them.

system of South American Indians is, in fact, identical with the better-known totem-system of North American Indians. It is hardly necessary to add that each family is of course marked by no very great difference in language; yet, because of the great scope for divergence in pronunciation which is allowed by the fact that the language is unwritten, and that each of the families by which it is spoken lives to a certain extent secluded from the others, small differences of pronunciation, not sufficiently fixed to be regarded as dialectic, are often acquired by the separate families. There is some importance about the last-mentioned fact, in that possibly the family, when it becomes numerous and changes its locality, becomes a tribe, which, in the course of long periods, may, by splitting, possibly develop into a branch; and if this is so, the small peculiarities of pronunciation belonging to the family develop, as it becomes a tribe, into the dialect of that tribe, and afterward, as this tribe becomes a branch, into the distinct vocabulary of that branch.

It being very important to make these divisional terms clear, they may be tabulated thus:—

Order	Differentia	Example
1. Race	Language, whatever the vocabulary, of uniform (polysynthetic) structure	American.
2. Branch	Language in structure that of the race, but with a distinct and peculiar vocabulary	Carib.
3. Tribe	Structure and vocabulary of language like that of the branch, but with peculiar dialectic variations	True Carib.
4. Family	Each with a distinct family name, the distinctness of the family marked by certain regulations as regards intermarriage	Onisidu (an Arawak Family).

As has already been indicated, I am fully aware of the danger of trusting solely to differences of language as a means of classification. But it is far the most ready means; and if a classification thus made is confirmed by such differences as

can be found in the bodily structure and appearance of the
Indians, in their customs and habits of thought, it may, I
think, be safely adopted. It must, indeed, be adopted, and
all effort must be made to elaborate it more and more—unless, as is not likely to happen, some new and more satisfactory method is discovered. We shall find that, though
there are no very great differences other than those of language among the Indians of Guiana (which fact shows that
they are all not very divergent members of the same race),
yet that there are physical differences— as, for instance, in
height, in build and strength, in features and in colour of
skin ; that there are also differences in custom—as, for instance, in the objects and methods of manufacture, and in
care for cleanliness and modesty; and, lastly, that all these
differences correspond with those in language. To this it
may be added that corresponding differences in the degree
of mutual hostility between the various groups lends further
evidence; for though every group ignores all others as far
as it can, and when perforce it must meet others, regards
these as hostile, yet this feeling of aversion is greater between two tribes of different branches—for example, between
True Caribs and Arawaks—than between two of the same
branch—for example, Macusis and Arecunas.

Using the tests of difference and of degree of difference
with which we have thus provided ourselves, we find that,
omitting for the present certain groups which are either
fragmentary or little known, there are in Guiana four
branches of the American race—the Warraus, Arawaks, Wapianas, and Caribs ; further, that two of these, the Warraus
and the Arawaks, cannot be distinguished into tribes ; that
the third, the Wapianas, is probably represented by three
tribes—the True Wapianas, Atorais, and Amaripas; and, lastly,
that the fourth branch, the Carib, is represented by four
tribes—the True Caribs, Ackawoi, Macusi and Arecuna. One
or two of these tribes have attached to them various small
groups, which may perhaps be regarded as sub-tribes. The
following table will make the matter more clear —:

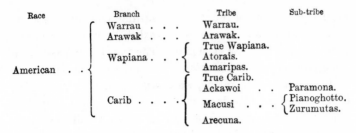

Race	Branch	Tribe	Sub-tribe
American	Warrau	Warrau.	
	Arawak	Arawak.	
	Wapiana	True Wapiana. Atorais. Amaripas.	
	Carib	True Carib. Ackawoi	Paramona.
		Macusi	Pianoghotto. Zurumutas.
		Arecuna.	

If this table is compared with the list of groups given on
p. 159 it will be found that the only omissions from the
classification here suggested are the Maopityans, Tarumas,
and Woyowais. Without vocabularies, and indeed without
almost any knowledge of these three tribes, I am unable
to class them. The Tarumas appear to be a tribe—perhaps
not belonging to any of the branches which I have distinguished in British Guiana—which, according to Sir
Robert Schomburgk and the Brazilian traveller Von Martius,
reached their present position from the south, by way of the
Rio Negro; and the fact that the Maopityans live with the
Tarumas, the two conversing with a common vocabulary,
seems to indicate that the two are tribes of the same
branch, whatever that may be. Of the Woyowais only the
name is known.

Some explanation is necessary of the terms True Carib
and True Wapiana, which I am the first to use. The
Indians of the True Carib tribe are in Guiana known simply
as Caribs or as Caribisi, and they call themselves Carinya.
But none of these three terms are satisfactory. Not only this
tribe, but several others in Guiana—namely, the Ackawoi,
Arecuna, and Macusi tribes—belong to the Carib branch; to
use the simple term Carib indifferently of the tribe and of
the branch is therefore apt to confuse. An attempt has
been made to distinguish between branch and tribe by
calling the former Carib, the latter Caribisi. But this latter
term seems to have originated in a mistake. The word Caribisi is Arawak, and means the 'Carib's place,' or 'Carib's
home;' just as Ituribisci, the name of a small river of Guiana,

means 'the home of the ituri or howling monkey;' and as
Aroabisci, the name of a well-known district in Guiana, means
' the home of the aroa or jaguar.' The traveller in passing up
some river often has his attention called to some settlement
by his Arawak companions, who, with bated breath, point to
it and ejaculate 'Caribisi,' which merely means to say that
(True) Caribs live there; or, as I have again and again experienced, if the traveller himself asks who lives at some
settlement which is in sight, the answer of the Arawaks
invariably is ' Caribisi;' by a not unnatural mistake,
travellers have therefore supposed that Caribisi is simply
the name of the tribe. The term may therefore be ex-
punged from ethnological lists. But we have not yet found
a name for the Carib tribe, as distinguished from the Carib
branch, in Guiana. It might seem natural to use ' Carinya,'
their own name for themselves, for this purpose; but this
term has the disadvantage of being unfamiliar to ethnologists. Every purpose is answered by calling the tribe True
Caribs, and extending the term Carib to the whole branch.
Just in the same way, as it appears that there are several
other tribes belonging to the branch of which the Wapianas
are the largest and best known tribe, it is convenient to use
the term True Wapiana of the tribe, Wapiana of the branch.
It may be added that very possibly the Warrau and Arawak
groups are each of them really only of tribal rank,[1] but as,
in each of these two cases, the other tribes which go to
make up the branch are unknown or unrepresented in
Guiana, it is more convenient for our present purpose to
regard each of them as a complete branch represented only
by a single tribe.

We turn now to the marks of difference in language, in
physical characters, and in habits, which distinguish these
groups, as either branches or tribes. In the following
chapters, more or less of these differences will be recorded;

[1] For example, I believe that if materials were available for a comparison of South American groups generally, it would be found that the
Warraus are a tribe of the Guarani branch.

but here may be collected, as a necessary preliminary, just sufficient of these to show the distinctness and values of the groups.

The languages of the four branches, Warrau, Arawak, Wapiana, and Carib, will be found to be quite distinct from each other; or, if a few common words are found, these are so few that they may be explained as due to accidental borrowing by one branch from the other. But within the languages are dialects differing more or less from each other. In the Warrau and Arawak languages respectively, this diversity amounts to no more than very slight differences of pronunciation adopted by separate families of each group. The Wapiana language and the Carib are, again, distinct from each other and from either Warrau or Arawak. But differing dialects of the Wapiana language are spoken by the True Wapianas and the Atorais, and possibly a third by the Amaripas. So, too, of the Carib language there are four different dialects spoken by the True Caribs, Ackawoi, Macusi, and Arecuna respectively; and these dialects have been commonly, but quite wrongly, spoken of as distinct languages. The Macusi dialect is very closely similar to the Arecuna, from which it differs chiefly in the mode of pronunciation; and a similar dialect, with a few exceptional differences, principally in the lower numerals, is used by the Ackawoi. A Macusi, an Arecuna, and an Ackawoi speak quite intelligibly the one to the other. The remaining dialect of this language—that of the True Caribs—is, though the relationship is very recognisable, somewhat more distinct; for while most of the words are identical with those of the three former dialects, yet some are altogether distinct.

A few examples must here suffice to explain the matter :—

EXAMPLES OF THE CHIEF INDIAN LANGUAGES OF GUIANA.

English.	Branch; Warrau — Tribe; Warrau	Branch; Arawak — Tribe; Arawak	Branch; Wapiana — Tribe; True Wapiana	Branch; Wapiana — Tribe; Atorais	Branch; Carib — Tribe; True Carib	Branch; Carib — Tribe; Ackawoi	Branch; Carib — Tribe; Macusi	Branch; Carib — Tribe; Arecuna
Wood	dow	àda	atomònah	?	wey-weh	ye-hi	yè	Unfortunately I have no Arecuna vocabulary at my disposal; but the language differs merely by very slight varieties of pronunciation from the Macusi. Robert Schomburgk says the same of it. (See *Reisen in Britisch Guiana,* vol. ii. p. 523.)
Arrow	a-tà-bu	simàra	bihiri	?	puròwah	purrow	perrow	
Water	ho	oomiaboo	win	honih	toona	toona	toona	
Fire	y-kung	ikihi	teekari	teekehr	wah-toh	apo	apo	
Sun	ya	adaili	kamoo	kamozh	weya	weyana	wey	
Moon	wa-ne-ka	katchi	kai-er	kaihr	noo-nah	kapoo-i	kapoo-i	
Medicine-man	wisida-a	semtchehi	marinow	?	puyai	peartsan	peartsan	
Jaguar	tobi	aràa	baidookori	kitenhur	kaikushi	kaikushi	kaikoosi	
One	ishakka	abaro	bai-dap	baidepah	ohwin	tewin	teween	

NOTE.— In reality an Indian word is rarely exactly synonymous with an English word. The shade of difference is often difficult to understand; and even when it is understood I find it difficult to explain, without the aid of lengthy notes. The above words have been selected only on the ground that they are the simplest I can find, *i.e.*—there is least danger of difference in meaning between the Indian and English equivalents.

It is not very easy to describe the distinguishing physical characteristics of these groups, for, after all, all being of the same race, the differences are but small. A stranger invariably finds it impossible to distinguish, merely from appearance, the members of the different tribes, or even branches; yet after a time the eye becomes accustomed to the task, and recognises instinctively the tribe of any given Indian.

Though all are, according to the ordinary English standard, short, the Warraus are the shortest. They have, too, even less developed muscles than the other tribes. They are thickly built, and the neck especially is short and thick. The trunk is unusually long in proportion to the legs; and the feet, perhaps in consequence of the soft and muddy nature of the ground about the usual homes of these people, are unusually flat and broad. The expression of the face is strikingly dull, unintelligent, and gloomy. The colour of the skin is apparently very dark; but this is in reality due to the filthy state in which they live, and the dirt which encrusts them. The Arawaks are slightly taller than the Warraus; their bodies, though short and broad, are far better proportioned; their skin, not only appears much lighter in colour, because of their more cleanly habits, but in reality is slightly so; and the expression of their faces is far brighter and more intelligent. The Wapianas are, for Indians, unusually tall; their bodies are slight and well-built, and their faces, because of the regularity and better form of the features, are far finer. The tribes of the Carib branch are all in a greater or less degree marked by a darker skin. The True Caribs are somewhat taller than the Arawaks; their bodies are better built and, both in appearance and reality, have far greater strength; their features are coarser, but such as to give the appearance of greater power. The Ackawoi are like the True Caribs, but somewhat shorter and slighter in the body; and perhaps owing to their habits, they are somewhat miserable in appearance. The Macusis are even darker than the True Caribs and

Ackawoi in colour, but are taller, slighter, and better made ; their features are more regular, and their expression is bright and intelligent, but somewhat timid. The Arecunas have the darkest skins of all; their bodies are like those of the Macusis, but more powerful; and similarly their features are like, as is their expression, but that the latter is far more bold and warlike.

Evidently these physical differences would by themselves be insufficient to distinguish the groups. Nor are the differences in habit very great.

The Warraus are timid people, despised by other Indians, and, apparently, with but a poor opinion of themselves. Except in the rare cases in which they have been partly civilised, their personal habits are, as is rarely the case among these Indians, very filthy.   They live, or did till lately live, in miserable houses, raised on piles over swampy ground, or even over water.   They are the great canoe-builders for the surrounding tribes.   It must be added that a considerable number of the tribe have lately been induced to settle round the mission stations. As the Warraus are the filthiest, so the Arawaks are the cleanliest of all the Indians.   This may be partly due to the fact that the latter, living just in the district which was earliest, and has been continuously, occupied by Europeans, and having always held friendly relations with these Europeans, have, more than any other tribe, become to a certain extent civilised; that is to say, though they still use houses of their original pattern, these are cleaner than those of other Indians, are sometimes made partly private by partitions, and are even furnished occasionally with a wooden table and benches. With very few exceptions they can all speak English, and, at least in the presence of white men, they wear European clothes. This degree of civilisation has greatly obscured their proper habits, as is well and significantly illustrated by the fact that they are the only tribe which has not, at the present time, any special manufacture of some kind of object useful for trade with the other Indians, such, for instance, as the canoe-building of the

Warraus. One of their old habits is, however, still very discernible, and this is their aversion from other tribes, and especially their hatred of the True Caribs. The Wapiana, with the allied groups of Atorais and Amaripas, none of which is it any longer possible to distinguish in habit, are, as usual, averse to intercourse in most matters with other tribes, but yet they are the great traders of the district, serving as middlemen, through whose hands the manufactures of each tribe pass to the other. They are themselves, moreover, the great canoe-makers of the interior, as the Warraus are of the coast. Another respect in which they differ from the other tribes of Guiana is, that they alone eat much of the cassava, which forms the chief vegetable food of all the tribes, in the form, not of bread or cakes, but of that rough meal which is common in the Brazils under the name of farine. All the Carib tribes are, though in various degree, more warlike than any of the other tribes, and are consequently especial objects of dread. Most warlike in reputation, and most dreaded of all, are the True Caribs. There appears to be a special feeling of enmity between them and the Arawaks. They are peculiar among the tribes in that they occupy no special district, but are scattered more or less thickly through the country. They are the great makers of pottery, though this is also made, to some small extent, by their kindred the Ackawoi. The last-mentioned tribe are perhaps chiefly peculiar for the fact that they make almost all that they want for themselves, and have but little communication with other Indians. Just as the True Caribs are dreaded as the most warlike tribe, so the Ackawoi are as the most harmful, in a sly, underhand way. Perhaps, because of their seclusion, they are, though by no means so filthy in their habits as the Warraus, yet far less cleanly than any of the other tribes. The Macusis and the Arecunas are in habits, as in language, much alike. A strong hostile feeling, however, separates them, and this is mani-fested by the gentler Macusis chiefly in their dread of their fellow tribe, and by the bolder Arecunas chiefly in contempt for the Macusis. Both are cleanly in their habits, but the

Macusis excel in this respect not only the Arecunas but also all other tribes, with the possible exception of the semi-civilised Arawaks.

The differences which we have now seen in the languages, physique, and habits of the tribes, if taken together, are sufficient, on the one hand, to show the distinctness of the groups, and, on the other, to class them as tribes, or branches, according to the table given on p. 163.

Accepting this classification, the next point to be considered is the geographical position now occupied by these tribes. The distribution of the tribes is as follows. For our present purpose the whole country may be regarded as consisting of three regions, parallel to each other and to the coast. In the earlier part of the book it was convenient to distinguish four of these regions; but now we may regard two of these—the timber and the forest-region—as one whole, which we may call the forest-region. Nearest the sea, therefore, is the coast-region; within that the forest-region; and within that again the savannah-region, passing without break into the great savannahs of Brazil. The northernmost part of the coast-region, toward the sources of the Orinoco, and nearest to the West Indian islands, is inhabited by the Warrau Indians, and the rest of it by the Arawaks. Here and there, however, throughout the whole region, but far more commonly in the north than in the south, are single settlements of True Caribs, who occupy no distinct territory, but live more or less scattered among the other tribes.

The forest-region is almost entirely inhabited by the Ackawoi, though in this district also a few scattered True Caribs may be found.

The savannah-region is peopled by several tribes. Beginning from the north, toward the Orinoco, these are the Arecunas, Macusis, the Wapianas (with whom live the Atorais and the Amaripas), the Tarumas (with whom live the few remnants of the Maopityans), and lastly, occupying a very isolated position, the Pianoghottos. With the exceptions of the Atorais and the Amaripas, who live intermingled in the same settlements with the Wapianas, and the Maopityans, who live with the Tarumas, each tribe occupies a distinct territory. But these territories are in no way distinguished by marked geographical boundaries, and are probably not even exactly defined in the minds of the Indians. Here and there also travellers report the existence of other groups; but these are in reality not tribes, but groups of hybrids between two tribes. For instance, where the Arecuna territory borders on the Macusi is a hybrid people called Engaricos.

Here may be inserted an explanation of two terms which it will be convenient to use frequently in the ensuing chapters: these are 'forest Indians' and 'savannah Indians.' The customs of these people are naturally considerably affected according as they live on the open savannah or in the recesses of the forest; e.g. we shall find that very different houses are built on the two places respectively. It is therefore evident that it will be convenient to speak of the savannah Indians and of the forest Indians, though it must always be borne in mind that these terms do not correspond with any difference of race—for instance, of the Ackawoi and Macusis, both of Carib race, the former tribe includes none but forest Indians, the latter none but savannah Indians.

The last point with which I have now to deal is the way in which these tribes reached the positions which they at present occupy. In the first place, the branches may, I think, be distinguished into two sets. The Carib tribes seem to me to represent migrations into the country already occupied by the other tribes. In the absence of better terms, the one set, including the Warraus, Arawaks, and Wapianas, may be distinguished as *native tribes*; the other set, including all the Carib branch, as *stranger tribes*. That there is some difference between these two groups seems indicated both by the fact that the native tribes, though they belong to three distinct branches, with languages mutually unintelligible, are yet all united by a common feeling of aversion from the stranger tribes greater than that which they feel for each other; and also by the fact, which will be explained in greater detail in a future chapter, that the native tribes all make their hammocks, which, it must be remembered, are, next to food, the chief necessary of life to the Indians, of the fibre of a palm (*Mauritia flexuosa*) which is excessively common in Guiana, while the stranger tribes make their hammocks of cotton ; and moreover, the two, as will also be explained later, spin the threads respectively of palm-fibre and cotton, of which their hammocks are made, differently.

As to the native tribes, it must of course not be taken for granted that they were, in any real sense of the term, aboriginal ; but in our present state of knowledge it is impossible even to guess either the quarter whence, or the time when, they reached Guiana. It has indeed been suggested that the Arawaks reached the mainland from the West India islands ; but the evidence for this is too slight to be worth considering. All that we can suppose is that the Warraus at the time of the Carib immigration, as chiefly now, occupied the swamps south of the mouth of the Orinoco ; that the Arawaks occupied a long line of coast stretching south-east from the Warrau country ; and that the Wapianas, with the Atorais and Amaripas, and, probably, with some other tribes which are now either unrepresented or are represented only by the fragmentary tribes to which I have alluded as existing on the outskirts of Guiana, occupied the whole of the savannahs of the interior, which are now partly occupied by the Macusis and Arecunas. Such I suppose to have been the distribution of the tribes before it was disturbed by the arrival of any of the warlike Carib branch.

Then came the Caribs. There are two theories as to this Carib migration. One is, that all the Carib tribes reached Guiana by land, and that certain of the branch crossed from there to the islands, where they formed the ' Island Caribs ' who inhabited the Antilles at the time of their discovery by Europeans, and of whom a very few still remain in Dominica and St. Vincent. The second theory, which I much prefer, as apparently substantiated by many of the facts which I shall have to tell in the following chapters, is, that all the Carib tribes now in Guiana reached that part of the mainland from the islands. How, before that, they reached the islands is a matter that does not at present concern us. Our immediate concern is with the probability of the fact that the Macusis and Arecunas, the Ackawoi and the True Caribs, first reached the mainland of Guiana from the islands.

These four tribes represent, I think, four distinct immigrations. Perhaps each of these tribes acquired tribal distinction by living in a different island; or more probably their distinctness is merely due to the long intervals which elapsed between their migrations to the mainland and to the seclusion in which each party lived after its migration. A glance at the map will show that Trinidad, the last of the long chain of the West Indian islands, between no two of which intervenes a longer distance than might easily have been traversed by Caribs in their canoes, lies close to the mainland, opposite to the country about the mouth of the Orinoco. That, therefore, is the point of the mainland which the Indians would first reach. But instead of land suitable and pleasant to Indians, there is there only a huge swamp, in which the miserable Warraus drag out a wretched existence. The Macusis therefore, on their arrival, passed up the Orinoco, on the banks of which they were living, as Robert Schomburgk has shown, probably as lately as Sir Walter Raleigh's time.[1] After the Macusis, the Arecunas came from the islands and passed, as the latter had done, up the Orinoco. In their advance they drove the Macusis, first, further up the river, then from the river, and lastly southward on to the savannah ; and they occupied each successive district in which the latter had lived. Traces of this long chase still remain in the dread which the Macusis feel of the Arecunas, as in the contempt which the latter feel for the former. Whether the Ackawoi reached Guiana before or after the Macusis, or even before or after the Arecunas, is a question which will probably never admit of solution, if, as is

[1] *The Discoverie of Guyana.* By Sir Walter Raleigh. Edited by Sir Robert Schomburgk for the Hakluyt Society, p. 78, *note* 1.

most likely, they proceeded, on reaching the mainland, in different directions. The Macusis and Arecunas, as has been said, proceeded up the Orinoco, but the Ackawoi, on the other hand, probably passed downward along the sea-coast, through the country then and now occupied by the Arawaks ; and, not being able to drive these latter out, they wandered into their present home, behind the Arawak country, at some distance from the sea. We shall find strong evidence for the supposition that a similar divergence down the coast, instead of up the Orinoco, was at a later period—almost indeed within historic times—made by the True Caribs. It seems almost certain that these latter represent a later, and probably a much later, migration than do the three others. They reached Guiana about the end of the sixteenth century. That they did not try to settle on the mainland much earlier is sufficiently shown by the fact that they, with a warlike reputation and a real power which would most certainly have enabled them to gain for themselves a distinct territory such as that occupied by the other, less powerful tribes, had they not arrived simultaneously with the earliest European settlers, were, owing to the presence of the more powerful white man, unable to drive out the former inhabitants and to take possession of any distinct tract of country ; so that to this day they, the most powerful of all the tribes, live scattered amongst the other tribes, but far more numerously in the district between the Orinoco and the Pomeroon—the district, that is, in which they first arrived—than elsewhere.

Such appears to me the most probable explanation of the present position of all the tribes, both those which took part in the great and comparatively recent migrations of the Caribs from the islands to the mainland, and those which were settled at an earlier time in the country.

In conclusion, I can only excuse the dryness of the details given in this chapter on the ground that they are intended to provide a knowledge which may make the facts, which will, I trust, be more generally interesting, of the succeeding chapters intelligible.

CHAPTER VII.

FAMILY-SYSTEMS AND MARRIAGE-SYSTEMS.

Arawak System as Type—Description of the System—List of Family Names—Origin of the Names—Method of keeping Families Distinct— Co-existing but Contradictory System of Bride-lifting—Evidence of Existence of this latter System—Two possible Explanations.

As in very many other parts of the world, within some of the tribes of Guiana there are more or less strong indications of further subdivision into families ; and where this occurs there are traces of certain laws regulating the inter-marriage of members of these families. It may safely be assumed that between members of different tribes there was formerly no intermarriage, except such as took place when a woman captured in war was taken to wife by her captor ; and even now tribal intermarriage is, except at missions, a rare event. The marriage is now therefore almost always, as formerly it was always, except in cases of capture, between members of different families. In most tribes it is now very difficult to trace these different families, and it is correspondingly difficult to understand the laws prohibitory and permissive of intermarriage, especially as these are now very laxly observed. The Arawaks alone of all the tribes have till very recently preserved their lines of family descent somewhat strictly ; but even they have now become so lax in the matter that the outlines of their system are already much blurred. Their system, as far as it can be discerned, may, however, serve as a type of those which, probably with some differences, once prevailed in several, if not all, the other tribes.

It has long been known that the Arawaks are divided

into a great number of families. A certain traveller in Guiana, named Hillhouse, having, about the year 1830, published a list of twenty-three names of such families, it has been stated by writer after writer, up to the present time, that twenty-three is the exact number of the families. This is far from the case. Mr. McClintock, a man well known in Guiana, who has lived longer among the Arawaks, and has mixed more freely with them than any other European, was good enough to supply me with a list of fifty of these names. It is true that on analysis it appears that among these are one or two instances of duplicates, one name having been corrupted into two; yet after allowance has been made for this the number of distinct family names as yet ascertained amounts to at least forty-seven; and it is almost equally certain that there are others yet to be recorded.

Before giving the list of names it may be as well to point out that each name occurs under three forms, which, however, differ only in the termination : a plural or collective form which expresses the whole family; a singular, masculine form expressing one individual man of the family; and a singular feminine form expressing one individual woman of the family. For example, in a family the collective name of which is *Karuafona* any individual man of this family is spoken of as a *Karuafodie*, and any individual woman as *Karuafodo*. The final syllable in each of these three cases is evidently merely an additional qualifying suffix, and has nothing to do with the real name of the family. These suffixes, collective, male, and female, occur in each of the names. As in the above case, *die* is generally the masculine, *do* the female, and *na* the collective termination; but occasionally the masculine and feminine forms are, for some unexplained reason, *tie* and *to* respectively. Of course, in seeking the derivation of the names these terminations must be rejected.

In the following list of known names where the masculine and feminine terminations are regular—that is, are *die* and *do* respectively—they are omitted.

1. *Karuafona*.   One informant gives the meaning

of this as '*from the grassy land*,' from *karau* or *karow*—grass. He adds that a man who lived on the open savannah —which, by the way, is a very rare position for an Arawak house—is called *karoa kondi*. The derivation of the name is, as he says, obscure, and must remain so unless the legend which is doubtless connected with it can be discovered. Another suggestion is, that it is from *karaowkoan*—'*not weight enough*'—but there is little evidence in favour of this.

2. *Onishèna*. The meaning of this is given as '*from the rain or water*.' Another suggestion is '*rainhead*,' from a word *onishi*. What the meaning of 'rainhead' may be does not appear. Yet another gives the meaning as '*he who sends rain*,' and adds that 'if rain fall inopportunely the Arawak Indian sometimes curses the "*œnicidu*"—thus, "*balhitu œn'cidu*."' At any rate, the root involved seems to be the important *un* or *oon* which, with the meaning of rain and water, is common to many of the Indian languages of South America.

3. *Koiarno*. This is peculiar in that its collective termination seems to be *no* instead of *na*. The masculine and feminine terminations are *tie* and *to* respectively. In Hillhouse's list, in Montgomery Martin's 'West Indies,' it is spelled '*Queyurunto*.' The meaning seems to be, '*from the deer*' (*cuiaro*). Another improbable derivation given is '*the turners back*,' from *koiaroina*—'to turn back.'

4. *Urahkàna*, '*from the ourali or bloodwood tree*.'

5. *Hairèna* (mas. *tie*, fem. *to*), '*from the wild plantain tree*.' The plant usually known under this name is the very striking *Ravenala guianensis*, but the same name is also applied to several species of *Heliconia*.

6. *Yobotàna*, '*from the black monkey*.' I am not sure, but I think the species referred to is *Ateles beelzebub*.

7. *Haiawafòna*, '*from the hyawa tree*' (*Icica heptaphylla*)—a species of tree which, because of the abundant and highly perfumed resin which it produces, which is much used by the Indians for such purposes as the rapid kindling of fire, the making of torches, and to scent the oils with

which they anoint their bodies, is well marked to Indian eyes from other trees of the forest.

The syllable *fo*, which intervenes between the root-word and the terminal syllable in this and other cases (*cf.* No. 1), is puzzling.

8. *Demarèna.* Various interpretations are given of this name. One is that it means '*from the water-mama*,' or rather '*from certain spirits*,' dwelling usually underground. There is much confusion as to these legendary beings, there being supposed to be many of various sorts living in various places. The water-mama, one of these kinds of spirits, which is supposed to live under the water of rivers, is often used for supernatural beings in general. Two other interpretations of the name, both very unlikely, are that it means 'rivals,' and another that it means 'from the Demerara river.'

This family are said to intermarry with the *Karobahana* family (see No. 25), in accordance with an old legend. This case of the especially lawful intermarriage of two particular tribes is curious and deserves attention. It is possible that it is the last trace of a marriage regulation which is known to have existed elsewhere in similar societies. For example, in Morgan's 'Ancient Society' (p. 90) it is stated that among the Iroquois of North America, which *tribe* was divided into a number of *families* or *clans*,[1] it was originally the custom that each man of one of these families might marry a wife, not from his own family, or even from *any* one of the other families, but only from certain of these other families. Thus, a man of the Wolf family might not marry a woman of the Wolf, Bear, Beaver, or Turtle families, but he might marry one of the Deer family. The legend among the Arawaks of the custom of intermarriage of the Demarena and the Karobahana may be referable to a former regulation similar to that among the Iroquois.

---

[1] It will be observed that I have here used the terms *tribe*, and *family* or *clan*, as being the terms which I have used throughout as the equivalents of the terms used in the passage referred to by Mr. Morgan.

9. *Wakuyàna.* The family sprung '*from the redbreast bird*' (*Leistes americana*), called *wakuya* in Arawak. This bird is one of the commonest and most striking in the coast region of Guiana, to which the Arawaks are confined.

10. *Kamikaihimikìna,* otherwise given as *akamikina* (mas. *tie,* fem. *to*). There is almost certainly some error in the transcription of this name. No one can afford a satisfactory interpretation. It has been suggested that it has something to do with *kannakain,* '*it can take more*;' and another correspondent says '*kannakimukina*' means '*good eaters*;' but I can give no opinion on the word.

11. *Dakamokàna,* '*from the dakáma tree*,' a tree bearing a nut like souari (*Pekea tuberculosa*), the kernel of which is grated and baked with cassava meal when cassava is scarce.

12. *Madayalèna,* also given as *moukina* (mas. *tie,* fem. *to*)—the family coming '*from a treeless place*,' perhaps '*from a savannah.*'

13. *Hekorowàna,* '*from a tortoise.*' *Hekorie* is the Arawak name of the tortoise.

14. *Awarakàna,* '*from the awara palm*' (*Astrocaryum tucumoides*)—a very common palm near Indian settlements on the coast, the fruit of which is eaten with great relish and is also used for the production of oil. The young leaves are also used to make the fans for blowing the fire which are an indispensable property of all Indians. The tree is, therefore, one certain to have attracted their notice.

15. *Kaiokàna,* '*from a rat.*' The word *kaio* is the Arawak name for a species of rat. Another informant, on the other hand, says this family takes its name from a tree, but gives no information as to the kind of tree.

16. *Ematàna* (mas. *tie,* fem. *to*). The meaning of this has not been traced.

17. *Ebesowàna.* This seems to mean '*the changed or transformed.*' The word *ebesoa* means 'to change.' The name might just possibly refer to an admixture of Carib blood. The members of the family, however, deny that

there is any foreign blood in them.   They derive their name
from the tradition of a change or magical transformation
undergone by an ancestress.   Mr. Brett says that the legend,
a wildly romantic one, is in his collection ;[1] but I fail to find
it.   As to the actual word *ebesoa*, another informant says,
'A legend of the Demerara rapids called the "Lucadaia
falls" is, that when the *lucadaia*, or plant from which the
Arawaks sprang into existence, was cut down, it was *ebesoa*
or *transformed* into the rapid.   Caterpillars are " *ebesoa* "
or *transformed* into butterflies.'

As regards the suggestion that the name may refer to
'changed blood'—*i.e.* blood mixed with that of Caribs—
Mr. Brett tells me that *arantucino* is the word most frequently used for people of such mixed race.

18. *Babowna*, from a tree producing a juice like milk,
and used medicinally as a dressing for ulcers.

19. *Eeyicòno*.   This form is said to be common to male
and female alike and to be plural !   The meaning seems to
be ' *the newly come family*.'   The root of the word is said
to be found in *eeyato* = ' raw ' or ' fresh.'   Mr. McClintock
notes that the family is extinct, in the Pomeroon district at
least, the last survivor having died in 1876.

20. *Ebesolèno* (mas. *tie*, fem. *to*).   This is another abnormal termination in *no* instead of *na*.   There is a conflict of evidence as to the meaning.   One makes it the
' *faithful, truthful, or heedful family* ; while others concur
in interpreting it as ' *the changed*,' or ' *the family with
changed skin* '—*i.e.* a family of mixed blood and abnormal
complexion.

21. *Warerokàna*, ' *from a wild plantain*.'   This wild
plaintain appears to be not the same as the *Ravenala* mentioned above (see No. 5), but a species of *Heliconia*.

22. *Pariàna*, ' *from a kind of bee*.'   It is perhaps worth
noting that on the borders of Guiana, but within the Brazil,
there is a *tribe*, members of which I have myself seen, of

[1] *Legends and Myths of Guiana*, by William Henry Brett, B.D.
London, 1879.

this name. It is curious that the same name should be claimed by a distant tribe and by a family of the Arawak tribe.

23. *Yabièno*, or perhaps *Sabieno*. The termination is noticeable as being in *no* instead of *na*. The meaning is '*the family sprung from the mocking-bird*' (*Cassicus persicus*). Here again the bird chosen as name-father is one of the most prominent in the district.

24. *Kabolifòna*. In this case also two very distinct meanings are given—'*from the wild thorn tree*,' by Mr. Brett, and '*from a kind of white winged ant*' by Mr. McClintock.

25. *Karobahana*—the family *related to the Coriaki parrot*. It has already been noted that this tribe inter-marries with the Demarena (No. 8).

26. *Maratakayòna*, sprung ' *from a (small) bee.*'

27. *Miekariòna*. I have heard no suggestion as to the meaning of this name.

28. *Barakàna* (or *Barakatana* ?) (mas. *tie*, fem. *to*), ' *from an armadillo*' (sp. ?). *Barakata* is the Arawak name for one species of armadillo, but which is unknown.

29. *Tahatahabetàno* (or *Tatabetàno* ?). The family sprung ' *from a hawk* ' (?).

30. *Turubalèna*, ' *from the turu palm*' (*Ænocarpus baccaba*), ' the seed of which, being dark, represents persons of dark complexion.' This name is also given as *Turubalolu*.

31. *Aramokèna*. Another form of the name is given as *Aramokiyu* (pl.); *Aramokite* (mas. sing.); *Aramokitu* (fem. sing.). ' *From the arara tree*' (sp. ?) An old man of this family told Mr. Brett that this is the meaning of his name; and that once upon a time several persons of different families met to settle various matters, and among others to give names to their respective families. Each took the name of some object near; and the representative of this family took the arara tree, the leaves of which were then on the ground on which he sat.

32. *Kamonèna.* No suggestion has been made as to the meaning of this name.

33. *Dahati-betàna,* sprung '*from the pepper plant.*' The red-pepper, or capsicum, is grown and used in very great quantities by the Indians.

34. *Kaboribetàna,* said to mean sprung '*from the kabori tree.*' What tree this may be I do not know. On the other hand, another informant asserts that the name means '*from the wild yam,*' the fruit of which is much used by the Indians as bait for fish. The weight of evidence is in favour of the latter interpretation. A third interpretation is that the name means '*from the kaboreeshe,*' a kind of fish unknown to me; the weight of evidence is against this.

35. *Mibibitàna,* '*from the bush rope called mibi*' (*Carludovica*), which is much used by Indians to make their quakes and other rough baskets, and also in binding together the various parts of which their houses are formed.

36. *Bakuriekàna,* said to be '*from another, smaller kind of bush rope;*' or, according to another informant, the word is connected with the word *bakarie*—a mother-in-law. The former is the more probable explanation.

37. *Yobakaquàna* means '*the deformed family,*' and seems to refer to some such deformity as a lame foot.

38. *Atiyokàna* (or, perhaps, *Antiyokàna*)—a family sprung '*from the wild cherry tree.*' This tree is not uncommon in the forest; its fruit, which in shape and colour resembles a cherry, is much relished by Indians. Mr. McClintock thinks that the name refers to a peculiar redness of skin in this family.

39. *Arase* (perhaps *Haraschino* from *harasche*—*without hair*). No other interpretation has reached me. The form of the word is altogether abnormal.

40. *Seàna,* said to mean sprung '*from a bee*'—*i.e.* another of the numerous species (*cf.* No. 26).

41. *Seima.* This family is said to be of no antiquity, and its name to refer in some way to an admixture of Spanish blood. Many Arawaks were driven to Guiana from

the region of the Orinoco by the cruelty of the Spaniards. Possibly the name refers to these so-called Spanish Arawaks.

42. *Sewenana.* A family sprung '*from the razor-grinder,*' an insect remarkable for the extraordinarily loud noise with which it makes the forest resound.

43. *Yatéyo.* The form of the word is quite abnormal. Mr. McClintock says that it means '*the offspring of a cannibal.*'

44. *Waruwakàna,* '*from the waruwaka, or wild liquorice tree.*' The tree is *Cassia grandis.* It grows to a large size, and is one of the most beautiful in the colony; when in flower every branch is covered with a small, delicate pink flower. It is common on the Essequibo coast.

45. *Korikurèna.* This name is said to be referable to the word *korikuri,* or, more probably, *karukuri* = gold.

46. *Tetebetàna,* a family sprung '*from a kind of nightjar,*' or goatsucker. There are several species of this bird in Guiana, all of which are more or less very remarkable for the extraordinary cries with which they make night hideous.

47. *Arubunoòna* (or *Harubunoòna*), '*from the velvet-leaf plant,*' common about Indian houses. On the other hand, another authority says that the name refers to some mixture of Ackawoi blood with the true Arawak.

Even after this list of the names had been obtained it was extremely difficult to procure information as to their original meaning. In default of better means of attaining this desirable end, I caused the list to be printed, and sent copies to the several persons who were living, either as missionaries or magistrates, among the Arawaks. Four of those to whom the lists were thus sent most kindly exerted themselves greatly in getting all possible information on the subject from the Indians in their respective neighbourhoods. They all, however, declared that many of the names are from forms of expression now obsolete, and that the meanings of the rest are now known only to a few very aged persons. For example, one of my correspondents wrote to me : ' I do not hope to do very much, as their grandfathers, with whom I discussed the matter over Hillhouse's list thirty-five years ago, and their fathers, whose aid I called in when Mr. McClintock had made his additions to that collection, pronounced them "old-time talk"—that is, obsolete.' In further illustration of the difficulty of procuring the desired information, I may mention the fact that two of my correspondents, having accidentally consulted Arawaks from the same settlement, these Indians differed as to the meanings of some of the names; and this gave rise to strife so great, that the settlement was nearly broken up and abandoned. Yet, notwithstanding these difficulties, some fragmentary information was supplied to me; and this has been incorporated, by way of putting it permanently on record, in the list of families just given.

The fact chiefly evident is that the names are generally those of animals or plants common in Guiana.

Two traditionary explanations of the origin of the names are given by the Arawaks themselves, one simple and the other marvellous. Some say that when the Arawak families in Guiana were increasing in number, at a meeting of the heads of these families, each arbitrarily chose a distinctive family name. One chief, specially mentioned, chose the name of the tree called *arara* (see No. 31), the leaves of which happened to be on the ground on which he sat; another chose the name of another which grew behind him; a third chose the name of a bird which happened to be heard at the moment; and a fourth that of an insect which was at the moment in sight. Most Arawaks, however, emphatically deny this account, and assert that each family is descended— their fathers knew how, but they themselves have forgotten— from its eponymous animal, bird, or plant. It is a matter of much regret that I have been unable to find examples of these legends of descent. In the present state of knowledge, all that can be observed is, the names are evidently almost invariably derived from natural objects, animal or vegetable, and that almost as invariably these eponymous objects are such as are in some way very prominent in Indian life.

But, as we shall elsewhere have occasion to point out, the common language of these Indians changes with so great rapidity, that, within little more than one generation, words often change very greatly in form, or even fall completely out of use. On the other hand, a word once given as a name to a family is much more fixed. One and the same word, when used as the name of a common object by the whole tribe, the members of which live widely scattered and never see each other, soon varies greatly from its original form, though, when used as a name by a family, the members of which live in comparatively close and constant communion, it long retains its original form; thus it is not surprising that the meaning of some of these family names is unknown to the Indians to the present day, and that they are regarded merely as meaningless names.

Each family is, or was, kept distinct by the fact that the descent is solely and rigidly in the female line, and that no intermarriage with relations on the mother's side is permitted among these Indians. The first of these regulations, the descent in the female line, is doubtless founded on the fact that, while there can be no doubt as to the mother of a child, there may be considerable doubt as to the father. The fundamental idea of the second regulation, which forbids the intermarriage of those related on the mother's side, is not so apparent. According to it, a child may marry a husband or wife, as the case may be, of its father's family, or of any other family but that of its mother. If the said child is a man, the offspring of his marriage belong to his wife's family, and bear her name; if it be a woman, the offspring of her marriage belong to her family, and consequently to her mother's. It is evident that the two regulations, taken together, ensure the purity of descent in each family.

Quite in accordance with this system of retaining the descent in the female line is the fact, which will be noted in due course, that an Indian, when he marries, goes to live in the house of his father-in-law, and works for him; he becomes, in fact, a part of his wife's family.

Side by side with this Arawak system of marriage, there are in Guiana a few traces of a totally opposed system, that according to which the bride was captured from a hostile tribe. The fact that the island Caribs had two more or less distinct vocabularies—one of which was used by the men, and by the women when speaking to the men, the other being used only by the women between themselves, or by the men when repeating *oratio obliqua* some saying of the women—has long been known, and has been plausibly explained by the fact that the women were captured from foreign tribes and retained their own language for use amongst themselves. The same fact, liable to the same explanation, may still be noticed in some slight degree in Guiana. And the fact that at least the Caribs did lay waste the homes of other tribes in Guiana, and carried off the women as wives, is told in many a legend. But such a system of 'bride-lifting' is obviously opposed to that of marriage by families. The question therefore arises, how the two occur side by side in Guiana. Two explanations are, I think, possible. One, that it was not a normal habit of any of the tribes of Guiana to steal their wives, but that such bodies of Indian men as went marauding into an enemy's country and there settled, having brought none or few of their own women with them, naturally used their female captives as wives. On excursions of warlike purpose, and only on these, Indians go without their women. When, therefore, for example, a body of Carib men crossed from the islands to the mainland, carrying destruction before them, and then found it convenient to settle in the country they had laid waste, they would naturally take their captives as wives. The second possible thing is, that the tribes of one branch used the system of marriage by family, the tribes of another branch used the system of marriage by capture. If this were so, as we know that the Arawaks used generally, if not exclusively, the former system, the Caribs sometimes, if not always, the latter, it might be natural to suppose that the tribes earlier in Guiana married by family, and that the later-coming Carib immigrants captured their wives. This suggestion cannot, however, be accepted, as some of the Carib tribes, notably the Macusis, show traces of the system of marriage by family. On the whole, though proof cannot at present be afforded of either of these two theories, the former seems the more probable.

CHAPTER VIII.

APPEARANCE AND DRESS.

Physical Characters and Appearance—Artificial Modifications of the Body
—Ordinary Dress—Body-painting—Ornaments—Regard for Personal
Appearance—Partial Adoption of European Dress.

IN trying to realise the appearance of Indians, the first
essential is always to remember that they are decently naked,
and that there is no chance, as with us, of the clothes making
the man. The Indian, man or woman, whatever the tribe,
is not a fine animal in appearance. All are of small stature,
though there is considerable difference in this respect in the
various tribes, the Arecunas being the tallest, the Arawaks
the shortest.[1] The trunk and limbs are generally well
formed, though, except in rare cases of individuals during
the prime of life, a protuberant stomach, due apparently
to the habit of drinking paiwari in excessive quantities,
makes the whole body ugly. But the most striking feature
of the physique is the sleekness and fulness of the flesh, and
the apparent absence of any considerable development of
muscle. This appearance is partly due to a real deficiency
in the development of muscle by constant and regular exercise, but partly also to the fact that the form and play of
such muscle as is there is hidden by the thickness of the skin,
and by the large quantities of fat deposited by the cassava
which forms so great a part of the diet of these people. The
matter was well illustrated to me when for some time among

[1] It is rather curious, though I do not attach much importance to the
fact, that the Arecunas lead the hardest lives and have been least affected
by European influence, while the Arawaks have been longest and most
exposed to the enervating effects of that influence.

PLATE VII.

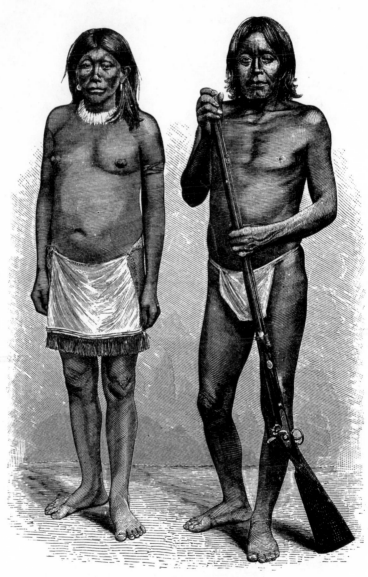

ACKAWOI MAN AND WOMAN.

my canoe-crew of pure-blooded Indians was a young cobungru, half-Indian, half-negro, who, though certainly not unusually muscular, as he moved and worked among the Indians, always looked like an athlete among sybarites. It is very difficult to describe the colour of the skin. It is usually said to be ' copper-coloured,' and the Indians themselves are sometimes called ' red-skins.' Both these expressions refer to a real appearance of the skin, for the colour is, as nearly as I can express it in words, very red cinnamon. The shade differs considerably in the different tribes. Perhaps it differs according to the localities inhabited by the different tribes; for the forest Indians, except the Warraus and some few individuals of other tribes whose colour is obscured by dirt, are fairer than those on the open savannahs. Moreover, as I have said in a previous chapter, I have seen the skin of an Indian, who, after wearing clothes for about two years, then rejected them, pass gradually, but within six months, from a shade very remarkable among Indians for its fairness to a shade quite undistinguishable from that exhibited by his fellows. The hair on the scalp is thick, long, very straight, and very black, and is generally cut to an even edge, at right angles to the neck, round the head. The features of the face are strikingly like those familiarly known as Chinese (Mongolian). The expression is decidedly gentle; and a habit which almost all Indians have of keeping their eyes turned rather to the ground than upward, gives somewhat the appearance of timidity. The expression, probably because Indians have for many generations trained themselves to repress all show of emotion, is very changeless and monotonous. As a rule the faces of neither men nor women appear to the European handsome or beautiful; but in rare cases one sees both men and women with features so regular and well-formed that they would anywhere be considered pleasing and taking.

Physically and constitutionally, the Indians, in spite of the severe labour which they occasionally undergo, are but weak, as might, indeed, be guessed from their appearance.

They can work, provided the exertion is not very great, for very long periods. For instance, they can paddle—an exercise which, as practised by them, when once the knack is acquired requires very far less exertion than rowing—for several consecutive days and nights, with wonderfully short intervals of rest. But any severe work very soon tires them ; though they think nothing of walking over the savannah day after day, from morning to night, yet they cannot walk any given distance even in twice the time required for the purpose by the ordinary European or negro. The well-known fact, about which I shall presently have to say more, that after a hunting excursion Indians lie idly in their hammocks for days, arises from their real need of apparently excessive rest after any unusually violent exertion. Moreover, their vital powers seem but weak ; many a slight chill, or blow, or wound, that would be insignificant to a negro or ordinarily healthy European, is fatal to some Indians. They very rarely attain any considerable age, probably never old age. Of course, as they have no idea of estimating their own ages, it is impossible for a traveller to determine with absolute certainty the average duration of their lives; but it is probably hardly ever more than from forty to fifty years. They never become bald. Light yellow hair, which is to an Indian as white hair is to a European, is of very extreme rarity. I have seen it in but two instances; and the brothers Schomburgk, during a much longer experience than mine, saw it hardly oftener.[1] But such beauty as the Indian ever has, is very early lost. It has been said that the protruding stomach is the ugliest feature. There is a very short period, probably about the twentieth year, when the vital powers are strongest, and the amount of exercise taken is greatest, during which this feature becomes, at least in many cases, almost unnoticeable ; but it soon reasserts itself, and between the thirtieth and the fortieth year in the case of men, and even earlier in the case of women, the rest

---

[1] Schomburgk, *Reisen in Britisch Guiana*, vol. ii. p. 54.

of the body shrinks, the fat disappears, and the skin hangs in hideous folds from the bones.

A pleasing point about Indians is that, with some exceptions, they are extremely clean in their personal habits.

Early in the morning, and many times during the day, men and women troop down together to the nearest water, be it river, stream, or pool, and there, in company, splash about in the water. They evidently feel real pleasure in being in the water. Men and women alike swim splendidly, but with a peculiar action. The legs are hardly spread; but the thighs are bent downward at right angles to the trunk, the lower part of the legs being of course parallel to the trunk, and then the legs are again suddenly straightened, thus driving forward the body of the swimmer. It is, by the way, rather curious that Indians make a point of bathing *immediately* after every meal, apparently without ill effects.

Owing to these constant washings, their skins are very fine and smooth. The exceptional cases in which these habits of cleanliness are not observed are to be found in the whole tribe of the Warraus, and in some few families, apparently especially on the Potaro river, of the Ackawoi, who go to the opposite extreme and never wash. The skin and the appearance of these is therefore anything but pleasant.

So far, only the natural physical condition of the Indians has been described; but, as among so many other people in a state of savagery or barbarism, many of them artificially distort their bodies. In one of the most remote parts of the colony, or perhaps beyond its limits, near the sources of the Essequibo, lives a little-known tribe, the members of which are in the habit of tying boards on to the heads of their young children in such a way that the skulls assume, and permanently retain, an extraordinarily flat shape. And even among the more important tribes of Guiana, with which we are more especially concerned, this habit is said, both by early travellers and by Indians themselves, to have prevailed among all the Caribs. However that may be, it is no longer practised. But a somewhat similar habit is yet in full use.

Among the True Caribs a two-inch-broad belt of cotton is knitted round each ankle and just below each knee, of very young female children; and this band is never throughout life removed, or if removed is immediately replaced. The consequence is that the muscles of the calf swell out to a very abnormal degree between these bands, while those parts

FIG. 1.

COBUNGRU WOMAN, SHOWING LEG-BANDS.

of the leg which are actually constricted remain hardly thicker than the actual bone (Fig. 1). The whole leg below the knee looks like the pedestal of a chessman of the conventional form. The arms are occasionally, though much more rarely, treated in the same way. Of the other Carib tribes, the Macusi and Arecuna women have one such constriction above each ankle, but not the second below the knee. Apparently none of the other tribes, not even the Ackawoi, though these are also Caribs, distort their legs in this fashion; but all Indians, men and women alike, generally, if not always, wear a piece of string or a band of cotton or beads round their ankles and round their arms, just below the shoulder, and this may possibly be a recently adopted substitute for permanent distortion of the limbs. Another way in which all Indians interfere with their bodies is by pulling out by the roots the very few hairs which grow anywhere but on their scalps. Even the eyebrows are not unfrequently sacrificed in this way. Moreover, the True Carib and Ackawoi women, and more rarely those of other tribes, pierce one or more holes in their lower lips, through each of which they pass, point outward, a pin or sharpened piece of wood. What the object of this may be I do not know, as kissing is unknown among Indians; but the effect is, that the lips are protected by a dangerous-looking row of spikes. Similarly the men pierce one hole just under the middle of their lower lips, through which they pass the loop of string, fastening it inside the mouth, to which is attached a bell-shaped ornament, which hangs down over the chin; and they pierce the cartilage of the septum of their noses, from which they suspend a half-moon shaped ornament (Fig. 2). The

FIG. 2.

MACUSI, WITH
NOSE AND LIP
ORNAMENT.

ears too of men, and sometimes of women, are pierced, and pieces of stick or straw are passed through the holes.

In turning now to the body-coverings put on by Indians, we will consider first such very simple clothing as they ordinarily wear, and then that of many and various kinds which they put on occasionally for ornament.

Indians, after babyhood, are never seen perfectly naked [1]

---

[1] The Zurumutas, a sub-group in the interior, in some way allied to the Macusis, are said by Sir Robert Schomburgk to live in a state of actual nakedness.

When they want to change their single garment, they either retire from the sight of others to do this, or, if this is inconvenient or impossible, they put on the fresh garment over the old, and then withdraw the lower one. Every man wears a long narrow strip of cloth, called a lap, which is passed between the legs, the ends being brought up at the back and front of the body respectively, and then suspended over a rope-like belt worn just above the hips. Every woman wears a tiny apron, called a queyu, suspended by tying its strings round her waist. (See Plate 7, opp. p. 189.) It is worth noting that very young children before they wear even so much clothing as this, usually have a string round the waist. That is absolutely all the clothing worn on ordinary occasions. It is a most curious but certain fact that these people, even as they wander in the streets of Georgetown, do not appear naked.

The lap of the man is, with very rare exceptions, now formed of blue salemporas cloth, procured directly or in-

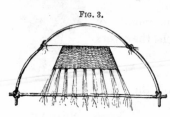

FIG. 3.

METHOD OF MAKING QUEYU.

directly from Europeans. The exceptions occur among the Warraus, who still sometimes wear laps made of the inner bark of a tree (*Lecythis ollaria?*), which has been beaten until it is comparatively soft and of the texture of thick rough cloth. Most probably this tribe, and perhaps some others, used this bark as a rule before the arrival of Europeans; and, as some of the other tribes, especially those of Carib origin, have peculiar methods, as will presently be told, of preparing for themselves a rude sort of cotton-cloth, it is also probable that some laps used to be made of cotton. The queyu (Fig. 3) of the woman is now almost invariably made of European beads fastened together into a cloth-like fabric. But the Warrau women still generally make their queyus of bark; and some few Arecuna women make them of loose strings of cotton arranged in a deep fringe; and the rude Pianoghotto women make them as those of beads are made,

but of small bright-coloured seeds. All these are probably
survivals of old indigenous customs.

It should perhaps be noted that, according to their
different tribes, the women generally make their bead queyus
of particular colours and patterns—for instance, those of the
Ackawoi women are generally dark blue, with one row of red
and another of white beads at the bottom; while among the
Macusis they have generally a white ground, on which is a
simple pattern in red or blue.

Before passing to those parts of the dress which are
both merely ornamental and occasional, one article claims
mention in that, though it is only very occasionally worn,
yet it is for use and not ornament. This is the pair of
sandals, cut from the leaf-stalk of the æta palm (*Mauritia
flexuosa*), which is worn on very stony parts of the savannah
to protect the feet. The string which keeps the sandal on
the foot passes between the great toe and the next; and
where these foot-coverings are much worn the flesh between
these toes soon becomes callous and as hard as horn. A very
few hours' use wears out the sandals, but this does not much
matter, for a new pair can be cut from the nearest æta palm,
and can be ready for use in a few minutes. Rough as these
sandals are, they are made to the measure of the foot; on
several occasions when I was reduced to wearing them myself,
the Indians measured me for each pair as carefully as though
they had been European shoemakers.

Turning now to mere ornaments, we shall find that
among Indians, as throughout almost the whole animal world
exclusive of civilised man, these are far more abundantly used
by the males than by the females.

As to the occasion of the wearing of ornaments, there
are Indians who are never without more or less of these of
some kind, and there are others who never use them except
on special occasions, such as feasts and visits of ceremony.

Painting the body is the simplest mode of adornment.
Tattooing or any other permanent interference with the surface of the skin by way of ornament is practised only to a very

limited extent by the Indians; is used, in fact, only to produce the small distinctive tribal mark which many of them
bear at the corners of their mouths or on their arms. It
is true that an adult Indian is hardly to be found on whose
thighs and arms, or on other parts of whose body, are not
a greater or less number of indelibly incised straight lines;
but these are scars originally made for surgical, not ornamental purposes. Painting is, however, much practised.
Several pigments are used for this purpose, but chiefly red
faroah and blue-black lana among the savannah Indians, and
carmine caraweera and lana among those of the forest; white
clay and a yellow substance of uncertain nature are also
used more rarely, but by all tribes. As a vehicle for these,
various oils, scented with natural resins, are used. The paint
is applied either in large masses or in patterns. For example,
a man, when he wants to dress well, perhaps entirely coats both
his feet up to the ankles with a crust of red; his whole trunk
he sometimes stains uniformly with blue-black, more rarely
with red, or he covers it with an intricate pattern of lines of
either colour; he puts a streak of red along the bridge of his
nose; where his eyebrows were till he pulled them out he puts
two red lines; at the top of the arch of his forehead he puts
a big lump of red paint, and probably he scatters other spots
and lines somewhere on his face. The women, especially
among the Ackawoi, who use more body-paint than other
ornament, are more fond of blue-black than of red; and one
very favourite ornament with them is a broad band of this,
which edges the mouth, and passes from the corners of that
to the ears. Some women especially affect certain curious
little figures, like Chinese characters, which look as if some
meaning were attached to them, but which the Indians are
either unable or unwilling to explain.

There are two ornaments which are worn by men of all
tribes more frequently than any others. These are a necklace of bush-hogs' teeth and the pair of armlets of which
mention was made a page or two back. Of the first of these
one is possessed by every adult Indian, and is almost

constantly worn everywhere but in the house. The even row of teeth, whiter than ivory and filed to uniformity, as it hangs against the chest of the Indian, contrasting with his dark red skin, is really a beautiful ornament; but the special value which the Indian attributes to it is not because of its beauty, but because, as each man is supposed to wear only the teeth of such bush-hogs as he has himself killed, the more numerous, the finer, and the larger the teeth are, the more successful do they show their Indian owner to have been in hunting. It is, indeed, only in the last extremity that the Indian will part with this necklace. The armlets, worn just below the shoulder, on the other hand, are of small value and are frequently replaced; the fact that they are very generally worn perhaps indicates, as I have already suggested, that they represent a permanent constriction of the flesh which used formerly to be made round the arm. Sometimes they are in the form of broad cotton bands, but more often each is simply a loop of string which encircles the arm, and is furnished at the knot, in front of the arm, with a flat disc of bone, shell, or metal, from which the long loose ends of the string hang down.

The other ornaments seem to have no special significance, and are used in more or less profusion according to the individual taste of each Indian, but chiefly on the occasion of feasts.

The men wind long single strings of seeds, or now more often of beads, red, white or blue, evenly round and round their ankles and their wrists. They smooth their hair and make it shiny with palm oil, and, parting it in the middle of the forehead, in the arch made by the parting they daub a thick mass of red paint, and on this they stick some white down from under the feathers of the curassow bird (*Crax alector*). Among the toilet properties of an Indian is a small bag made of skin, full of this down, from which small pieces are pulled out and used as required. A long straw, or a stick of letter-wood, sometimes ornamented with humming birds' and other feathers, is passed through a hole in

the lobe of each ear in such a way that one end rests on the
cheeks and reaches nearly to the mouth. A crescent-shaped
or round piece of silver or copper, flat and highly polished on
one side (Fig. 4), is suspended from a small stick passed
through the cartilage of the nose, so as to hang down over
the mouth. Apparently, the crescent-shaped nose-pieces
are proper to the Carib tribes, the round to the Wapianas.
Sometimes they are so large that the wearer has to hold up
this ornament with one hand, while he lifts the calabash of
liquor to his mouth with the other. A small, bell-like ornament, made of white bone or shell, with a long streamer of
white or red cotton in place of the clapper (Fig. 5), is hung
by a string passed through the middle of the under lip.
Beautiful crowns of feathers, of two shapes, the colours

FIG. 4.

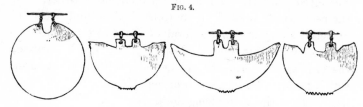

NOSE ORNAMENTS.

varying with the tribe to which each Indian belongs, is
worn on the head. (See Frontispiece.) Several strings of
cotton hang from the back of this down to the heels, where
they are finished off with skins of toucans, fire-birds, cocks-
of-the-rock and other such bright-coloured birds, or with
tassels, made of iridescent beetles' wings, which tinkle like
tiny bells at each movement of the wearer. Strings of jang-
ling seeds are fastened round the ankles and the arms, and
two others are worn over the shoulders, crossed saltire-fashion
in front and at the back of the body. Round his neck the
Indian puts not only his necklace of bush-hogs' teeth, but
also necklaces of the teeth of other animals and of seeds.
Round the waist is sometimes put a skirt of young yellowish-
green palm leaves, neatly plaited.

Ruffs made of the long tail-feathers of macaws are fas-

Plate VIII.

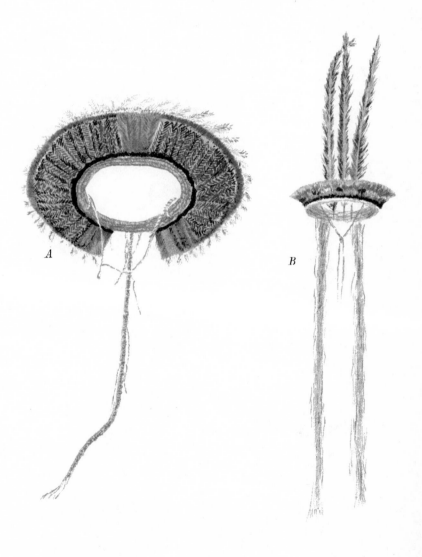

A

B

Two Feather Head-dresses.

A. Macusi.   B. Tarurna.

tened on to the shoulders so as to stand out almost at right angles to the body. (See Frontispiece.) Other very short mantles of woven cotton, from which hang long cotton cords, ornamented at frequent intervals with tufts of white down, are occasionally worn (Fig. 6, p. 200); but the art of making these is said to have been lost. Collars made of white heron feathers, or the black feathers of the curassow bird, are sometimes worn, especially by those engaged in races.

FIG. 5.

c

LIP ORNAMENT.

The toilet of the women is more simple. They wear no feathers, and very seldom any teeth, except those of the acourie, but they load themselves with astounding quantities of seeds and beads in great ropes round the neck, and as girdles round the waist, and in bands round the ankles, the wrists, and upper arms; and they wear a simple cotton fillet at festivals.

As to the children, the ornaments which are put on them are very much like those of their elders, except that special kinds of seeds are principally used for their necklaces, or, if these are made of teeth, they are generally of jaguar's teeth.

The Indians differ individually in the degree of care which each takes of his or her personal appearance as much as do members of civilised communities. One whole tribe, the Warraus, are, or were, distinguished by utter disregard of all cleanliness and neatness, but in the other tribes more or less attention is always paid to such matters. It is rather curious that dandies, male and female, occur among them about as frequently, comparatively, as in more civilised communities, and in as pronounced degrees. A young Indian in the prime of his life, conscious of a fine figure and good looks, often takes infinite pains with his person, and manages to put on his oils, paints, feathers, and teeth so delicately and becomingly that, despite his nakedness, he gives himself exactly that neat and well-dressed appearance which one is accustomed to associate with a young, well-bred civilised gentleman, very careful in the matter of clothing. And just as there are young Indian men of this temper and habit, so there are young women.

FIG. 6.

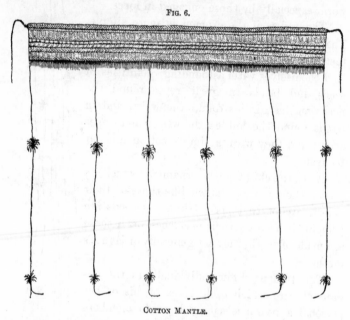

COTTON MANTLE.

As one of the earliest ways in which the Indian mimics the European is in the adoption of clothes, even though he generally only uses these while he is among white men, rejecting them with a sigh of relief as soon as he is alone with his fellows, it may not be out of place to say a word here as to how far this matter has yet gone. The new habit seems to be adopted in three stages: first, beads are used by men and women alike; then the men obtain and put on by way of show some single European garment, generally an ordinary flannel jersey or a hat, and the women wear a garment made like a flannel petticoat, worn round the neck, the band over one shoulder, under the other; and lastly, the men wear shirt and trousers, the women an ordinary dress, in each case without other clothing. Beads have already penetrated almost throughout the colony, enormous quantities finding their way, in barter, year by year into the interior. As is evident from what has been said, they are used chiefly to replace the seeds or teeth, which were formerly all that the Indian had of this sort to make into body ornaments. The second stage, marked by the occasional possession and use of a single European garment, has not yet spread beyond the Ackawoi and True Caribs of that part of the forest region which is near the coast, and even there prevails only in rare cases. The third stage has fairly established itself among the Arawaks, and other Indians living round mission stations of the coast region.

CHAPTER IX.

HOUSES AND SETTLEMENTS.

Distribution of the Settlements—The Three Chief Types of Houses—Warrau
Pile-dwellings—Open Houses in the Forest—Walled Houses on the
Savannah—Communal House in rare instances—Pile-houses occasionally
built on the dry Savannah—Benabs, or temporary Huts—Probable
History of Development of House-building among Indians—Various
Thatch-materials.

THE homes of the Indians are widely scattered both in the
forests and on the savannahs, but there is some difference in
their mode of distribution in these two different regions.
In the forest each family generally lives in a separate settlement of one or more houses, often far from the nearest
neighbours. How far apart these settlements are may be
gathered from the fact that in the two hundred and fifty
miles of the course of the Essequibo from the first falls—at
Aretaka—upward, there are not half a dozen of them. On
the savannahs also, separate widely scattered family settlements occur, but more often several families have united and
formed villages, which sometimes consist of as many as from
twenty to thirty houses, each containing a separate family.

The houses are everywhere almost equally simple in structure, for the materials are everywhere much the same and admit
of but little difference in combination ; and such differences as
exist have evidently arisen in consequence of natural efforts
to meet the special requirements of each kind of situation.
Three chief types of houses are distinguishable. In the low
and swampy coastlands occupied by the Warraus, there were
not long ago many houses built on piles over water ; and
though many of the Warraus, taking advantage of the quiet
times and security from enemies in which they now live, have

migrated to places rather more inland and on higher, dry ground, some of them still build pile-dwellings in the swamps. In the forest region the Arawaks, Ackawoi, and True Caribs, sheltered from cold winds by the surrounding trees, build wall-less houses. And on the open savannah in the interior, the Macusis, Arecunas, and Wapianas build houses with thick clay walls as a protection against the cold winds which, especially at night, blow from the mountains across these plains. But between these three types of houses—those on piles, those in the forest, and those on the savannah—there are, as we shall see, many gradations.

My travels never having led me into the swamps occupied by the Warraus, I cannot write of their pile-dwellings from experience. Richard Schomburgk's description of one such place is as follows: 'The whole settlement was surrounded by water, and the miserable huts, seven or eight feet long, stood on a platform, formed of interlaced stems of the manicole palm (*Euterpe oleracea*), and supported on piles or tree-trunks of five or six feet in height. In the centre of each hut a heap of earth did duty as a hearth, and prevented the fire, which was kept continually burning, from finding its way through the wooden floor. The low roof was thatched with palm-leaves, and a notched tree-trunk, leaning against the hut, served as a ladder, to which, when the water is high, the canoe is tied. Even in the dry season the ground is so swampy that a narrow raised path leads from the settlement to the nearest somewhat higher ground.' [1]

The forest Indian's house, or group of houses, stands in a clearing abruptly walled in by tall forest trees. Irregularly planted cassava, sugar-cane, pine-apples, and other plants which the Indian cultivates, grow intermingled with wild seedlings and shoots from the stumps of the trees which once stood there; and the whole is matted together by thickly growing yam-vines, and by razor-grass, passion-flower, and other wild creeping plants. Charred trunks of felled trees lie in all directions amongst this dense mass of

[1] Schomburgk's *Reisen in Britisch Guiana* (Leipzig, 1847), vol. i. p. 195.

vegetation. A very narrow and much-trodden path leads from the house, through the clearing, into the forest, and then down to the nearest water.

Very rarely the house is round; it is far more usually square, or at least rectangular. The four posts and the cross-beams support a sloping thatch of palm-leaves. The two gable-ends are usually entirely open; but on the two sides the eaves of the thatch almost touch the ground. The floor is the natural earth, often a loose white sand. The most conspicuous objects inside each house are a huge canoe-shaped wooden trough, to hold paiwarie, some clay pots for cooking, a few bottles made of clay, some hollow gourds, baskets, implements for making cassava bread, and some low wooden benches—like footstools—roughly carved into the likeness of animals. Resting from cross-beam to cross-beam are bundles of arrows, a bow or two, perhaps a blow-pipe. From some of the uprights hang a few necklaces of teeth and other body ornaments. There are two or three fires on the ground, one under each hammock, and an extra one for cooking. From the beams hang many red-dyed cotton hammocks slung side by side, and one over the other. In one Ackawoi house of but twenty feet by thirty, I counted as many as eighteen hammocks; and as a few of these were occupied by more than one person—by a husband and wife, and even by a child or two—the number of people belonging to the house could not have been less than twenty-two or twenty-three. Nor is this an unusually large number of inhabitants for an Indian house.

Of all the forest houses, those of the Arawaks are far the cleanest and most cared for. A partition, made of palm leaves or bark, often makes part of the house private. Sometimes, indeed, these Arawak houses, standing in clearings floored with glittering white sand and bordered with coffee and cashew trees, among which beautiful crimson lilies (*Hippeastrum equestre*) grow thickly, are as pleasant places as any in which one need wish to stay. But in these, as in some other respects, the Arawaks have adopted a considerable amount of civilisation from their white neighbours.

Sometimes, where the forest houses stand in very extensive clearings, where therefore there is some need of shelter, a wall of plaited palm-leaves or of bark is added to the house on the side most exposed to the wind, or even all round.

The savannah houses are almost invariably round or oval. There are no signs of cultivation round them, with the exception, perhaps, of a few stunted and untended white-podded cotton plants or faroah shrubs loaded with their beautiful crimson fruit; for the fields belonging to these houses are far away, in the centre of one of the thickets which line the gullies or edge the streams of the savannah country. The house is provided with very substantial walls of wattle-work thickly plastered with mud, often two feet in thickness; and above these rises the high conical thatch of palm-leaves. A few feet off the main house is a rude dome-shaped building, entirely smothered in palm-leaves, and looking like a gigantic English haycock, which serves as a kitchen, and in which the women often sleep. Generally there is a third building, a mere shed, which is intended for the use of such strangers as visit the settlement.

Near each house is a shallow pit, evidently artificial. This is where the clay for the walls of the house was prepared. The wattle-work of the walls being ready, this pit was dug; and in it was put clay and water. The women and children went into it, and all stamped and danced vigorously until the clay was kneaded to a proper consistency.

The history of the adoption of these walls is clearly seen in the fact that sometimes, especially when a new house is first built, it is walled only with plaited palm-leaves, as has been said is sometimes done in large clearings in the forest, and on the further fact that these palm-leaves are sometimes roughly daubed with mud as a temporary expedient before they are pulled down and the substantial permanent walls are built.

For a few minutes after entering the main house, it is

impossible to distinguish anything. There are no windows; and the very narrow doorway, which is the only apparent opening in the walls, is blocked with loose posts, or sometimes with a rude door of leaves or skin. Sometimes there is another, smaller, concealed door at the other end of the house, by which it is said the women and children escape when the house is entered by anyone with hostile intentions; but such hostile visits being extremely rare, this door always remains closed. Gradually the eye accustoms itself to the gloom and darkness, and the interior becomes visible. The floor is of mud, trodden by much traffic to the hardness and likeness of stone. The smoke from many fires has dyed the roof a deep highly polished black. Like the forest houses, the place is crowded with hammocks. Under each of these are the ashes of a fire; for all Indians, whether at home or travelling, sleep with a fire so directly under their hammocks, that the flames seem to lick the naked skins of the sleepers. Here and there, about six feet from the ground, a few sticks, their ends resting on the cross-beams, are placed so as to form rude shelves, on which are dried fish, bows and arrows, baskets, and a confusion of other similar objects. Some grave-looking parrots walk gingerly about among piles of cassava-roots, balls of cotton, surianas of bread, seeds of the æta and cokerite palms (*Mauritia flexuosa* and *Maximiliana regia*) which litter the floor. Some fowls scrape among this litter in search of food. One or two men lie in their hammocks; some women are nursing babies, others are cooking at the fire which burns in one corner.

Towards the Brazilian border, where the influence of the Rio Negro tribes has made itself felt, the houses are similar to those just described in most respects, but are much larger. One house, indeed, often shelters a whole settlement, each family having a special place in it. In that district, too, the platform of parallel sticks under the roof, which elsewhere serves only as a shelf for goods and stores, is occasionally made much larger, and serves as a sort of upper floor, to which the Indians retire at night.

A most remarkable fact is that houses on piles are not unfrequently built, for no apparent reason, on the savannah; and this is done not by any special tribe, but occasionally by Arecunas, Macusis, and by other Carib tribes. They stand not in swamps, but on dry ground, sometimes on top of a hill. Except that they are much larger, they are exactly like the Warrau houses already described; and it is a note-worthy fact that the platform on which the house stands is, as in the case of the Warrau houses, made of the stems of manicole palms (*Euterpe oleracea*), though this moisture-loving palm is very locally distributed in the savannah region, and the Indians fetch it from long distances, although other, apparently equally suitable, material is at hand. It is probable that these savannah pile-builders revert to a form of house which they saw—and perhaps used—on the coast land, when they first reached the main-land from the islands.

After all, each of these houses is but a variation of the same idea. Four or more poles or posts, fixed upright in the ground, connected by cross-sticks lashed with pieces of the stems of creeping plants from the top of one upright to that of another, and surmounted by other poles lashed on to the cross-pieces, so as to slope from these to a common ridge-pole, in the case of the rectangular houses, or to a common centre in the case of the circular or oval houses, forms the entire framework. A thatch of leaves is then fastened on to the sloping roof-poles. Then the house is complete. Sometimes, however, it is raised from the ground on piles, by making the upright corner-posts of unusual height, and by hanging a platform half-way up these corner posts by way of a floor. In other cases, the house is on the ground, but it is enclosed with walls, made, like the roof, of leaves; in yet other cases these leaf-walls are plastered with mud, or are replaced by sheets of bark; and in yet other cases, the leaf-walls are replaced by wattle-work, and on this stronger framework much more substantial walls of mud are laid. That the houses on the savannah are round instead of rec-

tangular may be due to the wish to present as few points of
resistance as possible to the wind; or the shape may simply
have been copied from Indians of other Brazilian tribes.
And the occasional habit of building one large house for
many families, instead of a small house for each family, is
probably also copied from other tribes.

As yet, only permanent dwelling-houses have been
described. But whenever an Indian is on a hunting or fishing expedition, or is for any reason away from home, during
the rainy season, he builds for himself at night a temporary
shelter, called in the colony a ' benaboo, or 'benab.' A
benaboo is less or more substantially built according to its
occasion. Sometimes it is only intended to afford shelter
from rain for an hour or two; and then it only consists of a
very few leaves of some palm, laid flat one upon the other,
and the stalks, which are bound together, stuck into the
ground at such an angle that the natural curve of the leaf
affords some shelter.[1] Sometimes a benaboo is built to
afford shelter to several men for a whole night when heavy
rain threatens, and then it is made by sticking three poles
upright in the ground in the angles of a triangle, by joining
the tops of these by three cross-sticks, and by then laying
over the whole a bunch of palm-leaves, like, but bigger than,
that used in the earlier described benaboo. Sometimes,
again, a benaboo is built for occasional brief use at some
place of repeated resort—either a good fishing ground, or
where turtle abound, or where some desirable plant grows, or
for some similar reason; and in that case it is made as is
that last described, except that the upright poles are four,
arranged at the angles of a square, and that these support
not only cross-pieces, but above that a ridge-pole, and that
two bundles of leaves are arranged, one on each side of the
ridge-pole, to which they both slope up. Thus it is easy to

---

[1] When travellers describe the miserable houses of some of the forest
tribes of Brazil (see E. B. Tylor's *Anthropology*, p. 230), I am inclined to
think that possibly not the real, but only temporary shelters, such as these
' benabs,' have sometimes been seen.

trace the whole history of the development of house building among these Indians, from the first rough shelter made by sticking a few leaves into the ground, to the most complete mud-walled house on the savannah. It may not be unsuggestive to add that this most complete Indian house is in all essential points similar to the simpler houses built in other parts of the world—such, for instance, as is the Highland hut.

Lastly, as regards the materials of which Indian houses are built, the only point which needs further explanation is the thatch. Different kinds of leaves are used for thatch, not necessarily by different tribes, but each as it is most easily attainable in any district. Various kinds of palm are the chief thatch plants. Each gigantic undivided leaf of the troolie palm (*Manicaria saccifera*) is really a shelter in itself; and a few of these laid, without further preparation, so as to overlap like tiles, make a most perfect roof. Indeed, before corrugated zinc was introduced for the purpose, a large trade was carried on between the Indians and the planters on the coast in these troolie-leaves, with which most of the buildings on the sugar estates were thatched. Where troolie does not grow, there is often an abundance of a dwarf palm (*Geonoma baculifera*), with small, almost transparent leaves, called by the Indians *dealibanni*. The leaves of this afford a thatch which is, in one respect, still more convenient than troolie. They are gathered and fastened by their stalks, so as to hang close together, and with their sides overlapping, from a long lath cut from the stem of the booba-palm (*Iriartia exorrhiza*). Such rows of leaves, ten or twelve feet long, and two or three feet deep, are arranged one above and overlapping the other. The great advantage of this plan consists in the fact that the entire rows of leaves can be taken down in a few moments from the roof or walls of a house, can be removed, and can be tied on to a new framework almost as speedily. One Indian I knew, who had a small house thatched in this way in his field, which was far from any settlement, in which he used to live for a day or two at a time when cultivating the ground, used to carry the thatch with him each time he went to or came from his field, in order that the house might not afford shelter to any other Indians during the absence of the owner. Moreover, this kind of thatch is so convenient that it has been adopted by many of the negroes, and other Creole settlers on the coast, who buy the laths ready set with leaves from the Indians; and the trade in these articles on some parts of the coast is so brisk, that the Indians have learned to cheat, by substituting, in the article made for trade, laths cut from the manicole palm (*Euterpe oleracea*) for those from the booba (*Iriartia exorrhiza*), the former being much more easily procurable though less durable.

In other parts of the country, thatching is done with the young leaves of the cokerite or turu palms (*Maximiliana regia* and *Œnocarpus baccaba*), which are cut before the leaflets have spread from the midrib, so that when the leaflets are separated artificially, they hang limp and loose from the midrib. Sometimes the leaves, without further preparation, are then tied on to the roof, the one above the other; but sometimes the leaflets from the two sides of the midrib are first plaited together. The young fan-leaves of the æta palm (*Mauritia flexuosa*) are also sometimes used, the leaflets being cut from the leafstalk, and used just as straw or rushes are in England. But, beside palm-leaves, the huge oblong leaves of the 'wild plaintain' (*Ravenala guianensis*) are also sometimes used for thatch; and where no other materials are easily procurable, the comparatively small broad leaves of a common aroid (*Anthurium acaule*) are used, strung together many on a stick. In any case the thatch is made much more enduring by the smoke of the fires which are constantly kept up in inhabited houses, so that on such a house, the thatch lasts for some years, while in a deserted house or temporary benaboo, it falls to pieces in a few months.

CHAPTER X.

SOCIAL LIFE.

Ruling Authorities—Observance of Mutual Rights—Treatment of Women—
The Story of a Day—The Story of a Life—Birth— *Couvade*—Childhood—Personal Names—Marriage—Death—Burial.

THE system of authority which prevails in Indian societies
is very simple. Each family, whether living apart or in a
settlement, is ruled over by the father, whose authority
is great. As long as he lives, or at least while he is strong
and active, his wives, his daughters and their husbands, and
his sons, until they marry and thus pass from their own
family under the rule of a new house-father, are almost
completely under his sway. Thus, wherever one family lives
by itself the sole authority rests with the father. But the
father of each, while retaining his authority over his own
family, is to some extent under the authority—that is, under
the fear and influence—of the peaiman, and, where several
families live in one place, he is also under the authority of
the headman of the settlement. The authority of the peaiman, which will presently be explained in greater detail,
depends on the power which the man is supposed to exercise
over spirits of all kinds and, as all diseases are supposed to
be the work of spirits, over diseases, and, yet further, consequently over the bodies of his fellows. The headman, on
the other hand, is generally the most successful hunter,
who, without having any formal authority, yet because he
organises the fishing and hunting parties, obtains a certain
amount of deference from the other men of his village. He
settles all disputes within the settlement, and in the not distant days when Indians were in the habit of waging war, the one

on the other, he used, according to Richard Schomburgk, to determine on the commencement of hostilities. His orders to any of the men of his settlement to go anywhere or to do anything are implicitly obeyed. And after a successful hunting or fishing excursion, he always receives a larger share than the others of the booty. This system of authority—that of the peaiman, of the head man of the settlement, and of the father of each family—is probably the remnant of the system which was in use before the intervention of the white men. There is nothing to show whether or not there was originally a higher authority, that of a chief over each tribe ; but none such now exists.

On this original Indian system, a new system has been imposed by the colonial government. In each of certain very vaguely defined districts, some one Indian of each tribe is officially recognised as " captain " of all Indians of his own tribe living in that district. He who would be captain or chief of a district, if his influence was sufficient to persuade a number of his tribe to support his claim, travelled to Georgetown and appeared before the Governor. If it seemed the wish of the majority of the Indians concerned, he was nominally made captain of the Indians of his district ; really he was, comically enough, commissioned to be ' rural constable.' From that day, wherever he went, he carried with him his certificate, a most potent and mysterious document to the Indians, and a huge staff of letter-wood, as signs of authority. His power is strangely real, considering that to enforce it he has to depend but on his own influence, on a sheet of paper, and a stick such as every Indian might cut for himself. The document is far the most dreaded of his insignia. His orders to any Indians of his district are almost unhesitatingly obeyed. It is to be regretted that this system, inadequate as it was, is now being allowed to fall into disuse, without the substitution of any better method. The system is at least useful to the traveller, who, if he is able to secure the good-will of these captains, can at once obtain any requisite number of Indians that he may require, and any amount of provisions ; and it was of use in creating some sort of order among these people.

A far clearer idea of Indian social life will be gained by first obtaining some knowledge of the moral character of these people. The ordinary Indian in his natural state, and before he feels the influence of white men, is of decidedly admirable morality. There are, of course, exceptions ; but such individuals are very rare, and are soon killed or driven out from the tribe. To women and children, and to those weaker than himself, the Indian is gentle ; he is very observant of the rights of his equals, from whom, he in turn, receives a like observance. To his superiors, the head of his family, and the head-man of his settlement, he is as obedient as a good child. The last fact was made manifest to me in a curious manner. When living, on generally very friendly terms, with a party of Indians, of whom the head-man and one or two of the others spoke a few words of English, I, on more than one occasion, gave slight, very temporary offence to the chief, who used to indicate his displeasure by forgetting his English for a time, and so forcing me to fall back on my small stock of Indian words ; and on such occasions the others, though still very friendly, used to refuse absolutely to speak English, however much I might tempt them, and however far we were from the ken of the headman. Within their own families Indians are affectionate, though not in a demonstrative manner. They are grateful for any kindness, and, though proud and very ready to take offence, are easily pacified. In the absence of anything corresponding to police regulations, their mutual relations in everyday life are very well-ordered by the traditional respect which each individual feels for the rights of the others, and by their dread of adverse public opinion should they act contrary to such traditions. The kenaima system—the duty, that is, of revenging all shedding of blood, the explanation of which I must defer to a separate chapter—also helps greatly to keep order. Nor is it only that homicide must be paid for by death. In theory, if not in practice, a complete system of tit-for-tat, of eye for eye, has saturated the mind of the Indian and regulates his whole life. The smallest injury done by one Indian to another, even if unintentional, must be atoned by suffering a similar injury. Of course all this refers chiefly to the mutual relations of members of the same tribe; for the Indian has no dealings with tribes other than his own, except occasionally to barter, when his dealings are regulated by the ordinary laws of honesty, and the strangers with merchandise are for the time being treated as members of the tribe.   Yet even in dealing with white men, the Indian cannot shake himself free from the ideas generated by this tit-for-tat system.   Two curious illustrations of this fact came under my notice. One was when the Macusi boy Möe, of whom mention has already been made, overheard me ' beg pardon' of a companion whom I had accidentally struck.   Möe immediately asked, ' what that you say, " beg you pardon " ? '   After I had explained to the best of my power, I asked the boy to translate the words into his own language.   Then there was a great consultation between Möe and the other Macusis, and only after that was I told a Macusi version of ' I beg your pardon.' It turned out to be ' me hit you again.' The second instance was this.   An Arawak named Robert, belonging to the Corentyn River, undertook to accompany a young fellow from New Amsterdam on a shooting excursion. Some monkeys being seen at the top of a tree, the white man fired and apparently killed one, which, however, as is often the case, remained clinging to the bough. Robert climbed for it, and when near enough shook the branch to make the animal fall. The man below hearing the rustle and thinking that the monkey had revived and was escaping fired his second barrel straight into the tree.   Unfortunately that part of Robert's body which, as the man told of in ' Tom Cringle's Log ' said ' is nearest the chair,' being directly overhead, received the charge. Down came the Indian, furious and vowing that if the white man did not stand to receive an exactly equivalent shot he would shoot and hit him in a more vital part. It was long before the culprit, who appears to have been really unnerved by the mischief he had done, could persuade the Indian to forego his just retaliation.

The fact, of which we shall presently have abundant evidence, that the men leave to the women a far larger share of the necessary work than appears to us proper, may seem somewhat to contradict the favourable verdict on the mutual relations of Indians.   In reality the men's work, hunting, and cutting down trees where cassava is to be planted, is at least equal to, though accomplished more fitfully than, that of the women.   And, moreover, no different distribution of labour has ever entered into the thoughts of Indians, and the women do their share of work willingly, without question, and without compulsion.   The women in a quiet way even have a considerable amount of influence with the men ; and even if the men were—though this is in fact quite contrary to their nature—inclined to treat them cruelly, public opinion would prevent this.   Moreover, the women, just because they have been accustomed to labour hard all their lives, and because this has been the rule for an unknown number of generations, are probably very little, if any, weaker than the men ; and if a contest arose between an average man and an average woman, it is very doubtful with which the victory would be.

The life led by forest and savannah Indians alike, is very simple and unvaried.   The day begins before dawn.   Men and women turn out of their hammocks and stretch themselves.   The first thing done is to wash.   The morning bath over, the men, if it does not happen to be a day for hunting, throw themselves back into their hammocks and there spend almost the whole day, smoking cigarettes made of home-grown tobacco wrapt in the inner bark of a tree, and leisurely fashioning arrow-heads or some such article of use or of ornament.   The hard work falls on the women.   They clean the house—so far as cleaning is considered necessary— fetch water and firewood, cook the food, make the bread, nurse the children, plant the fields, dig the produce; and when any of the men travel, the women carry whatever baggage is necessary. When not engaged in cultivating their fields, in feeding their fathers, husbands, brothers, or sons, the women fetch water for the house from the nearest stream in clay bottles or in goobies (gourds), or they take surianas—large baskets which fit on the back and are supported by a band placed across the forehead—and fetch heavy loads of firewood. When all these things are done, they yet, if there is but little cassava bread left, have to replenish the stock. This last labour—no easy one—seems almost incessant. It is rare to enter an Indian house without seeing some, sometimes all, of the women engaged in making bread.

But the list of the woman's labours is not yet complete. They make the hammocks, both for the use of their own people and for exchange with other Indians and with white traders; and even if it does sometimes happen that there is yet a little time after these many household cares have been fulfilled, they at once sit down to make *queyus*, aprons of beads—their only dress;—or to spin cotton, or weave the small hammocks which serve as cradles for their children. With all these occupations an Indian woman finds but little time during the day to be in her hammock.

When the day has at last come to an end, and the women have gathered together enough wood for the fires during the night, they too throw themselves into their hammocks; and all talk together. Till far into the night, the men tell endless stories, sometimes droning them out in a sort of monotonous chant, sometimes delivering them with a startling amount of emphasis and gesticulation. The boys and younger men add to the noise by marching round the houses, blowing horns and playing on flutes. There is but little rest to be obtained in an Indian settlement by night. These people sleep, as dogs do, without difficulty, for brief periods, but frequently and indifferently by day or night as may be convenient. The men, having slept at intervals during the day, do not need night-rest; the women are not considered in the matter. At last, in the very middle of their stories, the party drops off to sleep; and all is quiet for a short while. Presently some woman gets up to renew the fires or to see to some other domestic work. Roused by the noise which she makes, all the dogs of the settlement break into a chorus of barks and yelps. This wakes the children, who begin to scream. The men turn in their hammocks, and immediately resume their stories, apparently from the point at which they left off, and as if they had never ceased. This time it is but a short interruption to the silence of the night; and before long everything again becomes quiet, till some new outbreak is caused, much as was the last. In the very middle of the night there are perhaps some hours of quiet. But about an hour before dawn, some of the men, having to go out to hunt, effectually wake everybody about them by playing flutes or beating drums as they go to bathe before leaving the settlement.

Turning from the story of the day to the story of the life, we may begin at the beginning, that is, at the birth of the children. And here at once we meet with perhaps the most curious point in the habits of the Indians; the *couvade* or male child-bed. This custom, which is common to the uncivilized people of many parts of the world, is probably among the strangest ever invented by the human brain. Even before the child is born, the father abstains for a time from certain kinds of animal food. The woman works as usual up to a few hours before the birth of the child. At last she retires alone, or accompanied only by some other women, to the forest, where she ties up her hammock; and then the child is born.[1] Then in a few hours—often less than a

---

[1] Richard Schomburgk says (of Macusis): 'Der Nabelstrang wird von der Mutter oder der Schwester der Gebährenden abgeschnitten; ist das neugeborne Kind ein Knabe, so geschieht dies mit einem scharf geschnittenen Bambusrohr; ist es ein Mädchen, mit einem Stück Pfeilrohr (*Gynerium saccharoides*), worauf er mit einem baumwollenenen Faden unterbunden wird" (*Reisen in Britisch Guiana*, vol. ii. p. 313). According to the same authority the teeth of the mother are, among the Warraus, used instead of the bamboo. (Ibid. p. 166.)

day—the woman, who like all women living in a very
unartificial condition, suffers but little, gets up and re-
sumes her ordinary work.   According to Schomburgk, the
mother, at any rate among the Macusis, remains in her hammock for some time ('bis dem Kinde die Nabelschnur ab-
fällt'), and the father hangs his hammock, and lies in it, by
her side; but in all cases where the matter came under my
notice, the mother left her hammock almost at once.   In
any case, no sooner is the child born than the father takes
to his hammock and, abstaining from every sort of work,
from meat and all other food, except weak gruel of
cassava meal, from smoking, from washing himself, and,
above all, from touching weapons of any sort, is nursed and
cared for by all the women of the place.   One other regulation, mentioned by Schomburgk, is certainly quaint; the
interesting father may not scratch himself with his finger
nails, but he may use for this purpose a splinter, specially
provided, from the mid-rib of a cokerite palm.   This continues for many days, and sometimes even weeks.

Couvade is such a wide-spread institution, that I had
often read and wondered at it; but it was not until I saw it
practised around me, and found that I was often suddenly
deprived of the services of my best hunters or boat-hands
by the necessity which they felt, and which nothing could
persuade them to disregard, of observing couvade, that I
realized its full strangeness.   No satisfactory explanation
of its origin seems attainable.   It appears based on a belief
in the existence of a mysterious connection between the
child and its father—far closer than that which exists between the child and its mother,—and of such a nature that
if the father infringes any of the rules of couvade, for a time
after the birth of the child, the latter suffers.   For instance,
if he eats the flesh of a water-haas (*Capybara*), a large
rodent with very protruding teeth, the teeth of the child
will grow as those of the animal; or if he eats the flesh of
the spotted skinned labba, the child's skin will become
spotted.   Apparently there is also some idea that for the

father to eat strong food, to wash, to smoke, or to handle
weapons, would have the same result as if the new-born
baby ate such food, washed, smoked, or played with edged
tools.

The child is not weaned till an extraordinarily late age,
sometimes not till the third or fourth year; and, according
to Schomburgk—though I never saw such a case myself—
when there are too many children claiming food from one
mother, the grandmother occasionally relieves her of the
elder. While the child is young a great deal of affection is
bestowed upon it by both father and mother. The latter
almost always, even when working, carries it against her hip,
slung in a small hammock from her neck or shoulder. The
father, when he returns from hunting, brings it strange
seeds to play with, fondles it, and makes it necklaces and
other ornaments. The young children seem fully to recip-
rocate the affection of their parents; but as they grow older,
the affection on both sides seems to cool, though in reality
it perhaps only becomes less demonstrative. Only once have
I seen grown-up Indians mingling in the games of their
children. Indians rarely, if ever, ill-treat their children, of
whatever age they may be. As soon as the children can
run about, they are left almost to themselves; or rather,
they begin to mimic their parents. As with the adults, so
with the children. Just as the grown-up woman works incessantly, while the men alternately idle and hunt, so the
boys run wild, playing, not such concerted games as in
other parts of the world more usually form child's-play, but
only with mimic bows and arrows; but the girls, as soon as
they can walk, begin to help the older women. Even the
youngest girl can peel a few cassava roots, watch a pot on
the fire, or collect and carry home a few sticks of firewood.
The games of the boys are all such as train him to fish and
hunt when he grows up; the girl's occupations teach her
woman's work.

The system under which the Indians have their personal
names is intricate, and difficult to explain. In the first

place, a name, which may be called the proper name, is always given to a young child soon after birth. It is said to be proper that the peaiman, or medicine-man, should choose and give this name; but, at any rate now, the naming seems more often left to the parents. The word selected is generally the name of some plant, bird, or other natural object. Among Arawak proper names may be mentioned *Yambenassi* (night-monkey) and *Yuri-tokoro* (tobacco-flower), and among Macusi names *Ti-ti* (owl), *Cheripung* (star?), and *Simiri* (locust-tree). But these names seem of little use, in that owners have a very strong objection to telling or using them, apparently on the ground that the name is part of the man, and that he who knows the name has part of the owner of that name in his power.

To avoid any danger of spreading knowledge of their names, one Indian, therefore, generally addresses another only according to the relationship of the caller and the called, as brother, sister, father, mother, and so on; or, when there is no relationship, as boy, girl, companion, and so on. These terms, therefore, practically form the names actually used by Indians amongst themselves. But an Indian is just as unwilling to tell his proper name to a white man as to an Indian; and, of course, between the Indian and the white man there is no relationship the term for which can serve as a proper name. An Indian, therefore, when he has to do with a European, asks the latter to give him a name, and if one is given to him, always afterwards uses this. The names given in this way are generally simple enough—John, Peter, Thomas, and so on. But sometimes they are not sufficiently simple to be comprehended and remembered by their Indian owners, who therefore, having induced the donor to write the name on a piece of paper, preserve this ever after most carefully, and whenever asked for their name by another European, exhibit the document as the only way of answering. Sometimes, however, an Indian, though he cannot pronounce his English names, makes it possible by corruption. For instance, a certain Macusi Indian was known to me for a long time as Shassapoon, which I thought was his proper name, until it accidentally appeared that it was his 'English name,' he having been named by and after one Charles Appun, a German traveller.

After a by no means unhappy childhood, comes the age for marrying. The young men choose their wives. The choice is restricted by certain regulations to which allusion has already been made.

Boys and girls are often betrothed at a very early age; and the boy or young man brings the game that he shoots, and such other presents as he can obtain, to the girl. But when the proper age of marriage comes, the youth is free to choose his wife, and need not necessarily take the girl to whom he was betrothed. Strangely enough, if he deserts his old love, he, as a matter of course, reclaims from her all the durable presents, such as beads and other ornaments, which he has given her. But before he is allowed to choose at all, he must prove that he is a man, and can do man's work. Without flinching, he suffers the infliction of wounds in his flesh; or he allows himself to be sewn up in a hammock full of fire-ants; or by some other similar tests he shows his courage. And he clears a space in the forest to be planted with cassava, and brings in as much game and fish as possible, to show that he is able to support himself and others.

Unfortunately the nature of the bargain for a wife is another obscure point. It is certainly sometimes, if not always, by purchase from the parents. I was once offered a wife in this way; and that it was at an exorbitantly high price was probably owing to the fact that I was rich in such wealth as an Indian covets. The price asked was two guns, two cutlasses, an axe, two razors, some knives, and a piece of the blue cloth called salemporas for the father, and twelve bunches of beads for his daughter. Sometimes, again, a girl is given by her parents to a man in recompense for some service done. The marriage once arranged, the husband immediately transports his possessions to the house of his father-in-law, and there he lives and works. The head of his family, for whom he is bound to work, and whom he obeys, is not his own father, but his wife's. A complete and final separation between husband and wife may be made at the will of the former at any time before the birth of children ; after that, if the husband goes away, as very rarely happens, it is considered not lawful separation, but desertion. When the family of the young couple become too large to be conveniently housed underneath the roof of the father-in-law, the young husband builds a house for himself by the side of that of his wife's father ; and to this habit is probably due the formation of settlements. And when the head dies, it being uncanny to live where a man has died, the various house-fathers of the settlement separate, and build houses for themselves, each of which, in its turn, forms the nucleus of a new settlement.

Possibly each tribe once had certain ceremonies with which they were accustomed to celebrate such events ; but these are now rarely discernible. On one occasion a marriage took place among the people of the Macusi village in which I was living. The old father, very conservative of the customs of his tribes, refused to allow his daughter to be married at all, unless her husband would take her with the old orthodox Macusi ceremony. A few square yards of the savannah were cleared of grass and stones. Over this mats, made of parallel strips of the pith of the æta palm (*Mauritia flexuosa*), were spread. When all was ready, the bride and bridegroom were placed in the clearing, round which the whole population of the village gathered ; and the marriage was there and then carried out.

One other detail, in connection with the ceremony of marriage, as practised by the Macusis, came under my notice : possibly it obtains among other tribes also. The man for some time before marriage abstains from meat. Probably this habit is founded on an idea similar to that which gave rise to 'couvade.' Once, during an expedition with Macusi Indians on the savannah, we were for some days entirely without provisions except a little venison; but one of my companions, who intended to take a wife as soon as the expedition was over, refused to take his share of the meat, and went without food rather than break through the restrictions entailed upon him by his coming marriage. Indian husbands and wives are as a rule very faithful to each other; even on the comparatively rare occasions on which there has been some looseness before marriage there is none after. Husband and wife, without being demonstrative, are decidedly affectionate towards each other; and this, though the woman is held to be as completely the property of the man as is his dog. He may even sell her if he chooses. Yet, as I have before said, the wife—in this, too, like a good and faithful dog—manages to obtain considerable influence with her husband. Polygamy prevails among some, but not all the tribes. Warraus are the most uxorious, some of them having as many as eight or ten wives; and the Wapiana are also polygamists. Macusis and Ackawoi are not, except perhaps in the cases of individuals who choose to break through the customs of their tribe. I am by no means sure, but am inclined to think, on the whole evidence, that the Carib tribes are not usually polygamists, and that some or all the others are, or were. Even when there is more than one wife, the first is almost always chiefly regarded and favoured; those that are married afterwards seem to be taken more as domestic helpers of the first and real wife. From what has already been said of the length of time during which the Indian wife suckles her children, it will be evident that her power of doing all the household work is thereby much diminished. As, however, it is very common for an Indian to marry a woman much older than himself, as his first wife, this wife often grows inactive and useless from sickness or old age. In such cases one or more young girls are generally taken into the house, nominally as wives, but really rather to be taught their domestic duties by the old wife, so that when the latter dies, or becomes perfectly useless, one of them may take her place.

The peaimen, taking advantage of their power, seem,

at least at the present day, to indulge in a very large number of wives. The immense influence which they exercise over the other Indians enables them to acquire any number they please; for an Indian, when asked for his daughter, or even sometimes his wife, by his peaiman, dare not refuse. In this way it happens that the house of the peaiman is generally full of women. These are very useful, for the peaiman in the exercise of his calling has to travel often and far; and on such occasions the women, as is usual among Indians, serve as beasts of burden to carry all the necessary baggage, while the peaiman himself, fantastically adorned with feathers and paint, marches ahead, burdened only with his magic rattle, and perhaps with his bow and arrows.

The life of almost constant exposure which Indians lead, acting on very weak constitutions, kills them at an early age, generally by dysentery or consumption. And even when one does live longer, life can hardly be enjoyable to them; for powerless old age meets with no respect. When old and past work, they are indeed allowed to remain in their hammocks in the houses which once, perhaps, belonged to them, and are fed by their younger relations in a rough and grudging manner; but no further care or kindness is shown to them.

When death comes, either to the old or to the young, the survivors, except in rare instances, show but very few outward signs of grief. More than once I have seen an Indian die—husband, or wife, or son—and sometimes under most painful and distressing circumstances; but the surviving wife, husband, or parent, apparently almost unaffected, within a few hours fully resumed his or her usual habits and cheerfulness. Yet, Indians being always so exceedingly reticent in the expression of emotion, there is some reason to believe that even in such cases the survivors feel a grief which they do not exhibit. Occasionally, however, a terrible wailing is raised over a dead body and is kept up for many days, sometimes even after the burial. On such occasions the survivors crop their hair; and, according to Schomburgk, they paint themselves in excessive degree with faroah. The ceremonies of burial differ slightly in each case; but they are, in the main, as follows: The body, wrapped in the hammock which belonged to it when living, is put into a hole dug in the house and lined with palm-leaves. If the hole is large enough, the body is buried in a sitting position or, in the case of the Ackawoi, in a standing position; but if, as sometimes happens, the survivors do not trouble themselves to dig a large hole, the body is bent and placed in any position that may be most convenient. It is said that the True Caribs were in the habit of cleaning and preserving the bones of their dead relations in their houses; but they certainly no longer do this. Various properties of the deceased are put into the grave. Schomburgk mentions a curious case of a man who had been, or was supposed to have been, murdered, into whose grave a cord was put with which he might bind his murderer should he meet him on the further side of the grave. It is to be feared that the respect for the grave has now diminished; for, if the hammock in which the body is wrapped happens to be new and good, it is now not unfrequently withdrawn from the body. The grave is then filled in.

Fire is then made over the grave; a feast is celebrated, with dancing, drinking, and singing of songs in which the good qualities of the deceased are lamented; and the house is then deserted for ever. To this practice is chiefly due the great number of deserted and ruined Indian houses which are to be seen in the forest tract. That the forest Indians always do this, while those of the savannah occasionally shirk the ceremony, is probably due to the fact that the houses of the former, unlike those on the savannah, are so slightly built that but little provocation is sufficient to induce their owners to desert them and build anew.

But wherever the body is buried, the grave, when once covered with earth, is regarded as sacred, and no Indian— unless it be some vile kenaima, whose reason for body-snatching will presently be explained—ventures to disturb it.

The bodies of peaimen—at least among the Macusis—

are disposed of in a somewhat different manner. Their graves are dug not in the nearest convenient spot, but on a special hill, of somewhat peculiar shape, and well-wooded, which stands isolated on the savannah in front of the northern face of the Canakoo mountains. The Macusis of the village of Karenacroo, on the Roopoonooni savannah, have a special place for burying their dead; but this seems quite an exceptional instance.

CHAPTER XI.

HUNTING AND FISHING.

THE Indians of Guiana, with many other tribes, have been put into a class, and labelled as 'the hunting tribes of South America.' The name is, however, misleading, at least as far as the Indians of Guiana are concerned; for these tribes live as much by a rude, but not unproductive, kind of agriculture as by hunting. Probably their lives are supported in about equal degree by the produce of their fields and by their gains in the chase. An opportunity will be found in another chapter to describe their agriculture; at present their methods of capturing fish and game will be told.

Hunting is the most important occupation in the life of an Indian man. In the very simple system of life followed by these people, food may be said to be the chief thing for which they have to exert themselves. Their wants in the way of clothing and shelter are very easily satisfied. Only food has incessantly to be provided. The women, with but very little help from the men, gain part of this by cultivating certain plants, especially cassava, and the men contribute their share by hunting. So important to them is this latter, that an Indian takes rank in his village or settlement according to his skill in the chase; and even the boys, as soon as they are no more than mere babies, have no other toys than small bows and arrows and such mimic weapons of the chase, which become bigger and bigger, more like the real things, as the boy grows older. Every boy, almost as soon as he can walk, can send his arrow into a frog ; a little later, lizards are his aim ; and again a little later, small birds.

Hunting is not, however, a constant occupation. The Indian leaves his home and spends many days hunting in the forests or on the savannahs, or fishing on the rivers ; but when he returns he spends many days almost incessantly in his hammock, until, in fact, he and his family have consumed the produce of his chase.

He never goes on these expeditions alone. He is too timid, and fearful of the attacks of enemies. If he fails to induce another man to accompany him, he takes his wife, his mother, or even a child, who, if unable to do anything else, at least supply a second pair of eyes to watch the approach of danger. Often, however, hunting parties, especially when the object sought is fish, consist of a large number of individuals.

Before an Indian sets out to hunt, he goes through one or more strange performances to ensure success. Round his house he has planted various sorts of 'beenas'[1] or plants, generally caladiums, which he supposes to act as charms to make the capture of game certain. These are for his dogs, which are made to swallow pieces of the roots and leaves. Sometimes the poor brutes have to undergo more painful operations. For example, two holes are dug in the ground, and by pushing a stick from one to the other of these, and then withdrawing this, a tunnel or covered passage is made between the two holes. A fire, in which parings of the hoofs of tapirs and other animal substances are burned, is then kindled in one hole ; ants and wasps are also put into this hole, and it is then covered over with sticks and earth. The ammoniacal smoke from the burning hoofs, the ants and the marabuntas of course pass through the tunnel into the

---

[1] 'Beenas' is the Carib word. I do not know the equivalent in the other languages.

second hole. The poor dog is then caught, and its head is
held down in this second hole, until the
animal sometimes drops senseless from
pain. Or, probably when there is less time
to spare, ants and other insects are, without other preparation, made to bite the
nostrils of the dog. But the Indian, cruel
to his dog, does not spare himself in his
desire to ensure successful sport. At some
previous time he has woven a number of
strings of fibre, called *emnaki*, each a yard
and a half long, or more, and tapering
from a very small point at one end to a
considerable thickness at the other end,
where the fibres hang loosely in a bunch
(Fig. 7). He now takes one of these strings,
and passing the thin end up his nostril,
manages to bring it out through his
mouth, and thus pulls the whole length of
the string in at the nostril and out at the
mouth. To judge by appearance this must
be a most painful operation.   Or he takes
a small mat, about six or eight inches
square, made of narrow parallel strips of
the skin of a reed-like plant (*Ischnosiphon*), tied together somewhat as are the
laths of a venetian blind (Fig. 8, p. 230).
Between each two of these strips he inserts
a row of living ants, their heads all one
way. The strips are exactly at such a distance apart that the ants when once inserted cannot extricate themselves. The
huntsman then presses the whole mat, on
the side on which are the heads of the
ants, against his own chest ; and the ants,
which are of a large and venomous kind,
bite most painfully. Or, in other cases,

FIG. 7.

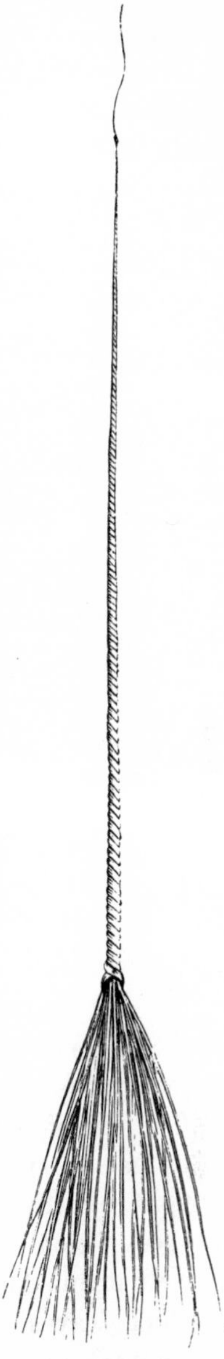

NOSE BEENA.

the huntsman looks for certain large and very hairy caterpillars, the hairs of which break off very readily and have a
great power of irritating flesh. These caterpillars he rubs on
his chest or thighs, and thus produces a considerable and very
painful-looking rash. I have seen all these means of torture
employed by Macusis, Arecunas, and Ackawoi, either on themselves or on their dogs ; and, though I have had no experience,

FIG. 8.

ANT BEENA.

I have little doubt that these or similar methods are employed by the other tribes also.

The use of beenas is very curious. The avowed purpose
is, as has been said, to ensure success. But the line of
thought by which the hunter mentally connects success in
the acquisition of game with pain previously inflicted on
himself or his dogs is not obvious. For such cases as those
in which leaves or other parts of certain plants are rubbed
into wounds on the noses of the dogs, it seems at first sight

probable that this is done on the supposition that the power of scent in the dogs is thereby improved. But such cannot be the explanation of the other forms of beena which have been described ; and, as the term beena is applied to all the forms indiscriminately, it is probable that there is only one explanation for all the forms. I can only suggest that the custom was adopted with the idea of preparing to meet without flinching any pain or danger that may arise during the chase. Perhaps the matter may be made clear by one or two illustrations drawn from more familiar experiences. A living novelist has made one of his male characters say that among men he has known are some who are very good fellows and friendly, but who are not the sort of men to stand by a friend in an exciting tussle with a tiger. The meaning of this is not that such men are in any way cowards, but that, never having experienced pain, such men flinch involuntarily in moments of danger. Just in the same way, one occasionally sees a man, physically strong and morally brave to an unusual degree, but who, just because of his strength, has never before suffered the pains of illness, flinch and moan when he for the first time becomes ill, far more than another man, really a coward but who is accustomed to such pain, does under similar circumstances. Again, if a man is accidentally burned, he shrinks and shows sign of pain ; but if with full forethought and determination he puts his hand into the flame, he can hold it there for any length of time without flinching even in the least degree. Of course the Indian has not analysed this psychological fact, but yet he knows empirically that by accustoming himself to bear pain voluntarily inflicted, he prepares his nerves to withstand the shock of any pain or danger that may come suddenly. The same reason explains the fearful tortures which, as Catlin has most vividly depicted, North American Indians voluntarily undergo when they put away childish things and become men, and also the similar, but slighter tortures which South Americans inflict on themselves at the same epoch in their lives ; and lastly, the same reason perhaps explains the use which the Indians of Guiana make of beenas on the frequent occasions on which they prepare to hunt.

A word must be said as to the dogs used by Indians in hunting. Indigenous species of dogs exist in America; but our own domestic dog, which is used by the Indians, was, of course, first introduced into America by the Spaniards. The best hunting dogs are, however, said, and apparently with truth, to be cross-bred with one or other of two species of wild dogs (*Canis cancrivorus* and *C. azaræ*). The breed of the Indian dogs is, however, so very mixed, that the parentage is never very evident. Almost every Indian house now swarms with an undue number of miserable-looking curs, most of which are never fed at all, but have to live on the very few scraps of food which they can manage to pick up for themselves. But such dogs as show an aptitude for hunting are treated very differently, and are carefully trained. They are fed with the best food that is to be had. Often they are not allowed to lie on the ground (which generally swarms with jiggers (*Pulex penetrans*) and other noxious vermin), but are tied so that they can stand or lie only on raised platforms of sticks. The best of these hunting dogs—which, like the others, are of no particular breed—are bred by the Tarumas, a remote tribe living near the head waters of the Essequibo, and especially skilful as trainers. Hunting dogs form a regular article of barter, and are very highly valued. A hunting dog, a good gun, and a large canoe are of about equal value in Indian economy. As a rule, each dog is only trained to hunt one sort of game; so that one is a deer-dog, another a labba-dog, and so on. It is said that when one dog hunts various kinds of animals, he gives tongue, when on the scent, differently for each kind of game. When hunting, these dogs are generally turned into the forest on the bank of the river, while the Indian himself remains in his canoe on the water. The game, when once started, is driven by the dogs down to the water, where it is killed by the Indian.

There is a very curious superstition connected with

hunting dogs, that if a pregnant woman eats of the game caught by their means, they will never hunt again.

The variety of game for which the Indian seeks is large. In the forest there are deer, tapir, two kinds of wild hogs or peccaries, labba, acourie and adourie; and there are tortoises. There are also many birds, among which the powis or curassow-bird, maroodie or wild-turkey, and the various species of maam, are especially sought. On the savannahs is another kind of deer, and, in the reeds at the edges of ponds, numbers of ducks of various kinds. In the river are fish and turtles of many sorts; and on the river-banks are small alligators and—though these are not eaten by many of the tribes—water-haas or capybaras.

Let us suppose that the Indian hunting party is ready to start. If fish is sought, these are obtained either by poisoning some creek or side stream, or by shooting them with arrows, by netting, by fish traps, or by hook and line. The first is, however, the chief, as it is the most picturesque, mode of fishing.

A suitable creek or an inlet from a larger river having been chosen, a dam is built across the mouth of this, to prevent the fish which happen to be within the creek from passing back into the main river. Sometimes the dam is made merely by heaping stones and earth; but more often a number of straight stakes are tied together, parallel to each other, as are the laths of a venetian blind, and the palisade thus produced is fastened across the mouth of the stream. Roots, stems, or seeds of plants are then beaten until the fibres are loosened, and these are put into the stream at a point some distance above the dam. The narcotic juices of these particular plants saturate the water, and stupify but do not kill the fish. Along the banks the Indians stand watching. Before long a few tiny fish rise to the surface, gasp, leap out from the water, fall back into the stream, turn on to their backs, and at last float motionless down the stream. Gradually larger and larger fish show similar signs of discomfort. They dart quickly down the stream, trying

to escape out of the poisonous water which surrounds them ;
then, checked by the dam, they turn, struggle violently, and
in a little while they too float motionless on the water. If
there are many fish in the creek, the water gradually becomes white with their up-turned sides. Meanwhile, the
Indians on the bank busy themselves in shooting such of the
large fish as might in their struggles escape over the dam,
and in collecting those which are already motionless. Very
large quantities of fish are often procured in this way, and
these, in spite of the poison, are in no way unfit for food.
Of the small fish which are left in the water, the very
smallest die, but the others after a time recover from their
stupor, and remain to restock the stream.

The fish-poisons most generally used are the roots of the
haiari (*Lonchocarpus densiflorus*), the seeds of the connami
(*Clibadium asperum*. Dec). Less common poisons are the
haiari-balli of the Arawaks (*Mullera moniliformis*), and
the yarro-conalli of the Macusis (*Tephrosia toxicaria*), and
many others.

Another method of procuring fish is perhaps best mentioned here. When the rivers sink, fish are sometimes
naturally left, without possibility of escape, in the pools ;
and sometimes when this is not the case the Indians
enclose part of a stream or river by dams. In either case
the water is baled out in hollow gourds until the fish, struggling and panting at the bottom, can be seized by the hand.

Far greater skill is required to shoot fish with arrows;
indeed, the skill with which the Indian in this way pierces
his prey, often hardly visible through the water, is most surprising. The arrows used for this purpose differ—partly
according to the circumstances under which they are to be
used, partly according to the tribe by which they are used.
The most important of these is the harpoon-arrow (Fig. 9 *a*),
which is used almost exclusively by the True Caribs to shoot
one particular kind of fish, which frequents the rushing
water of cataracts or rapids. In this, one end of a long
string or line is fixed to the head of the arrow, into which

the shaft is only very
loosely inserted, and this
line is again attached, at
about half-way along its
length, to the shaft, and
finally, at its extreme end,
to the arm of the shooter.
The result of this arrangement is that the head of
the arrow when it hits the
fish becomes detached from
the shaft, which floats on
top of the water while the
line connects the arrow-
head in the fish, the floating shaft, and the wrist of
the shooter.

The harpoon-arrows are
used principally for shooting pacu. This fish (*Pacu
myletes*) abounds at all
seasons of the year in most
of the large rivers of
Guiana. When the river is
high and the water is tur-
bid with rain, the pacu are
distributed equally in all
parts of the rivers, and are
almost invisible. When,
however, in the dry season,
the river is low and the
water clear, when the rocks
which form the rapids are
partially uncovered, and
the 'pacu-grass,' a small
water-plant (*Lacis*), which
clothes these rocks, comes

FIG. 9.

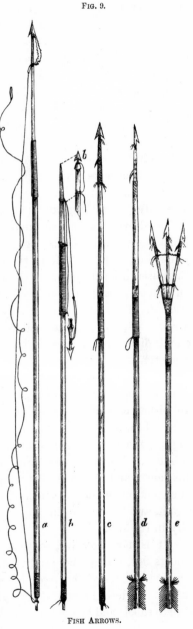

FISH ARROWS.

into flower, then the pacu collect at these falls to feed on
the leaves. Large numbers of Indians then camp at the
sides of the falls to shoot these fish. Such a scene is highly
picturesque. The place is generally a wide extent of river-
bed, apparently enclosed by the forested banks, and entirely
occupied by a curious confusion of rocks and white rushing
water. On a rock in the midst of, and almost covered by,
the tumbling water, stands an Indian, his feet crushing the
delicate, star-shaped, pink flowers of the *Lacis*, and every
muscle in his naked cinnamon-coloured body bearing witness
to the intentness of his watch. His bow is half drawn; the
arrow is in position, but its point rests idly on the rocks.
The water is rushing and tumbling so wildly that an unpractised eye can see nothing below its surface. But the
Indian sees. Quickly the bow is raised, aim is taken, the
arrow flies, and its shaft is there, dancing and tumbling in
the water, carried here and there by the terrified rushes of
an unseen pacu, in the body of which the arrow-head is embedded. But the line not only connects arrow-head and
arrow-shaft, but its other end is held firmly in the hands of
the Indian, who now easily hauls the fish on to the rock.
Sometimes, instead of waiting on a rock, in his eagerness he
stands waiting in the midst of the almost overwhelming
rush of the water, stooping, the better to resist its force.
In either case, if he is skilful, he gets a large number of
fish. I have seen fifteen pacu, averaging about seven or
eight pounds in weight, shot by one man in about twenty
minutes. When enough have been taken, the Indian loads
his canoe, and returns to his temporary camp. The fish are
then cut open and cleaned, their sides are slit again and
again, salt is rubbed in, and they are put on the rocks to
dry in the sun.

It is not, however, only in the falls that the Indian
shoots fish, though he rarely gets pacu elsewhere. In the
smooth reaches of the river he shoots other fish of various
kinds. Indeed he can almost always and everywhere find
fish to shoot; and he rarely fails to hit them when they are once

seen. Where the water is smooth, two other fish-arrows are used. Of these two, one (see Fig. 9 b, p. 235) differs from the harpoon only in that a short line connects only the head —which in this case also is only slipped on to the shaft—and the shaft, instead of being carried on to the arm of the shooter. The struggles of the fish when hit immediately cause the shaft to slip out of the head ; and the former, which is very long and light, floats on the top of the water, but remains connected with the fish by the line, and so serves as a buoy and mark of the position of the fish. In the second (see Fig. 9 c and d, p. 235), which is used chiefly by the Macusis and other savannah tribes, there is no line, for the head is permanently attached to the shaft.

In all three cases the arrow-head is either doubly, symmetrically, barbed, or has only a single barb on one side, according to the fancy of its owner.

When the river is high, and heavy rain still frequently falls and dulls the colour of the water, so that even the Indian can hardly see the fish under the surface, a stratagem is used. A basket of open wicker-work, filled with the green apple-like fruit of the lana (*Genipa americana*), is thrown into the river and allowed to swim with the stream. Standing in the bow of his canoe or wood-skin, while another man paddles, the Indian follows the floating basket. The lana seems to be a very attractive bait to fish, for they rarely fail to rise to it. As soon as this happens, a rush through the water indicating where the fish is, the arrow flies, and the fish is almost invariably transfixed.

Another form of fish-arrow (see Fig. 9 e, p. 235), used principally for shooting small fish in the shallows left by the falling river, ends, trident-like, in three singly barbed prongs, each of which is several inches in length. Fish of larger size which have resorted to the shallow waters to spawn are also a favourite aim for these arrows. Fish-roes are a great delicacy to the Indians, who in the spawning-season shoot an immense number of heavy fish, the bodies of which are of little account when the roes have been extracted. The

roes are then smoked; and in this state large baskets of
them may often be seen in their houses.

A store of hooks and lines for barter is almost necessary
to a traveller.   Whether this mode of fishing has or has not
been learned from Europeans, it is now frequently practised.
Most beautifully finished hooks of large size (2–4 inch) are
even sometimes made by the Indians themselves.   These
large hooks are used for such gigantic fish as the low-low
(*Silurus*, sp?), sometimes from ten to twelve feet long, and
the aropaima (*Sudis gigas*), which often attain a length of
eight or ten feet.   One fish, the haimara (*Erythrinus*),
which frequents certain parts of the river, is generally
caught with a hook attached to a short line and a spring rod.
The whole apparatus is fastened on some rock and left overnight.   Where haimara abound the rocks may occasionally
be seen covered with a thicket of old rods.   The bait used
in fishing with hook and line is sometimes a piece of meat,
but more often the seed of some plant.   Indians are perfectly aware that fish gather in large numbers in water over
which hang certain trees and other plants, at the time when
the ripe fruit drops, to eat the seeds.   For instance, one
tree thus attractive to fish is the Hatie ' india-rubber ' plant
(*Hevea Spruceana*), and among creepers may be mentioned
Smilax cayannensis.   Acting on this knowledge the Indians
use the seeds of this and other plants similarly attractive
as bait on their hooks.   Small hooks are in great request
among Indian children, and are used also by the Arecunas,
who live on the savannahs about Roraima, often far from any
but very small streams, and who are consequently obliged to
content themselves with very small fish.

In these small streams are shoals of fish a few inches in
length.   To catch these the Arecunas use two methods
which are apparently not in general use among the other
Indians.   Sometimes they catch them in nets made like
landing-nets, the hoop being made of a pliant piece of wood
or strip of bark; sometimes in small wicker-work traps, not
unlike English eel-baskets in principle.

Less legitimate, but far more dexterous, was the occasional fishing of a Macusi Indian who was with me on the Roopoonooni; and who, when the canoe was near the bank, used to watch for a particular kind of fish, and as soon as one appeared, would dive from the canoe, chase the fish to the bank, drive it into some hole there, seize it with his hands, and then bring it up.

Turtles and iguana lizards are also often shot by the Indians. A special arrow (Fig. 10), with a small, but very strong head, only slipped on to the shaft with which it is connected by a long line wound round the shaft, is used for shooting turtle. The Indian aims not directly at the turtle, but up into the air, in such a way that the arrow in its descent hits the animal with wonderful precision, and, gathering force in its fall, pierces the shell. The turtle immediately dives. The shaft of the arrow slips out of the head, the line which connects shaft and head unwinds, and the former floats on top of the water. By the line, thus buoyed by the shaft, the turtle is readily drawn into the canoe. The Indian, having learned the tenacity of life of these creatures, generally has a turtle-pen near his house, where he keeps a living stock for use.

The iguanas, climbing up the bushes overhanging the edges of the river, lie sunning themselves on the highest branches. In this position they can hardly be detected by an unpractised eye. But the Indian, passing in his canoe, keeps his eye fixed on the banks. The cry of 'waiamucka,' the Carib name for the animal, is one of the most frequent interruptions to the water journey. As soon as it is heard, the surest shot among the Indians seizes his bow and arrow—by preference an arrow pointed with bone—and shoots. Sometimes the creature drops unhurt, or but slightly touched, into the water, and

FIG. 10.

f

TURTLE ARROW

there easily escapes among the mass of roots and dipping branches; sometimes it falls, transfixed by the arrow; but most often, if badly wounded, it remains motionless on the branch, and the Indian has to climb for it. To seize it, if it is not dead, is dangerous work; for the iguana can give a very bad bite. When once seized by the back of the neck, a few blows with a stick or cutlass put an end to its struggles.

Hunting for game is quite as important to the Indians as fishing. For this purpose, he now as often as not takes a gun, instead of the bow and arrows or the blow-pipe which are his own proper weapons. The ambition of almost every Indian is to obtain sufficient money, or goods exchangeable with white men, to buy a gun. For this purpose he will undergo far more labour than he will endure for any other end, and will travel almost any distance. Large numbers of very inferior guns are imported into the colony to meet this demand, and are sold at a retail price of from one to two pounds. The chief point to which an Indian looks to in choosing his gun is its length. The longer the barrel is, the better he is pleased. The reason for this seems to be that an Indian, in order to make sure of his game, likes to make as big a hole in it as possible. He therefore not only stealthily approaches bird or beast, until the muzzle of his gun almost touches the body of the animal, before he fires, but he likes a very large gun in order that the whole mass of the shot may enter unscattered. Owing to this circumstance, of a bunch of ten or twelve pigeons, which were shot and brought to me on one occasion by an Indian, scarcely a shred of flesh was left on the breast of any one. Another somewhat remarkable thing, and one of which I can offer no explanation, is that as soon as a gun is his, the Indian takes off and throws away the cap of the screw-worm at the end of the ramrod.

But we are more concerned with the Indian's own weapons. These are bow and arrows and the blow-pipe.

The arrows used for shooting game, as for fish, are of

several kinds. For big game, such as bush-hog and deer, the Indian uses an arrow with a diamond-shaped head, like that of a spear, but occasionally somewhat varied in detail of shape, and of very various sizes. (Fig. 11, *g*, *i*, *j*, and *k*.) These spear-headed arrows are used by most of the tribes ; but they seem more common among the Caribs and Ackawoi—i.e. the coast Caribs—than among the Macusi and Arecunas, the savannah Caribs. All the arrows, whether intended for fish or for game, which have at present been mentioned, are now filed by the Indian out of a piece of the iron hoop of a barrel, or of any other old metal on which he can lay hands. Formerly, and not so very long ago, they were probably made of the bones of turtle or other animals, of the shells of certain molluscs, or of stone. A True Carib, of about forty years of age, who served as captain during several of my expeditions, has often assured me that as a boy he used to see these bone, shell, or stone-pointed arrows in common use. He himself still uses a bone-pointed arrow for a special purpose. I first questioned him on the subject when I saw him fashioning a piece of bone into

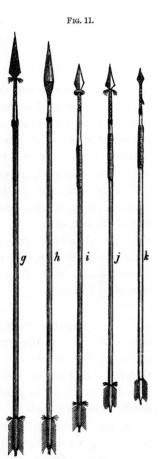

FIG. 11.

g   *h*   *i*   *j*   *k*

GAME ARROWS.

an arrow-head ; and he told me that this was to shoot iguanas (*Iguana tuberculata*), and that bone arrows are especially adapted for that purpose. On one occasion I saw similar arrows, headed with stone, in the possession of some Arecunas.

It is to be noted that all the arrows which yet remain to be mentioned are tipped, not with iron, but with wood.

To return to the subject of game-arrows : the savannah tribes, instead of the iron diamond-headed arrows, for big game use arrows (Fig. 11 *h*, p. 241) with very long lance-shaped heads made of a bamboo called by the Indians ' rappoo.' This bamboo—which only grows in a few places—is cut and carefully dried. The arrow-head is then shaped, and is hardened in the fire ; when fixed into the reed shaft, it is ready for use, and is supposed to possess poisonous qualities. The Indians assert that these arrows are as poisonous as those smeared with the deadly ourali; and this statement seems confirmed by Richard Schomburgk and by C. B. Brown. The latter tells the story of a peccary hunt, during which he saw one of these animals, when struck by a rappoo arrow, stand still, apparently paralysed, for a time, and then fall dead. Wishing to try the experiment, I have more than once caused one of these arrows to be shot gently into a fowl, so that it entered only a very little way and not in a vital part. The fowls were certainly, and naturally, frightened, but showed no more fatal signs than would have been the case if the wound had been made by the most harmless splinter of wood or other weapon. When I pointed this out to the Indians who were standing round, they explained that the poison only took effect if the arrow went in far enough ; that is, probably, if it touched some vital spot. I think, therefore, that the poisonous character attributed to this bamboo-wood may be considered as doubtful, until more accurate experiments have been made.

A far more deadly weapon, used also by the savannah tribes, sometimes for animals, sometimes for birds, is the ourali arrow. The points (Fig. 13, *pp* and *ppp*), which are long, narrow, and flat strips of light wood, smeared with a vegetable poison called ourali, more or less jagged according to the purpose for which they are intended, are inserted in the socket at the end of the reed shaft (Fig. 12 *b*). These points are either carried separately from the shaft, in a small

quiver (Fig. 13 *s*) made of hollow bamboo, and are only inserted in the shaft the moment before the arrow is to be
used; or, if they are carried in the shaft they are covered
with a sheath of hollow bamboo (Fig. 12 *d*).   In either case,

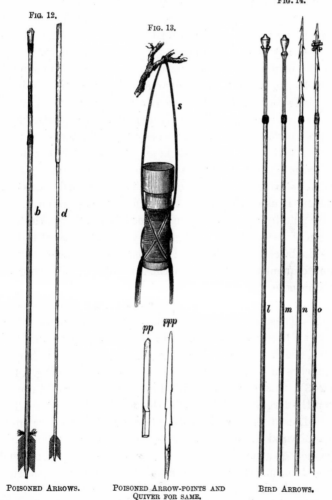

FIG. 12.

FIG. 13.

FIG. 14.

POISONED ARROWS.

POISONED ARROW-POINTS AND
QUIVER FOR SAME.

BIRD ARROWS.

whether the points are carried separately or whether they are
protected by a sheath, the object of the precaution is to protect the hand of the Indian from any chance of contact with

the deadly poison with which the points are smeared. In
another place I shall have occasion to speak of the making of
this ourali poison, which is used both for these arrows and
for the darts of the blow-pipe ; for the present it is sufficient
to say that it is a vegetable substance prepared by the Indians
themselves, and especially by the Macusis ; and that its effect
is gradually to diminish, and finally to stop, the action of the
heart of any animal into the blood of which it enters.

The points of these arrows are of two forms : the stouter
(Fig. 13 *pp*, p. 243), with only one or two notches, is used
especially for ' baboons '—i.e. red howling monkeys (*Mycetes
seniculus*), and for other monkeys; the more slender (Fig.
13 *ppp*, p. 243), with many notches, is used for birds. A very
slender variety of the latter kind, smeared with but little
poison, is also used for such birds and small animals as are
not to be eaten, but to be tamed. Whether in such cases any
antidote is used to counteract the effects of the poison, I was
never able to learn ; but I am inclined to think that the real
reason of recovery (for though many animals treated in this
way doubtless die, a few live) is that there is only a very
minute quantity of poison on the arrow used in shooting for
this purpose.

Four varieties of unpoisoned arrows are also used for
birds. These may be conveniently described in pairs. The
first pair are those used chiefly by the savannah Indians. Of
these, one has a round tapering wooden point, often five or
six inches in length, armed with several notches (Fig. 14 *n*,
p. 243); this, when shot with force, will penetrate through
even the largest bird found in the forests of Guiana. The
second, used for smaller birds, differs only in that four small
slips of wood are fastened, cross-wise, round the point, at a
distance of about a quarter of an inch from the sharp end
(Fig. 14 *o*, p. 243) ; these prevent the arrow from entering
too far into the bird.

The second pair differ from each other but slightly, and
are used respectively by the Arawaks and the True Caribs
(Fig. 14 *l*, *m*, p. 243). Both end not in a point of any sort,
but in a large wooden knob. The creole children on the coast

imitate these arrows by fixing an empty cotton-reel at the end of the shaft of an ordinary arrow, and the imitation is very close. These arrows are intended to knock birds down, not by entering and wounding them, but by stunning them. The slight difference between the two forms used by the Arawaks and True Caribs respectively is merely in the form of the fore-shaft and the blunt head.[1]

The blow-pipe is, I believe, peculiar among the Indians of Guiana to the savannah tribes, and on the rare occasions in which it is found in the possession of the forest tribes, the fact is probably only due to the chance acquisition of the weapon by some idiosyncratic Indian. It is, however, common to many other tribes of South America. The Macusis, Arecunas, and other savannah tribes of the Carib family probably found the weapon in use among the tribes formerly inhabiting the territory now occupied by them, and themselves adopted it; while the True Caribs and Ackawoi, the coast tribes of the Carib family, with the Warraus and Arawaks, having been but little in the interior, were not brought in contact with the original users of this weapon, and so never adopted it.

[1] The following list of the various arrows—some of which occur in several slight varieties—which are used in so small a district as British Guiana, may not be without interest to the ethnologist.

No.	Description	Purpose	Used by	Name
1.	harpoon		True Caribs (only ?)	'Harrapoona' (Carib) [1]
2.	with loose head	Fish	All forest tribes	Sawoto (Carib) / Atoom (Arawak ?)
3.	with fixed head		Savannah tribes	Takooya (Carib)
4.	with three prongs	Small fish	All tribes (?)	Samoroo (Carib) / Sarapa (Arawak ?)
5.	with loose head attached by long string to shaft	Turtles	All tribes	Pooya (Carib) / Waibacash (Arawak ?)
6.	spear-headed iron	Game	Forest tribes	Tefoking (Carib ?) [2] / Sebrali (Wapiana ?) [2] / Siparara (Arawak ?) [2]
7.	„ bone	„ especially Iguana	True Caribs (now rare)	
8.	„ stone	Game	Arecuna (now rare)	
9.	lance-head of bamboo	„	Savannah tribes	Rappoo (Carib)
10.	poisoned (fixed head)	„ and birds	„ „	Ourali-eboo (Carib)
11.	„ (loose head)	Monkeys	„ „	„ „
12.	„ „	Birds	„ „	„ „
13.	unpoisoned wooden point	„	Forest & savannah tribes	Tarau (Macusi)
14.	„ (with guard)	Small birds	Savannah tribes	Toommarai (Macusi)
15.	with blunt head	Birds	Arawaks	Marowa (Arawak)
16.	„ „	„	True Caribs	

[1] The name is evidently European.

I am inclined to think that distinct varieties of this arrow exist under different names; e.g. the tefoking and the sebrali are not quite the same.

These blow-pipes (Fig. 16) are tubes of very great length, often from 12 to 16 feet or more, through which a small dart (Fig. 25, p. 302) is blown. The manner of manufacture of both tube and dart will be afterwards explained. When setting out to shoot with this weapon, the Indian takes not only the tube, but also a quiver (Fig. 15 *A*) containing a large number of darts—sharply pointed splinters of wood, five or six inches in length, each tipped with ourali—and the jaw-

FIG. 15.

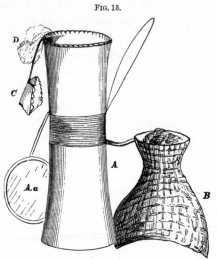

QUIVER FOR DARTS OF BLOW-PIPE.

bone of a perai-fish (Fig. 15 *c*) (*Serasalmo nigra*), and also a small basket (Fig. 15 *B*) filled with the natural fibre of cotton or of some other plant. The fibre of the silk-cotton tree (*Eriodendron*) is often used for this purpose. When game is seen, one of the darts is placed between two of the sharp teeth of the perai, and is twisted sharply round in such a way that a very small portion of the point is almost, but not quite severed from the main part; this is in order that the point may break off in the body of the animal, that the dart may again be used. A little of the fibre is then wound round the other end of the dart—i.e. the dart is 'feathered'—care being taken not to destroy the balance. The dart is then inserted in the blow-pipe, aim is taken, the dart is blown, and the bird almost invariably falls. The certainty with which an Indian can take aim with these hugely long weapons, even when supported by only one hand, is really wonderful. The range of the weapon is as much as from forty to fifty feet.

For its special purpose the blow-pipe is much superior to the gun. The best way of getting a heavy bag of birds with it is to find some tree the fruit of which is attracting large numbers of birds to feed. If the birds sought are parrots, it is especially easy for an Indian with a practised ear to discover such a tree. As he walks through the forest he hears a sound like the fall of heavy rain-drops. Parrots feed in a very wasteful way; the flock flies screaming to a tree, and then each bird silently begins to pick the fruit, and after once biting each fruit lets it fall. Thus a constant shower of the fruit falls from the tree on to the dry leaves on the ground. In this way, though they do not scream while actually feeding, parrots betray their presence. The Indian, as soon as he hears this sound, creeps stealthily up to the tree, and aims his blow-pipe at the bird lowest on the tree. When this falls the rest of the flock are not much alarmed; seeing one of their number suddenly disappear, they perhaps cease feeding for an instant and chatter, but, hearing no noise, they turn again to the fruit. In this way the Indian can bring down a very large number of birds before the flock is really alarmed, and, rising, flies screaming away; whereas with bow and arrow he could, owing to the twang of the bowstring, get but few shots, and with a gun he could get but one.

Much of the Indians' success in killing both birds and beasts is due to their wonderful skill in

FIG. 16.

9 Feet

BLOW-PIPE.

calling birds—in imitating, that is, the note of any bird which they think may be in the neighbourhood, and so attracting them to their destruction. The Indian name for a bird is almost always an imitation of its cry. This Indian habit of mimicry was well illustrated on one occasion, when two of my Indians started from our camp in two directions to shoot a maam (*Tinamus*), neither knowing that the other was going. Presently one, hearing the cry of a maam some distance on his right, began to imitate it to draw the bird nearer. The other heard a maam cry on his left, and he too began to imitate it. Each mistook the cry of the other for that of a real bird, and the two continued calling each other and drawing nearer through the thick bush, until they met ; each, thinking that he was just about to see his bird, found the other had mimicked the cry of the maam only too well. They came back to camp in very bad temper.

From what has been said it will be sufficiently evident that the objects for which the Indian hunts or fishes are many and various ; and it is very rarely that he is unsuccessful. It is, however, noticeable that the Indian can generally hunt successfully only in a district which he knows, and that Indians in travelling through a strange country seldom attempt to hunt, and when they do, meet with but small success. As the provisions which he thus gets have to be carried home, often a journey of some days, and as even after that they have to last for some time, the meat and most of the fish is smoked or babracoted ; the rest of the fish is salted, as has already been described in the case of the pacu shot in the falls. A babracot is a stage of green sticks, built over a fire, on which the meat is laid and exposed for a long time to the action of the smoke. Meat, fish, and even eggs treated in this way become very tasteless, but retain their nutritive powers for a long while, and may either be eaten without further preparation or may be further cooked.

Land tortoises being very common in the forest, the Indian collects these, slings them with a piece of bush-rope across his shoulders, and so carries them home alive. Sometimes also he carries with him one or two of the round, porcelain-like eggs of these tortoises. In the open savannah country, where such a signal may be seen from a long distance, the hunters, when yet far from home, make a big fire, as a signal to announce their coming to their women-kind at home, that due preparation in the shape of a large amount of bread and drink may be prepared. At last they arrive at home, deliver over the meat into the hands of the women, and sink into their hammocks to rest for several days.

CHAPTER XII.

AGRICULTURE.

An Indian Field—Method of Cultivation—Cassava—Abandonment of Field—Maize in the Mountains—Drought and Famine.

THE Indians living in the forest use the clearings in which their houses stand as chief provision fields; but even they generally have one or more other fields at favourable spots in the neighbouring forest. The fields of the savannah Indians are, on the contrary, almost invariably at some considerable distance, often indeed very far from their houses; for the ground round the houses is unshaded, stony, and unproductive, and it is only in the moist and shady coppices that provisions flourish.

One only uses the word 'field' of the spots cultivated by the Indians in default of a more apt term. A stranger on first seeing an Indian field, with its surrounding wall of natural forest, might well think it a place no longer cultivated, but some former clearing in the forest in which the natural growth had once more sprung up unchecked. The cassava and other cultivated plants are lost among the bushy off-shoots which have sprung from the stumps of felled trees, the trunks and branches of which lie just where they fell among the tangled growth. The bark has fallen from some of these trunks, and their white wood glistens in the sun; others are blackened and charred by fire; others again have retained their bark, as on the day they fell. Often, among all this, it is almost impossible to discern the narrow foot-trodden track which, winding in and out among the fallen trunks and the cassava plants, leads through the field.

This is how the field was made. A fitting place having

been chosen—cassava, the main object of cultivation, flourishes best in sandy soil—the men cut down the undergrowth and fell the trees. Then, when it seems likely that
the weather will be dry, they set fire to the fallen refuse.
The leaves and smaller branches of the trees, together with
the cut and now withered undergrowth, slowly burn; but
the tree-trunks and the larger branches are only more or less
charred. The fire smoulders long, often for many days; and
when at last it dies out, there is an open space in the forest,
floored with hot white ashes, and empty but for prostrate
trunks, the crooked branches of which stand up into the air,
and but for any palms which may have been there—for these
are always allowed to stand if they are of a kind with edible
fruit. The men have now finished their share of the work.

At the beginning of the following wet season the women
come, guarded, if the field is far from home, against sudden
attacks of jaguars or snakes by a few wretchedly lean dogs,
and carrying on their backs baskets heavy with a load of
cassava sticks to be used as cuttings. Here and there, at
somewhat irregular intervals, they loosen small patches of
the soil, hardly more than a foot in diameter, and in each of
these they insert three or four cassava sticks. The field is
then virtually formed.

From time to time, while the cassava is growing, the
women do just so much weeding as is absolutely necessary to
prevent the cultivated plants from being choked by the wild
growths which spring up side by side with them; and while
so doing, pine-tops, banana, and plaintain suckers, pumpkin
and water-melon seeds, yams, sweet potatoes, sugar-cane,
papaws, cashews, tobacco, and, above all, red and yellow
podded peppers (*Capsicums*) are planted wherever there is
space.

During the ten months which generally pass before the
cassava reaches maturity, not only shoots from the wild
plants which formerly occupied the ground, but also those
creepers and other plants which in this, even more than in
most other climates, are never seen while the land is left in

a natural state, but always appear wherever man makes a
clearing, spring up with new and surprising vigour. Of
these weeds which infest Indian fields, first the razor-grass
(*Scleria scindens*) throws its endless stems and grass-like
leaves, stems and leaves alike as keenly edged as knives,
over the cassava and other plants, and then, having overrun
the clearing, flings itself up on to the trees which edge the
surrounding forest and, finding no yet higher thing to which to
reach, hangs its tangled ends like a curtain from branch and
bush.   Passion-flowers send out long tendrils, which creep
along the ground and up on to the bushes, where they hang
their flowers, according to their kind, some large and purple, others crimson, others white (*Passiflora laurifolia*),
and one (*P. fœtida*) the small pale-coloured petals of which,
buried in large moss-like green sepals, remind one of a
flower common in old-fashioned English gardens, called
with quaint variety 'Love-in-a-mist' and 'Devil-in-a-bush'
(*Nigella damascena*).   Various kinds of pea-flowers and convolvulus add to the confusion.   Before long, the hollow and
straight stems of the trumpet-wood (*Cecropia peltata*), each
crowned with a single rosette of a few big maple-shaped
leaves, rise over everything, and with marvellous rapidity
reach a height of from twenty to thirty feet.

     At last, in the ninth or tenth month, seeds appear among
the hemp-like leaves at the ends of the straggling branches
of the cassava plants.   This is a sign that the roots are ready
for use.   Again the work is done by the women.   They cut
down the cassava and the weed-bush, and dig up the roots,
not all at once, but as they are required.   Some short straight
lengths of the stems of the cassava—sufficient to reproduce
the number of plants which have been dug up—are cut and
inserted in the ground as before, and in the same spots.   By
the way, an old Indian tradition tells that when cassava was
first given to the Indians, after their first appearance upon
earth, they knew not how to make it reproduce itself; when
they tried to sow the seeds or to plant the tubers, it always failed to grow; but, just as the stock was dying out,

it was discovered by chance that cuttings of the plant, if stuck into the ground, grew. So this method of propagation has been followed ever since.

The field is deserted after three or four crops have been taken from it; and a new clearing is made and planted. The reason of this periodical desertion of the old, and clearing of new ground is uncertain, but it is perhaps connected with some superstition. But so little trouble is, indeed, involved in this sort of cultivation, that a field is often deserted in consequence of a mere whim, often before even the first crop has been gathered. In one instance, a very flourishing field of cassava in the Canakoo Mountains had been deserted, its owners refusing even to approach it, because kenaimas —mysterious murderers, half human, half supernatural— had been heard near it.

The produce of these fields is of the finest quality. This is especially the case in the Pacaraima and Canakoo Mountains, and generally on the savannah, where the plantains and the sugar-canes especially attain a size far greater than in the coast lands. In the sandstone mountains about Roraima maize is more abundantly cultivated than cassava, the Indians affirming that the latter plant does not flourish well in that district.

As the life and prosperity of the Indians depend so much on the produce of their fields, it may not be without interest to tell what becomes of these people when their crops fail. This happens, sometimes, owing to the improvidence of the Indians, who use their cassava freely, so long as it lasts, not only for making bread but even for making paiwari, without any regard to the quantity left; sometimes in consequence of prolonged drought.

The failure from the first of these two causes is met by the habit of mutual hospitality which prevails among the Indians. When a family finds its stock of cassava exhausted, the goods are packed up, and all walk to some other settlement, inhabited by Indians of the same tribe in whose fields there is still plenty. Without invitation, and without excuses, the strangers take up their quarters in the new settlement, where, as a matter of course, there is a stranger's house ; and it is an understood thing that the present hosts will return the visit when they have need ; and there they live and eat as long as the cassava lasts, or until some one of their own fields is again ripe.

Failure of the crops owing to long-continued drought is far worse in its effects. A very severe famine of this sort prevailed in March and April of 1878 throughout the greater part of the savannah region, where the effects of dry weather are of course far worse than in the damp forest. Gradually the cassava and provisions failed, and the young crops made no advance or even died. Even the hardy savannah plants were withered up and burned. The famine was very great. Most of the settlements and villages were entirely deserted, their inhabitants having wandered away into some damper and more favoured part of the country. Those who remained —chiefly the women who were too old to walk far, the sick, and here and there a family who were inclined to trust to chance—were reduced to skeletons.

CHAPTER XIII.

THE PREPARATION OF FOOD.

Cooking done by Women—Fire-making—Staple Food: Meat chiefly in form of Pepper-pot; Cassava as Bread, Farine, and Paiwari—Effect of Cassava on Indian Physique—Salt—Occasional Food: Eggs, of Birds, seldom eaten; of Reptiles, often; Insects; Fruits—Various Drinks.

THE staple food of Indians includes both animal and vegetable substances. The men provide the former by hunting and fishing; while the women, almost unassisted, provide the latter. As the pursuit of game generally leads the men for several days' journey from home, and as the booty must be at least roughly preserved on the spot, this preliminary operation, by smoking the meat on a babracot or by salting the fish, is done by the hunters. These rough processes, which are not the final cooking of the meat, but are only meant to preserve it till it can be handed over to the women at home, have been described in connection with the methods of hunting. As regards the meat which the Indian consumes during these excursions, when he is naturally without cooking utensils, the method of preparing this is extremely simple. The meat is indeed often eaten just in the half-roasted, half-smoked state in which it is taken off the babracot; or, at most, it is cut into small fragments, which are fastened into a cleft stick and so held or fastened over the fire until they are roasted. All other cooking, not only of the dried meat brought home and of meat procured near enough to the settlement to be cooked while fresh, but also of bread, the only staple vegetable consumed, is done by the women. If by some chance a man is obliged to cook, except so far as is absolutely necessary on an ordinary hunting excursion, and is seen to do so by some other Indian, he feels as much shame as if he had been caught in some unworthy act. For example, on one occasion when we were forced by famine to take cassava roots from an Indian field which we found ownerless, it was with great difficulty that any of my Indian companions, who were all men, were persuaded to make these roots into bread, and those who at last did this were ever after scornfully pointed at as ' old women.' In now discussing the preparation of food, it must be remembered that this, when done at home and under normal conditions, is wholly women's work.

Cooking is perhaps the most frequent occupation of these women. Indians eat not at regular times, but whenever and as often as they feel inclined. Fortunately for the women, no variety of food is demanded. Except on rare occasions, when a very large store of meat has been obtained, pepper-pot and cassava-bread invariably form the meal. All the meat or fish obtained is put, with cassareep and peppers, into a buck-pot and boiled to a thick soup. This pot is never emptied, but more meat is added whenever necessary. This mess is boiled again and again, and is ready for use at a few minutes' notice. A store of cassava-bread is also at hand whenever required; for large quantities are made at each baking. Whenever the men feel hungry, the women bring the pepper-pot, with some cassava on one of the fans which are used for blowing the fire, to the side of the hammock. The men often do not trouble themselves to get out of their hammocks, but simply lean over the sides to eat; at other times they get up and sit on one of the low wooden stools or on one of the turtle-shells which lie about the floor; or they squat before their food with their knees drawn up almost to their heads in the invariable sitting posture of an Indian. The bread having been dipped into the mess in the pot, the sodden piece is bitten off. Very little is eaten at a time; and when the meal is over, the men roll back into their hammocks, and the women fetch away the remains of the food. The women never eat with the men; indeed, as often as not the former take their food out of the pot, while cooking.

First, a word must be said as to the making of fire. Fire has very seldom to be made afresh ; for it is continually kept burning in every house, and even on long canoe-journeys a large piece of smouldering timber is usually carried. Even when walking across the savannah an Indian sometimes carries a firebrand. But sometimes, especially during hunting excursions, it becomes absolutely necessary to make a new fire. This is done either with flint and steel, or rather with jasper and an old knife, or—and there is every reason to believe that this is the original Indian fashion—by friction of two pieces of wood.

It is a well-known fact which has attracted much interest and notice, that uncivilised people all over the world have been, or are still, in the habit of producing fire by the friction of two pieces of wood.[1] Several different kinds of wood are used, but all these have some special fitness for the purpose. That used by the Macusis appears to be from a species of *Apeiba*.[2] That used by the Warraus is cut either from a plant called by them *Yoarno* (*Gaultheria uregon*, Aublet), or from the 'bone' (mid-rib) of the troolie-palm (*Manicaria saccifera*), or from the *Yari-Yari*, or Lancewood tree, or from at least one other tree of unknown name. Two long thin sticks of one of these, when thoroughly dried, are used in the operation. A small pit is dug on the side of one of the sticks close to one end ; and a groove is cut from this pit half-way round the stick (Fig 17, A, p. 258). One end of the second stick having been cut evenly at right angles to the length of the stick, a few inches at the same end are peeled (Fig. 17, B). A knife or flat piece of wood or stone

[1] Much has been written about the source from which men first obtained fire ; and it has been suggested that the first fire originated in the natural friction of two boughs of trees rubbing against each other in a high wind. It is worth mentioning that the West Indian negroes affirm that bamboo stems do often thus make natural fire ; and if anyone will carefully watch a big clump of bamboos in the tropics during a high wind, he will understand that if any plants can really thus cause fire, it is these.

[2] Schomburgk, *Reisen in Britisch Guiana.*

is now placed on the ground. Across this the first stick
is laid so that the pit is uppermost and immediately over
the blade of the knife. The Indian then grasps this stick
with the toes—always very prehensile—of one foot, and thus
holds it steadily in position. The second stick is held at
right angles to the first, the peeled end being in the pit,
the other end between the palms of the operator's hands.
The left hand being held motionless, the right palm is rubbed

FIG. 17.

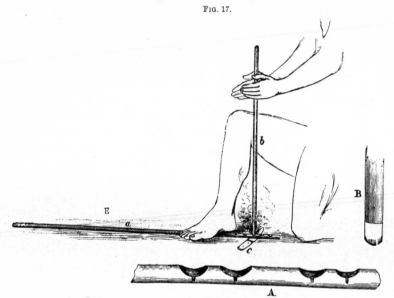

FIRE-STICKS, A AND B, AND METHOD OF USING THE SAME, E.

steadily and somewhat rapidly backwards and forwards against
the left (Fig. 17, E). This of course twirls the upright stick
rapidly round and round in the pit of the other. The friction wears away the sides of the pit and enlarges it. The
groove which passes half round the stick, consequently becomes an open channel through which the dust-like fragments worn away from the inside of the pit fall on to the
knife or board below, where they form a small heap. After
about a quarter of a minute, smoke arises; and at the end of
half a minute the heat within the pit, acting through the

open channel, ignites the little heap of dust. The fire, once ignited, smoulders for about half a minute, during which time it is easily blown into a flame. No great exertion is required in the operation.

These particular woods are chosen for the purpose by the Warraus because of their peculiarly friable grain. The *Apeiba* wood used by the Macusis makes but little of this inflammable dust, so that tinder has to be placed under the stick to catch the fire. The beauty of the Warrau operation consists in the fact that the tinder is formed by the wood itself.

When travelling, the second stick—that which is held upright in the hand—is kept unpeeled ; and each time that it is used only so much is peeled as is necessary for the operation. In this way it is always dry and in a fit state for use.[1]

Even when the spark has been procured, it is difficult, if much rain has lately fallen, to find wood dry enough to make a fire. Under such circumstances the patience of the Indian overcomes the difficulty. He collects fallen wood and carefully strips off with his knife the outer parts of this until he obtains so much of the heartwood (often very little indeed) as is dry. Round the fire thus laboriously made he heaps other wood, and this in time becomes dry and is added as fuel to the fire. Instead of bellows a fan of definite shape, woven of the young leaflets of a palm (*Astrocaryum tucumoides*) is used.

Except the flesh of animals introduced by Europeans, which are always considered unclean, and a very few tabooed indigenous animals, which—different kinds by different tribes—are also considered unclean, all mammals, birds, and fish are meat to the Indian. There is, if we disregard for a moment the rougher method of cooking employed by men

---

[1] It may not be uninteresting to add that, having brought to England sticks which have actually produced fire in Guiana, I utterly failed to rub fire with these here. I believe a similar experience has fallen to the lot of other travellers. Mr. Tylor tells me that the Zulus lately exhibited in London succeeded in rubbing fire, but that the operation took considerably longer than it does in Zululand.

when away from home or without a cooking utensil, but one way of cooking this—whether it is still fresh or has been previously smoked, whether it is meat or fish—and that is, by boiling it down into a sort of thick soup, with peppers (chilis) and cassareep. The nature of this last ingredient will be explained presently ; at present all that need be said is, that it reduces all flesh to one common flavour, its own, and that it has antiseptic qualities which keep meat boiled in it good for a long time. The result of this method of cooking meat is the far-famed pepper-pot, which, first made by the Indians, all settlers in the West Indies have now learned to make and like. The one proper Indian meat dish is therefore pepperpot.

The one staple vegetable food of the Indians is afforded by the roots of the cassava-plant (*Manihot utilissima*), which are made into bread, like oatcakes, by most of the tribes ; into farine, a rough sort of meal, by others. No scene is more characteristic of Indian life than that of the women preparing cassava.

One woman, squatting on her hams, and armed with a big knife, peels off the skin of the cassava roots which lie in a heap at her side. Each root, after being peeled, is washed and then thrown on to a new heap. A little way off, another woman stands and, grasping one of the peeled roots with both hands, scrapes it up and down an oblong board or grater studded with small fragments of stone, and so roughened, like a nutmeg-grater. One end of the grater stands in a trough on the ground, the other rests against the woman's knees. It is violent exercise. As the woman scrapes, her body swings down and up again from her hips. The rhythmic ' swish ' caused by the scraping of the juicy root is the chief sound in the house ; for the labour is too heavy to permit of talking. The cassava, which slips as pulp from the scraper into the trough, is collected and put into a long wicker-woven matapie, which hangs from the roof. This matapie or cassava-squeezer (Fig. 18), is in principle exactly like the not uncommon toy known as a ' Siamese Link.' It is a cylinder, seven or eight feet long and five or six inches in diameter, made of closely woven strips of pliant bark. The upper end is open, and has a loop by which the matapie may be suspended from one of the beams of the house; the lower end is closed, but it also has a loop, the use of which will presently appear. The cassava, saturated with its highly poisonous juice, is now forced into the matapie; through the loop at the bottom of this, a heavy pole is passed, one end of which is allowed to rest on the ground and is there fastened by means of a heavy stone or some such device, while the other is raised into the air. A woman now sits on the raised end of the pole, and her weight stretches the matapie downwards. In proportion as the length of the cylinder increases its diameter is of course reduced. The pressure thus applied to the cassava pulp immediately forces the poisonous juice out through the walls of the matapie. The juice drops down into a buck-pot which stands on the ground; and it is this which when it is afterwards boiled becomes cassareep, a thick, treacle-like liquid, which is no longer poisonous, and the use of which in the manufacture of pepper-pot has already been described. Cassareep when but slightly boiled is sometimes eaten by itself and without further preparation; but if it is meant for pepper-pot it may either be used at once, or, if boiled to a high degree of density, not for some considerable time. The cassava, now dry and free from juice, is taken from the matapie, broken into a sieve (Fig. 20, p. 279), and sifted, so that it becomes a coarse flour. This is either wrapped in leaves and put away for future use, or is at once made into bread.

A large circular iron griddle or plate, of European manufacture, is now placed over the fire; by some of the remote Indians a flat slab of stone is used for this purpose, and there

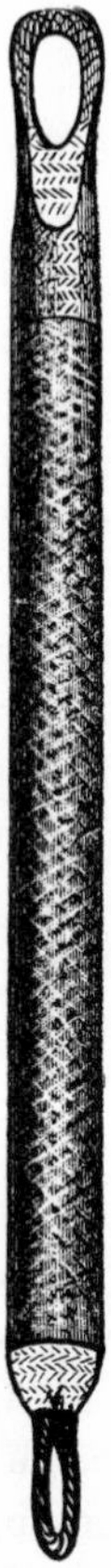

FIG. 18.

CASSAVA
SQUEEZER.

can be little doubt that this stone was originally universally used. On the griddle, whatever its material, a thin layer of the meal is spread. A woman, fan in hand, sits by the fire, watching. With her fan she smooths the upper surface of the cake, and makes its edges round. In a very few minutes one side of the large round white cake is done; and when it has been turned, in yet a couple of minutes the bread is ready. When a sufficient number of these oatcake-like pieces of bread have been made, they are taken out of the house and thrown up on to the roof to dry in the sun. I have often admired, and vainly tried to imitate, the skill with which an Indian woman 'quoits' up these large and thin cakes (which, until they are well sun-dried, are limp and flabby) on to the roof, often high above her head. When thoroughly sun-dried the bread is hard and crisp, with a flavour like that of freshly gathered nuts; in this state, if guarded from damp, it will keep for an indefinite time.

Not quite all the cassava meal, freed from juice by means of the matapie, passes through the sifter—a small residue, consisting of the more starchy matter, adheres together in particles too large to pass through the close-woven wicker-work. This coarse starchy residue, called by the Caribs *Emoo*, which is always small in quantity, is at once made into a cake, which differs from the ordinary cake made of the sifted meal in that, if eaten at once, it has a half-gelatinous consistency, and a pleasant sub-acid flavour; while, if it is allowed to become cold, it acquires a leathery consistency, and is taste-less and uneatable.

Some of the True Caribs slightly diverge from this method of making bread in that they pound the meal in a mortar before sifting it, and, if it is to be kept, they slightly smoke it. The bread thus produced is much more friable and much more easily digestible than that made by the ordinary process.

When cassava is very scarce, its bulk is sometimes increased by mixing the chopped leaves of the cassava plant, or the pounded seed of the mora tree (*Mora excelsa*), or of

the greenheart tree (*Nectandra Rodiœi*), or even pounded
rotten wood, with the meal.

Sometimes, especially by the Arecunas, cakes like those of
cassava are made of maize.

The cassava root is eaten chiefly in the form of bread by
all the tribes except the Wapianas, Atorais, and Tarumas.
These latter tribes make most of their cassava into farine.
It is to be noticed that these tribes live on the frontiers of
Brazil, and that this form of bread-stuff is almost universal
throughout that country.   Up to a certain point the cassava
is prepared as for bread.   The difference is in the baking,
for instead of being allowed to consolidate into an entire
cake, the cassava meal is kept continually stirred as it rests on
the iron griddle, so that in drying it assumes the form of an
accumulation of small dry crumbs of wheaten bread.

Much cassava, after being made into bread, is further
transformed into paiwari, the chief Indian beverage.   Astounding quantities of this are consumed at special drinking
bouts, of which we shall hear more presently.   But paiwari
is also largely used at other times ; and indeed as long as
there is any cassava to be had, a stock of this liquor is
always kept ready.   Whenever the men return from hunting, and whenever a stranger comes into the house, it is
drunk.   And the women and children—even the youngest
babies—drink it.

Cassava bread which is to be transformed into paiwari,
is made as is that for other purposes ; but it is thicker, and
is baked, or rather burned, until it is quite black.   It is
then broken into small fragments, and mixed with water in
a large jar or pot.   The larger fragments are picked out and
chewed by the women, who do this work while moving about
and performing their usual household work ; and the chewed
masses are again replaced in the jar.   As soon as this jar is
sufficiently filled, its contents, after being well stirred, are
slightly boiled, and are then poured into the trough.   More
and more is added to the liquor in the trough until it is full.
The mixture is then allowed to stand for some days, until it

is sufficiently fermented—a process which is said to be much accelerated by the mastication of the bread.[1] Sometimes a little juice of the sugar-cane is added to sweeten the liquor. The result is a brownish liquor—looking like coffee with a great deal of milk in it—with a sub-acid, but not unpleasant taste. Some of the True Caribs, it is said, and some of the Brazilian tribes, manage to prepare paiwari, and to procure a proper degree of fermentation, by simple boiling, without resorting to the very disagreeable but more orthodox chewing process; but paiwari produced in this way is said to be of very inferior flavour.

In some parts of the country, instead of paiwari, both for festivals and for ordinary occasions, a much pleasanter drink is used. This is casiri, which is made of sweet-potatoes and sugar-cane. A little cassava is sometimes added. Generally, though not always, it is prepared simply by boiling the ingredients, and allowing them to ferment. It has a pretty pink colour, due to the sweet-potatoes; and when well made it tastes not unlike thin claret.

To the large proportion which cassava, in the form of bread, or farine, and of paiwari, bears to the rest of the food of the Indians, are probably due two very marked physical peculiarities of these people. Even at first sight, nothing is more striking in the appearance of the Indians than the extraordinary protuberance of their stomachs; and after only brief companionship with them, the European is struck by the rapidity with which Indians—usually so sleek and fat—lose flesh and strength when cassava fails, and as suddenly regain these when circumstances become more favourable. Cassava seems to have a great tendency to extend the paunch, and to puff out the flesh and make the whole body look fat and round, without giving any real stamina; and as soon as it fails, even for a few days, the paunch hangs

---

[1] It must be noted that paiwari differs essentially from the khava of the South Sea Islanders, with which it has sometimes been identified, in that, though the operation of chewing is performed in both cases, paiwari is never drunk until it has fermented, whereas khava is not a fermented liquor.

like an empty sack, and, the fat disappearing, the skin hangs in folds, and every bone in the body becomes prominent.

Before turning from the subject of the regular food supply of the Indians, a word must be said as to the salt which almost invariably forms part of it. Indians are extremely fond of salt, and large quantities of this substance—procured originally from the English on our own coast, or from the Brazilians—are passed from owner to owner as a highly valued article of barter. Moreover, in the Wapiana country salt of a very pungent quality occurs naturally on the savannah; and this is carefully collected, and used or bartered by the Indians of that district. Salt, however procured, always forms an ingredient in pepper-pot, though never in bread. It is also largely eaten by itself, just as an English child eats sugar.

But beside these regular food articles—bread, meat, and salt—there are many others which are occasionally procured, and are regarded either as delicacies, or are eaten when the regular supplies fail. Most of these are either eggs, insects, or fruits.

It is rather curious that birds' eggs are seldom eaten. The fact that the eggs of the ordinary domestic poultry, which generally abound in every Indian settlement, are not eaten, is simply another manifestation of the habit of regarding all introduced animals as unfit for food; but it might have been supposed that the eggs of indigenous wild birds, especially of the many kinds of game-birds, would have been eagerly sought as food; but this is rarely the case. On the other hand, the eggs of certain reptiles are largely consumed and appreciated. When, twice a year, the turtles and the iguana-lizards lay their eggs on the sandbanks in the rivers, large parties of Indians gather from all quarters, not only living upon the eggs for a time, but also smoking and drying others for future use. Sometimes I have seen an Indian canoe weighed almost down to the edge of the water by its load of turtle- or iguana-eggs. Tortoise-eggs are much less commonly found; but these too are readily eaten. Moreover, in a previous chapter I have told how the True Caribs boil and greedily eat the musk-flavoured eggs of the cayman and alligator; on the other hand, this last habit is regarded with disgust by members of most other tribes.

Of insects, true ants and white ants (*Termes*), grass-hoppers, grubs of wasps and beetles, and caterpillars, are eaten. When, at the beginning of the rainy season, the winged individuals of the colonies of white ants leave their nests, the Indians make large fires at evening, and the insects, attracted by the light, swarm round, scorch their wings, and fall like rain to the ground, from which they are swept up by the Indians, and are eaten in handfuls. The winged individuals of true ants, especially of the common coushie (*Ecodema cephalotes*), are also gathered in the same way. At other seasons of the year, if an Indian hankers after ant-meat, he pushes a sharply pointed stick into some nest of ant or termite, and then, withdrawing this, licks off the living insects which are sure to have crawled on to the intruding wood. Possibly this trick has been learned from the ant-eaters (*Myrmecophaga*), who gain their livelihood by inserting their long slender tongues into such nests, and eating the ants which adhere. The wingless individuals of a large black ant, of a kind unknown to me, but, I believe, a *Ponera*, which become very prominent at times, are eaten in very unceremonious fashion: the living insect is held by the head, and its abdominal segment is bitten off. I once ventured to taste one of these latter delicacies, and found it to affect the palate very much as dry corn-husks probably would. Various grasshoppers, especially a beautiful scarlet and black kind, are also picked up and eaten without further preparation. Wasps'-nests are knocked down from the trees, and the grubs are picked out from the cells and eaten. Of beetle-grubs, apparently the only one commonly eaten is the great yellowish-white 'gru-gru worm,' called *tacooma* by the Arawaks, *ewoi* by the Carib tribes, which, disgusting as it is in appearance, is also eaten, and even regarded as a great delicacy, not only by the negroes, but also by European colonists. It is the grub of a beetle (*Calandra pal-marum*)[1] very destructive to palm-trees, in the heartwood of which it lives.[2] Caterpillars are apparently not ordinarily eaten; but in times of famine the smooth-skinned kinds are collected, boiled, and used as food.

Of fruits, those of various palms are most largely used. The fleshy covering round the seeds of the cokerite (*Maximiliana regia*), and of several species of *Astrocaryum* is scraped off and eaten; and even after that the kernels of the former kind of palm are eaten. The cokerite seeds, called *mareepa* by the Carib tribes, sometimes, indeed, during famines, form almost the sole food of the Indians; and at such times they are boiled before eaten, in order that their bulk may be increased. The fleshy covering round the seeds of the æta palm (*Mauritia flexuosa*) is also eaten, being first scraped off and pressed into a sort of cake, in which condition it tastes something like strong rancid cheese. These are all wild palms. The Arawaks, and a few other Indians on the coast region, often have a plant or two of the famous peach-palm (*Guilielma speciosa*) growing near their houses, though this is not indigenous, nor do the Indians now know whence it came. The soft seeds of this, which grow in large bunches, are boiled and eaten as we eat potatoes.

A few other wild fruits are eaten, such as the plum-like fruit of the bullet-tree (*Mimusops balata*), certain small guavas, called by the Caribs 'billicoes,' which look and taste very like gooseberries, and which grow on bushes (*Nigritia Schomburgkii*) on many parts of the savannah, and the nut— the most delicately flavoured of all nuts—of the souari-tree (*Pekea tuberculosa*).

Yams and sweet-potatoes, plantains and bananas, sugar-cane and maize, are grown and eaten by the Indians, but in

[1] See p. 146.

[2] It is perhaps suggestive that the Arawak name for the grub, *tacooma*, is really identical with their name for the heartwood of any tree (*tacooba*); and the insect is possibly regarded as really part of the wood in which it lives.

no very large quantities; moreover, these were, according to the Indians themselves, derived from Europeans.

Lastly, various beverages, beside the paiwari and casiri which have been mentioned, are prepared. A kind of wine or toddy is procured from the æta palm, though only where the tree is plentiful, for one is very unnecessarily sacrificed each time that this wine is to be procured; and, because these trees produce so many things valuable to the Indian, this is done reluctantly. After the tree has been cut, a large groove is made in that part of the trunk which lies uppermost, and this groove is covered over with loose leaves. In a few hours the sap of the tree collects in this trough, and is collected and drunk without further preparation. If this juice (called by the Macusis *gwy*[1]) is kept for a few days it ferments, and then forms a pleasant, wine-like drink which is not unlike thin sauterne. Another drink is made by boiling maize, crushing it, and allowing it to ferment in water. And the pleasantest of all is made simply by crushing the large and very juicy fruit of the wild cashew (*Anacardium rhinocarpus*), which has a strawberry-like flavour, in water. Wild honey, too, which is very abundant, is also mixed with water and drunk. Even in its natural state this honey differs from that of European bees in that it is not viscid, but almost as fluid as water, and has a sub-acid, highly fragrant taste.

---

[1] The æta tree and the drink procured from it are alike called *gwy* by the Macusis, *æta* by the Warraus. As regards this common name for various parts of the same thing *cf.* note 2, p. 267.

CHAPTER XIV.

MANUFACTURES.

General Considerations—Pottery—Basket-work—Spinning : Three kinds of
Fibre ; two Methods of Spinning ; Explanation of Co-existence of two
Methods—Weaving : Hammock-weaving ; Rude Cloth-weaving—Boat-
building — Bench-making — Weapon-making—Ornament-making—Mu-
sical Instruments—Poison-making—Preparation of Oils, Pitches, Dyes—
Tobacco-production.

No little ingenuity is displayed by the Indians in making
their simple household utensils, weapons, and ornaments.
Yet many of the arts practised by their ancestors, such as that
of shaping stone into knives and for other purposes, have disappeared already ; others, such as the making of bows and
other weapons, are even now gradually, but rapidly, disappearing in consequence of an ever-increasing distribution of
goods of European manufacture throughout the interior.

It has already been remarked that the life of the Indian
man is made up of alternate fits of energy and of comparative
inactivity ; during the former he hunts or prepares a plot of
ground for the women to cultivate, while during the latter he
lolls for days together in his hammock, occupied only in most
leisurely manner in fashioning weapons or ornaments. The
amount of time spent in this latter way is very striking ; and
it is at first sight still more striking that the Indian is ready
to part with the articles which have cost him so much time
for almost anything. It has again and again been pointed
out that this inactivity and carelessness of time are not due
to any blameworthy idleness. The Indian exerts himself to
obtain all that he needs—food, a very moderate amount of
clothing, a good deal of ornament, a shelter of no very elaborate

kind from the weather, and weapons for defence or for hunting ;
of the advantage to him of anything beyond these things he
is ignorant, and he cannot therefore be blamed for not striving
to obtain more.   But the acquisition of these things occupies
comparatively little of his time; and it is therefore not
laziness if he spends the rest of his life in dawdling.   This is
true not only of the Indians of Guiana, but also, as has frequently been pointed out, of savages generally.   But there
is another circumstance connected with the same subject of
Indian industry which has, I think, attracted less notice.
Wherever white men go among Indians—wherever, that is, we
learn anything of the life of that people—goods manufactured
by the white men soon pass into the hands of the red men.
For example, in Guiana, the Indians instead of laboriously
shaping stones, as their fathers did, into knives, axes, and
other cutting implements, now very easily procure substitutes
for these implements from white men.   Thus one former
source of occupation has long been lost to the Indian.   Again,
at the present time, he is in the very act of relinquishing his
bows and arrows and his blow-pipes, things the making of
which occupied much of his time, in favour of European guns
—guns which, being of the cheapest kind, he receives from
the European in return for a very small amount of labour.
Nor has any new industry been taught him to occupy the
time thus set free.   Thus the necessity to the Indian to
work to obtain all that he needs or desires is now much less
than it was, and he has even more time than his fathers had
that he cannot occupy.   On the old and true principle that
work is good for man, this fact, too, probably explains in some
considerable degree the very common degeneration of savages
in the presence of civilisation.

    And from another point of view these Indians' arts are
interesting.   There exists among the tribes of this, as of
probably every other similar district, a rough system of distribution of labour ; and this serves not only its immediate
purpose of supplying all the tribes with better-made articles
than each could make for itself, but also brings the different

tribes together and spreads among them ideas and news of general interest.

The startling rapidity with which news spreads through vast tracts in which there seems to be no organised system of communication, and in which civilisation is altogether wanting, has surprised travellers in all quarters of the world. If, for instance, an event, possibly quite trivial in itself, but yet of interest to the Indians, happens in any part of the interior of Guiana, news of it reaches even the most remote of the Indians with a rapidity almost as great, if not as certain, as could be achieved by the best system of postal communication. Naturally, Indians of one tribe constantly visit each other, and these carry news of all that has passed in their own neighbourhood. It is more strange that news is as rapidly passed from tribe to tribe, however hostile the one may be to the other. The reason of this is to be found in the system of division of labour, which has arisen in quite a natural way.

Each tribe has some manufacture peculiar to itself; and its members constantly visit the other tribes, often hostile, for the purpose of exchanging the products of their own labour for such as are produced only by the other tribes. These trading Indians are allowed to pass unmolested through the enemy's country. When living among the Macusis, I was often amused by a number of those Indians rushing into my house, in the walls of which we had had windows pierced, who, with bated breath, half in joy, half in terror, used to point through the window to some party of their enemies, the Arecunas, coming with cotton-balls and blow-pipes for exchange. It is these traders who carry with them the latest news.

Of the tribes on the coast, the Warraus make far the best canoes and supply these to the neighbouring tribes. They also make hammocks of a peculiar kind, which are not, however, much in request except among themselves. In the same way, far in the interior, the Wapianas build boats for all the tribes in that district. The Macusis have two special products which are in great demand amongst all the tribes. One is the ourali used for poisoning arrows and the darts of blow-pipes, the other is an abundance of cotton hammocks— for, though these are now often made by the Wapianas and True Caribs, the Macusis are the chief makers. The Arecunas grow, spin, and distribute most of the cotton which is used by the Macusis and others for hammocks and other articles. The Arecunas also supply all blow-pipes; for these are made of the stems of a palm which, growing only in and beyond the Venezuelan boundary of their territory, are procured by the Arecunas, doubtless by exchange, from the Indians of the native district of that palm. The Tarumas and the Woyowais have a complete monopoly of the manufacture of the graters on which Indians of all the tribes grate their cassava. These two remote tribes are also the great breeders and trainers of hunting dogs. The Tarumas and Woyowais, however, though it is said that they sometimes pass down the rivers of Dutch Guiana towards the sea-coast of Surinam, do not travel from their own territories into any other part of British Guiana, but distribute their cassava-graters and their dogs through the Wapianas, who act as middle-men.

The True Caribs, again, are the most skilful potters; and though the Arawaks frequently, and the other Indians occasionally, make vessels for their own use, yet these are by no means as good as those which, whenever possible, they obtain from the Caribs. The Arawaks make fibre hammocks of a kind peculiar to them. They also make a good deal of pottery for their own use. Possibly in former times they produced some other manufacture of more importance to the other Indians; but now they have become so far civilised, and have so far adopted habits similar to those of the colonists, that they no longer have need of much intercourse with other Indians; for which reasons few traces of any arts peculiar to them are discoverable. The Ackawoi alone, so far as I know, have no special product interchangeable for those of their neighbours. These Indians are especially

dreaded and disliked by all the others; and it is possible
that the want of intercourse thus occasioned between this
tribe and the others forced the Ackawoi to produce for themselves all that they required. It is, further, possible that to
this enforced self-dependence is due the miserable condition of most of the Ackawoi.

To interchange their manufactures the Indians make
long journeys. The Wapianas visit the countries of the
Tarumas and the Woyowais, carrying with them canoes, cotton hammocks, and now very frequently knives, beads, and
other European goods; and, leaving their canoes and other
merchandise, they walk back, carrying with them a supply
of cassava-graters, and leading hunting dogs—all which things
they have received in exchange for the things which they
took. The Macusis visit the Wapiana settlements to obtain
graters and dogs, for which they give ourali-poison and cotton hammocks; and they again carry such of these graters
and dogs as they do not themselves require, together with
more of their own ourali and of their cotton hammocks, to
other Indians—to the Arecunas, who give in return balls of
cotton or blow-pipes; or to the True Caribs, who pay in
pottery. In this way, travellers with goods and with news
constantly pass from district to district.

Richard Schomburgk has suggested that a higher degree
of ornament is apparent in the manufactures of each tribe
the further that tribe lives from the sea-coast. There is
some slight ground for this suggested theory. The hammocks of the coast tribes, indeed of all the tribes of British
Guiana, are strong, but without ornament. On the frontiers
of Brazil live tribes who introduce blue and yellow threads
into their hammocks; and but very little farther away, on
the Rio Negro, hammocks edged with the beautiful feather
work of the Indians of Brazil begin to appear. Again, even
within British Guiana, as one advances from the coast inland,
more and more elaborate patterns are to be seen on paddles,
on pottery, and on utensils of all sorts, and more and more
feathers are worn as personal ornaments. On the other

hand, the Indians of the coast, with the exception perhaps
of the Warraus, certainly surpass those more inland in the
neatness and strength of their weapons, especially their
arrows, which, after all, are the most valuable and important
of their possessions.

The ornaments which the Indians paint upon their
pottery, weapons, and sometimes upon the posts and walls
of their houses, are of a very simple kind. Generally they
are mere lines, curved or straight, drawn free-hand and
according to the will of the artist, combined in very irregular patterns. Sometimes a rude and childish drawing of
a figure of a man or of some other animal may be distinguished. It is somewhat curious that Schomburgk thought
that all such ornamentation, even of weapons, was done by
women; but, however that may have been in his time, it is
now certainly as often the work of men as of women.

We must now glance, as briefly as the subject admits, at
the various Indian products, and learn the ways in which
they are made.

The pottery first claims attention. The clay vessels made
by the Indians are all of a few very simple and unvaried forms.
The 'buck-pot' (see Fig. 19 *A*) is the most universal. In form
this is not unlike an ordinary fish-globe, but has a wider lip or
rim; it stands in a saucer, which serves also on occasion as
a lid. It is in these vessels that all the food of the Indians
is cooked. One or two vessels, like 'buck-pots' in form, but
very much larger—being often two feet in diameter and two
and a half feet in height, and without a saucer—may be
seen in almost every house (see Fig. 19 *B*). These are for
holding casiri or paiwari, the two favourite beverages of the
Indian. The casiri-jar is so large and heavy that to prevent
the body, or belly, from breaking away from the rim when
the vessel is full of heavy liquor, the lower part is bound
round with a network of bush-rope, the tough and pliant
stems of certain creeping plants. It seems not impossible
that in some, though not all cases, where, in other parts of
the world, pottery is found marked *on the outside* as though

with basket-work, and this is regarded as evidence that pottery was originally made by lining baskets with clay, the real explanation may be that, as in the case of the casiri-jar, the pottery was bound with basket-work for the sake of greater strength.

Goglets (see Fig. 19 c and d), clay bottles with globular bodies and long straight necks, are made, and used to contain liquids by the forest tribes, but not by the savannah Indians, who use the empty skins of gourds and calabashes in their stead.

Another vessel (see Fig. 19 e), made chiefly by the True Caribs and Arawaks, and seldom used by the other tribes, is

FIG. 19.

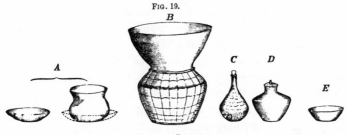

TYPES OF POTTERY.

the sappoora. This is shaped like an ordinary basin, and is used, not for cooking, but for holding food.

Various degrees of skill are shown by the women of the different tribes in making pottery. As has been said, the True Caribs are the most skilful. Moreover, the success of the potter seems also in part due to the place from whence the clay is obtained; for it differs much in different places. The clay from certain places on the Cuyuni river is said by the Indians to be the best in the colony; and more goods are always asked in exchange for a vessel made of this clay. The clay from the Pomeroon river is said to be of very bad quality; vessels made of it are certainly remarkably fragile.

The best of the vessels are, in appearance, as perfect in shape and as truly curved as though made with the potter's wheel; and yet they are formed by the hand alone, guided only by the eye.

A flat, circular sheet of clay, the foundation of the intended buck-pot, or goglet, is first laid on a small piece of board. The rest of the clay has been rolled between the palms of the hand into long cylindrical pieces as thick as a man's thumb. One of these rolls is now laid round the edge of the foundation so as to stand up round it like the rim of a tray. This rim is now manipulated between the finger and thumb; it is amalgamated with the clay of the foundation; it is flattened and smoothed; and, with great nicety, exactly that curve is given to it which it will have to bear as a part of the body of the vessel. On top of this another roll is now applied; and this is manipulated in the same way. In this way the vessel is gradually built up piece by piece; and its walls, though moulded only by the fingers, acquire a perfectly true curve. To smooth the edge or lip of the vessel, a piece of the shell of a calabash is used. A piece is carefully cut out from one side of the shell, so that the space left exactly corresponds with the intended lip of the vessel. By means of this nick, the shell is then fitted on to the edge of the vessel, and is passed round its circumference. This of course smooths away any inequalities in the clay, and leaves a perfectly smooth edge. In the same way, either a projecting ledge or a groove is sometimes made in the soft clay by way of ornament, entirely round the body of the growing vessel. In such cases, according as a ledge or groove is to be made, a groove of the required shape and size is made in the edge of the calabash-shell, or a projection is left on its edge.

After the vessel has been shaped, it is smoothed and polished by much rubbing with a water-worn pebble—preferably a piece of porphyry or, if it can be had, an old Indian stone axe-head. Suitable porphyry pebbles rounded by the action of water, occur in many of the smaller rivers of the interior; these are collected and form a regular article of trade. If I am not mistaken, the so-called 'charm stones' which Schomburgk and others obtained from the Indians under the impression that they were worn into their present shape merely by being long held in the hands of Indian children, in a form of divination, are in reality the natural water-worn pebbles used by potters. After being polished the pot is dried in the sun. Some time after this, a pattern is drawn on the vessel with pieces of the bark of various trees, the juice of which produces markings of red, brown, pink, or black. Rude figures of animals are often drawn in this way, and, at other times, geometric patterns of spiral, curved, or straight lines. Some of the True Caribs have the knack of producing a fine glaze on the vessel, by the application of certain juices to the clay in this stage of its manufacture. The vessels finally are slowly baked over a fire. This brings out the glaze or the pattern, if any is prepared, or if, as is often the case, the bark of a certain tree, called by the Arawaks *kawta* (*Artocarpus?*), burned and ground to powder, has been mixed with the clay, leaves the vessels quite black; or if neither of these precautions have been taken, leaves the vessels hard, but of the natural yellow colour of the clay. They are then finished.

The labour and care devoted to building up an enormous casiri-jar, bit by bit, with inch-broad strips of clay, and the wonderful skill shown in keeping the walls of the growing structure perfectly round, are worthy of notice. Often, indeed, the women fail in many attempts before they successfully fashion one of these large vessels; and even after one has been made, it often cracks or breaks during the baking. A perfected casiri-jar, especially if it is much ornamented, is highly valued; one especially fine specimen, which I had often tried in vain to get, I only secured at last by bargaining for it one day when I happened to find its owner merry and good-humoured after a long drinking feast.

It is only vessels of the two or three shapes which she and her ancestors have long been accustomed to make that the Indian woman can make well and perfectly round.

Asked or unasked, the women who come in contact with
white people frequently imitate such vessels of European
structure as they may see, such as teapots, cups and saucers,
tumblers, or wineglasses; but these articles are always mis-
shapen and untrue in curve.

Before passing from the subject of Indian pottery, it
must be noted that the vessels made are strikingly similar
in form to the ruder forms of those found in the North
American earth-mounds. The 'buck-pot' and the goglet are
exactly matched in shape by vessels from these mounds; but
those made by the present Indians of Guiana are more
highly finished than most, at any rate, of those left behind
by the old North American mound-makers. Another significant fact is that, while the Indian women of Guiana are
shaping the clay, their children, imitating them, make small
pots and goglets. Many of these toy vessels may be seen in
and about almost every Indian house. The large number of
vessels too small for practical use which occur in the North
American mounds, and the object of which has long been a
question, were, judging by analogy, probably made by the
children of the mound-makers.

The Indians—this time the men—are very skilful
basket-makers. Baskets of various shapes are used by them
for many different purposes. The material used for all fine
basket-work is the split, reed-like stems of a kind of
maranta (*Ischnosiphon*), called *iturite* by the Indians. For
rougher work other species of iturite are used; and for
the roughest of all, the unsplit stems of certain creepers,
especially one called by the Indians *mamoorie* (*Carludovica
plumierii*) are used.

The so-called pegalls [1] are made to contain all loose
arrow-heads, a ball of cotton for binding, some wax, such
beads and other ornaments as are not in use, and all the
other smaller properties of the Indian. The pegalls of the

---

[1] The word *pegalla* is possibly a genuine Carib word; but the form
pack-all which is used by colonists, is, when the object of this basket is
remembered, suspicious.

Arawaks, Ackawoi, and Warraus are generally square in shape. The basket itself and its lid are of exactly the same shape, and the latter, being rather the larger, slips over the former and entirely covers it. It is, perhaps hardly neces-

FIG. 20.

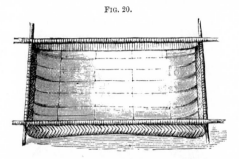

CASSAVA SIFTER.

sary to observe that the 'nests' of these pegalls, which are often exported, are only made as curiosities for Europeans. Many True Caribs make their pegalls of a peculiar oblong shape, with very gracefully curved lines, and adorn them with long strings of thick white cotton on which are knots of coloured feathers. Round pocket-shaped baskets, without

FIG. 21.

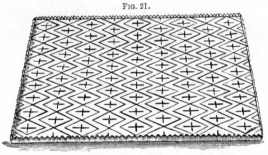

MACUSI BREAD BASKET.

lids, but covered with loose leaves if there is need of protection, are chiefly used by the Indians of the savannah, instead of the more ordinary pegalls.

Sometimes, especially by the True Caribs, each pegall, basket and lid alike, is made double, and between the two

layers of basket-work certain leaves (*Ischnosiphon*) are inserted, to render the whole basket waterproof.

Most of the implements used in making cassava-bread
are of basket-work. The *matapie*, a very peculiar basket, by
means of which the bitter, poisonous juice is expressed from
the cassava, has already been described (Fig. 18, p. 261).
The square sieve (Fig. 20, p. 279) through which the cassava-
meal is sifted before it is strewn on the baking-iron is made
of basket-work. To hold the cassava-bread when made, large
square tray-like baskets (Fig. 21, p. 279), with little or no rim,
are made by the Macusis and Arecunas, and similar, but much

FIG. 22.

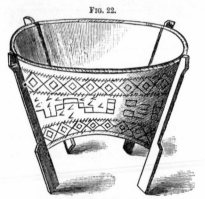

ARAWAK BREAD BASKET.

deeper baskets (Fig. 22), raised some distance above the ground
on wooden legs, are made and used for the same purpose by the
Arawaks, True Caribs, and most other Indians of the forest.

Another basket in common use is the suriana, which is
used for carrying heavy loads of cassava and other roots
home from the fields, for bringing in firewood, and for
carrying hammocks, cooking utensils, and all other goods
when travelling. This basket is shaped like a slipper; the
flat side, answering to the sole of the slipper, fits against the
back of the carrier; a string is laced backward and forward
across the open side, so as to keep the contents of the basket
from falling out; and a strong and broad band, cut from the
inner bark of a tree, passes from the two upper corners

of the basket across the forehead of the carrier so as to support the whole weight. The quake, again, is a much-used basket with rounded bottom, and is made of very open wicker-work. Quakes are used for storing provisions; they also serve as cages to confine young birds and animals which are being tamed; and they are used for half a hundred other everyday purposes. Special baskets are also made to hold the cotton fibre when it has been separated from the seeds before being spun. These are round, shaped like flat basins, or, rather, saucers.

Most of these baskets—all indeed, except some of the surianas and quakes, are made in much the same way, and of the same material. The very strong stems of iturite, which grows commonly in the forest, are split into many parallel pieces. These pieces are sometimes used in their natural state, sometimes peeled and bleached, sometimes stained black. They are closely woven together, so that the walls of the basket are as dense as cloth. If the materials used are of various colours, the different kinds are so carefully interwoven as to produce very intricate patterns in the finished basket.

Waist-belts, to support the cloth lap, are also made of these strips of iturite stems by the Macusi.

The rougher surianas and quakes—those which are only intended for very brief use—are woven either of certain sorts of bush-rope, which are especially strong and suitable for the purpose, or of strips of iturite, as described above, but very roughly prepared; or again, if they are required for some emergency, and only for a very brief time, they are rapidly woven of the leaflets of a single palm-leaf.

The quake, which, next to the buck-pot, is the most used of all the possessions of the Indian, is, as has been said, much used for packing provisions, such as farine, salt, and cassava bread which is to be kept for some time. But the quakes are loosely woven, and have large holes, through which such things as farine—coarse meal made of cassava —and salt would certainly fall out. They are, therefore,

lined with the broad oval leaves of the iturite. The bottom of the basket having been lined with a single layer
of leaves placed in beautifully regular order, a line of the
leaves is placed, their stalks on the bottom, their upper part
against the sides of the baskets. As much farine or salt is
then poured in as reaches nearly to the top of the first line
of leaves. The lining is then carried up higher, one more
row of leaves being added, their stems secured in the farine.
More farine is poured in, and the processes are continued
until the basket is full. A covering of leaves is then added
and tied down. In this way the contents of the basket are
entirely guarded against all damp.

The Nikari-karus, a curious hybrid tribe of Indians, living
on the Brazilian borders, are peculiar in making their pegalls
of the leaves of a palm (*Orbigignia*) very rare in British
Guiana, but growing near the Oorooa rapids on the Roopoonooni. These pegalls are square or oblong in shape, like
those of the Arawaks.

Indian basket-work is so beautifully neat, that it is much
to be regretted that the art of producing it is fast dying
out, at least wherever the influence of white men is felt.
Missionaries would certainly be doing good work if they
endeavoured to revive and retain this and all other such
native arts.

Having so lately spoken of the baskets used in the manufacture of cassava bread, it may be as well to find place here
for some account of the cassava-graters. These are, as has
been said, made only by the Woyowais and Tarumas, and are
distributed throughout the interior of the colony by the
Wapianas. They are oblong boards, with a slight curve
parallel with their length. On the concave surface of this
many small holes are drilled, and in each of these a small
and angular fragment of granite or other hard stone is inserted, so as to project slightly. The whole is then rubbed
over with a strong black vegetable pitch, called *karamanni*,
so that the holes are entirely filled up; and the stones, as
soon as the pitch is dry, are firmly fixed. The result is that

this side of the board is roughened like a large nutmeg-grater, and on this the cassava roots are scraped up and down, and are thus reduced to pulp. Sometimes the top of the board is painted and carved. Before handing them over to the Wapianas, the makers pack each carefully in a single layer of the waterproof iturite leaves.

Thread, or string, is one of the first of human wants, being needed for fishing-lines, bow-strings, and for tying purposes; and in a very slightly higher stage of civilisation the art of twisting this thread into some sort of cloth is attained. The Indians of Guiana have, therefore, of course provided themselves with string to be used in the first-mentioned simple ways; and they have even attained some slight knowledge of its use for the latter purpose. Their string is made of but three kinds of fibre. These are cotton, the fibre called *tibisiri*, which is obtained from the æta palm (*Mauritia flexuosa*), and that called *crowia*, which is procured from the silk grass-plant (*Bromelia* and *Anannassa*).

A small quantity of cotton is grown and spun by almost all Indians, but by far the larger part of that used by them is prepared by the Arecunas, and is distributed by them among the other tribes. Æta palms grow, sometimes in very considerable quantity, in swampy places throughout the colony. Silk-grass, though also an indigenous plant, is cultivated in almost every Indian field. Tibisiri and crowia are gathered and prepared by each Indian as they are required.

Æta fibre, the tibisiri of the Arawak Indians, is prepared from the young leaf of the palm (*Mauritia flexuosa*). The leaf, when fully developed, is fan-shaped, but it first appears folded in a spike which springs from the very centre of the plant. It is from this spike that the fibre is obtained. Fibre taken from the spikes of old plants is not nearly as strong as that taken from young plants. Each leaf, or spike, is taken singly; a sharp dexterous rub at the top separates the outer skin, and the whole of this is then torn off. This is the fibre, the rest is waste. It is further prepared by boiling, drying in the sun, and twisting into strings, in a way which will presently be explained. The fibre from a dozen such spikes is sufficient to make a large hammock.

Crowia—called silk-grass fibre in the colony—is ingeniously extracted from the leaves of a bromelia, and sometimes of various species of anannassa, plants like huge pineapples. A string, from which hangs a small noose, with a slip knot large enough to allow the pointed top of one of the leaves to pass through, is tied round a tree. A single leaf is then split up the midrib from the point where it was cut from the plant nearly to the top ; and each of the two halves thus separated is bent back so as to lie flat against the unsplit top of the leaf. The latter is then passed through the noose, so as to hang down on one side of the string, while the split parts of the leaf hang down on the other. The noose, by means of the slip knot, is then made smaller, so as to confine the leaf tightly. The Indian then takes the point of the leaf in his hand, and by a sudden and strong pull, forces the whole leaf toward him, through the loop. The green skin and soft matter are torn or rubbed off against the string of the loop, and only the long tough fibres pass through and remain in a neat bundle in the hand of the Indian. After this the fibre is washed, to free it from what remains of the green matter, is dried in the sun, and is then ready for use. It assumes a very white colour, and, unlike tibisiri, which turns yellow in the water, washes well. It is a remarkable fact that, at least among the Arawaks, the men peel the leaf from the bottom upward, the women from the extreme point downward to the base of the leaf.

Both these fibres—tibisiri and crowia—are twisted into string in a very simple and ingenious way, but one which would be impossible to all except people such as these Indians. A proper number of the parallel fibres are held firmly by one end in the left hand, the remainder of the fibres resting across the naked right thigh. The palm of the right hand is laid across the fibres and, therefore, parallel to the thigh. By a very rapid downward and sideward motion of the right hand, followed by a slight backward motion, the fibres are rolled downward along the thigh and become spirally twisted. And this spiral is retained. The single strand thus produced is used for making hammocks; but three strands are rolled together, in the same way, to make the string used for bow-lines; and three of the triple cords—sometimes nine strands—are used in making hammock-ropes.

The bodily form and the habits of the Indian are such as render the making of the string in this way easy; for not only are their thighs naked, but their skins are smooth and hairless. If a European tries to do this same thing, the small hairs on his skin are caught up among the fibres and are twisted in with them; and this is not only painful, but it also prevents the work from being done quickly and evenly enough to be successful. Similarly, the Indian women, whose duty it is to prepare the twine for hammock-making, so soon as they become so far civilised as to wear dresses, have to give up this work.

The string prepared from the æta is strong, but is not nearly so even and regular as that from the silk-grass. The latter kind of fibre is made in much smaller quantity, and is only used for the most important purposes.

The cotton is gathered and spun by the women. The fibre having been carefully extracted from the pods and freed from seeds, is pulled by hand into a long, uneven, and loose band. One end of this is fastened to a hook at the end of a small spindle—one of a pair—which is held between the thumb and one finger of the left hand. About six or eight inches of the band of cotton hangs freely from this spindle, and the remainder is wound loosely round the right wrist.

Each of the spindles is a round wooden stick, about eight or ten inches in length, which passes, at about two inches from the end which is held in the hand, through a circular disc, or whorl, of bone. This whorl serves as a guard, beyond which the spun cotton when wound round the spindle cannot pass. At the other end of the spindle is the small hook to which the end of the loose cotton band is fastened.

The spindle, after the cotton has been arranged as described, is twirled rapidly round between the finger and the thumb; and at the same time the right hand is raised and removed further from the left. The circular motion given by the twirling of the spindle twists the fibres together; and the band, being extended by the gradual separation of the hands, is reduced to the thickness of the required thread. But certain parts of the compact thread thus produced are thicker than others. These thicker parts are, therefore, pressed in with the fingers of the right hand; and the thread being yet more extended, the whole becomes even and of one thickness. The part of the strand thus finished is then wound round the spindle without breaking its connection with the band round the right wrist. More of the latter is now unwound and spun in the same way. The first spindle, when as much as it will carry has been wound round it, is put aside till the second has been filled in the same way. The thread thus prepared is of course but a single strand.

Cotton of three thicknesses is used for three different purposes. Very fine cotton is used especially for binding the heads on to the shafts of arrows; a thicker kind is used, somewhat as in knitting, for making various articles, such as the bands worn round the arm and leg; and the thickest kind is made into hammocks. All these consist of but two strands; but the strands themselves are more or less thick according to the kind of cotton into which they are to be combined. If, for instance, a very fine strand is to be made, for arrow cotton, very little cotton is put into the original band; and while the spindle is being twisted, this band is much further extended than would be the case if a thicker strand were being made.

Whatever the thickness of the strands, they are twisted together from the two spindles on to a third and larger spindle, exactly in the same way as the fibres were spun into the single strand. The cotton, when it has been wound from this third spindle on to a ball, is then ready for use, and is carefully wrapped in leaves, tied round with string, and put aside until it is required.

Attention will doubtless be at once attracted to the curious fact that in each one of the tribes these two distinct methods of twisting fibres into threads are employed side by side: one, the rude, laborious, and often painful method of rolling the fibres on the thigh; the other the much more apt, simple, and less laborious method by use of the spindle. It might naturally be supposed that a tribe which had once attained to a knowledge of the better of these two methods would at once cease to use the worse; and I believe it is really an unusual thing in other parts of the world to see tribes long retaining two such methods side by side. But I think there is a very simple and significant explanation of the anomalous state of the art of spinning in Guiana. Two facts must be observed: that the spindle is used only for cotton, the other fibres being twisted on the thigh; and that, though all the three fibres are used by each of the tribes, yet cotton is used especially by the Carib tribes, the other fibres especially by the other tribes. In illustration of the latter of these two facts, it is sufficient to point out that the hammock, which is the most important, and indeed the only considerable form of woven work used by the Indians, is, as we shall presently see, made of cotton by all the Carib tribes, of palm or other fibre by the other tribes. Now, we have elsewhere found many reasons for supposing that the tribes not of Carib origin were the earlier inhabitants of Guiana, and that the various Carib tribes came into the country later. It therefore requires no great stretch of imagination to suppose that the Carib tribes brought with them the habit of using cotton and the spindle; and that the tribes previously in Guiana had before used only palm and silk-grass fibre, and had twisted these on their thighs. The two sets of people, the thigh-twisters and the spindle-users, having, if not intermingled, yet come into proximity, each adopted, for certain minor purposes, the kind of fibre used by the other; and with the fibre they adopted the method of preparing it. Thus not only is an explanation afforded of the simultaneous use of the better and the worse method, but additional light is thrown on the Carib migration into Guiana.

Each of the three kinds of fibre is used in the simple form of string. Tibisiri, which is coarse and makes but rough strands, is used for the rougher purposes, as for the laces of the sandals used on the stony parts of the savannah, for hammocks, and occasionally for hammock-ropes. It may perhaps be as well to note here that for rough tying purposes —as, for example, in lashing together the beams and posts of his house, in fastening on the thatch, in fastening together the various parts of his boats, and in many other such ways —the Indian uses no artificial rope or string, but the natural ropes or strings afforded by the larger or smaller stems of certain pliant creepers. Crowia fibre, since it can be made into much stronger and more even string, is used for all more important purposes—for bow-strings, fishing-lines, and especially for hammock-ropes. Entire hammocks are occasionally, but very rarely, made of it. Cotton is used for many such purposes as binding on the heads of arrows, and for ornament, as in the numerous long streamers which float from the feather head-dress of the Indian and hang from his necklaces and other ornaments, and from his arms.

It is in the manufacture of their hammocks that the Indians first exercise the art of weaving their thread into textile fabrics, though only of a very simple kind.

The three kinds of hammocks chiefly produced in British Guiana are made either of cotton or of tibisiri fibre. Cotton hammocks are made by the Macusis and Wapianas, and occasionally—though in a slightly different way—by the True Caribs. They are made on a square frame, formed of four bars of wood. These bars are so fitted together that two of them—those forming the top and bottom of the frame— can be slid along the other two, so as to reduce the size of the rectangular space which they enclose and make it correspond with the size of what the intended hammock is to be (Fig. 23).

A continuous length of cotton thread is then wound round and round the frame, from side to side, or from top to bottom, in such a way that the threads lie parallel, and are equidistant from each other. These lengths of the thread form the longitudinal bars of the hammock. The cross-bars are then put in. Three reels, or shuttles, charged with cotton thread, are provided. Each cross-bar consists of three strands of cotton—from the three reels—which are simply plaited together, each of the longitudinal bars of the hammock being successively inserted into one of the plaits. When the first cross-bar has been carried entirely across the width of the hammock, its three threads are broken, and a new

FIG. 23.

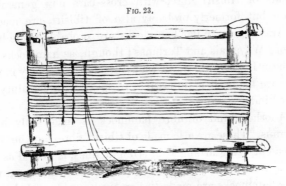

CARIB METHOD OF MAKING A HAMMOCK.

cross-bar is begun parallel to, and a short distance from, the former. When all the cross-bars have been inserted, the hammock is taken off the frame. So far the work has been done by the women. The hammock is then handed over to the men, who always prepare and add the scale lines. These scale-lines are of much thicker cotton than is the hammock; to fit them properly, so that the hammock hangs evenly, is an operation requiring extreme care. At each end of the hammock is a series of loops, formed by those parts of the longitudinal threads which passed round the side-bars of the wooden frame. The scale-line having been fastened to the first of these loops, a certain length of it is allowed to hang loose; it is then passed through the second loop and a slightly longer length is allowed to hang loose, and in the same way it is passed through each successive loop, a certain definite length being left to hang loose between each two. These loose loops of scale-line must be very nicely measured and adjusted; for only if the centre one is the shortest, and each successive one, on either side, is made longer than the one before it, so that the outermost is the longest, will the hammock hang evenly and comfortably. Lastly, when the ends of these scale-lines furthest from the hammock have been bound together, the hammock is finished.

Fibre hammocks, made in the same way, but of parallel threads of tibisiri fibre, with cross-bars now generally of cotton but formerly probably also of tibisiri, are made by the Arawaks. Similar hammocks are probably made by the remote Woyawais and Tarumas; though, as hammocks made by these Indians are never seen outside the country in which they are made, it is impossible to speak with certainty as to their kind.

Another kind of fibre hammock is made only by the Warraus. These are also made of tibisiri fibre, but the thread, instead of being arranged in straight lines, is netted as in an old-fashioned silk purse. The square wooden frame on which these hammocks are made lies on the ground; and the whole hammock is netted of one continuous string.

Each tribe, besides the large hammocks of its own peculiar kind, makes small hammocks, or rather broad 'endless bands' of the same kind, in which, being worn by the women over the shoulder, the children are carried.

All these hammocks, are, however, almost too loose in their texture to deserve the name of cloth. Cloth, indeed, as we have it, is but little needed by Indians, in that they wear hardly any clothing. Yet these people do make some fabrics of far closer texture than that of the hammocks above described. One example is to be seen in the so-called Brazilian hammocks, which are woven of cotton, often coloured, as closely as felt, by some few True Caribs; but it is certain that this art has merely been copied from some of the half-civilised Brazilian-Indian half-breeds who have settled on some of the rivers. A genuine Indian advance in the art of weaving is, however, to be seen in the broad cloth-like cotton bands which are worn by some tribes round the legs and arms, being, curiously enough, woven on to the limbs, and so without seam; and also in certain narrow cotton fillets, of equally compact texture, which the women wear round their hair, on certain festal occasions, and the men wear round the lower edge of their feather crowns. In both these cases the web is put together by means of a number of sticks like knitting needles; and the stitches are all of one kind. A further and very much greater advance in the art is to be seen in certain curious strips of cotton cloth worn by men (Fig. 6, p. 200) from shoulder to shoulder during feasts, in which, by means of various stitches, a distinct pattern is produced; but the art of making this particular cloth has already been lost, and the cloths themselves are exceedingly rare. Of the only two which I was able to procure, or, indeed, ever saw, one is now in Georgetown Museum, the other in the British Museum.

Before Europeans went westward and supplied the Indians with ready-made cloth, it is probable that some of these people wove for themselves, in the way that the leg bands are now woven, both the long narrow strip of cloth which, passed between the legs, forms the only garment of these men, and the small apron which serves a similar purpose in the case of the women. In some tribes, however, then, as now in very rare cases, the soft cloth-like inner bark of a tree (*Lecythis*) was used for these purposes. Some of the Arecuna women in very remote places still make their aprons of cotton, adorned with seeds instead of beads.

The invention of the simple art of plaiting probably is of older date than that of weaving; but it seems more convenient to speak of it, as practised by the Indians, in this place. It is employed chiefly, if not only, in making the belts which the men wear round their waists to support the cloth passed between their legs. These are plaited, apparently of different materials by different tribes, sometimes of cotton, sometimes of fibre, sometimes of strips of the material used for basketwork, and sometimes of hair, either of men or monkeys. Schomburgk speaks of human hair having been frequently used for this purpose only forty years ago; but, probably because intertribal war has now almost ceased to be waged, monkeys' hair is now far more commonly used.

Lastly, it may be pointed out as somewhat curious that, though the work of spinning and weaving is in other respects naturally enough distributed between the sexes, the cotton fillets worn by the women round their heads are made only by the men.

Not the least admirable of the simple arts of the Indians of British Guiana is that of working in wood. Only the men do this. The axes, scrapers, and chisels of stone which once formed their whole stock of wood-working implements are no longer used. Yet even now, as a rule, the only tools used to transform the rough block of wood into the required shape are an axe, a cutlass, and a knife. Sometimes a small adze is also used; nails too are now sometimes obtained from Europeans and used. But an Indian is quite capable of building his house, or hewing a beautifully neat boat, stool, or other such article, from a rough block of wood, without the use of any implement beyond his axe and cutlass.

So much of the life of these Indians being spent on the water, boat-building is the most important form of carpenter's craft practised by them. The boats made are of four kinds —the canoe, the corial, the buckshell, and the woodskin. Each of these forms was possibly once peculiar to a special tribe; but they are now nearly, though not quite, indiscriminately used. The Warraus on the coast, and the Wapianas in the interior, are the most apt boat-builders, and the canoes which these make form their principal article of barter with the other tribes.

When a canoe is to be made, a suitable tree is carefully

sought in the forest, often at a long distance from the nearest river or creek. I have known cases in which this distance was more than two miles, through dense, pathless bush. The tree is felled, and is roughly hewn, on the spot where it falls, into the shape of the required canoe. It is then hollowed, partly with axe or adze, partly by burning out the interior. Sometimes at this stage, but sometimes not till it is finished, it is carried down to the river. A path through the bush down to the water-side having been cleared and laid with cross-pieces of wood as runners, the canoe is laboriously dragged to the water. At this stage the two sides of the canoe are much closer together than they will eventually be, and are parallel to each other throughout the greater part of their length, so that, instead of the canoe ending in a point at the bow and another at the stern, there is a gap left at each of these points such as would be produced by cutting off the bow and stern of a boat of ordinary shape perpendicularly to the water-line. The Indian boat-builder has next to open the canoe further, to bend the sides from each other, and to give these sides the proper curve. The gaps at bow and stern are now explained; for the sides could not be forced sufficiently apart from each other if they were joined firmly at bow or stern. There are several ways of forcing the sides apart and giving them their proper shape. Sometimes the canoe is inverted over a fire till the action of the heat spreads the sides; sometimes it is filled with wet sand, the weight of which eventually forces the sides, softened by the moisture, outward; and sometimes the canoe is sunk for a considerable time in running water, and when the wood has thus been made pliant, the sides are forced asunder by driving large wedge-shaped pieces of timber in between them. In any case, as soon as the sides have been spread, bars of hard wood, about an inch and a half in diameter, are fixed firmly across within the canoe from side to side, so as to prevent the sides from again approaching each other. The benches, too, are at once fixed in their places and help the same purpose.

Two triangular pieces of plank-like wood are then cut and fitted into the gaps at bow and stern. The sides and 'squared' ends of the whole canoe are raised by the addition of a plank or 'extra-streak.' The junction of this streak with the dug-out body of the canoe is carefully caulked with shreds scraped from the inner bark of certain trees, and is pitched with hyawa—*i.e.* the resin of a common tree (*Icica heptaphylla*)—or with karamanni, which is a curious pitch-like substance, with very strong adhesive powers, much used by the Indians, not only as pitch, but also as glue. It is obtained from a very beautiful tree, the *manni* of the Indians (*Siphonia bacculifera*). Before it is used it is generally, if not always, mixed—by melting the two together —with the wax of a wild bee.[1]

[1] The following note, supplied by a correspondent, on canoe-building as it is yet practised in some of the West Indian islands, from which places the ancestors of many of the Indians of Guiana doubtless came, exhibits a marked case of the survival of old habits, notwithstanding the introduction of new, and presumably better, European methods : ' It may not be without interest to mention that in St. Vincent, St. Lucia, and Grenada canoes are generally used along the coast in lieu of built boats. These canoes are often of considerable size, capable of carrying ten or twelve passengers, with more cargo in the shape of barrels of flour, quintals of salt fish, &c., than their apparently frail construction would seem to warrant. They are rowed by a crew of four or six men, always creoles. The shells are invariably furnished—at all events in St. Vincent—by the Caribs. A small settlement of these people, distinguished as Black Caribs, sprung from intermarriage between the aboriginal yellow Carib and some Africans landed from a slaver wrecked on a neighbouring island some two hundred years ago, still exists on the leeward side. On the windward coast some of the more or less pure yellow-skinned Caribs are still to be found. These latter are invaluable as boatmen for the purpose of shipping produce. They are as much at home in the rolling breakers as on terra firma ; but rum, *cum annexis* as we say here, militates against their continued existence as a race. The tree used in St. Vincent is the " gommier," so called because it exudes a quantity of resin so fragrant as to be a chief ingredient in the incense used in the Roman Catholic churches. The tree is felled and treated much as Mr. im Thurn describes, but the practice in St. Vincent is to hollow out the trunk with fire and axe (formerly a stone implement) in the woods and to haul down the shell to the beach. There it is spread by wet sand—the bow is never split down—but a triangular board of white pine is let in and a streak of the same material superadded ; then "knees " of the white cedar (*Bignonia leucoxylon*) keep it in form, and seats of pine complete the craft. Thole-pins of tamarind and cars of "Shoemakers'

If the canoe is to be used for long journeys, a tent is added for the protection, not of the Indians themselves, but of their goods. A number of sticks are bent into semi-circles, and the two ends are fastened, one against each side of the canoe, so as to make a framework for the tent; these are held in place by cross-sticks tied on at right angles; and on the framework thus made a thatch of palm-leaves is laid. Sometimes—especially in the interior—instead of the thatch just described, two thin wickerwork mats, each large enough to cover the whole frame of the tent, are made; a layer of leaves (*Ischnosiphon*) having been placed between them, the two are fastened one over the other, and the one mat thus produced, which is perfectly waterproof, can be laid on to the framework of the tent or taken off in a few minutes. This latter method of making tent covers seems to have been learned from the Brazilian Indians, and it is rarely seen far from the border land.

A 'corial' resembles the dug-out body of a canoe without the plank which raises the sides of the latter; as a rule, too, the corial is smaller than the canoe and is not flat—that is to say, its sides are not so widely opened. It is used more for short excursions, to fish or hunt, or to go to the field, while the canoe is used for long journeys.

The 'buckshell' is dug out from the trunk of a tree in the same way as the canoe and corial; but it is made with pointed and closed ends, so that it is impossible to spread its sides as widely apart. Buckshells, on account of their shape, are more cranky, and more easily upset, but lighter to pull and more speedy, than canoes. Those made by the Arawaks and True Caribs differ slightly in shape.

bark" (*Byrsonima spicata*) are usually preferred. For the latter, imported ash oars are sometimes substituted. A rudder of European shape is used. In St. Lucia the construction is much the same, only the upper streak is lower or sometimes entirely omitted, and the oar consists of a stick, with an oval board, perforated with two holes, lashed to it. A couple of cows, well lashed down, are often brought across to St. Vincent in one of these "pirogues"—a word some of us first learned from "Robinson Crusoe." These craft are wonderfully buoyant. The canoe rarely upsets; the only danger arises from overloading and swamping.'

The lightest and most easily made boats in use among these Indians are 'woodskins.' These are usually made of the bark either of the locust-tree (*Hymenœa courbaril*) or of the purpleheart (*Copaifera pubiflora*). A strip of bark of sufficient length is first carefully taken from the tree, and this is cut to an oblong shape. The natural curve of the bark is carefully preserved. From each of the two long sides of this, between two and three feet from either end, a wedge-shaped piece, the base of which corresponds with the outer edge of the bark, is cut out. The two ends of the whole strip of bark—that is to say, the short piece between each end and the nearest wedge-shaped incisions—are raised till the edges of the wedge-shaped slits meet; and these edges are then sewn together with bush-rope. This, therefore, raises the bow and stern at an angle from the water, while the body of the craft floats parallel to the water-line. Sticks of strong wood are sometimes, but not always, fastened round the gunwale inside the woodskin, to keep the bark in shape. Two or three small square pieces of bark are then laid, the rough side upward, on the floor of the woodskin; these serve as seats for the passengers and rests for any goods carried. The craft is then ready.

Woodskins are made and used chiefly by the Ackawoi and Arecunas, and also by such other Indians as live on rocky rivers much interrupted by falls and rapids. A woodskin, even when large enough to carry three or four Indians, with their goods, is so light that it can easily be taken from the water and carried past a fall or other obstruction to navigation in a few minutes. When not in use, woodskins are kept sunk under water, to prevent their splitting or warping under the action of the sun.

The paddles, by which alone all these kinds of boats are generally propelled, are hewn merely with cutlass or knife, sometimes out of a solid block of timber, but more often, because more easily, out of one of the board-like natural buttresses of the 'paddle-wood' tree (*Aspidospermum excelsum*). In appearance this tree is one of the most peculiar in the forest; the trunk resembles a number of boards standing on end, one edge of each going to form the common centre from which they all radiate. In the South American forests there are many kinds of trees which have these queer board-like trunks, but in no other of these is this habit of growth so strongly developed as in the paddle-wood. The mora (*Mora excelsa*) for example, has board-like buttresses, but these radiate from a main trunk of considerable diameter and of the ordinary approximately round form; but in the *Aspidospermum* the whole trunk, at any rate for some distance from the ground, often consists merely of boards. It will readily be understood that one of these buttresses can easily be shaped into a paddle. In shape the paddles vary but little throughout Guiana. All the tribes, with one exception, make and use paddles with broad, oblong blades and round shafts; at the top of the shaft is a small semilunar handle, into which the hand of the paddler fits most readily and comfortably. The one exceptional tribe is that of the Wapiana, who use paddles with perfectly circular blades, rounded shafts, and straight cross-handles. Similar paddles are in fashion among the Brazilian Indians of the Rio Branco, from whom, doubtless, the neighbouring Wapiana learned to use them. The paddles, whatever the shape, are often roughly ornamented with painted figures and patterns.

Sometimes, though rarely, and principally on the lower, broader parts of the rivers near the sea-coast, square sails made of strips of the pith of the æta palm (*Mauritia flexuosa*) tied together somewhat as in a venetian blind, are used to drive canoes. The Warraus seem more apt at making and using these sails than any other Indians; but True Caribs and Arawaks, at any rate now, occasionally use them.

Next in importance among the wooden articles made and used by the Indians are the low seats or benches common in their houses, which are also hewn in spare moments from solid blocks of wood. The very desirable object of these seems to be to raise the hams of the Indian, when sitting, out of the reach of the jiggers which usually abound on the floors of the houses, and are painful enough when they enter the flesh of the feet, but are far more inconvenient in other parts of the body. These benches are from six to ten inches high, and they are often so carefully scooped out and shaped to fit the body of the sitter that they are as comfortable as any cushioned stool could be. They are often formed into grotesque figures of tortoises, frogs, armadilloes, alligators, and other animals. One in the Christy collection, which, though not from Guiana, is Carib, is in the form of a man on all fours, the middle of his back forming the seat. Bright-coloured seeds, and occasionally pebbles, are inserted to represent the eyes.

But, after all, the greatest time and care is spent in fashioning weapons, both offensive and defensive. These, instead of being roughly finished, as are boats, benches, and such large articles, are smoothed and polished as carefully as any piece of European furniture. For the first rough smoothing the palate bones of certain fish are used in place of files; for the final smoothing the rough leaves of the trumpet-wood (*Cecropia peltata*) are used in place of sand-paper by the Forest Indians, the somewhat similar leaves of a shrub (*Curatella americana*), very common on the savannahs, by the Savannah Indians.

Of weapons of war the only kind now to be seen is the war-club, called *tiki* by the Carib tribes; and even these are probably no longer made, and are carried more as ornaments than for use. They are made of hard heavy wood, and are often highly ornamented, being covered with a pattern formed by engraving and filling the lines thus made with a white earth, brightly polished, and neatly bound with large quantities of red or white cotton from which fringes and streamers, tasselled with bright-coloured feathers, hang loose. Originally, apparently, they differed in shape according to the tribe which made them; but these differences, as in so many other similar cases, seem now to be somewhat lost, and most of the various forms of tiki may be seen in possession of any one of the tribes. The commoner forms are three in number. One is four-sided; that part which is grasped in the hand is square, but from that point the sides gradually curve outward, the one end much more than the other, until they are abruptly cut off and end in both directions in flat surfaces at right angles to the sides (Fig. 24 c and d). This form appears to have been appropriated by the Macusis. Another type is shaped somewhat like a paddle, with a thin

FIG. 24.

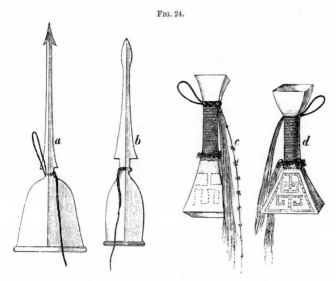

WAR CLUBS.

rounded shaft and a broad, flat, somewhat oval blade; but the shaft, unlike that of a paddle, tapers to a very sharp point, which is said to be intended to stick into the ear of the enemy as a *coup de grâce* after he has been knocked down by a blow from the knife-like edge of the blade. Different varieties of this type seem to have been appropriated by the Wapiana and the Arecuna (Fig. 24 a and b). The third kind is wedge-shaped, the pointed edge being that which forms the handle. There is nothing to show to what tribe this form originally belonged, and it is the rarest of all. A very severe blow could cer-

tainly be inflicted with any one of these weapons. From
specimens existing in English and European museums,
derived from Guiana and the neighbouring parts of South
America, it would appear that these clubs were occasionally
made yet more formidable by the addition of a stone axe-
blade, or in later times a similar blade of iron, which was
occasionally fixed into the side (Fig. 43, p. 425).[1]

Hunting weapons, such as the blow-pipe with its apparatus, and bows and arrows, are made in much greater
number; for while warfare among the Indians is now almost
entirely at an end, hunting is as necessary to them as ever.

The blow-pipe is not complete without the quiver, with
its complement of darts, and a small basket of peculiar shape
containing cotton or other natural fibre, which, being wrapped
round the blunt end of the dart, serves, as the 'feathering'
of an arrow, to balance it. The gigantic hollow reed (*Arun-
dinaria Schomburgkii*) of which the main part of the blow-
pipe itself is made, is said to grow only in the country about
the sources of the Orinoco. Of all the tribes of British
Guiana the Arecunas live nearest to that district; and it is
these, therefore, who procure the reeds and make the blow-
pipes, or perhaps sometimes procure ready-made blow-pipes
from yet more remote Indians, which they distribute among
the other Indians. A straight piece of the reed of length
sufficient for the blow-pipe, which may vary from eight to
fourteen feet, is cut from between any two of the widely
separated nodes, and is thoroughly dried, first by fire and
then in the sun, care being taken to prevent warping. This
reed forms the required barrel. It would, however, if left
unstrengthened, bend after a time. To obviate this, the
straight slender stem of a certain palm, which is also procured from a distance, by means of barter, is bored throughout its length, with a long sharply pointed stick; and within
the rigid tube thus made the reed is inserted, as in a sheath.
The end to which the mouth is to be applied when the pipe

---

[1] Since this was written I have been fortunate enongh to procure one of
these wooden war-clubs with a stone blade, from the Essequibo River.

is used is left as it is, or at most it is neatly bound with string; but on the opposite end, to prevent dirt from getting into the tube when it stands on that end on the ground, the cup-like half of a round hollow palm seed is fixed, like the lip of a trumpet. Generally, but not always, two peccary teeth are fastened, close together and parallel to each other, on the outside of the tube, near the end; and these serve as 'sights.' The blow-pipe is then complete in all essential points. But sometimes, merely for the sake of ornament, a close covering of basketwork—the so-called pegall work, which has been already described—is put round it. Most of the examples in European museums have this added ornament; but such are, according to my own experience, rarely actually used by the Indians. To prevent any chance of the tube losing its straightness it is very seldom allowed to rest on its end on the earth, but, when not in use, it generally hangs, passed through two slings, parallel to the ground.

The quiver (Fig. 15, p. 246) in which the darts are carried is in shape exactly like a dice-box, but larger. It is made of wickerwork thickly coated on the outside with the black pitch-like substance which is made and used by the Indians for so many purposes. Attached to the quiver by a string is a lid, made of the tough hide of the tapir (*Tapirus americanus*). Inside the quiver is a bundle of darts, the whole lower jaw of a perai-fish (*Serasalmo niger*), and some crowia fibre. The darts, each about eight inches long, are made simply of splinters of the woody midrib of the cokerite palm (*Maximiliana regia*), as sharp as needles, which are dipped in urari poison. They are fastened together, palisade-fashion, by means of two parallel plaits of string (Fig. 25, p. 302); and the band of darts thus made is wrapped lightly round a stick, the upper end of which—that towards which are the points of the dart—is provided with a few sticks tied together into the form of a wheel; the object of this latter arrangement being to protect the hand of the Indian from any chance contact with the poison-smeared points of the darts (Fig. 26, p. 302).

It will easily be understood that any single dart may readily
be slipped out from the bundle the moment before it is to be
used. With two or three crowia fibres, sufficient cotton, or
whatever fibre is used for the purpose—which is carried in a

FIG. 25.

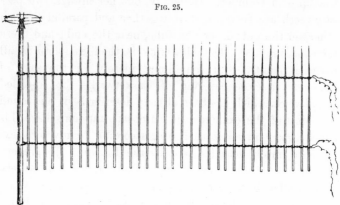

DARTS FOR BLOW-PIPE, UNROLLED FROM GUARD.

small wicker-basket, bottle-shaped, or like a sack tied in near
its mouth, which hangs by a string from the side of the quiver
—is tied on to the blunt end of the dart to fill the diameter of
the blow-pipe ; so that when the Indian blows into the tube

FIG. 26.

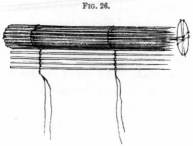

DARTS, ROLLED AS CARRIED IN QUIVER.

behind the dart the latter is propelled with force and expelled into the air. It is thus apparent that the whole apparatus, though so admirably suited for its purpose, is very
simply but skilfully made.

Of the ourali, called also curare and urari, the poison used for these darts and also for certain arrows shot from the bow, it will be more convenient to speak later, when telling of the methods by which Indians prepare other substances from plants.

The forms of the various arrows have been described in telling of the methods of hunting. The very long shafts are of a peculiar reed; and these are generally provided with a short fore-shaft of hard wood, which is forced into the reed and fastened with karamanni pitch. The point of union is then very neatly bound with cotton, which is often arranged in a sort of pattern and finished off with one or two short loose streamers. In some arrows the fore-shaft, being sharpened and cut into notches or small barbs, forms in itself the point. More generally there is a distinct point of iron, hardened bamboo, or, in rare cases, of turtle-bone, which is laboriously filed from the rough material. The arrow is feathered or not, according to the fancy of each maker. The notch at the end of the arrow, which fits on to the bowstring is made in this way: Two slits, crossing each other at right angles, are made across the end surface of the reed, and are continued down the length of the shaft for rather more than an inch; the pith having then been removed from between these split parts, a short, thin stick of hard wood, one end of which has been cut into a proper notch, is then inserted in place of the pith; and the four pieces of the rind of the reed are tightly bound with cotton round this plug. The Indians of the various tribes differ much in the degree of neatness with which they make their arrows, the neatest being made by the Arawaks, Ackawoi, and True Caribs. The bows, which are very long and straight, are made of various sorts of hard wood, generally of purple-heart (*Copaifera pubiflora*) or, when ornament is intended, of letter-wood (*Brosimum Aubletii*). The bowstring is, as has been said, twisted of crowia-fibre.

Passing to the making of ornaments, these are generally so simple, consisting of feathers, teeth, or seeds, tied together, that little art is exhibited in them. The feather ornaments consist chiefly of two kinds of headdress and of ruffs, or mantles, worn round the shoulders. The former are ingeniously made. They are of two shapes: in some the feathers stand, crown-like, round the head; in others they stand straight out from the head (see Plate), like the halo round the head of a saint in some old picture. In either case a frame of light wickerwork is used. The frame of the crown is like a round bottomless and lidless basket, some three inches high, with a broad lip turned outward at right angles to its sides. A band is woven of cotton, much in the same way that the ordinary cotton hammock is made, as broad as the height, and as long as the circumference, of the frame; across each end of this band a stick is fastened so as to project slightly both above and below the band; and beyond the sticks the cotton is continued in a loosely twisted rope for three or four feet. The feathers, from two inches to half an inch long, having been carefully sorted according to colour and size, a row of the longest, all of one colour, are tied evenly side by side on a string; and this string is fastened along the top of the cotton belt. A second row, of rather shorter feathers and of a different colour, is then prepared, and is fastened on to the band so as to cover the base of the first row; and this process is repeated until the whole cotton band is covered by feathers lying as closely and evenly over one another as they do on the breast of a bird. To cover the base of the lowest row of feathers, a very narrow fillet of cotton (see Plate 8, p. 198), coated with a white pipeclay-like earth, is then added at the bottom. The whole band, thus prepared, is then applied round the outside of the frame, and is fastened by slipping the projecting ends of the cross-sticks, when they meet at the back of the headdress, into the wickerwork of the frame. The cotton ropes in which the band ends hang down side by side from the back of the frame. Three long red feathers from the tail of a macaw are then fastened each on to a separate stick, and, by slipping these sticks into the wickerwork of the frame, are fixed side by side, so that they rise straight up from the back of the headdress. The tips of these long feathers are sometimes clipped into fantastic shapes, or are sometimes removed and replaced by tips cut from white feathers. When the headdress is not in use, the band of feathers is slipped without trouble from off the frame, and is rolled up in very compact form; and the long feathers are also removed, and put, for safety sake, in a cylinder of closely plaited wickerwork.

The other kind of feather headdress—that which has been described as like the halo of a pictured saint—has a much smaller framework, a simple, very narrow, circle of wickerwork which stands out round the head. Round the outer circumference of the frame is a deep groove. The feathers are fastened together in rows, three or four in number, as in the former case; but these rows are not attached to any common band, but are drawn, one after the other, base inward, into the groove in the frame. The row first applied—that which is uppermost when the headdress is worn—consists of long, white, half-fluffy hackle-feathers from the backs of white cocks. The next row consists of shorter parrot's feathers; the next of yet shorter, and the next of the shortest feathers. In the one figured (Plate 8, p. 198) there are four rows of feathers—white, green, red and green, and black respectively.

Each tribe makes these headdresses of special colours. In the crown-shaped headdresses of the Macusis, the top row is yellow; then come one or two rows of crimson feathers from the breast or tail of toucans; and last and lowest is a band of black-green feathers from a powis or curassow-bird. The yellow feathers used in this work are mostly grown by artificial means on living birds kept for the purpose; and the chief reason for which Indians keep domestic poultry is to supply themselves with the white hackle-feathers for the same purpose. It seems probable that each of the two kinds of headdress was originally peculiar to certain tribes; but both are now used indiscriminately. I once, and only once, saw a headdress of a third form—a row of long feathers from the tails of macaws, erect and encircling the whole head.

The feather shoulder-ruffs and collars made by the Indians
are of three kinds. One consists of a closely placed row of
tail-feathers of one or other of the two reddish kinds of
macaws, arranged side by side, their bases connected by a
string, while another fine thread passes across them in a
straight line, at a certain distance up their length, to keep
them parallel to each other and in the same plane (Fig. 27).
This mantle of gaudy feathers, the top of which is as wide as

FIG. 27.

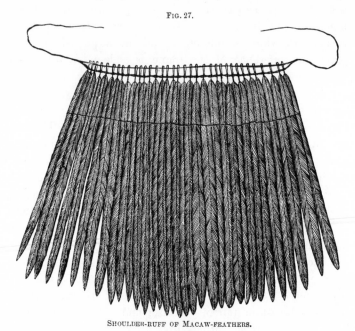

SHOULDER-RUFF OF MACAW-FEATHERS.

a man's back across the shoulders, is stretched from shoulder
to shoulder, so that, the string being brought under the arms
and drawn very tight, the feathers stand out from the body
of the Indian like a gigantic ruff. (See Frontispiece.) The
two collars are more simple; and they only differ from each
other in that one is made of the feathers of a white heron, the
other of the black feathers of the powis. In either case the
web of the feather is stripped from the quill, and the long pieces
of web are made into a fringe which, when hung round the

neck, covers the shoulders and upper part of the chest. The
heron's feathers are worn especially by men engaged in running foot races; the black when dancing, and sometimes when
paddling in canoes. But that the part of the body sheltered
by these feathers is not especially delicate, it might be supposed that the original reason for the custom might have
been to obtain some slight shelter from the heat of the sun
by men engaged in violent exercise.

Of necklaces the most important is made of a very large
number, sometimes over a hundred, of teeth of the bush-
hog or peccary; and as only the two upper canine teeth are
used, such a necklace would represent the spoils of fifty
animals. The fact that every Indian possesses one such
necklace consisting of more or less teeth, is some indication
of the enormous abundance of these animals in the forests
of Guiana. Each tooth is filed down till its four sides are
square; and the top is filed to a point; the bases of the
whole are then firmly embedded, side by side and quite close
to each other, in a thick fibre-woven cord. The two ends of
the row of teeth thus formed are bound together; and from
this point of junction, which is that which, when the necklace is worn, rests on the back of the neck, two long cords of
cotton, the ends ornamented with tassels of bird-skins and
beetle-wings, hang down. The teeth are kept very white;
and that they may be more readily cleaned, the necklace is
occasionally taken to pieces and the teeth reset. There
seems to be some slight difference in the way in which these
teeth are put together by the different tribes; for on one
occasion when I tried to induce a Macusi to put on a necklace which I had obtained from a source unknown to him, he
refused angrily, on the ground that it had been made by a
True Carib. But the difference is so slight that it is unnoticeable to any but an Indian eye.

Other necklaces are made by simply piercing and stringing
together the teeth of acourie, caymans, jaguars, or sometimes
water-haas (*Capybara*). True Caribs make them also very
prettily of deer's teeth, separating each two by a couple

of brown seeds or red beads. Other necklaces are made in
the same way, but of seeds instead of teeth. One Indian
often has many necklaces of various kinds, but none except
that first described is regarded as of any special value.

Turning to the musical instruments of the Indians, but
few words need be said. Their drums, which are of the
ordinary shape, are made at the cost of much labour. A
suitable tree, generally an æta palm, is felled, and a piece of
the trunk, of the right height for a drum, being cut off, this
is hollowed into a cylinder with a very thin wall. Two pieces
of jaguar, deer, or monkey-skin, for the top and bottom of

FIG. 28.

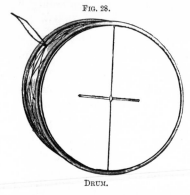

DRUM.

the drum, have been previously stretched in a wooden frame
and thoroughly dried in the sun. One of these is now fixed
on to either end of the cylinder. A very fine double thread,
in the middle of which is a slip-knot, is then stretched
diagonally across the skin at one end of the drum, and
before this is finally drawn tight an excessively slender
splinter of wood is passed through, and secured in the slip-
knot, so that it rests on the skin at right angles to the line
of the thread (Fig. 28). The result is that the two ends of
the drum when beaten produce different sounds; for the one
on which is the string and splinter returns a metallic sound,
caused by the vibrations of the splinter against the skin.
The skin of the baboon, or howling monkey, is preferred by
the drum-maker, because it is supposed to possess the power

of emitting the rolling roaring sounds for which this monkey is celebrated.

Another instrument, akin to the drum, but ruder, is made by stretching a piece of baboon-skin over one end of a four-feet-long piece of a hollow bamboo, of a particular and rare species. This instrument, when repeatedly struck against the ground, produces a drum-like sound (Fig. 32 D, p. 322).

Flutes are made simply by piercing the necessary holes

FIG. 29.

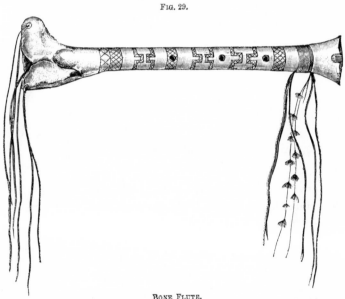

BONE FLUTE.

in the bone of a jaguar or deer, or, though such are no longer common, a man. Intricate patterns are sometimes engraved on these flutes, and are coloured black or red, to contrast with the pure white of the bone; and very long tassels of white cotton are fixed at each end of the instrument (Fig. 29). Wooden flutes, always used in pairs, are also made in somewhat the same way, of short pieces of bamboo-stem (Fig. 30, p. 310).

Pan-pipes are made of hollow reeds. Rude wooden trumpets are said to be made; and I once saw the fragments of one in an Indian house.

One other very curious instrument is made and used on the savannahs. This is a sort of Æolian harp, formed from the leaf-stalk of the æta palm, by picking and separating, without severing, four or five feet of several of the parallel fibres of which the skin of the stalk consists; a bridge, like that of a fiddle, is then placed under each end of these fibres,

FIG. 30.

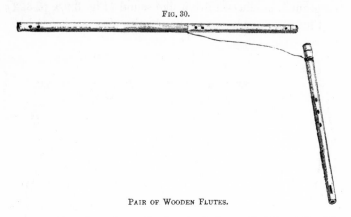

PAIR OF WOODEN FLUTES.

so as to raise them from the level of the stalk (Fig. 31). The leaf-stalk thus prepared is fastened upright in some exposed place, and the wind passing through the strings causes a soft musical sound, which rises and falls as the strength of the breeze varies.

FIG. 31.

ÆOLIAN HARP.

Last of the simple arts of the Indians may be mentioned their ways of preparing the chief poisons, oils, resins, dyes, and the tobacco which they use.

The poison used for the darts of the blow-pipes, as also for various kinds of poisoned arrows, is the far-famed ourali. The various properties of this curious poison have, in spite of much research, not yet been fully traced.[1] Its

[1] For an elaborate account of this poison, the reader is referred to a pamphlet by Richard Schomburgk, published in Australia.

very name is but confusedly known. In Europe it is variously called *curare, curari, urari, urali,* and *ourali.* The two first of these forms have probably arisen from a mere blunder; but the three latter are various attempts to pronounce the Indian name. The letters *r* and *l* are very commonly interchanged in Indian, as in other languages; and of Indians, not necessarily of different tribes, but perhaps only of different settlements, some use the word *urali,* or even *ulali,* some *urari.* The Macusis are the chief makers of this poison in Guiana, and they distribute it to the other Indians. But even of the Macusis it is only a man here and there who can make ourali, and the recipe is carefully kept and transmitted from generation to generation; so that the poison-maker is a great and important man in his district. The recipe appears to be known to other Indians of the tribe, and the fact that these do not prepare poison appears to be due, not to ignorance of the method, but to a superstitious feeling of the unlawfulness of its practice except by duly qualified practitioners, or perhaps to a feeling akin to the professional etiquette which in more civilised communities prevents members of one branch of a profession from doing work more proper to another branch of the same.

Ourali is made with much ceremony, probably intended to enhance the importance of the maker. A small hut is built especially for the occasion; and no woman or child is allowed to approach this. Many ingredients are used, such as several kinds of barks, roots, peppers (*Capsicum*), ants, and the poison-fangs of snakes; but of these, only one, the bark of a creeping plant (*Strychnos toxifera*), is alone essential, as appears from an experiment made by Sir Robert Schomburgk, who produced poison of an effective kind from this substance alone. The Indians, however, as far as I have seen and heard, always use a variety of barks and one or more roots; and this is confirmed by Sir Richard Schomburgk, who also saw the poison prepared. The latter traveller mentions the ingredients which he saw used, as follows:—

Bark and albumen of Urari-plant (*Strychnos toxifera*)	.	2 lbs.
,,	,,	Yakki (*Strychnos Schomburgkii*)	.	¼ lb.
,,	,,	Arimaru (*Strychnos cogens*)	.	¼ lb.
,,		Tarireng (?)	.	¼ lb.
,,		Wokarimo (?)	.	¼ lb.
Root of Tarireng			.	½ oz.
Tararemu			.	½ oz.
Curamu (*Cissus*, sp. ?)			.	?

A few small pieces of Manuca wood.

I myself saw the first of these (*Strychnos toxifera*) used together with the fleshy roots of a caladium, and with certain other barks, which may or may not have been the same as those mentioned by Schomburgk, as I only saw these in a dry state and after they had been scraped into small fragments. The caladium root which I saw used replaced, I presume, the fleshy cissus root of Schomburgk's formula.

Water was fetched especially for the poison-making from a stream nearly a quarter of a mile distant; and care was taken, in carrying this to the house, to rest it on the ground every few yards. For, say the Indians, a bird wounded by a poisoned dart will fly only as far as the water with which the poison was made was carried without rest.

The shreds of scraped bark were placed in a large and new earthenware buck-pot, which contained three or four quarts of water; and the mixture was allowed to simmer gently for many hours, during which the poison-maker carefully tended the fire, and every now and then blew into the boiling liquid. As we shall see elsewhere, the Indians believe greatly in the virtue of the breath of certain individuals—as, for instance, of the peaiman who blows away the spirit of disease from invalids, and the evil principle from meats otherwise unclean. After twenty-four hours the pot was taken off the fire. By that time the contents had been reduced to about a third of their original bulk, and were thick and syrup-like. This syrup was now strained through a new cassava-strainer, and was then exposed in a flat vessel to the heat of the sun. The juice of the caladium roots, which had in the meantime been boiled in a separate pot, on a separate fire, was now mixed with the other ingredients, with the immediate result of making the poison darker in colour and thicker in consistency. It was placed in the sun for some hours, till it at last darkened to a deep coffee-colour and to the consistency of a thick jelly. In this state it was put into the small gourds, in which it is kept, and, after four days, it was declared to be ready for use. Experiment proved its effectiveness. A fowl slightly pricked with a dart on which the poison had been smeared, ceased to live (for that is the only way to describe the apparent symptoms of the poison) in about six minutes. The poison, if kept warm and dry, retains its power for several years. That without these conditions it soon becomes powerless, I learned on two occasions. The first lesson was when I happened to pick up a stick in the forest, and accidentally pricking myself with the sharp end I found that it was an old blow-pipe dart with the poison still visible on it; exposure to the weather had, however, deprived the poison of its proper effect. On the second occasion, a bundle of poisoned darts which I had taken out of the quiver of an Indian two years previously, and had brought into the cold climate of England, fell so that the points entered the flesh of my hand. Richard Schomburgk was told by the Indians that the deadly power could, though once lost, be restored to the poison by mixing some cassava-juice with it and burying it.

This poison is prepared by particular Indians in several parts of South America. The materials apparently vary; but a *Strychnos* with poisonous qualities such as those of *S. toxifera* always forms the essential basis. Where ourali is made, Indians from distant parts of the country come to barter for it. That it is only made in these centres appears to be due to the belief of the Indians that the poisonous species of *Strychnos* grows only very locally. For example, in Guiana it is believed that *S. toxifera* grows only in certain places on the Canakoo mountains in the Macusi country; and the poison is only there made. But as Richard Schomburgk pointed out, the plant grows also on the Pomeroon and

Waini rivers, where it is unrecognised and unused by the Indians.

Another poison, called ' wassi,' is said by Richard Schomburgk to be prepared by the Ackawoi. From the description given of this it appears to be the white powder with deadly qualities which, as is told in many an Indian story, all kenaimas, and especially all Ackawoi kenaimas, are said to rub into the flesh of their victims.

A considerable quantity of oil is used by the Indians to anoint their bodies and to polish their bows and other weapons of hard wood. Among the Indians of the forest, most of this oil is prepared from the nuts of a very common tree, the crab-wood (*Carapa guianensis*). At the season when the nuts fall they are gathered, and, after being boiled, are put aside until they become half-rotten. When they are in proper condition they are shelled and kneaded into a coarse paste. Troughs are prepared of naturally curved tree-bark, one end being cut into a point : the shape of these troughs is in fact exactly that of the steel nib of a pen. These, having been filled with the nut paste, are fixed in some sunny place, slanting, and with the pointed end over some vessel. The oil oozes from the paste, runs down the trough, and drips from the point into the vessel below. The smell of this oil is very strong and unpleasant; but it is one of the characteristic scents of an Indian house. When rubbed on the body it keeps even mosquitoes and flies away from the flesh. Sometimes the smell is partly overcome by mixing some sweet-scented resinous or other vegetable substance with the oil. Crab-oil finds a ready sale in the towns ; and in September, at which season the new crop of oil is ready for use, Indians bring it down to the coast, coming down then in larger numbers than at any other time of year.

On the savannah, where crab-nuts are less easily procured, the seeds of the cokerite palm (*Maximiliana regia*) are used instead. These are crushed, and boiled in water ; and the oil which then rises to the surface is skimmed off by means of small pads of cotton fibre. This oil is very pure, and has no very disagreeable scent. Occasionally the seeds of other palms, especially of the various species of *Astrocaryum*, are treated in the same way.

One of the most remarkable substances prepared by the Indians is the karamanni wax or pitch, of which mention has already several times been made. The basis of this is a resin which is drawn, by tapping, from a very beautiful tree (*Siphonia bacculifera*), and is mixed with bees-wax, to make it more pliable, and with finely powdered charcoal, to make it black. While still semi-liquid it is generally run into a hollow bamboo; but it is sometimes allowed to take shape and to harden in the bottom of a buck-pot. One very curious and beautiful piece of karamanni, which is now in the Kew Museum, seems to have been prepared in this way. The resin has evidently been mixed with an unusually large quantity of bees-wax; and the whole has then been melted and allowed to drop into a buck-pot partly filled with water. The result is a circular tablet of wax, the lower side smooth, and of the shape of the buck-pot, but on the upper side wrought into the most beautiful coils and folds of infinite variety. It is like a beautiful medallion carved in high relief in coal-black wood. It was prepared, apparently accidentally, by Arawak Indians.[1]

Karamanni is used in place of pitch and glue to fill up crevices in woodwork, as, for instance, in boat-building, and to fix the heads of arrows into the shafts, and for all similar work. Its strength, when it is not mixed with too large a proportion of bees-wax, is very great. No better illustration of this quality can be given than the fact that on one occasion when our men were sawing timber, and the handle of the whip-saw parted from the blade, the two parts were, on the suggestion of an Indian, stuck together so firmly with karamanni that the saw again became effective.

Another substance, of very similar nature, called by the

[1] I have since met with other specimens of karamanni in this form, and am now inclined to think that their preparation is intentional.

Macusis 'tuara,' is sometimes, but very rarely, used in place of karamanni.   Except that it is a whitish resin, I know nothing further of its nature.

A deliciously scented white resin exudes from the hyawa-tree (*Icica heptaphylla*), which grows abundantly in sandy soils.   The rough masses of this, which is very inflammable, are often collected and stored by the Indians for the pur-pose of lighting fires.   Sometimes, too, it is broken up into small pieces which are put into hollow sticks, to be used as torches.   Made pliable by the admixture of a little oil, it is formed into balls, like cannon-balls, and in this state is stored and used to scent oil for anointing the bodies and hair of Indians.

The dyes used by the Indians to paint their own bodies, and occasionally to draw patterns on their implements, are red faroah, purple caraweera, blue-black lana, white fel-spathic clay, and, though very rarely, a yellow vegetable dye of unknown origin.

Faroah is the deep-red pulp round the seed of a shrub (*Bixa orellana*), which grows wild on the banks of some of the rivers, and is cultivated by the Indians in their clearings. Mixed with a large quantity of oil, it is then either dried, and so kept in lumps which can be made soft again by the addition of more oil, or is stored in a liquid condition in tubes made of hollow bamboo-stems.   When it is to be used, either a mass of it is taken in the palm of the hand and rubbed over the skin or other surface to be painted, or a pattern of fine lines is drawn with it by means of a stick used as a pencil.   The True Caribs also use faroah largely to stain their hammocks.

Caraweera is a somewhat similar dye, of a more purplish red, and by no means so commonly used.   It is prepared from the leaves of a yellow-flowered bignonia (*B. chicka*), together with some other unimportant ingredients.   The dried leaves are boiled for a few minutes over a fire, and then some freshly cut pieces of the bark of a certain tree and a bundle of twigs and fresh leaves of another tree are added to the mixture. The whole is then boiled for about twenty minutes, care being taken to keep the bark and leaves under water. The pot is then taken from the fire, and the contents, being poured into bowls, are allowed to subside. The clear water left at the top is poured away, and the sediment, of a beautiful purple colour, is put into a cloth, on which it is allowed to dry; after this, it is scraped off and packed in tiny baskets woven of the leaves of the cokerite palm. The pigment is used for body-painting, with oil, just as is faroah.

Lana is the juice of the fruit of a small tree (*Genipa americana*), with which, without further preparation, blue-black lines are drawn in patterns, or large surfaces are stained, on the skin. The dye thus applied is for about a week indelible.

One or more of the three body-paints already mentioned is used by most Indians, and in large quantities. But the white, and still more the yellow, pigments are used only rarely, in lines or dots, and very sparingly, by some of the Savannah Indians. The white substance is simply a very semi-liquid felspathic clay, which occurs in pockets in one or two places on the savannah; this is collected and dried in lumps, which are then pierced, threaded, and so put aside for future use. The nature of the yellow dye I was never able to trace; all that the Indians could or would say was that they received it in small quantities from a tribe living beyond the Wapianas, who extracted it from a tree which only grows in that neighbourhood.

We turn last of all to tobacco. Every Indian man, and nearly every boy, smokes. The tobacco is grown in the clearings. The leaves are picked, and are sometimes, though not always, dipped in honey; under any circumstances, they are hung up under the roof of the Indian house till they are partly dry. After that the leaves are evenly arranged side by side, and are lightly tied in bundles. As the leaves dry, the strings round the bundle are drawn tighter and tighter, until it is evident that no further diminution will take place in the bulk. The quality of this tobacco varies much, but some of it is most excellent. It is smoked only in cigarettes, made, each as it is required, by wrapping half a leaf, uncut, in a paper-like substance procured either from the cakaralli-tree (*Lecythis ollaria*) or from the manicole-palm (*Euterpe oleracea*). The method of preparing this paper from the cakaralli is most ingenious. A long strip of bark of exactly the width required for the wrapper of the cigarette is cut from the tree, with straight sides and ends. From this the outer rough bark is removed. With a thick, short stick the Indian then repeatedly strikes the cut edge of one end of the inner bark, with a peculiar but indescribable knack, so as to separate it into a great many even-surfaced sheets. Thus a number of bands of paper, called by the Indians *queeka*, are produced, and it is only necessary to cut these into proper short lengths, to make them into cigarette wrappers. The knack of preparing queeka is said by the Indians to be acquired only after much practice. Often, when camping in the neighbourhood of cakaralli-trees, I have seen the younger men and the boys spend the greater part of the night practising the art. The other kind of cigarette wrapper is procured simply by tearing the skin off the inside of the spathe of the manicole-palm.

CHAPTER XV.

PAIWARI FEASTS.

Feasting and Drinking and Games—The Invitation to the Feast—Quippoo-
writing—Preparations—Arrival of the Guests—Feasting—Dancing—
Brawls—Racing and Ball-play—Arawak Whip-game—Warrau Shield-
game.

THE festivals, the dances, and the games originally peculiar
to any people, often remain but little altered long after most
other matters which distinguished that people from the rest
of the world have disappeared. Probably this is as true of
the Indians of Guiana as of other races. But it is seldom
easy for a stranger to see and note such festivities in their
original and proper form. Indians are very shy; and in the
presence of a white man they are seldom willing to throw
aside their reserve sufficiently to enter freely and un-
restrainedly into the spirit of their games. It is, therefore,
not possible to give a minute and detailed account of their
amusements of this sort.

All the festivals among all the tribes being occasions for
much drinking of paiwari—the national beverage—they may
all be called Paiwari Feasts. Sometimes these feasts are
given on special occasions, as, for instance, to celebrate a
marriage or a funeral, or to mark the establishment of a new
settlement. But often they are held for no special reason,
but simply because the headman of some settlement feels
inclined to entertain his neighbours, and has sufficient ripe
cassava in his fields for the purpose.

When a paiwari feast is to be held, invitations are sent
to the people of all neighbouring settlements inhabited by
Indians of the same tribe as the givers of the feast. The

latter prepare a number of strings, each of which is knotted as many times as there are days before the feast day. One of these strings is kept by the headman of the settlement where the feast is to be held; the others are distributed, one to the headman of each of the settlements from which guests are expected. Every day one of the knots, on each of the strings, is untied; and when the last has been untied, guests and hosts know that the feast day has come.

Sometimes, instead of knots on a string, notches on a piece of wood are used. This system of knot-tying, the quippoo system of the Peruvians, which occurs in nearly identical form in all parts of the world, is used not only, as in the above instance, for calendar-keeping, but also to record items of any sort; for instance, if one Indian owes another a certain number of balls of cotton, or other articles, debtor and creditor each have a corresponding string or stick, with knots or notches to the number of the owed article, and one or more of these is obliterated each time a payment is made, until the debt is wiped out.

To return to the preparations for the feast: while the knots were daily decreasing in number, all who are to be present have been busy. The guests have been making bread, and have been hunting game and fish, and smoking meat, in order to contribute their share to the general entertainment; for the hosts supply the paiwari, but cannot supply all the food for their visitors. And the hosts have been busy—the men in getting together as much provisions as they can, the women in preparing the paiwari.

The one or more wooden paiwari-troughs which stand in the middle of nearly every house are shaped somewhat like canoes; indeed, canoes are often used for the purpose. Each trough holds from 150 to 200 gallons; so that, as all available troughs, as well as all spare bottles, gourds, and jars, are filled for the feast, no small quantity of paiwari has to be made. For this reason, and because paiwari does not acquire a proper degree of mellowness and fermentation for a day or two after it has been made, the women, whose duty it is to prepare it, begin to work some days before that on which their guests are expected.

By the time the guests begin to arrive sufficient liquor has been prepared. The visitors arrive in family parties, men, women, and children, in their canoes, corials, or wood-skins; and they bring their hammocks and their provisions—for the entertainment lasts some days, often for a week. Often they also bring such hammocks, balls of spun cotton, live stock, or other goods as they have for barter—for these gatherings seem to serve not only as feasts, but also as fairs. As the boats approach the settlement, the men give notice of their coming by loudly uttering the cry peculiar to their tribe—for each tribe has a distinct cry. The people of the settlement, with the exception of the headman, who goes to his hammock and there awaits the coming of his guests, flock down to the landing-place to receive the new-comers. The men of the newly arrived party make their way up to the houses, leaving the women to unload the boats. The latter patiently carry up the goods, and without a word sling their husbands', brothers', and children's hammocks, and then their own, in some of the houses.

The reception of the men by the headman of the settle-ment is tedious and formal in the extreme. The leader of the strangers first addresses his host—who during the recep-tion never stirs out of his hammock—and remarks that (he has come); to which the captain grunts assent. The first speaker then, in a number of short abrupt sentences, tells any news that he may have to give; and after each of these sentences, the captain from his hammock utters the same monosyllabic grunt of assent. At last, when this first speaker is done, he is bidden to sit down. Then the next in authority tells his news in the same manner, and is answered with exactly the same grunts of assent; and he in his turn is bidden to sit down. And so, in long and tedious order, each one of the new-comers addresses the captain. In the meantime, the women of the house bring to each man, as he sits down, a large calabash filled with paiwari. While he drinks, the woman keeps her hand on the calabash ; and when the vessel has been emptied, at one draught, she re-fills it. Another woman then brings the pepperpot and some bread, the latter on a fan, and sets these before the man. At last, when all the new-comers have had their say

FIG. 32.

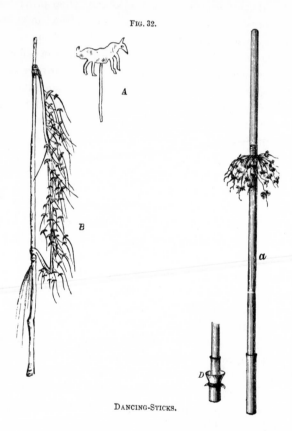

DANCING-STICKS.

and have eaten, they disperse, and retire to their hammocks; probably to make way for a new set, who are welcomed in exactly the same way.

The feast begins the next morning. By daybreak men, women, and children are busy painting and ornamenting themselves. On these occasions, Indians paint themselves to an unusual degree and load themselves with any ornaments which they happen to possess. Even the women are allowed on this occasion to put a fillet of cotton round their heads, besides putting on, as a matter of course, all their beads, teeth, and seeds. Each puts on what he has got, and seems to think himself the more successful the more finery he has put on. The result is as varied and picturesque a crowd as could well be imagined.

The children, too, are painted and dressed much as are their parents; and sometimes even the monkeys of the settlement are got up in the same way.

Quaint and varied as is the dress of the feasters, a further element of picturesque variety is added when they take their weapons and instruments. Some whirl sticks to which are tied bunches of certain seeds (*Thevetia nereifolia*) which, when struck against the ground, clash and rattle (Fig. 32 B); some beat time with hollow bamboos covered at one end with skin, like a drum, and ornamented with bunches of these same seeds; some have small rattles ornamented with bright-coloured feathers; some have drums; some have much-ornamented flutes made of animals' bones; some have flutes made of hollow reeds; some have pan-pipes; and some have sticks topped with a rude wooden and painted image of some bird, fish, or animal (Fig. 32 A).

At last all is ready for the carousal. All form a procession, and march slowly round the liquor trough, droning out a chant, keeping step, and waving their instruments in slow, measured time. Round and round the trough the strange procession winds, all feet stamping in time with the monotonous chant of *Hia-hia-hia*. Suddenly the chant gives place to loud discordant cries, and the procession breaks up. The women bring calabashes with paiwari for the men to drink. Then the women drink. And then the procession re-forms, and continues as before, till there is a new interruption, and a new drinking. The actual quantity of liquor consumed by each individual is tremendous. By long practice they have acquired the knack of bringing up the liquor almost as soon as it has been drunk. And so an enormous bulk of liquor fills and re-fills the stomach, but of this only the very small proportion of alcohol which it contains remains in the stomach to fire their spirits. In time this tells, and the drinkers get more and more excited. Then they leave the house and dance in the open space outside.

These dances seem to differ in each tribe; and, moreover, each tribe seems to have several dances more or less peculiar to it. In some the body is moved in a slow and stately manner, which contrasts oddly with the grotesque position in which the head and limbs are held. Very often the dance, if it deserves the name, is simple enough. The men range themselves in a long line, each linking his arms in those of his neighbours, and the women, standing opposite to them, do likewise. For hours together the two lines continue to advance toward each other and to retreat, keeping up a monotonous chant, each individual stamping in time with the others, and so hard, that one wonders how their naked feet bear the shock on the hard ground. Only now and then the lines break up for very brief intervals to allow opportunity to drink. Occasionally, too, a man and a woman link arms and strut about slowly together, bending their bodies forward and backward, this side and that, very grotesquely. Certain of the dances are imitations of the movements of animals. One, of an unusually lively kind, mimics the capers of monkeys; others, called tiger-dances, imitate the slow stealthy gliding of the jaguar. In these last, a man, supposed to represent the jaguar, creeps round and round the other dancers, and in and out among them, until he suddenly springs with a loud roar upon some one of them, and carries him off from out of the circle; then he returns and carries off another; and so continues, until he himself remains alone. The Ackawoi have one dance in which each of the performers represents a different animal; and in this each carries a stick on which is the figure of that animal. This seems to be the origin of the dancing-sticks mentioned above (Fig. 324, p. 322).

While dancing, they always chant songs; and the end of each dance is marked by a loud and discordant uproar, which is a signal for renewed drinking.

Often, as the fun grows fast and furious, men and women reel and stagger, and some dispute at last arises. As a rule, Indians never quarrel, and never fight among themselves. However much one Indian has been offended by another, he satisfies himself by ceasing to speak to his foe, or perhaps speaks of him in his absence as a 'bad man.' But when inflamed by paiwari, the quarrel is more violently followed up. Abuse is passed freely from one to the other. Sometimes even blows are exchanged; but that this is an acquired habit, and not one natural to the Indians, is shown by the fact that in such cases they do not double their fists, but, in imitation of the negro, swing forward the extended arm, so as to slap the opponent with the palm of the hand. But before Indians resort even to this mild form of fighting, they are generally so overcome by paiwari that the one who is struck falls at the blow, and he who strikes loses his balance and falls too. There they generally lie; but if one or other of the fallen ones shows signs of giving further trouble, the least intoxicated members of the party take him or her—for it is as often a woman as a man—and sew him up in a hammock, in which position, though quite helpless and harmless, he adds by his shouts to the din of the revel, which is still continued.

But at last, when all are either too drunk or too tired to keep up the dance and the shouts, they retire to their hammocks for what little remains of the night. The next morning, however, the revel of the previous day is renewed; and so it is for many days, until all the available stock of paiwari has been exhausted.

Among the Macusis on the savannahs, paiwari feasts are generally accompanied by foot-races. The racers, who wear collars made of long white herons' feathers, or of black powis' feathers, start, not abreast, but one behind the other, as in the ordinary 'bumping' boat-races of English universities.

Games of ball are also played on these occasions, the ball being made either of part of an ear of Indian corn or of native indiarubber.

The paiwari feasts—according to Schomburgk, though I am doubtful about this, only those held on funeral occasions—

FIG. 33.

MACQUARIE WHIP.

of the Arawaks were peculiar for a strange and painful dance, which is now probably nearly though not quite extinct. The dancers—who are all men—stand in two rows opposite to each other. Each man has in his hand a whip, called *macquarie*, with a hard strong lash made of fibre (Fig. 33). As they dance, the whips are waved. Every now and then a couple retires from the line and use their whips. One stands steadily, one leg in front of the other; the other swings back his whip, and, with all the force he can command, and with a spring forward, lashes the calf of the first man's leg; then, in his turn, the second man stands still, to receive a lash from the other. They lash each other in this way until their calves are striped with weals, and blood flows freely. The punishment is borne and inflicted with perfect good temper, and was probably originally devised as a means of testing endurance. Finally the dancers retire and drink together.

In the Christy collection and in that of General Pitt-Rivers, are some simple canes said to be macquarie whips from the Maiongkong, a tribe of Indians living on the outskirts of Guiana about the upper waters of the Orinoco. Perhaps this tribe also plays this game, using whips different from those of the Arawaks.

The Warraus, again, are peculiar for a kind of wrestling

which they practise at their paiwari feasts. A challenge is given and accepted. Each of the opponents is provided with a large square shield, called *ha-ha*, about four feet high by three wide, made of parallel strips of the pith of the æta palm lashed together by means of three long transverse sticks, the ends of which are ornamented with great tassels of loose fibre (Fig. 34). The two wrestlers, each behind his shield, which he grasps with his hands by its two sides, stands oppo-

FIG. 34.

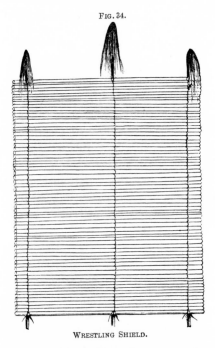

WRESTLING SHIELD.

site to each other, making feints and watching for a favourable opportunity. Suddenly one, seeing his opportunity, springs toward the other, and the shields meet and clash. Each now strives to push back the other. Each plants one foot firmly on the ground behind him and bends the other knee against the shield. Whoever succeeds in pushing back the other from his position is considered to have won the victory.

CHAPTER XVI.

KENAIMAS AND PEAIMEN.

Relation of Kenaimas and Peaimen—The Kenaima—The Vendetta System
—Real and Imaginary Powers of Kenaimas—The Kenaima's Method of
Work—The Peaiman—His Education and Powers—His Method of
Cure—Wide Extension of the Peai System.

KENAIMAS and peaimen,[1] the most marked and influential
characters in everyday Indian life, stand to each other in the
relation of evil and its cure. From the kenaimas come
nearly all injuries; and these the peaiman cures. It is only
by studying them in this inter-relation that the enormous
power exercised by these two characters can be understood.
Very nearly all bodily evil that befals an Indian is, he thinks,
the work of a kenaima, known or unknown; and his only
hope of guarding against such evil, or of curing such as has
come upon him, is by the help of the peaiman. The latter
is therefore the doctor of Indian societies. But he is more
than this, for as evil of all sorts is believed to be the work of
beings, men or other, with the power of working evil either
with their bodies or with their spirits, and as the peaiman
has therefore to contend with foes not merely physical but
half-physical half-spiritual, he is not simply the doctor, but
also, in some sense, the priest or magician.

It will be convenient to notice the kenaima first. In a
future chapter, in describing that which is as religion to the

---

[1] As regards these two names, the word *kenaima* is a genuine Indian
word of the Carib languages, and possibly (for such words generally have
a wide extension) of other languages; the word *peaiman*, on the other
hand, is an Anglicised form of the genuine Indian words *puyai* or *peartzan*—
two different forms of the same word belonging to different dialects of the
Carib language, and occurring in several other, but by no means in all,
languages of South America.

Indians, I shall have to enter somewhat in detail into the
nature of the conception formed by these people of the whole
spirit world; but it is absolutely necessary here to premise
that all tangible objects, animate (including man) and inanimate alike, consist each of two separable parts—a body and
a spirit; and that these are not only always readily separable
involuntarily, as in death, and daily in sleep, but are also, in
certain individuals, always voluntarily separable. A kenaima
is one who uses this last-mentioned power for the purpose of
inflicting vengeance. He is a man who, having devoted himself to slaying some other man, has this power of separating
his spiritual from his bodily substance. He is, as has been
said, the real or supposed cause of almost every evil, and
especially of every death. Other sources of evil believed in
by the Indians are certain beings, such as rocks, stones, and
tree-trunks, and monstrous crabs, eagles, jaguars, or other
animals, also and alike consisting of body and spirit; but
these will be more properly described as part of the whole
system of religion, or rather animism, of the Indians.

Travellers are apt to suppose that the motive of the
kenaima is merely that of an ordinary murderer. But though
there are probably murderers of this sort, for Indians, gentle
as they are, do sometimes commit murder—that is, homicide
prompted by a personal feeling of anger—yet such cases are
probably far from common. Such murderers, however, also
pass as kenaimas; but they are not so in any strict sense.
It is necessary, therefore, to distinguish the true nature of
kenaimas, and to add to this some knowledge of the belief in
their uncanny powers.

In the first place, as probably the original conception,
must be noticed the kenaima as the slayer—he must not be
called a murderer—who is bound to slay by a fixed and, in
a certain stage of society, undoubtedly salutary custom.
Indians have a high sense of the imperative duty of retaliation; and this fully suffices to keep crime in check amongst
them. He against whose nearest relative a wrong has been
done, either intentionally or unintentionally, by any other

Indian, devotes himself to follow and kill the wrong-doer, or, if he cannot be found, some one of his relatives. Richard Schomburgk[1] mentions a striking case in which a Warrau boy of twelve years old took upon himself, and boldly executed, the duties of a kenaima, as a matter of course and with the full approval of his tribe. In all primitive societies where there are no written laws and no supreme authority to enforce justice, such vengeance has been held as a sacred duty; for, in the absence of laws enforced by society, the fear of this vengeance to be inflicted by the injured individual, or by those nearest of kin to him, alone deters individuals from crime. Outside America, at various times in the history of the world, a custom in every way similar to this Indian kenaima system has prevailed. The best known instances are the vendetta, the Israelitish law of retaliation which gave rise to the ' cities of refuge,' and the Saxon system which resulted in the law of blood-money or were-gild, which was money paid to buy off just vengeance. This custom of recognised retaliation yet exists among the Indian tribes of Guiana, and must continue to exist until some system for the administration of justice is established in the districts inhabited by them. The kenaima, in the original and true sense of the word, is one who is thus compelled to retaliate.

Kenaimas of this kind are realities. But beside these there are other kenaimas, the imaginary nature of which we can recognise, but who to the fanciful Indian are equally real. Every death, every illness, is regarded not as the result of natural law, but as the work of a kenaima. Often indeed the survivors or the relatives of the invalid do not know to whom to attribute the deed, which therefore perforce remains unpunished; but often, again, there is real or fancied reason to fix on some one as the kenaima, and then the nearest relative of the injured individual devotes himself to retaliate. Strange ceremonies are sometimes observed in order to discover the secret kenaima. Richard Schomburgk[2] describes a striking instance of this. A Macusi boy

---

[1] *Reisen in Britisch Guiana*, vol. i. p. 158.   [2] *Ibid.* p. 325.

had died a natural death, and his relatives endeavoured to discover the quarter to which the kenaima who was supposed to have slain him belonged. Raising a terrible and monotonous dirge, they carried the body to an open piece of ground, and there formed a circle round it, while the father, cutting from the corpse both the thumbs and little fingers, both the great and the little toes, and a piece of each heel, threw these pieces into a new pot, which had been filled with water. A fire was kindled, and on this the pot was placed. When the water began to boil, according to the side on which one of the pieces was first thrown out from the pot by the bubbling of the water, in that direction would the kenaima be. In thus looking round to see who did the deed, the Indian thinks it by no means necessary to fix on anyone who has been with or near the injured man. The kenaima is supposed to have done the deed, not necessarily in person, but probably in spirit.

As regards the kenaima's method of doing his work, there is a way in which the real kenaima really does his, and other ways in which the imaginary kenaima is supposed to do his.

The real kenaima, wherever his intended victim goes, follows until he finds an opportunity of killing him, either with the club of hardwood which he carries, or with an arrow, or, more frequently, as the Indians say, by poison, which he finds an opportunity of administering, and which slowly destroys his victim. An Indian, if he thinks that he is being followed by a kenaima, tries never for a moment to be without friendly companions; but if ever—probably on some occasion when with others he is on his way home from making a field or from hunting—he lingers for a minute or two behind the others, and some thicket or a turn in the path hides him from their view, or if he is caught asleep by his enemy, in that minute he is lost. The kenaima who, though hardly ever seen, has followed him like a shadow for days, or weeks, or even months, strikes him down. According to the Indians, the kenaima, after he has struck down his victim, sometimes binds him while yet alive and rubs a burning and deadly poison into his flesh, or hopelessly dislocates his limbs; and in this state, alive, though with the certainty of speedy death, the poor wretch is found by his companions, if they return to look for him. This latter part of the process is really probably seldom, if ever, practised; but it is at least certain that Indians have a considerable knowledge of the use of vegetable poisons.

The method of the imaginary kenaima differs in that he works invisibly. It will presently be shown that Indians believe that each individual man has a body and a spirit within that body; and they think that kenaimas use their power of separating spirits and bodies and of sending these spirits to obey their orders, to whatever place they please, and of directing the actions of these spirits. It is, therefore, in the imaginary cases, not the kenaima in the body, but his spirit, which kills or injures.

The belief is probably partly based on the fact that the commonest forms of death among Indians are consumption, dysentery, and a horrible disease known as 'buck-sickness,' all of which diseases kill their victims by a slow, wasting process, not unlike the effects of poison; and poison is supposed to be in an especial degree a weapon of the kenaima. Whenever, therefore, an Indian dies in such illness, it is said that the spirit of the kenaima came and administered poison.

Nor is it only in his own proper body or as an invisible spirit that the kenaima is supposed to be able to approach his unsuspecting victim. He has the power of putting his spirit into the body of any animal he pleases—a jaguar, a serpent, a sting-ray, a bird, an insect, or anything else. It is not to be wondered at that an Indian, when attacked by a beast of prey, by a serpent, or other harmful animal, should regard it as a kenaima. But it is more remarkable that he regards certain small harmless birds in the same light. One small bird which in the early morning and in the evening flits, with a peculiar and shrill whistle, over the savannahs and sometimes approaches the Indian settlements, is looked upon with especial distrust. When one of these is shot, the Indians suppose that they have one enemy less, and they burn it, taking great care that not even a single feather escapes to be blown about by the wind; on a windy day on the savannahs I have seen upwards of a dozen men and women eagerly chasing single floating feathers of these birds. Again, kenaimas, in the form of worms, insects, or even inanimate objects, are supposed to enter into the bodies of their enemies and there cause all headaches, toothaches, and other such bodily pains.

The idea that pains are caused by foreign bodies embedded in the flesh of the sufferer is widely spread among uncivilised people throughout the world, as has long been known; but, as far as I know, it has not been noted that this foreign substance—at least among the Indians of Guiana—is often, if not always, regarded, not as simply a natural body, but as the materialised form of a hostile spirit.

The kenaima system seems to be partly the cause of the strict retention of the distinctions between the many tribes which live side by side in British Guiana. The kenaima— the real one—is probably rarely of the same tribe as his victim; and the imaginary kenaimas who mysteriously cause every death, are naturally thought of as of a tribe different from that of their victims. Thus the feeling of mutual suspicion and hatred which has arisen naturally between the tribes is fostered and retained. And while each tribe suspects the tribe which lives immediately next to it, they all seem to have a peculiarly hostile feeling toward the Ackawoi, who have an especial reputation as kenaimas.

Such are the foes against whom the peaiman—to whom we must now turn—has to fight on behalf of the people of his settlement or district. Of course, against the real kenaima his arts can afford no protection: it is the imaginary attack of the kenaima that he has to counteract. But, it must not be forgotten, the Indian conceives no difference between their real and their imaginary powers. It is almost impossible to over-estimate the dreadful sense of constant and unavoidable danger in which the Indian would live were it not for his trust in the protecting power of the peaiman.

In addition to the influence derived from this fact, the peaiman has power depending on his knowledge of the medicinal value of herbs—though it is doubtful whether this knowledge is not largely shared by the other, lay, Indians—and on the fact that he is supposed to be able to tell the place in which there is most game. The importance of the peaiman and the fact that he deals both with body and spirit, that he is both doctor and priest, will now easily be understood.

According to tradition, the office of peaiman was formerly hereditary. If there was no son to succeed the father, the latter chose and trained some boy from the tribe—one with an epileptic tendency being preferred. At present, however, the office seems occasionally to be undertaken without any hereditary claims—not because they have been chosen, but simply of their own wish—by the most worthless Indians, who choose it as the easiest, pleasantest, and best-paid way of life. But to become a peaiman the candidate has to undergo a painful and severe trial of endurance. He has to undergo long fasts, to wander alone in the forest, houseless and unarmed, and with only such food as he can gather; and he has gradually to accustom himself to drink fearfully large draughts of tobacco-juice mixed with water. He is trained to use and command his voice in a manner the sustained power of which might be envied by the most brilliant operatic singer, and the command of which would make his fortune as a ventriloquist. Maddened by the draughts of nicotine, by the terrors of his long solitary wanderings, and fearfully excited by his own ravings, he is able to work himself at will into those most frantic passions of excitement during which he is supposed to hold converse with the kenaimas and to control them. It has been said that epileptic subjects are by preference chosen as peaimen, and are trained to throw themselves at will into convulsions; and it is at least certain that the peaiman, when in the midst of his frantic performance, seems as though overcome by some fearful fit, or in the extreme of raving madness.

The second, and more sober, part of the education of the peaiman consists in learning the traditions of the tribe, which he, in his turn, will have to hand down to his successor. He is also taught the medicinal and poisonous qualities of plants; and he is taught rules by which he is supposed to be able to find out where game is to be had.

An instance of the peaiman's method of cure—one which I have good reason never to forget—may be given.

On one occasion, when living with Macusi Indians on the savannahs, and suffering from slight headache and fever, a peaiman, with whom I had endeavoured to establish friendly relations, offered to cure me. It was too good an opportunity to be lost, and I accepted. An hour or two after dark I carried my hammock to the house where the man was living, and there re-slung it. According to request, I had brought with me a pocketful of tobacco-leaves. These were now steeped in a calabash of water, which was then placed on the ground. The peaiman had provided himself with several bunches of green boughs cut from the bushes on the savannah. The entrance to the house having been closed, we were completely shut in—for the house, as usual among the savannah Indians, was walled and without windows or chimneys. The fires were put out, and all was dark. Besides the peaiman and myself, there were about thirty people in the house, most of them attracted by such a novel performance as the peai-ing of a white man. We all lay in our hammocks; and I was especially warned not to put foot to the ground, for the kenaimas would be on the floor, and would do dreadful things to me if they caught me.

All was now ready for the performance; but there was a pause. At last it appeared that the peaiman was shy of working in the presence of a white man. I did what I could to reassure him; and at last succeeded in this, by promising that I would not stir out of my hammock, that I would not look at anything—a promise which it would have been hard to break in that utter darkness—and that I would not attempt to lay hands on anything that might touch me. Then the ceremony began.

For a moment all was still, till suddenly the silence was broken by a burst of indescribable and really terrible yells and roars and shouts, which filled the house, shaking walls and roof, sometimes rising rhythmically to a roar, sometimes sinking to a low distant-sounding growl, which never ceased for six hours. Questions seemed to be thundered out and answers shouted back; words and sentences, questions and answers, following each other so closely that there was no pause in the sound. To me, knowing very little of the Macusi language, the meaning was unintelligible; but as long as I kept my senses a Macusi boy who spoke English, and who had slung his hammock close to mine, did his best to whisper into my ear some sort of a translation. It was the peaiman, he explained, roaring out his questions and commands to the kenaimas, and the kenaimas who were yelling and growling and shouting their answers.

Every now and then, through the mad din, there was a sound, at first low and indistinct, and then gathering in volume, as if some big winged thing came from far toward the house, passed through the roof, and then settled heavily on the floor; and again, after an interval, as if the same winged thing rose and passed away as it had come. As each of these mysterious beings came and went, the air, as if displaced by wings, was driven over my face. They were the kenaimas coming and going.

As each came, his yells were first indistinctly heard from far off, but grew louder and louder until, as he alighted on the floor of the house, they reached their height. The first thing each did was to lap up some of the tobacco-water, with an ostentatious noise, from the calabash on the floor. But while he lapped, the peaiman kept up the shouts, until the kenaima was ready to answer. When each kenaima had given an account of itself, and had promised not to trouble me, it flew rustling away. They came in the form of tigers, deer, monkeys, birds, turtles, snakes, and of Ackawoi and Arecuna Indians. Their voices were slightly different in tone, and they all shouted in voices which were supposed to be appropriate to their forms—but oddly enough, all hoarsely.

It was a clever piece of ventriloquism and acting. The whole long terrific noise came from the throat of the peaiman; or perhaps a little of it from that of his wife. The only marvel was that the man could sustain so tremendous a strain upon his voice and throat for six long hours. The rustling of the wings of the kenaimas, and the thud which was heard as each alighted on the floor, were imitated, as I afterwards found, by skilfully shaking the leafy boughs and then dashing them suddenly against the ground. The boughs, swept through the air close by my face, also produced the breezes which I had felt. Once, probably by accident, the boughs touched my face; and it was then that I discovered what they were, by seizing and holding some of the leaves with my teeth. Once, too, toward the end of the performance, and when I had lost nearly all consciousness, a hand was, I thought, laid upon my face. That, as will presently appear, was the crisis of my illness.

The effect of all this upon me was very strange. Before long I ceased to hear the explanations of the boy by my side, and passed into a sort of fitful sleep or stupor, probably akin to mesmeric trance. Incapable of voluntary motion, I seemed to be suspended somewhere in a ceaselessly surging din; and my only thoughts were a hardly-felt wonder as to the cause of the noise, and a gentle, fruitless effort to remember if there had once been a time before noise was. Now and then, when the noise all but died away for a few moments, during the intervals in which the peaiman was supposed to have passed out through the roof and to be heard from a great distance, I woke to half-consciousness. But always as he came back, and the noise grew again, I once more gradually fell into a state of stupor.

At last, when, toward morning, the noise had finally ended, I awoke thoroughly. The bars being taken away from the entrance of the house, I rushed out on to the open savannah. It was a wild and pitch-dark night; rain fell heavily; thunder pealed incessantly; and every now and then lightning, flashing behind the far-off Pacaraima range, for a moment vividly showed the rugged edge of the dark mountains against the sky. Bare-headed, bare-footed, and coatless, I spent the short time before dawn out in the storm; and the savannah, the night, and the storm seemed strangely fresh and pleasant after the dark, close, noise-filled house.

It is perhaps needless to add that my head was anything but cured of its ache. But the peaiman, insisting that I must be cured, asked for payment. He even produced the kenaima, a caterpillar,[1] which, he said, had caused the pain, and which he had extracted from my body at the moment when his hand had touched my face. I gave him a looking-glass which had cost fourpence; and he was satisfied.

Such, with occasional slight variations, is the performance by which the peaiman professes to cure his patients. The variations introduced are slight, and chiefly depend upon the tribe to which the peaiman belongs. For instance, among some tribes the peaiman works, as in the above instance, in an ordinary house, and in the midst of the people; but among others, the performances take place in slight, temporary huts of palm-leaves, without door or window, in which the peaiman is alone, the people standing outside the house, talking and laughing. In neither case, whether he works by himself or in a crowd, is the respect of silence paid to his incantations. Again, instead of the simple bunch of boughs which is sometimes used, a peculiar rattle made of a

---

[1] It is a legitimate question whether, when a kenaima having, as in this instance, entered into his victim, in the body of a caterpillar, and when that caterpillar has been removed and killed, the kenaima is at the same time killed or injured. I think not; his spirit simply passes out of the caterpillar back into his own body, or into any other body into which he chooses to send it. Cf. the story of Pau-Puk-Keewis in *Hiawatha*.

gourd-shell, containing some hard seeds, and ornamented with long wreaths of bright-coloured feathers is used. This rattle is different somewhat in shape according to the tribe. Sometimes, also, a drum is used.

One other power, in addition to that of summoning, banishing, and correcting kenaimas, the peaiman is supposed to possess. He is able to call to him and question the spirit of any sleeping Indian of his own tribe. So that if an Indian wishes to know what an absent friend is doing, he has only to employ the peaiman to summon and question the spirit of the far-away Indian. Or the peaiman may send his own spirit, his body remaining present, to get the required information.

There is a peaiman in each of the larger villages, and in each of the districts in which the inhabitants are more scattered. As soon as an Indian is ill he sends for the peaiman. The latter first blows three times on the invalid, under the idea that he is blowing away the evil spirit of the illness ; and if that fails he attempts to work a cure by the long and painful performances above described. If the first peaiman fails, a second is sent for ; and the two fill the second night with their noise. Sometimes, in very obstinate cases, three peaimen perform on a third night.

Sometimes, when there is no definite case of illness, but the whistling of certain birds or other equally certain signs of the presence of kenaimas have been observed in and about the village, the peaiman is employed to drive these enemies away. To do this, he walks round the houses by night, shouting, beating a drum, or shaking a rattle. Many and many a night is made sleepless in this way in an Indian settlement.

For each supposed cure, and for each ejectment of kenaimas from a village, the peaiman is paid. But by far the larger part of his reward is indirect, and consists in the immense amount of influence which he gains. Whatever he takes a fancy to—from some trifle of food to any other

Indian's wife—he asks for, and gets; for no Indian dare refuse him anything.   And thus he leads a lazy life, doing nothing except when peai-ing, living on all the good things of Indian life, and enjoying more wives—or, in other words, workers—than anyone else.

CHAPTER XVII.

RELIGION.

TRAVELLERS have again and again asserted of various peoples in the condition of savagery, that they were without religion; and ethnologists have as often disputed for and against the truth of this statement. This strife has generally arisen where the one single word 'religion,' on which the whole matter depends, has not been clearly defined at the outset. At the one extreme, the word 'religion' may mean a knowledge of a Supreme Being and Creator, together with a certain theory and practice of life which such knowledge is supposed to induce; at the other extreme, it may be used to express merely a recognition of the existence of spirit as opposed to body; and between these two meanings an infinite number of others, which are in fact intermediate between the two, may be attributed to the word. To deny religion, in the simplest meaning of the word, of any people, is obviously very different from denying it in any of its higher senses, or still more in its highest sense; and it may safely be affirmed that no people have been found without religion in its simplest form. Because of the ambiguity of the word 'religion,' a convenient term has been brought into prominence by Mr. E. B. Tylor, to express that which the word means when used in its simplest sense. This term is 'animism'; which means simply a belief in the existence of spirits as distinct, not necessarily as separate, from bodies. This animism is the universal and earliest form of religion, and is the germ from which religion in the highest form in which it anywhere exists has developed by additions made gradually and often without notice. My present task is first to show that the Indians of Guiana are an abundantly animistic people, and then to trace the very slight degree in which their religious views have advanced beyond the stage of mere animism in the direction of higher religion.

Before entering into details, one other point about pure animism, as it occurs in Guiana, must be brought distinctly into notice. It is commonly taken for granted that religion and morality are inseparably connected. But as a matter of fact, the two have originally absolutely nothing to do with each other; and it is only in a society which has reached a comparatively high stage of civilisation—where, that is, religion and morality have separately developed to a considerable extent—that religion grasps morality, and insists that the latter is a necessary part of itself. Pure animism belongs to a stage of social development below that at which this combination takes place. Accordingly, though the Indians of Guiana observe an admirable code of morality, yet this code is a matter of social convenience; and though this code exists side by side with a simple animistic form of religion, the two have absolutely no connection.

The difficulty of studying animism such as that of these Indians, lies in the fact that it is almost impossible for the student sufficiently to realise that though it is a form of religion it is, in so far as it is pure, without those supernatural and moral accretions which the civilised man is wont to regard as the most important part of religion. And this difficulty is largely increased, owing to the fact that the civilised student generally sees the animism of savages through the eyes of Christian missionaries, who of all men are the most apt, but wrongly, to regard the undoubted importance of these supernatural and moral accretions as proof of their necessary and aboriginal connection with religion. The safest method of study is to begin from the beginning, to find the nature and extent of Indian belief in spirits, or, in other words, the extent and nature of their animism, and thus to notice, without expecting, any accretions which they may have made to this.

The first matter, then, is the nature of the Indian's belief in spirits. Every Indian believes that he himself, and consequently every other human being, consists of two parts—a body and a soul or spirit.[1] To one who has never given thought to such matters it may at first seem strange that a so-called savage should be able to form for himself a conception of so immaterial a thing as a spirit. Yet but very little reflection is needed to bring conviction that it is impossible that man, being rational and having once seen death, should fail to acquire such conception. When a man dies, something goes, something is left. The survivors necessarily distinguish in thought between these two parts, and they call them respectively by some such name as spirit and body. A curious illustration of this is afforded by the saying of the Macusis, as they point out that the small human figure has disappeared from the pupil of a dead man's eye, that ' his spirit (or, as they call it, his *emmawarri*) has gone.' This alone is sufficient reason to the Indian for belief in the distinctness of body and spirit, or the two parts that separate at death. But it is not only at death that the Indian sees these separate. It is a platitude among civilised people to remark on the similarity between

Death and his brother sleep;

---

[1] The reader will at once perceive that I have not distinguished between soul and spirit. It is wholly unnecessary here to make any such distinction, for it does not exist in the mind of the Indian. I shall therefore, in future, use only the word ' spirit.'

but great as the similarity is to us, it seems far greater to
the Indian. Suggestively enough, civilised men and savages
do not see this similarity from quite the same point of view.
To us it appears to lie in the fact that both in sleep and in
death there seems to be a rest from and a forgetfulness of
the things of life; but to the Indian it lies rather in the fact
that in both cases the spirit departs from the body only to
continue its labours under slightly altered circumstances.
This latter fact requires a little consideration. The dreams
which come in sleep to the Indian are to him, though not to
us, as real as any of the events of his waking life. To him
dream-acts and working-acts differ only in one respect—
namely, that the former are done only by the spirit, the latter
are done by the spirit in its body. Seeing other men asleep,
and afterwards hearing from them the things which they suppose themselves to have done when asleep, the Indian has no
difficulty in reconciling that which he hears with the fact
that the bodies of the sleepers were in his sight and motionless throughout the time of supposed action, because he
never questions that the spirits, leaving the sleepers, played
their part in dream-adventures. Dreams, in fact, are regarded as but part of the history of each man's life. Then,
as regards death, the Indian, when some man known to him
dies, still continues to see his dead friend in dreams—that is,
in parts of his own real life; and it therefore, not unnaturally,
seems to the survivor that the spirit of the dead man, yet
living, continues to act just as does the living man in
dreams.

It becomes important, therefore, fully to recognise the
complete belief of the Indian in the reality of his dream-life,
and in the unbroken continuity of this with his working-life.
It is easy to show this belief by many incidents which came
under my notice. For instance, one morning when it was
important to me to get away from a camp on the Essequibo
river, at which I had been detained for some days by the
illness of some of my Indian companions, I found that one
of the invalids, a young Macusi, though better in health,

was so enraged against me that he refused to stir, for he declared that, with great want of consideration for his weak health, I had taken him out during the night and had made him haul the canoe up a series of difficult cataracts. Nothing could persuade him that this was but a dream, and it was some time before he was so far pacified as to throw himself sulkily into the bottom of the canoe. At that time we were all suffering from a great scarcity of food, and, hunger having its usual effect in producing vivid dreams, similar events frequently occurred. More than once, the men declared in the morning that some absent man, whom they named, had come during the night, and had beaten or otherwise mal-treated them; and they insisted upon much rubbing of the bruised parts of their bodies. Another instance was amusing. In the middle of one night I was wakened by an Arawak named Sam, the captain or headman of the Indians who were with me, only to be told the bewildering words, 'George speak me very bad, boss; you cut his bits!' It was some time before I could collect my senses sufficiently to remember that 'bits' or fourpenny-pieces, are the units in which, among Creoles and semi-civilised Indians calculation of money, and consequently of wages, is made; that to cut bits means to reduce the number of bits, or wages, given; and to understand that Captain Sam, having dreamed that his sub-ordinate George had spoken insolently to him, the former, with a fine sense of the dignity of his office, now insisted that the culprit should be punished in real life. One more incident, of which the same Sam was the hero, may be told for the sake of the humour, though it did not happen within my personal experience, but was told me by a friend. This friend, in whose employ Sam was at the time, told his man, as they sat round the fire one night, of the Zulu or some other African war which was then in progress, and in so doing inadvertently made frequent use of the expression 'to punish the niggers.' That night, after all in camp had been asleep for some time, they were roused by loud cries for help. Sam, who was one of the most powerful Indians I ever saw, was 'punishing a nigger' who happened to be of the party; with one hand he had firmly grasped the back of the breeches-band of the black man, and had twisted this round so tightly that the poor wretch was almost cut in two.

Sam sturdily maintained that he had received orders from his master for this outrageous conduct, and on inquiry, it turned out that he had dreamed this. Many similar stories might be added, but enough has been said to illustrate the firm belief of the Indian in the separability of the spirit from the body during sleep. It must be noted that this belief extends not only to the idea that the spirit of the dreamer leaves him and does various acts, but also to the idea that the spirits of others with whom the dreamer fancies he meets in his sleep are really, not merely subjectively, present. For the Indian who wakes in the night with loud cries and assertions that he is being beaten by some enemy, is not convinced of the fallacy of his belief by the fact that his enemy is obviously not present, and could not have disappeared under the circumstances, but explains that it was not the body but the spirit of his enemy which did the harm. And he generally silently or in words adds a threat of vengeance on the body of the supposed culprit.

There is yet a third way in which the Indian sees the spirit leave the body. Visions are to him when awake what dreams are to him when asleep, and the creatures of his visions seem in no way different from those of his dreams. A distinction may be here drawn between natural visions, those, that is, which appear to a man in consequence of the abnormal condition in which his body happens accidentally to be at the moment, and artificial visions, that is, those which appear in consequence of the abnormal bodily condition into which he has brought himself by such means as fasting, stimulants, or narcotics, for the express purpose of experiencing visions. Innumerable instances of natural visions are recorded from other parts of the world where the reality of vision-life is believed; and, judging by analogy, such must occur among the Indians of Guiana. The following, which came within my own experience, seems almost certainly a case of the kind. One morning in 1878, when I was living in a Macusi settlement, some Indians of the same tribe came from a neighbouring settlement with the extraordinary request that I would lend them guns and go with them to attack some Arecunas of a settlement some twenty-five miles distant. Though there is an unusually strong feeling of hostility between the Macusis and Arecunas, this request seemed to me, remembering how peaceful the Indians now generally are, very strange. It was explained that a certain man named Tori, one of the suppliants, had a day or two previously been sitting alone on the savannah, outside his house, when, looking up from the arrow-head which he was fashioning, he saw some Arecunas, whom he knew by sight, and who belonged to the village against which war was now to be waged, standing over him with uplifted war-clubs, as if about to strike him down. According to the account given by Tori, his shouts brought his own people out from their houses, but by that time the Arecunas had vanished without effecting any harm. The story was utterly incredible to me; but after much cross-examination it was evident that Tori himself believed it, and I can only suppose that it was a case of a natural vision believed in as a reality. Artificial visions, on the other hand, are very frequent in Indian life, especially and perhaps only in one way. The peaiman, as has been described elsewhere, undergoes a long training of fasting and solitude, of stimulants and narcotics, in order to be able to raise himself at any moment into the ecstatic condition in which he is able to send his spirit where he will, to hold communion with other spirits. That the peaiman himself believes in this separation and departure of his spirit, would not be easy to prove; but after much inquiry from these practitioners, I am fully persuaded that in this, as in so many similar cases, the peaiman certainly partly believes, partly perhaps feigns to believe, in his own practice. But—and this is the important part—that the other Indians believe in the departure of the spirit of the peaiman is certain. That it is the spirit, not the body, of the man which is supposed to depart was made very plain to me in this way. On being assured that the peaiman in his practice passed up and outward through the roof, I expressed scepticism, and asked to be allowed to fasten one end of a thread to the body of the peaiman, to hold the other in my hand, in order that, though because of the darkness I could not see the ascent, I might by means of the thread be satisfied of its occurrence. The answer, which was given quite naturally, was that the body remained and that it was 'something inside him' which went up. Thus the peaiman when he communicates with spirits does this through his own spirit separated from his body.

Another feature in the practice of the peaiman throws some light on this conception of the reality of events apparently experienced during artificial excitement, by showing that the beings, whether patients or kenaimas, with whom the peaiman holds converse are communicated with as spirits separated from their proper bodies. I have elsewhere described the state to which I myself was reduced by the practice of a peaiman as akin to mesmeric trance; but it may equally well be compared to the state, known by experience to most men, in which man sometimes lies, between sleeping and waking, conscious and able to think somewhat rationally, yet either wholly unconscious of the existence of his body, or, even if conscious of this, wholly unable to produce any effect upon it by volition. It now seems to me that my spirit was then as nearly separated from my body as is possible under any other circumstances short of death. Thus it appears that the efforts of the peaiman were directed partly to the separation of his own spirit from his body, and partly to the separation of the spirit from the body of his patient, and that in this way spirit holds communion with spirit.

It may fairly, therefore, be assumed that the Indian believes not only in the existence of a spirit within the human body, but also in the separation, voluntary or involuntary of these two parts.

The next feature to be noted in Indian belief is that the spirit may be passed from the body of its proper owner into that of any animal, or even into any inanimate object. We have seen that the kenaima, while following his victim, does not necessarily keep his human shape, but often assumes the form of some animal, usually a jaguar, or, as it is commonly called, a tiger. The expression 'kenaima-tiger' is often heard from Indian lips; and again and again an Indian has been heard to say, 'I can kill a tiger, but how shall I kill a kenaima-tiger?' It has also been noticed that the object which the peaiman extracts from the body of his patient, which is said to be the cause of the disease—be it animate or inanimate, be it for instance, caterpillar, stick, or stone—is a kenaima; that is to say, it is the bodily form into which the spirit of the kenaima has passed in order to penetrate into his victim. It is evident, therefore, that a person may pass his spirit into a body not his own. Yet a reservation must be here made. No Indian, unless, possibly, a peaiman, believes that he himself is able at will thus to pass his spirit into another body, but he does believe that other men have this power. The transmission of the spirit seems to him something uncanny, something only to be done voluntarily, either by a kenaima, or by a peaiman to counteract the evil working of the kenaima. In this belief is exhibited some little natural logic. The Indian is never himself conscious of sending his spirit into another body—though, by the way, such cases of self-deception have been noted from other parts of the world—and he therefore believes that he has not the power; but on the other hand he sees certain animals which he has reason to believe are men in disguise, and therefore, knowing how loosely spirits are attached to bodies, he supposes that other men know how to acquire the power, denied to him, of transmitting their spirits into what bodies they will.

So far we have examined Indian animism only as far as it

is exhibited in a belief of the existence of spirits of men, of the separability of these spirits, as displayed in the case of all men, of the power of these spirits to wander away from their proper bodies, and of the power which some men have of transmitting their spirits to other bodies. But the fact that I began by speaking of the spirits of men, was only because man, whether he be Indian or other, naturally begins by thinking about himself; nor must the fact be understood to indicate that the Indian sees any sharp line of distinction, such as we see, between man and other animals, between one kind of animal and another, or between animals—man included—and inanimate objects. On the contrary, to the Indian, all objects, animate and inanimate, seem exactly of the same nature except that they differ in the accident of bodily form. Every object in the whole world is a being, consisting of a body and spirit, and differs from every other object in no respect except that of bodily form, and in the greater or less degree of brute power and brute cunning consequent on the difference of bodily form and bodily habits. Our next step, therefore, is to note that animals, other than men, and even inanimate objects, have spirits which differ not at all in kind from those of men.

Fully to realise this entirely natural conception of primitive man, the civilised student must make a great effort, and must forget for a time all that science from its origin to the present day has taught of the difference between man and other animals. It is very difficult for us to realise the Indian conception even of this identity in everything but bodily form of men and other animals; and it is still more difficult to realise that the Indian conception is wider even than this, in that it knows of no difference, except again in bodily form, between animate and inanimate objects.

The very phrase 'men and other animals,' or even, as it is often expressed, 'men and animals,' based as it is on the superiority which civilised men feel over other animals, expresses a dichotomy which is in no degree recognised by the Indian. The only dichotomy recognised by him is 'myself, that is the only thing I know, and the rest of the world, which is all unknown to me.' It is, therefore, most important to realise both how comparatively small really is the difference between men in a state of savagery and other animals, and how completely even such difference as exists escapes the notice of savage men.

In skill, in cunning, in courage, in social morality, which is based on fear and not on any knowledge of right, in all except bodily form—and the difference in that is not greater between man and other animals than it is between almost any two classes of these other animals—there really is no great difference between man in a state of savagery and animals, regarded class for class. And that the uncivilised man should overlook the real difference, *i.e.* the mental potentialities, is natural. It must be remembered that almost every Indian understands the ways and cunning of other animals round about him far better than civilised men, even than the few learned in such matters, even guess them; and on the other hand, the real differences, the mental potentialities, are just such as entirely escape the notice of the uncivilised man. To the ear of the savage, animals certainly seem even to talk. This fact is universally evident, and ought to be fully realised. In Longfellow's wonderful medley of ethnological lore, the child Hiawatha,

> When he heard the owls at midnight,
> Hooting, laughing in the forest,
> ' What is that ? ' he cried in terror ;
> And the good Nokomis answered :
> ' That is but the owl and owlet
> Talking in their native language,
> Talking, scolding at each other.'

But the complete identification in this as in all qualities of men and other animals is perhaps most strikingly illustrated in Joel Chandler Harris's recently published folk-lore stories of ' Brer Rabbit,' [1] in which ' Miss Meadows en de girls wuz in de tale ' without the slightest shade of human

---

[1] *Uncle Remus : or, Mr. Fox, Mr. Rabbit, and Mr. Terrapin*, by Joel Chandler Harris. London and New York, 1881.

difference distinguishing them from the other non-human actors. In Guiana countless Indian stories, fully believed, introduce the sayings of animals; and though the individual Indian knows that he no longer understands the language of the beasts and birds around him, yet he attaches but little weight to this, in that he is constantly meeting with other Indians of one or other of the many alien tribes which surround him, who speak languages at least as unintelligible to him as are those of birds or beasts; and in that, as he is fully persuaded, he constantly hears the peaiman still converse with birds and beasts. The whole belief is well illustrated in a curious custom which often came under my notice. Before leaving a temporary camp in the forest, where they have killed a tapir and dried the meat on a babracot, Indians invariably destroy this babracot, saying that should a tapir, passing that way, find traces of the slaughter of one of his kind, he would come by night on the next occasion when Indians slept at that place and, taking a man, would babracot him in revenge. It is not, therefore, too much to say that, according to the view of the Indians, other animals differ from men only in bodily form and in their various degrees of strength. And they differ in spirit not at all; for just as the Indian sees in the separation which takes place at death or in dreams proof of the existence of a spirit in man, so in this same death-analysis of body and spirit— all other qualities being in his view much the same in men and other animals—he sees proof of the existence in each other animal of a spirit similar to that of man.

Nor is it only real animals that are regarded as identical in all points, except that of mere bodily form, with men. In a chapter on folk-lore, mention will be made of various animals which civilised man knows to be fabulous. Perhaps the nature of these beings is best made clear by saying that they correspond very closely to the dragons, unicorns, and griffins, and to the horned, hoofed, and tailed devils of our own folk-lore. Of this kind, in Guiana, is the *di-di*, or water-mama, a being with a body not well described, who lives under water; the *omar*, a similar being, who also lives under water, with a body said sometimes to be like that of a gigantic fish, sometimes like that of a huge crab, and again at other times to be of various other forms; and there are many other beings of this class, not clearly distinguishable to us. The one common quality which these animals have for us is that they are all fabulous and non-existent. But our knowledge of this fact is derived entirely from science. The Indian, being without even the rudiments of scientific thought, believes as fully in the real existence of an animal as impossible as was ever fabled, as he does in that of animals most usual to him. In short, to the Indian the only difference between these monstrous animals and those most familiar to him, is that, while he has seen the latter, he has not himself seen the former, though he has heard of them from others. These monstrous animals, in short, are regarded as on exactly the same level as regards the possession of body and spirits as are all other animals.

It is somewhat more difficult to realise the Indian belief in the spirits of inanimate objects, such as plants, stones, and rivers. Perhaps the belief in the spirits of plants is merely an extension of the same belief as concerning animals : there is a vitality in plants which disappears at death, and serves as some evidence of the presence of a spirit. There cannot be the same reason for belief in the spirits of such lifeless things as rocks or stones. It might be thought that this bodily motionlessness would prevent any conception of the possession of spirits by such objects. But, in the first place, this absence of motion is less striking to the Indian mind than it would otherwise be, owing to the fact that comparison, if made at all, would be made, not directly between animals, with perfectly free powers of bodily motion, and stocks and stones, with no such power of motion, but indirectly through plants, which are intermediate in this respect, in that the sway of their branches gives them the appearance of some small power of bodily motion. Moreover, the Indian, always reasoning in the first place from what he knows of himself, remembers that, as, for example, in dreams, his own spirit moves with complete activity even when his body lies motionless; and he therefore sees no reason to doubt that the spirit within the motionless rock has the power of activity also. And, in the second place, the activity of this spirit of the rock is proved to his cost in various practical ways. The Indian is occasionally hurt either by falling on a rock, or by the rock falling upon him; and in either case he attributes the blame, by a line of argument still not uncommon in more civilised life, to the rock. In fact, he attributes any calamity which may happen to him to the intention of the immediate instrument of its infliction, and he not unnaturally sees in the action of this instrument evidence of its possession of a spirit. Then he carries this line of argument yet further: if his eye falls upon a rock in any way abnormal or curious, and if shortly after any evil happens to him, he regards rock and evil as cause and effect; and here again he perceives in the rock a spirit. As it is with rocks so it is with other inanimate objects: the belief in their possession of a spirit probably originates not in their evident vitality, but in the vitality which is presumed to exist in them from their supposed actions. But, whatever its origin, the fact of the belief is certain. In very dry seasons, when the water in the rivers is low, the rocks in their beds are seen to have a curious glazed, vitrified, and black appearance, due probably to deposits of iron and manganese. Whenever I questioned the Indians about these rocks, I was at once silenced by the assertion that any allusion to their appearance would vex these rocks and cause them to send misfortune. Again in mid-stream in the Essequibo river there is the curiously shaped rock called *paiwari-kaira*, the upper part of which is very large but rests upon a small pillar-like base. Not only do the Indians allow no mention of this rock to be made, lest it should be vexed, but they will not even look at it, nor, if they can prevent, allow others to look. Again, all the many sculptured rocks are objects of this awe. It is unnecessary to multiply instances, further than by saying that almost every rock seen for the first time, and any rock which is in any way abnormal whenever seen, is believed to consist of body and spirit. And not only many rocks, but also many waterfalls, streams, and indeed material bodies of every sort, are supposed to consist each of a body and a spirit as does man; and that not all inanimate objects have this dual nature avowedly attributed to them, is probably only due to the chance that, while all such objects may at any time, in any of the ways above indicated, show signs of the presence of a spirit within them, this spirit has not as yet been noticed in some cases.

But, after all, such arguments as those given above, by which it seems probable that a savage man strengthens his belief in the presence of spirits in all objects, are not primitive. The primitive habit of thought is of a much more simple and natural kind. It must have been acquired by the Indian, not by asking himself whether the objects around him were animate, but rather by his never doubting that, like himself—that is, like the only object known to him by personal experience—all other objects had bodies and spirits. In fact, the really primitive idea naturally would be that all objects are animate. And only then, as scepticism began to grow and primitive man began to question whether stones have spirits and power of action, then the more orthodox and conservative probably strengthened their faith in the old belief by such arguments as those given above concerning the apparent action of stones.

By some observers among these and other tribes in a parallel stage of civilisation, it has been supposed that all diseases are also personified and regarded as possessed of spirits, just as are material bodies, animate and inanimate. But it seems to me that, at least in Guiana, this is not quite the case. It is true that the peaiman in removing a disease from a patient removes a body, the nature of which has before been described, in which the spirit which caused the disease is supposed to be; and it is also true that diseases are believed to move about the world much as do men. As a curious instance of the belief in this latter power of diseases, it may be mentioned that, as Mr. Brett has told,[1] in 1856, when a horrible epidemic known locally as buck-sickness, attacked the Indians on the Pomeroon river, the True Caribs fled from the settlements far into the forest, and in so doing cut down large trees to obstruct the paths behind them. A similar notion of disease walking along a path, and of the possibility of preventing its so doing, has been noticed among many other people.[2] In this connection it must be noted that it is a common habit among the Indians of Guiana to obstruct in a similar way the paths which they are in the habit of using, to prevent dangerous animals, such as jaguars, or even hostile men, from using them. It seems to me that these diseases are not distinct beings, but rather forms, visible or invisible, assumed by the spirits of kenaimas, who, as has been explained elsewhere, are capable of throwing their spirits into any body they please. When, therefore, a disease-spirit situated in the bodily form of a stick or stone is removed from the flesh of an invalid, this bodily form is only one of an infinitely variable number which the kenaima is able to assume; and when a forest path is blocked against the advance of a disease, it is blocked against the bodily form of a malicious kenaima. In other words, diseases are not, I think, distinctly personified.

The Indian, therefore, believes that every object perceptible to his senses has, or may have, a body and a spirit; and he sees no difference in this respect between man and other objects, all being to him equally natural—or, in other words, no idea of that which we call the supernatural being known to him. Thus the whole world of the Indian swarms with these beings. If by a mighty mental effort we could for a moment revert to a similar mental position we should find ourselves everywhere surrounded by a host of possibly hurtful beings, so many in number that to describe them as innumerable would fall ridiculously short of the truth. It is not therefore wonderful that the Indian fears to move beyond

[1] W. H. Brett's *Indian Tribes of Guiana*, p. 225. London.
[2] E. B. Tylor's *Primitive Culture*, vol. ii. p. 179, *et pas.*

the light of his camp-fire after dark, or, if he is obliged to do so, carries a fire-brand with him that he may at least see among what enemies he walks; nor is it wonderful that occasionally the air round the settlement seems to the Indian to grow so full of beings, that a peaiman, who is supposed to have the power of temporarily driving them away, is employed to effect a general clearance of these beings, if only for a time.

That is the main belief, of the kind that is generally called religious, of the Indians of Guiana; and it is the same entirely pure form of animism which, as other comparative researches, into which it is impossible to enter here, show, has almost certainly been held by every people at some time during their earliest stages of civilisation; and this same form of animism is the earliest recognisable rudiment from which, by subsequent modifications and development, all higher forms of religion have grown. It will perhaps be easiest to proceed by examining how far the chief of these modifications are discernible among the Indians of Guiana. The chief modifications, throughout the world, are: (1) Acknowledgment of the everlasting, as distinguished from the merely continued, existence of the spirit after the destruction of the body; (2) a belief in a separate place of abode for the spirit when separated from the body, and, in close connection with this, a belief in the reward or punishment of the spirit for the good or evil deeds which it did when in the body; (3) a belief, which has arisen but very gradually, in higher spirits, and eventually in a highest spirit; and (4), keeping pace with the growths of these beliefs, a habit of reverence for, and worship of, spirits.

All these developments of animism appear in various early stages of civilisation and grow as the people advance in other matters. Hardly any of them, however, appear to have yet made much advance among the Indians of Guiana; though it is just possible that these have at some past time advanced among the ancestors of the present Indians to a point somewhat beyond that to which they have now reverted.

Though improbable, it is quite intelligible, for example, that these people may have attained a somewhat higher conception of religion, which their descendants have again lost. When, therefore, I speak of the religious belief and practice of the Indians, I must be understood to refer only to the present form of these matters, which, after all, is hardly likely to be very much lower than it ever was.

The remainder of this chapter will be devoted to an attempt to discover what advance, if any, from simple animism is traceable among the Indians of Guiana. It is as well here to state the fact that the key to the whole matter may be provided by remembering that these Indians look on the spirit world as exactly parallel to, or more properly as a part of, the material world known to them. Spirits, like material beings, differ from each other only, if the phrase is allowed, in their varying degrees of brute force and brute cunning, and none are distinguished by the possession of anything like divine attributes. Indians, therefore, regard disembodied spirits not otherwise than the beings still in the body whom they see around them.

The first advance from the simplest animism consists in the recognition of the *everlasting* existence of the spirit after the destruction of the body. The merely *continued* existence of this spirit is implied in simple animism. After death, as we have seen, the spirit appears in dreams to the survivors, and it is therefore believed still to exist. Confirmation of the existence of this belief is to be found in the custom of the Indians, elsewhere described, of burying their dead in the houses of the deceased, and then deserting these houses, that the spirit of the dead man may use his former dwelling without interference from the presence of his surviving relatives; further confirmation is afforded by the fact that various necessaries, but especially the hammock, the one chief necessary of life to the Indian, are buried with the dead for their future use; and perhaps the strongest confirmation of all is to be found in the stories which Indians tell of the existence and actions of their dead ancestors. On the whole, the belief in the after-existence of the spirit may be taken for granted. But no attempt is made to realise the duration of this after-death existence of the spirit. As long as the memory of a dead man survives, either in the minds of his former companions or in tradition, he is supposed to exist; but no question as to whether this existence is or is not to be prolonged for ever has ever been formulated in the Indian mind. It is not till a considerably higher stage of civilisation is attained than that at which these Indians are, that the memory of certain dead men surviving practically for ever, recognition is made of the everlasting existence of spirits, by a natural expansion of the earlier belief in continued existence.

A belief in the reward or punishment of spirits after death for the good or evil which they did when in the body, is created only by religion at the moment when it begins to absorb and enforce morality; and as this stage has by no means been reached by the Indians of Guiana, this particular belief does not concern us here.

The spirit continuing to exist after the destruction of the body, the question naturally arises as to what place Indians believe such disembodied beings to occupy. This question, when worked out during many ages by the methods of higher religion, finds its answer in heaven and hell; but Indians, having yet hardly begun to ask themselves this question, usually think of spirits as remaining disembodied on earth in the places in which they lived when in the body. Sometimes there seems to be some idea of a transmigration of the spirit into a new body. This must not be confused with the temporary transmission, elsewhere described, by a living being—for instance, by a kenaima—of his spirit into some body not his own. Several times I was told by Indians that they hoped to become white men, apparently in the sense that their spirits after death would reanimate the bodies of white men. Appun, who travelled in Guiana, reports a curious story which he heard from the Arecunas near Roraima, which, even if untrue, is at least often repeated, though with considerable variation, by other Indians. Once upon a time, they told him, a great peaiman named Becka-ranta, called all the Indians together to the neighbourhood of Roraima, with the secret purpose of making himself their chief. To carry out his purpose he found it necessary to get rid of large numbers of the more powerful men. Having therefore made all drink deeply of paiwari, he then announced that if certain of those present were killed they would revive after some days as white men. The result was a slaughter in which friend tried to benefit friend by killing him. The end of the story is that, after waiting in vain for some days for the return of the dead, the peaiman was himself killed by the survivors. This story may be, probably is, untrue, or at least greatly exaggerated, but the fact that it is told at all seems to indicate a very strong belief in the possibility of a transmigration of spirit. In these cases the spirit is, of course, supposed to remain on earth. The same idea is implied in such facts as that of the giving up of houses to the use of the spirits of dead men who once lived in them. Yet Indians have some idea of a place above the sky—'a heaven floored upon a firmament.'[1] In several of the legends which form their folklore there is mention of such a place. For instance, the Caribs say that they arrived in Guiana from sky-land through a hole. It is important to realise the idea which the Indian holds of this place. This is just one of the cases in which our own deeply engrained and popular notion of a *heaven* above the sky makes it difficult for us to realise the Indian conception. The Indian idea seems to me to be that beyond the sky, just as beyond the sea, there is, nothing akin to our heaven, but another country just such as that in which they live. Hunting is mentioned as a constant occupation there. The ordinary Indian knows that he cannot go beyond the sea, yet he occasionally sees other men come thence, and he hears from them of lands beyond those waters impassable to him. Just so, he sees an apparently firm sky, separated by

[1] E. B. Tylor, *Primitive Culture*, vol. ii. p. 69.

an ocean of air impassable to him, and to which he does not know the way, but to which he sees birds go, and even, as he thinks, he sees the spirits of his peaimen go. Above the sky he thinks, therefore, that there is a country attainable under certain conditions. Their ancestors came perhaps from that country by climbing down by a rope from the sky-land, perhaps from the islands by crossing the sea in canoes. Either way of travelling appears equally probable to them—either ancestral country equally natural. It is to be noted that the country beyond the sky is more often mentioned as that from which men come than as that to which men go; but, on the other hand, the spirits of individuals among their hero ancestors are sometimes said by the Indians to have gone to this place, sometimes said to have gone to the islands, just as individual Indians in the body occasionally travel away from their tribes and are heard of and seen no more. In either case the method of travelling is not by apotheosis, but by such natural means as are used indifferently by beings, whether encumbered by bodies or not—in short, the Indian knows of no heaven, but only of other countries. The whole matter—that is, both the conception of the Indian of the place of the spirit after death, and the difficulty which civilised man has found in understanding this conception, may be made more clear, by examining a passage by Rochefort, in which, writing of the Caribs of the West Indies, the ancestors of the True Caribs and of certain other tribes in Guiana, he says that their brave men would live after death in happy islands, where their enemies the Arawaks would be their slaves; but that the cowards of their own tribe would, on the contrary, serve the Arawaks as slaves in a barren land beyond the mountains.[1] This, as told by Rochefort, certainly seems at first sight to indicate not only a belief in a 'heaven' for all spirits, but also a belief, which I have already denied of the Indians, in retribution after death for conduct which is, according to

[1] Rochefort, *Iles Antilles*, p. 430; quoted by E. B. Tylor, *Primitive Culture*, vol. ii. p. 79.

the Indian standard, virtuous and vicious—that is to say, for bravery or cowardice. A little investigation makes the matter appear in an entirely different light. Rochefort wrote of a time when the Caribs were already, as far as Indians were concerned, in complete possession of the West Indian Islands, and the Arawaks lived on the mainland the mountains of which were visible from Trinidad. According to some accounts the Arawaks had been driven to the mainland from their former homes in the islands by these very Caribs. It is at least certain that the Caribs were in the habit of making hostile raids into the country of the Arawaks on the mainland, and that great mutual hostility and the habit of enslaving each other prevailed between these two tribes. Moreover, the dry, beautiful islands, might then as now be loosely described as indeed fertile in comparison with the flat swampy belt which lies on the mainland between the mountains and the sea. When, therefore, the Carib said that if he were brave in this life he would after death live, with Arawaks for slaves, in fertile islands, he spoke remembering how in previous raids on the mainland he had by his bravery captured Arawaks and brought them as slaves to his own happy islands; and when he said that, if he were a coward, he would after death live beyond the mountains, a slave to some Arawak, he spoke remembering the fate of perhaps some companion on his raids, who, having fought not well, was himself captured and retained as a slave by the Arawaks. In short, in describing his notion of future life, he was only describing exactly the state of things, among exactly the same scenes, to which he was accustomed in this life.

It may be added, that though the Indians have no notion of a heaven, and regard the place beyond the sky as merely another country, this knowledge of a country beyond the sky is probably the germ which, in a higher stage of thought than that attained by these people, develops, when the thinkers at last become puzzled by the fact that in the body they fail to find their way to that place beyond the sky, into a belief in its unearthly nature as a place which spirits only may attain.

The point next to be considered is whether Indians believe in any hierarchy of spirits, such as that which forms so important a feature in the higher religions. There is nothing to indicate that the Indians know of any spirits except such as are, or once were, situated in material bodies of some kind ; and these differ in rank and power only as one man or one animal differs in these respects from another. That is to say, of all the beings that fill the world, none, whether they are spirits still in the body or spirits which have left their former bodies, have any authority over others except such as they can gain and keep by—if such a term may be applied to spirits—their greater brute force. As religion grows this early form of belief develops into a recognition of higher spirits and lower, until, in the highest form of religion, a belief in one supreme spirit is attained. But on this belief, at a very early stage in the transition which it thus makes, is engrafted the very important idea of spirits, many or few, which have always been spirits, and were never specially associated with any material body. Up to the point at which this new idea is engrafted it cannot be said that there is any belief in a spiritual hierarchy. The Indians of Guiana have not yet reached this point.

The process by which the idea of a difference in the authoritative rank of spirits is attained seems to be by a generalisation of those spirits of equal power which form the earlier subjects of belief ; for example, the belief in a distinct spirit in each body of water—river, sea, rain, spring, or whatever its nature—passes by generalisation into a belief in one spirit powerful over all water. It will presently be shown that the Indians of Guiana have hardly made any advance even in this direction. The process by which the first idea is gained of gods—of beings, that is, who have always been spirits, is less easily explained ; but this is of little consequence here, in that all that it is necessary to show is that the Indians have not yet attained any such notion.

It is indeed fully recognised in Guiana that some spirits
are more to be feared than others. But this is only because
some excel in physical power and cunning. For instance,
the spirits of all rocks are supposed to be capable of harm ;
but again and again I have found cases, as, for example, the
rock Paiwarikaira and the sculptured rocks already mentioned, in which the Indians possessed special dread of
certain particular spirit-possessed rocks. But these rocks
are deemed more malicious than others. The matter may
be made quite clear in this way : Not only every river, but
also every bend and portion of a river, has a spirit, and
though all these are regarded as possibly harmful, in that
Indians have been drowned even in still water, yet those of
these spirits which belong to the falls, rapids, or cataracts
are especially dreaded, in that Indians have been much more
frequently drowned in such places. In short, though some
spirits are thus especially harmful, there is no notion of any
that have definite authority over any other spirits in general.

It has been presumed that traces of a belief in spirits
with definite authority, as distinguished from brute power,
over others have been found, among other peoples, in a
sun-spirit, a moon-spirit, a water-spirit, and so on. Traces
of these last-named spirits may perhaps be found in Guiana.
On one occasion, during an eclipse of the sun, the Arawak
men among whom I happened to be rushed from their
houses with loud shouts and yells. They explained that
a fight was going on between the sun and moon, and
that they shouted to frighten, and so part the combatants.
In many other countries exactly this proceeding of making
a noise to separate the sun-spirit and the moon-spirit, or
the sun-god and the moon-god, has been noticed ; and it is
generally supposed that in such cases a high degree of
authority is attributed to these spirits. But I see nothing
in this or in anything else which shows that savages distinguish, by attributing greater authority to them, such
beings as sun and moon, and very many other natural phenomena, as wind and storms, from men and other animals,

plants and other inanimate objects, or from any other beings whatsoever. All beings—and under this heading are included all personified natural phenomena—are, in fact, of the same kind, each with a body and a spirit. It is the old story—they differ from each other only that some are more powerful than others in the mere matter of brute force, and none have any other sort of authority over others.

It is true that when rain falls at an inopportune time, or when a sudden flood arises, the Arawak occasionally inveighs against a being called *Œnicidu*. They are unable to explain exactly who this being is, but he is apparently only that particular body of water, be it flood or rain, which happens to be under notice at the moment. Here is probably a germ which might develop, when the identity of water in its various forms is recognised, into a belief in a being having power over all water, and thus would first be attained a belief in an authoritative spirit. Though this latter belief does not seem yet to have been attained in Guiana, it must be added that in this matter, if anywhere, the Indians may have reverted to a point of belief below that at which they once were.

If there is no belief in a hierarchy of spirits, there can of course be none in any such beings as in higher religions are called gods—beings, that is, who have not only authority over others, but who have also always been spirits, unless when temporarily and for their own purposes they put themselves into bodies; and who in some, if not in all, cases, had some share in the creation of the world. It is true that various words have been found in all, or nearly all, the languages, not only of Guiana, but also of the whole world, which have been supposed to be names of a great spirit, supreme being, or god, in the sense which those phrases bear in the language of the higher religions. In Guiana, their names, as far as they are known to me, are—

Carib Tribes { True Caribs { Tamosi = 'the ancient one.'
Tamosi kabotano = 'the ancient one in the sky.'
Ackawoi; Mackonaima = ?
Macusi kutti (probably only Macusi-Dutch for ' God ').

Arawak	Wa murreta kwonci = 'our maker.
	Wa cinaci = 'our father.'
	Ifilici wacinaci = 'our great father.'
Warrau	Kononatoo = 'our maker.'
Wapiana	Tomingatoo = ?

It will be seen that of these I am only able to explain the exact logical meaning of the two True Carib words, of the Arawak word, and of the Warrau word. In these only three ideas are expressed—(1) One who lived long ago and is now in sky-land; (2) the maker of the Indians; and (3) their father. Now none of these ideas in any way involve the attributes of a god. On the contrary, they all point rather to a conception, which is certainly present in all Indian minds, that their remote ancestors, of whom they are accustomed to speak as their fathers or, by a very natural figure of speech, their makers, came into their present homes from some other country, which is sometimes said to be that entirely natural country which is separated from Guiana by the ocean of the air. And when, sometimes, these same ancestors are said still to exist in that other place which I can only call sky-land, this probably only means that these spirits have recrossed the same ocean and gone back to the old country. Thus these supposed gods are really but the remembered dead of each tribe; and where there is mention of one great spirit or god, it is merely the chief traditional founder of the tribe. It must be remembered that these names were first noted by missionaries, and were eagerly seized upon by them, and used to express the God whom they preached. The names have, therefore, to some extent acquired a sense which the missionaries thus imparted to them. While, therefore, it seems to me that there is nothing to show the existence of a genuine Indian word for a genuine Indian idea of that which we call God—while, that is, there is nothing to suggest an affirmative answer to the question, whether Indians have any idea of a God—there is this to suggest a negative answer to the same question, namely, that the conception of a God is not only totally foreign to Indian habits of thought, but belongs to a much higher stage of intellectual development than any attained by them. To repeat what has been said, perhaps, wearisomely often already, there are, according to Indian belief, no spirits but such as are, or originally were, embodied in material bodies; and no apotheosis has of these made gods or a God.

Once more, however, in the idea of ancestral spirits still existing, is the germ which might under certain circumstances develop into that leading conception of the higher religions which recognises one God, the creator and ruler of all.

Yet one more subject claims mention in connection with Indian animism. The belief in spirits and the worship of these spirits by certain rites and ceremonies are two very different things, though the fact that in the higher religions the two are almost invariably found in very close association has induced civilised men to regard them as nearly inseparable. Spirits may be regarded with indifference, as without power to affect men for good or evil, in which case they are not worshipped. Or they may be regarded either with dread as harmful, or with expectancy as beneficial, to man; and in either of these cases various attentions are paid to them, to avert their ill-will or to attract their good-will, as the case may be. Or, lastly, spirits of the good kind may be regarded with gratitude for benefits received, and in that case also a worship of thanks *may* be paid to them.

To understand the matter as it is exhibited in British Guiana, it is necessary to notice which of these attitudes the Indians hold toward spiritual beings. There are, the Indians think, harmless spirits and harmful; but while the latter are very active in exercise of their power of affecting men and other beings, the former are perfectly and entirely inactive in this respect. It is somewhat difficult to realise this Indian view. All that can be said of it is, that all the good that befalls him the Indian accepts either without inquiry as to its cause or as the result of his own exertions; but, on the other hand, all the evils that befall him he regards as inflicted by malignant spirits. This being his state of mind, the

Indian has no inducement to attract the good-will of spirits; but he naturally so acts and so avoids action as to avert the ill-will of other spirits. For example, he is, as has been told, very careful not to mention, or even look at, certain rocks and other objects. He avoids eating the flesh of certain sorts of animals, possibly because these are supposed by him to be especially malignant. It is somewhat curious that in this way different tribes avoid different animals; most tribes, for instance, refusing to eat the flesh of water-haas (*Capybara*) and sting-rays, though these are freely eaten by True Caribs. All tribes, however, agree in refusing to eat the flesh of such animals as are not indigenous to their country, but were introduced from abroad, such as oxen, sheep, goats, and fowls; apparently on the principle, with which we have met before, that any strange and abnormal object is especially likely to be possessed of a harmful spirit. It must, however, be added that, under great pressure of circumstances, such as utter want of other food, these meats are occasionally rendered eatable by the simple ceremony of getting a peaiman, or even occasionally an old woman, to blow a certain number of times on them; apparently on the principle that the spirit of the animal about to be eaten is thus expelled. But in connection with this subject one universal and very common custom of the Indians of Guiana is chiefly noticeable. Before attempting to shoot a cataract for the first time, on first sight of any new place, and every time a sculptured rock or striking mountain or stone is seen, Indians avert the ill-will of the spirits of such places by rubbing red-peppers (*Capsicum*) each in his or her own eyes. For instance, on reaching the Timehri rock on the Corentyn river, I at once began to sketch the figure sculptured thereon. Looking up the next moment I saw the Indians—men, women, and children—who accompanied me all grouped round the rock-picture, busily engaged in this painful operation of pepper-rubbing. The extreme pain of this operation when performed thoroughly by the Indians I can faintly realise from my own feelings when I have occasionally rubbed my eyes with fingers which had recently handled red-peppers; and from the fact that, though the older practitioners inflict this self-torture with the utmost stoicism, I have again and again seen that otherwise rare sight of Indians, children and even young men, sobbing under the infliction. Yet the ceremony was never omitted. Sometimes when by a rare chance no member of the party had had the forethought to provide peppers, lime-juice was used as a substitute; and once, when neither peppers nor limes were at hand, a piece of blue indigo-dyed cloth was carefully soaked and the dye was then rubbed into the eyes. These, I believe, are the only ceremonies observed by the Indians. One idea underlies them all, and that is, the attempt to avoid attracting the attention of malignant spirits.

Thus, if it is absolutely necessary to pass a rock or spiteful cataract, the Indian avoids attracting the attention of this by mentioning it. This idea is further developed and exhibited in an attempt to make himself invisible to the dreaded object. Just as an ostrich, according to the old story, is said to bury its head in the sand and so to blind itself to conceal its body from the hunters, so the Indian, if he can only avoid seeing the object dreaded by him, thinks that he himself is invisible to that object. To effect this purpose, he temporarily blinds himself with the juice of capsicums or other similar matter. This circumstance is further well illustrated by the fact, which I often observed, that when after much difficulty I had persuaded Indians to stand in front of such a terrible object as a camera, to be photographed, they again and again defeated my purpose by clapping their hands over their eyes at the moment the cap of the apparatus was withdrawn, lest the terrible eye of the camera should see them. This is also exactly parallel to the action of young children all over the world, who clap their hands to their eyes in the presence of some object dreadful to them.[1]

[1] This is another side of an Indian habit of thought before mentioned— I mean, of their belief in the reality of dreams. In the one case, that of sleep, they think themselves present among surroundings which have no

In conclusion, the whole religious belief of these Indians may be shortly summed up thus : Not only every human being but every object perceptible to the senses consists of a body and a spirit ; the spirits of all these are separable from their bodies, both during life and at death ; spirits thus separated after death continue to exist for an indefinite period upon earth ; of spirits, both while associated with their bodies and after, some are malignant and active, others are entirely quiescent ; all spirits may be communicated with, not by the ordinary individual, but by the peaiman when in an ecstatic condition. This constitutes a very simple form of animism, which has no connection whatever with the Indian's code of morality. Yet in this animism there are germs which might develop in the direction of higher religion. For instance, the belief of the Indians of the continuance of the existence of the spirit for an indefinite period after the death of the body is the germ from which might have developed a belief in the everlasting existence of the spirit. So, also, their knowledge of a country beyond the sky, difficult but not impossible of attainment by living man, is the germ from which might have developed a belief in a separate place for departed spirits. Their belief in the existence of a separate spirit in each portion of any natural phenomenon, for example in every portion of water, might eventually pass into a belief in one spirit supreme over that phenomenon ; and this would originate a recognition of spirits with authority over other spirits. Lastly, their belief in ancestral spirits is a germ from which might spring a belief in the existence of gods or even of a God.

Finally, the great lesson to be learned from a study of Indian animism is that the very pure form in which it exists in Guiana, common to a very large number of Red-men elsewhere, is much more primitive than has yet been suspected by most students of religious evolution.

real existence but are only the circumstances of a dream, because they see or fancy they see themselves among these surroundings ; in the other case, when they shut their eyes to avoid certain objects, they think themselves not present among the surroundings in which they really are, because they do not see them.

CHAPTER XVIII.

FOLK-LORE.

General Statement of the Nature of the Folk-lore—Elements of Error in reading the Folk-lore of Savages—Examples of such Error regarding God, Prayer, a Deluge, and a World-fire—Mythological Legends—The Arrival of Indians upon Earth—The Origin of Cultivation—Animals and their Doings—Fanciful Explanations of the Facts of Nature—Fabled Animals—An Indian Jonah—Historical Legends.

INDIANS, as they lie at night in their hammocks, or squat round the fire with knees drawn up to chin, listen to endless tales, told sometimes by the peaiman, sometimes by the headman of the settlement, sometimes by the old women— who in this, as in other societies, are great tradition-mongers; and these tales are always told with an amount of gesticulation, half seen and yet intensified in the fitful firelight, and with modification of the voice so varied that they have considerable dramatic interest even to a stranger, though ignorant of the language, who, on rare occasions, may happen to be present. Some few of these stories, which, in that they are handed down from generation to generation, may be conveniently classed as folk-lore, I was able to gather, and a far larger number have been learned and told by my friend Mr. Brett,[1] to whom I am indebted for very much information on this subject. Many of the stories are of course intimately connected with the subject of the last chapter, in which the religion of the Indians was described as a very extensive animism—as a recognition, that is, of the existence of a world full of non-supernatural beings, some of

[1] *Indian Tribes of Guiana*, by W. H. Brett, London; and *Legends and Myths of the Aboriginal Indians of British Guiana*. Same Author, London, 1879.

which *to us* appear animate, as men and other animals, others inanimate, as trees and rocks, others to be natural phenomena, as winds and storms—but of which each alike appears *to the Indian* to be alive and to have both a material body and a spirit. Much of their folk-lore tells of the acts of these beings. Other of their folk-lore consists of a few half-remembered traditions of comparatively recent historical events, as of battles and war between the tribes. In the present chapter an attempt will be made to give some idea of both of these phases of folk-lore, the mythological and the more purely historical.

Before telling any tales of the former of these kinds something must be said as to how far they are probably of genuine Indian origin; for some of those which have been recorded have undoubtedly been much affected by European influence; for example, in many of the tales there are points which in a very marked manner recall incidents belonging to Christian mythology, especially incidents of the Creation and of the Flood. It is not here necessary to make more than a passing allusion to the theory based upon these supposed common points, of the common descent of the Indians and of the rest of mankind from the actors of Genesis; for these apparently common points are themselves of very suspicious origin. It is true that they appear in the legends as the Indians themselves tell them at the present day; but it does not by any means follow from this that these details belonged to the tradition before the discovery of America. The Indian mind is like a highly polished mirror which reflects all that is shown it. If we can imagine such an incident as a civilised man glancing for the first time into a mirror, we must remember that at the first glance the man would realise the exhibition, not of glass, quicksilver, and certain optical laws, but of a duplicate of himself. So the student of Indian thought at first is apt to see not such things as the Indian thinks, but such things as he, the student, thinks. A partial explanation of this is that the Indian, unlike the civilised man, knows nothing of the supernatural or impossible, and is fully prepared to believe in the existence of everything even that he has not seen ; so when told by the European of the facts, simple or complex, of Christian theology, he undoubtingly and without the least mental effort assents to their existence.   To test this I have often asked Indians as to the existence both of animals never seen in America, such as elephants, and of animals the most impossible that my imagination could produce ; and the result invariably was that the Indian quietly assented to the existence of such animals, and that in many cases he was even prepared to describe the localities, to which, though near, he had never been, where such animals occur.   In the same way there can be little doubt that the early explorers of America described the Amazons of the Old-World legends to the Indians, and learned from the latter that such fighting women existed in the New World.   Again, in exactly the same way there can be little doubt that the early conquerors of America, who salved their consciences, whenever these were slightly disturbed by the knowledge of the cruelties which their owners practised upon the Indians, by proclaiming the mysteries of the most charitable of all religions, thus placed incidents of Christian tradition in the minds of these Indians.   Such alien facts, even if they were unenforced by sword and fire, were unhesitatingly accepted and engrafted on the Indian mind, and must have spread with a rapidity which will be appreciated fully only by those who by actual experience have realised the extraordinarily rapid rate at which news, even of a trifling kind, spreads amongst these people. And before long the new facts must have been fully amalgamated with the genuine Indian tradition.

In connection with the circumstance just described, it must be remembered that a very large proportion of those Europeans who have been much in contact with the Indians and have recorded their folk-lore, have, whether nominally missionaries or not, been more or less inspired by the purposes of the Christian missionary ; and these have rejoiced to find the Christian traditions which their own

forerunners had poured into the Indian mind. Every allowance must therefore be made by the scientific student of
folk-lore for the extreme probability that these missionaries
have very often mistaken such mere reflections for realities.
The amount of error thus introduced is largely increased by
the fact that not only each missionary by himself is liable
to err, but that the whole body of those who have spoken
of Christianity to the Indians since these were first seen have
been liable to the same error. It is too generally forgotten
that, though the present missionary efforts in Guiana are
hardly more than a generation old, other efforts of the same
kind, though not so fully organised and recorded, had been
made before. Though, therefore, the present missionary may
often meet with an Indian who has perhaps never seen a
white man before, he must not assume that in the stories
which this Indian tells there have not been incorporated,
generations before, incidents gathered from the preachings of
the earliest explorers, conquerors, and settlers of this part of
America.

It may perhaps be as well to give an illustration or two
of the more subtle forms which this error takes. How a conception, similar to our own, of an omnipotent and creating
God may have been erroneously read from the simple Indian
tradition of some great and powerful ancestor, has already
been explained.[1] A fact recognised even by missionaries is
that Indians make no prayer to any being whatsoever.
Mr. Brett again and again bears witness to this in his book
of legends; perhaps he most emphatically emphasises the
statement where he italicises his words in saying that they
'*never call upon*' their Great Spirit. Yet the same writer
in another passage[2] actually introduces a prayer for rain supposed to have been made by the earliest Warrau Indians. In
this case the discrepancy is probably to be explained in one
of the two following suggestive ways : either the missionary
was so saturated with the idea, more orthodox than religious,
of calling on God for rain that, forgetful of the fact that such

---

[1] See p. 366 *ante*.   [2] Brett's *Legends*, p. 62.

crying is so unnatural as to be utterly alien to Indian habits
of thought, he misread some part of the Indian story as a
prayer; or—as, remembering Mr. Brett's wonted accuracy, I
am induced to prefer—there actually was a prayer in the
story as he heard it, but this prayer was introduced into the
traditions after, and under the influence of, European teaching.   Other typical instances of error from a similar source
are to be found in the stories of world-floods and world-fires.
The calamity to which an Indian is perhaps most exposed is
to be driven from his home by a sudden rise in the river and
consequent flooding of the whole forest. His way to escape is
to get into his canoe with his family and his live stock, and
to seek temporarily some higher ground, or, as sometimes
happens, if none such can be found, the whole party lives
as best they may in the canoe until the waters disappear
from the face of the earth. It is well known how in all
countries the proverbial 'oldest inhabitant' remembers and
tells of the highest flood that ever happened. When therefore the Indian tells in his simple language the tradition of
the highest flood which covered all the small world known
to him, and tells how the Indians escaped it,[1] it is not
difficult to realise that the European hearer, theologically
prejudiced in favour of Noah, his flood, and his ark, is apt
to identify the two stories with each other, and with many
similar stories from many parts of the world. In the same
way the Arawaks, as Mr. Brett relates, have a tradition of a
world-fire which swept over the land.[2]   On the savannahs of
Guiana, and even in the forest, when a long season of drought
has dried up almost all vegetation, a fire sweeping over the
land is not a very uncommon event. In such cases the
Indian, if on the savannah, takes refuge on some patch of
ground where grass is the only vegetation, and where that
is too scanty to afford more than very momentary food and
delay to the flames; or, if he is in the forest, he hurries on
to some one of the many utterly barren sand-banks near the
rivers, and there waits until the fire has passed. When,

---

[1] Brett's *Legends*, p. 13.   [2] *Ibid*, p. 10.

376 AMONG THE INDIANS OF GUIANA.

therefore, the Arawak tells how a world-fire once devastated the land, the explanation is, *mutatis mutandis*, that which has been given of the world-flood. But as no world-fire has any place in Christian tradition, the missionaries disregarded the catastrophe as told by Arawaks, though they spent their whole energy on a supposititious world-flood told of by the same people.

From the folk-lore now to be told an attempt will be made to exclude, as far as possible, all that is of doubtful Indian origin; for the present object is solely to present some picture of Indian habits of thought as shown in these fireside tales.

It will be found that a very large proportion of the stories are attempts to account for the features of the world in which the Indian lives. Naturally these attempts are in no way founded on scientific grounds, but are just the simple thoughts such as would everywhere readily occur to man in a primitive state, and which would even now occur to any child of civilised parents who could be entirely guarded from all hereditary scientific knowledge. This being so, the fact of the recurrence of the same legend, in slightly varied forms, in different parts of the world, ought not to excite the slightest surprise. For example, to take the legend of a world-flood already explained, floods must have afflicted primitive man in most parts of the world; and that the tradition of such an event, and of the escape in a boat, has originated independently, but from similar circumstances and by a similar process, in various parts of the world, is not only not surprising, but was to be certainly expected.

The first group of stories is concerned with the origin of man, or at least with his appearance in Guiana. The Arawaks, according to Mr. Brett, say that, before men were, a being,[1] breaking off twigs and pieces of bark from a silk-cotton tree (*Eriodendron*), threw them far and wide around him. Some as they fell became birds; others fell into the water and became fish; others fell on land and became

[1] Mr. Brett of course identifies him with God.

beasts, reptiles, men, and women. The Warraus, on the other hand, without troubling their minds as to the first manufacture of the bodily shapes which we see, begin their story from a time when their ancestors lived in sky-land. Up there one of their number, named Okonoroté, was a famous hunter. On one occasion he followed a bird for many days without finding opportunity to shoot it. At length he succeeded, his arrow piercing the bird. But the game fell down into a deep pit, and was apparently lost. But Okonoroté, looking down into the pit, saw daylight below, and before long he was able to discern down below a land on which many kinds of four-footed animals were walking. With the help of his tribe he hung a long piece of bush-rope down toward the earth, and then climbed down this. After much successful hunting he climbed home again, taking with him some venison. The Warraus who had remained in sky-land, never having tasted such food before, appreciated it so highly that they determined to move to the land below. After many had descended, a woman—who according to some was with child, according to others was very fat—stuck in the hole in sky-land, and though the other members of the tribe pushed and pulled from above and below, it was never possible to move her. So the Warraus who were already on earth had to remain there, and those who were still in sky-land remained there. The True Caribs have a story which differs from this of the Warraus only in that the former represent that their object in coming down from sky-land to earth was to clean the latter place, which was evidently very dirty. This difference is of some slight interest in that, as has before been said, the Warraus are of filthy habits, while the Caribs are much more zealous in cleanliness.

The whole group of these stories, thus compared, have a considerable incidental significance. The Arawak story seems full of European ideas, and, as is natural in the case of this tribe, which was from the first, and has continued, in closer communion with white men than any other tribe, is no doubt much modified from its original Indian form. The story of the Warraus—and in a somewhat less degree this is also true of the Carib story—is not only much more in accordance with Indian habits of thought, but, owing to the fact that this tribe has till quite recently had hardly any communication with Europeans, is much more likely to be genuine and original. For myself, I do not believe that any idea of a general manufacture of animal bodies, much less of spirits, ever originated in the brain of an Indian, or any other man, in a state of savagery.

The next story is told by the Warraus of the origin of the first Carib, and fully accounts for the enmity between the Warrau and Carib tribes. It also incidentally illustrates the Indian way of thinking of inanimate objects, such as stumps of trees, as living beings hardly different from men.

Once upon a time there was a pond in which, as is often the case, the Warraus feared to bathe. At last two Indian women ventured into the water. Presently one of the women, named Korobona, touched the stump of a tree which rose over the surface of the water, and immediately the stump seized her and made her his wife. Then Korobona returned home, where after some time a child was born. The brothers, jealous of their sister's honour, wished to kill it, but eventually consented to spare it. The child, however, soon died. Then Korobona went back to the pond, and again saw the stump. Once more a child was born, this time a boy. The mother, remembering her brothers' threats on the previous occasion, hid the child in the forest. But the brothers discovered their sister's secret, and, having shot their arrows into the boy, left him as dead. But the mother nursed her child, revived it, and succeeded in rearing it. It was not till the child was a big boy that the brothers discovered that he still lived. Then they attacked him, and cut his body in small pieces. From the grave in which the mother buried the victim rose an Indian more powerful and more fierce than any Warrau had ever been. He was the first Carib, who, with his descendants, waged perpetual war on the Warraus and reduced them to their present miserable state.

Stories of how savages first learned to use plants as food are common in many parts of the world; nor are they absent from Guiana.

The Caribs say that when they first arrived on earth from sky-land, cassava, plantains, and all useful vegetables grew on one huge tree.[1] This tree was first discovered by a tapir, who grew fat on the fruits which fell from its branches. The Caribs, who as yet had found the new land a poor place and without food, were eager to find where the tapir fed. So they set the woodpecker to watch him. But the woodpecker as he flew through the forest after the tapir could not resist the temptation to tap the trees for insects, and the tapir, hearing the noise, knew he was followed, and went another way. Then the Caribs sent a rat, who stealthily succeeded in tracing the tapir to his food-tree; but the rat, having agreed with the tapir quietly to share the food, persuaded the Caribs that he too had failed in the quest. But the Caribs, finding the rat asleep one day with corn still in his mouth, woke him and compelled him to show the tree. Then the Caribs took their stone axes, and after many months' hard work, succeeded in felling it. Each man took pieces of the tree and planted them in a field of his own; so from that day each Indian has had his own cassava-field.

The Ackawoi, as might be expected from their near relationship to the True Caribs, tell a tale which, up to this point, differs from the above only in that they say that the acourie (*Dasyprocta aguti*) was the original discoverer of the food-tree, and that one single man, apparently their traditional ancestor, assisted by various animals, cut it down. The two tales then coincide in representing that from the stump of the felled tree—which, by the way, some say was of stone instead of wood—a flood began to flow out on to the land. But before much harm was done the flow of water was stopped, according to the True Caribs, by the aid

[1] The story, as I heard it, slightly varies from Mr. Brett's version.

of certain mysterious beings, neither men nor animals as we know them—according to the Ackawoi, by one man, who inverted an empty basket over the spring of water and so stopped its flow. From this point on we will follow the Ackawoi version of the legend, which is better known.

For some time the water was confined under the basket. But at last the brown monkey, curious, and suspecting that something very good must be hidden under the carefully tended basket, cautiously raised it and peeped under. In an instant the flood rushed out, carrying away the monkey, and overflowing the whole land. Then the man, with all manner of animals, took refuge up in a tall kokerite palm. Most of the fugitives remained patiently during the flood, but the red howling-monkey, getting excited, began to roar, and roared so loudly that his throat swelled, and has remained extended ever since. That is the reason of the curious bony drum in the throat of this animal. Meanwhile the man at intervals let single palm-seeds fall into the water, to judge by the splash of its depth. At last the flood seemed to have subsided, and all prepared to descend. But the trumpet-bird (*Psophia crepitans*) flew down in such a hurry that he alighted in an ants' nest, and the hungry insects fastened on his legs, which had before been fairly thick, and gnawed them down to their present spindle-like size.[1] The others having descended more cautiously and safely, the man began to rub two pieces of wood to make fire. Now the first spark generated in this way is very small. The bush-turkey (*Penelope marail*), at a moment when the man was looking away, swallowed this spark, mistaking it for a fire-fly, and then flew quickly away. The spark burned the bush-turkey's throat, and that is the reason why to this day

[1] In further illustration of how such thoughts may arise in Indian minds from familiar incidents, I may refer to an accident which happened to myself and frequently happens to the Indians. Jumping suddenly out of my hammock one morning, I alighted in the very middle of an enormous column of hunting ants (*Eciton*) which happened to be passing underneath at the moment. From my own sensations I can fully realise those of the trumpet-bird on the occasion recorded above.

those birds have a red wattle on their throats. Meanwhile, the man missing his spark, saw the alligator, who was then a gentle brute, but ugly, standing near. Immediately the other animals, agreeing in their abhorrence of the ugliness of the alligator, raised a shout that it was he who had taken the spark. Whereupon the man, angry and impatient, tore out the tongue of the supposed culprit. And this is the reason why alligators have ever since had such very rudimentary tongues, and also why they wage perpetual war on other beasts. That is all that is known of the story.

A large number of other stories, as in the last example, are evidently intended to account for certain peculiarities of certain animals. The following examples, told by Arawaks, have been collected by Mr. Brett.

The first once more concerns the alligator. The Sun one day came down to fish. Like any other Indian, he built a dam across the mouth of a fish-haunted stream to retain the prey. But in his absence the otters broke his dam, and the fish escaped. Then the Sun rebuilt it and placed a woodpecker to watch it. One day, the woodpecker tapping very loudly, the sun came to see what was the matter. This time it was the alligator who was trying to do damage. So the Sun drove him away by striking him again and again with a huge club. Thus were made those marks which we think are scales, which are to be seen on the alligator to this day.

A similar tale tells how a young Arawak chose as his wife a king-vulture (*Sarcoramphus papa*). Now an Indian man, when he marries, goes to live with his wife's father. So the Arawak went to sky-land and was well received by the vulture's people. But when after a time he announced his intention of paying a visit to his own people, the vultures were enraged, and set him on top of a tall awarra-palm (*Astrocaryum tucumoides*), the trunk of which, as is well known, is covered with terrible thorns. There he remained until some spiders, feeling pity, spun a cord by which he descended. Then for many years he tried to get back to his wife, but the vultures would have nothing more to say to him. But at last the other birds, taking compassion on him, carried him to sky-land and helped him to fight the vultures. The latter having been driven into their own houses, their whole settlement was burned over their heads. Then the other birds began to quarrel over the plunder. The trumpet-bird and the heron got so angry that they fought and rolled each other in the ashes, which is the reason why the former bird has ever since had a grey back, and why the latter has been grey all over. Taking advantage of the confusion, the owl, prowling about, found a package so carefully done up that he thought it must contain something very valuable. So he opened it, and out came the darkness in which he has ever since had to live. Meanwhile, a rather important incident had occurred. The Arawak on whose behalf this war was waged fought with, and was killed by, his own son by his vulture wife. It must be added that the hawks and other big birds found, when the war was over, that that generally bold little bird, the keskedie (*Saurophagus sulphuratus*), disinclined to fight just then, had bandaged his head with white cotton and, pretending to be ill, had remained at home, for which act he was compelled by the big birds always to wear his bandage. And this little bird still has the white marks on his head, and still avenges the indignity by attacking big birds whenever opportunity offers.

Yet another tale tells of war waged by the combined forces of men and birds. The enemy this time was a huge water-snake. An agreement was made that whoever began the attack should claim the skin as his spoil. For a long time no one would begin, but at last a duckler (*Plotus anhinga*)[1] darted under water and wounded the snake, who was then gradually drawn out and killed. Then the duckler claimed the skin. Calling his family, he made each take hold of the skin, and thus the whole party flew away with it. Then the birds agreed to divide the skin, which, except

---

[1] Mr. Brett makes the attacker the cormorant, which is not a Guianese bird.

at the head, was of very bright colours, each taking the part that was in its own beak. And when they had done this, each dressed himself in his own bit of skin. Most of them—all except the duckler who had actually began the attack on the snake, and to whose lot the head of the skin happened to fall—at once became various bright-coloured parrots and macaws. Only one, he who began the fight, remained dingy in colour and a duckler.

Other kindred stories account for peculiarities of other natural objects familiar to the Indian. One is of the haiarri (*Lonchocarpus*) root, which Indians throw into streams to narcotise the water and thus obtain the fish.[1] Once upon a time an Indian took his young son to bathe. Wherever the lad swam the fish died; and the father found by experiment that these fish were quite wholesome as food. So he made a practice of obtaining fish in this way. But after a time, the fish having taken council, chose a moment when the lad sat on a log just before plunging into the water, when, therefore, the fish could approach him safely, and then, all springing out of the water together, struck their spines into the lad. The wound made in this way by the sting-ray proved fatal. But as the father was carrying his dying son home, the blood dropped on to the ground, and wherever it fell there grew up a haiarri plant, which has ever since been used by Indians to poison the streams when they want to catch fish.

The scene of a second story of this kind is the Kaieteur fall, which has been described in an earlier chapter. There, in mid-stream, a few hundred yards below the fall, is a long narrow island, in shape much like one of the 'wood-skins,' or bark-boats, used by the Ackawoi of that river; and at the side of the river, close to the foot of the column of water, is a curiously regular rectangular rock of the shape of the 'pegall,' or basket, in which the Indian packs his properties. Once upon a time, say the Ackawoi, there was on the savannah above the fall an Indian settlement in which lived an

---

[1] See *ante*, p. 233.

old man so worn out and useless from age that in his feet the jiggers buried themselves unmolested. In short, the old man was a scandal and a nuisance to his fellows. So the latter put the old man with his pegall into a woodskin, which they then launched on the river and allowed to drift over the fall. The old man was never seen again ; but his woodskin became the island in the river below the fall, and his pegall turned to stone, and remains to this day.

Akin to these stories are the statements of the Macusis, that the dew that falls by night is the spittle of the stars ; and that the Southern Cross, which is of course a striking object on the bare and open savannah where those Indians live, is a being whose dwelling is the plain.

Another large class of fireside tales are of the existence of various fictitious men and animals. When travelling round the Canakoo mountains, I was often told by the Indians of a certain tribe of Indians who lived up among the highest rocks and who never came down into the plain except by night. Indians who have ventured up into the mountains have often heard sounds from the settlements of these people ; and even from below one may often see their fires by night. It is a very curious thing that, as I have seen, there actually is an appearance as of fire to be seen sometimes up in these mountains ; nor was I ever able to form any theory as to its cause. Other people of the same kind are the Hooronis, a tribe of Indians living beyond the Pacaraimas, who are men by night but fish by day. Even by day, however, they do not live in the water, but lie about their houses as do the fish caught for food by ordinary Indians. But if by chance an Indian of another tribe finds his way into the house of a Hooroni, and, thinking it empty, helps himself, as by ordinary custom he is entitled to do, to any of the apparent fish lying about, and if he tries to put this fish over the fire to roast, then all the fish change back into men and slay the intruder. Another favourite statement of the Indians is that there is another tribe, whom they locate anywhere, who live like ordinary Indians by day, but retire into the water at night and sleep standing, with only their heads above water. If the Amazons are not, as has been asserted, a suggestion made by Europeans and only then caught up and adopted by Indians, they should probably be classed with these fictitious tribes of folk-lore. It may be added that Humboldt has very plausibly suggested that the rumour of Amazons, which he thought was of genuine Indian origin, arose from the fact that in some of the tribes the men wear their hair long, as in other tribes only the women do.

Again, any extraordinary or inaccessible rock is always said to be inhabited by monstrous animals. For example, on Roraima the Indians say that there are huge white jaguars, huge white eagles, and other such beasts. To this class probably belongs the di-dis, beings in shape something between men and monkeys, who live in the forests near the river banks. To English readers this last being has some literary interest as being probably that which suggested to the vivid and quaint imagination of Charles Waterton the idea of constructing his famous nondescript, the real nature of which for a time puzzled too confiding zoologists at home. To this class also belong the omars, beings with bodies variously described as like those of exaggerated crabs and fish, who live under water in the rapids, and often drag down the boats of the Indians as they shoot these places. In connection with one of these last beings a story was told me at Ouropocari fall, on the Essequibo, which is worthy of record.

This omar used to feed on rotten wood, and he dragged down many boats merely in mistake for floating logs, but all the same the Indians were drowned. So one day an Ackawoi peaiman carefully wrapped up two pieces of the wood with which fire is rubbed, so that no water could make them damp. Then he dived down into the middle of the falls and got into the belly of the omar. There he found whole stores of rotten wood. So he set fire to this. Then the omar, in great pain, rose to the surface, belched out the peaiman, and died.

In the above story we once more find an instance of the

occurrence among the Indians of an idea which has recurred again and again in almost all parts of the world. Jonah in the belly of the whale, Hiawatha in the belly of the sturgeon Nahma, Brer Rabbit and Mr. Fox in the belly of the Cow Bookay,[1] the seven kids of the well-known story in the belly of the wolf, and the peaiman in the belly of the omar, form a curious set of parallels. Whereon the notion of men entering the bellies of animals and then escaping in safety is founded is not clear; but that these various instances have originated independently by a common process of reasoning from some similar and simple incidents of general occurrence is highly probable.

The last group of folk-lore tales to which I shall now turn differs entirely from those already told, in that the subjects dealt with are not mythological but historical. They represent all that the Indians themselves know of the unwritten history of their ancestors in comparatively recent years.

The Arawaks say that their ancestors had first to fight a fierce tribe called Meyanow; and after they had exterminated these they were harassed by the Caribs, who came first from the islands, but afterwards settled on the mainland and carried on an even more constant warfare. Every year the Caribs from all quarters gathered round the Arawaks on the Pomeroon and attacked them. One year, when the Caribs were expected, the Arawaks chose a chief to lead them against the enemy. This chief, having seen that large quantities of arrows had been provided, placed his men in ambush, some distance from the river, at each side of the path leading from the river to the settlement. When the Caribs came, they saw the canoes of the Arawaks tied up at the side of the river as usual; and, suspecting nothing, they left their own canoes and hurried along the path. Then they fell into the ambush. When the Arawaks had exhausted their arrows, they fell upon the enemy with their war-clubs, till the few survivors of the latter fled back to the water-side, only to find their retreat cut off by other Arawaks who had

---

[1] *Uncle Remus*, by J. C. Harris. London and New York, 1881.

crept round them through the forest. Not a Carib of that whole party escaped.

The next year another party of Caribs came against the Arawaks of the Pomeroon. The chief of the latter made all his men hide their women and children in safety away in the forest. Then he placed the huge trunk of a tree across the mouth of a side stream, just under water. On the banks of the stream above this hidden trunk the Arawaks concealed themselves. When word was brought that the invading Caribs were near, two or three of the younger and most active of the Arawak men got into a small boat of very light draught, and, pushing this over the boom under water, paddled about in the mouth of the stream. Before long the Caribs saw them, and, enraged at finding the settlements which they had come to plunder deserted and bare, they gave chase to the Arawak boat. The latter was quickly paddled by its crew over the boom and up the stream. The Caribs following, their large and heavy canoes, urged in the course of the chase at their utmost speed, struck heavily against the unsuspected barrier and were split. At that moment the Arawaks rushed out upon the enemy from their hiding-places and slew almost all. A few only escaped, vowing vengeance.

Yet a third time the Caribs came, and were again over-thrown. Their chief, having been struck in the face by a three-pronged fish arrow, was captured alive. Then the Arawaks consulted as to what they should do with the prisoner. At last they determined to let him go unharmed; and this was the end of the feud between the tribes.

It must be added to the above story that the peace does not seem to have been very complete. The Caribs still continued to oppress the Arawaks; and, according to the general belief of the Indians, the former till quite recently were even in the habit of cutting off the hand of any Arawak who was bold enough to settle near the banks of the river. It must also be added that the preceding story, so favourable to the Arawaks, is derived entirely from Arawak tellers; but, on the other hand, it is certain that the Arawaks to this day retain a timid dread of the Caribs, who repay the feeling with contempt.

With regard to these semi-historical tales of war between the tribes it need only be added, as significant when the general condition of the various tribes is considered, that only the Warraus seem to have no tale to tell of bold deeds done against hostile tribes.

CHAPTER XIX.

INDIAN ANTIQUITIES.

The Various Antiquities—Rock-Pictures—Painted Rocks—Two kinds of Engraved Rocks—Shallow Engravings—Deep Engravings—The most recent Rock-Engraving—Comparative Study of the Rock-Engravings of the World—Shell-Mounds or Kitchen-Middens—Probable History of the Shell-Mounds—Stone Implements—Manner of Occurrence in Guiana —Some Typical Examples—Some Peculiar Examples—Standing Stones —Sites of Ancient Villages.

In 1825 Charles Waterton, in his classic 'Wanderings in South America,' wrote : 'I could find no monuments or marks of antiquity amongst these Indians ; so that, after penetrating to the Rio Branco from the shores of the Western Ocean, had anybody questioned me on this subject, I should have answered, I have seen nothing amongst these Indians which tells me that they have existed here for a century, though, for aught I know to the contrary, they may have been here before the Redemption ; but their total want of civilisation has assimilated them to the forests in which they wander. Thus an aged tree falls and moulders into dust, and you cannot tell what was its appearance, its beauties, or its diseases amongst the neighbouring trees ; another has shot up in its place, and after nature has had her course, it will make way for a successor in its turn. So it is with the Indian of Guiana : he is now laid low in the dust ; he has left no record behind him, either on parchment or on stone or in earthenware, to say what he has done. . . . All that you can say is : The trees where I stand appear lower and smaller than the rest, and from this I conjecture that some Indians may have had a settlement here formerly. Were I by chance to meet the son of the father who moulders here, he could tell me that his father was famous for slaying tigers and serpents and caymans, and noted in the chase of the tapir and wild boar, but that he remembers little or nothing of his grandfather.'

This statement is only true in so far as it describes the ignorance of the Indian as to his own forerunners and their real history. In the half century which has elapsed since he who wrote these words wandered through the interior of 'Demerara,' many antiquities have been found in the country—enough, indeed, to make it highly probable that many more remain to be discovered. Unfortunately, those already known are not enough in number, and have not been sufficiently studied, to afford much information as to their history and as to the inter-relations of their makers ; and, perhaps yet more unfortunately, even the few facts known have been recorded so fleetingly, and chiefly in such scattered papers, that they are hardly generally available. An account of all known antiquities of British Guiana ought therefore to be useful, even if only to those who wish to look further into such matters.

The objects to be discussed may, for the sake of convenience, be classed under five heads : (1) Pictured rocks, (2) shell-mounds, (3) stone implements, (4) standing stones, (5) sites of ancient villages. Before dealing with each of these in turn, it may be as well to state that in no one case is it as yet possible to assign any one of these traces of past human life with any certainty to the tribe which produced them ; and only in one case is it possible to point to the producers with even some degree of probability. With regard to the pictured rocks and the shell-mounds, good reason will be shown for supposing that the former are the products of a forgotten art of some of the tribes now living in this part of the world ; and yet stronger reason for supposing that the latter are the work of the True Caribs.

PICTURED ROCKS.

The pictured rocks, which are certainly the most striking and mysterious of the antiquities of Guiana, are—and this has apparently never yet been pointed out—not all of one kind. In all cases various figures are rudely depicted on larger or smaller surfaces of rocks. Sometimes these figures are painted, though such cases are few and, as will be shown, of little moment; more generally they are graven on the rock, and these alone are of great importance. Rock sculptures may, again, be distinguished into two kinds, differing in the depth of incision, the apparent mode of execution, and, most important of all, the character of the figures represented.

Painted rocks in British Guiana are mentioned by Mr. C. Barrington Brown, well known as a traveller in the colony. He says, for instance, that in coming down past Amailah fall (in the same district and range as the Kaieteur), on the Cooriebrong river, he passed 'a large white sandstone rock ornamented with figures in red paint.' When in the Pacaraima mountains, on the Brazilian frontier, I heard of the existence of similar paintings in that neighbourhood, but was unable to find them. Mr. Wallace, in his account of his 'Travels on the Amazons,' mentions the occurrence of similar drawings in more than one place near the Amazons; and from these and other accounts it seems probable that they occur in various parts of South America. If, as seems likely, these figures are painted with either of the red pigments [1] which the Indians use so largely to paint their own bodies as well as their weapons and other implements, or, as is also possible, with some sort of red earth, they must be modern, the work of Indians of the present day; for these red pigments would not long withstand the effects of the weather, especially where, as in the case quoted from Mr. Brown, the drawings are on such an unenduring substance as sandstone. Some further account of these

[1] See *ante*, p. 316.

paintings is, however, much to be desired ; for, though they are probably modern, it would be very interesting to know whether the designs resemble those depicted on the engraved rocks, or are of the kind which the Indian at the present time ornaments both his own skin and his household utensils

FIG. 35.

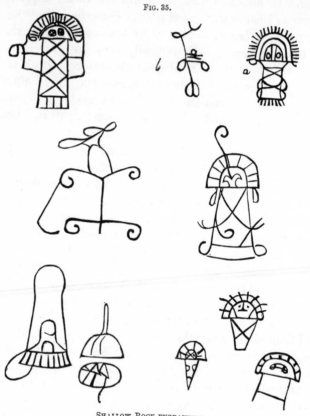

SHALLOW ROCK-ENGRAVINGS.

and paddles. It may be mentioned that in the Christy collection there is a stone celt from British Guiana on which are painted lines very closely resembling in character those which the Indian commonly paints on his own body.

The engraved rocks, on the contrary, must be of some antiquity ; that is to say, they must certainly date from a time

before the influence of Europeans was much felt in Guiana.
As has already been said, the engravings are of two kinds, and

FIG. 36.

DEEP ROCK-ENGRAVINGS.

are probably the work of two different people ; nor is there
even any reason to suppose that the two kinds were produced
at one and the same time.

These two kinds of engravings may, for the sake of convenience, be distinguished as 'deep' (Fig. 36, p. 393) and 'shallow' (Fig. 35, p. 392) respectively, according as the figures are deeply cut into the rock or are merely scratched on the surface. The former (Fig. 37) vary from one-eighth to one-half of an inch, or even more, in depth; the latter are of quite inconsiderable depth. This difference probably corresponds with a difference in the means by which they were produced. The deep engravings seem cut into the rock with an edged tool, probably of stone; the shallow figures were apparently formed by long continued friction with stones and moist sand. The two kinds seem never to occur in the same place, or even near to each other; in fact, a distinct line may almost be drawn between the districts in which the deep and the shallow kinds occur respectively. The deep form (Plate 9) occurs at several spots on the Mazeruni, Essequibo, Ireng, Cotinga, Potaro and Berbice rivers. The shallow form has as yet only been reported from the Corentyn river and its tributaries, where, however, examples occur in considerable abundance. But the two kinds differ not only in the depth of incision, in the apparent mode of their production, and in the place of their occurrence, but also—and this is the chief difference between the two—in the figures represented. This will best be explained by describing examples of each kind.

On Temehri rock, which lies in mid-stream some little distance below the Wanitoba cataracts on the Corentyn river, there is a very fine example of shallow engraving. (Fig. 37.) The Carib word *temehri* means 'painted,' or perhaps rather 'marked'; thus the figure now under notice has given name to the rock.[1] The engraving represents the single figure, the

---

[1] In connection with this word a curious fact is pointed out by Schomburgk. There is a tree in Guiana called 'letter-wood' or 'speckle-wood,' because of the curious marking of its heart-wood. Harcourt, in his *Relation of a Voyage to Guiana*, published in 1626, says of it, 'There is a hard, heavy, red-speckled wood in that country, called *Paira timinere*' (p. 48). Aublet's scientific name for letter-wood-tree is *Piratenera guianensis*. Schomburgk remarks, truly enough, that 'it is called by the Caribs and Macusis

PLATE IX.

ENGRAVED ROCKS AT WARRAPOOTA FALL.

outline of which is, with one exception, always represented in these shallow engravings. It may be described as a rectangular figure, of greater height than width, crowned by a semicircle marked with distinct radii. This outline is filled in by a pattern of straight lines; which, unlike the outline, is not always the same as at Temehri, and is indeed often considerably varied. The whole height of the figure

FIG. 37.

TEMEHRI ROCK, WITH ENGRAVING.

on Temehri rock is thirteen feet, its greatest width five feet seven inches; but figures of this sort vary very considerably in dimensions, though they are always much larger than are the figures of the deep sculptures. It is, as is indeed usual, very indistinct, and, except in certain lights, it is almost

Paira; and *timinere* (or *timehri*) signifies painted; ' and this writer adds, by making a slight error, that this term of 'painted' is given to it 'to distinguish it from a species which is not speckled.' As a matter of fact, the name of the letter-wood-tree is simply *Paira*; and *Paira temehri* is used to distinguish the marked or 'painted' heart-wood from the unmarked sap-wood. But the important point is, that Aublet made his scientific generic name for the tree by corrupting the Indian term *Paira timinere* into the pseudo-Latin word *Piratenera*, and thus ran the risk of offering a most hard nut to future etymologists to crack.

invisible until water has been poured over the surface of the rock. To obtain a photograph, it was necessàry carefully to mark the lines of the figure with white chalk, and one or two of the lines being accidentally left unmarked, these are not shown in the photograph.

In Downer's map of Berbice, published in 1844, are shown two rock-drawings supposed to occur on Temehri island, which is also in the Corentyn river, some little distance below Temehri rock. Both of these, as represented on the map, are very peculiar. In one, an upright line has several volutes starting from each side of it. Nothing of this sort occurs elsewhere, either in the shallow or the deep drawings. The other is an extraordinary combination—also such as has been seen nowhere else—apparently of straight-handled tridents. In the map it has a most suspiciously modern look, but as after careful search I failed to find any such figure on the island—which is very small—I need say no more about it. The original of the figure of six volutes I found. At first sight it does look as in the map ; but if carefully traced—for it is very indistinct—it becomes evident that it is of quite different nature. Curiously enough, however, though, according to depth of gravure, it certainly belongs to the shallow class of engravings, yet the figure represented bears little resemblance to the figures otherwise universal in this class ; it must, however, be added that it is still more unlike the character of the figures represented in the deep engravings.

Several other shallow drawings, apparently hitherto unrecorded, occur on this island. Some are so indistinct that I was unable to decipher and draw them. Another, which was almost entirely hidden by a tree which had grown over it, and which had to be cut down before the figure became visible to any but the sharp eye of the Indians, is a fine example of the common figure of the shallow class.

Another very good example of a rock-drawing of the shallow class exists at the side of the first fall on the Cabalebo, a large tributary running into the Corentyn on the eastern side. At first sight I saw that this engraving, though evidently of the shallow class, did not represent the normal figure. It is distinctly visible from a distance, but hardly perceptible from any point, but one, near the rock. It is on the eastern face of a gneiss boulder—five feet high at its highest point and seven and a half feet wide—which stands at the edge of the fall, and is partly surrounded by shallow water. When the river is full, the rock and the figure must be partly submerged. The incision is very slight indeed and much worn, indeed some parts of the figure have evidently been worn away. After carefully examining the rock from all points of view and from all distances, I could trace, partly by sight and partly by touch, some additional strokes, and these additional strokes, now almost obliterated, bring the figure very near to that represented on Temehri rock.

Scattered along the Corentyn and also on the Berbice rivers—in which latter place, however, there are also apparently examples of deep engravings—are other shallow examples, more or less resembling those which I have described. They may, therefore, be said to be confined, as regards Guiana, to the eastern district.

They seem always to occur on comparatively large and more or less smooth surfaces of rock, and rarely, if ever, as the deep figures, on detached blocks of rock, piled one on the other. The shallow figures, too, are generally much larger, always combinations of straight or curved lines in figures much more elaborate than those which occur in the deep engravings; and these shallow pictures always represent not animals, but greater or less variations of the figure which has been described. Lastly, though I am not certain that much significance can be attributed to this, all the examples that I have seen face more or less accurately eastward.

The deep engravings, on the other hand, consist not of a single figure, but of a greater or less number of rude drawings (Fig. 36, p. 393). These depict the human form, monkeys, snakes, and other animals, and also very simple combinations of two or three straight or curved lines in a pattern, and occasion-

ally more elaborate combinations. The individual figures are
small, averaging from twelve to eighteen inches in height, but
a considerable number are generally represented in a group.

Some of the best examples of this latter kind are at Warrapoota cataracts, about six days' journey up the Essequibo.
At that place a large number of figures occur scattered over
the surfaces of a group of granite boulders in the very midst
of the cataracts These rocks when the river is high are
covered by water; but the drawings are exposed during the
dry season. The engravings often occur on several sides of
the same block, but never on the side or sides which show
signs of most recent fracture. From the fact that they are
on two or even three sides of the blocks, it is evident that
the drawings were not, as might have been supposed, executed
on the face of a cliff, or on one large rock surface which has
since broken up into these boulders. Often they are on that
surface which now rests on other rooks of the pile; thus
showing that the blocks are no longer in the position in
which they were when the drawings were made. Again the
fact that the blocks, all of which are under water in times of
high rains, are many of them always below water-mark except in the very driest seasons, affords further strong ground
for presuming that the rocks have been displaced since the
engravings were executed.

The commonest figures at Warrapoota are figures of men,
or perhaps sometimes monkeys. These are very simple, and
generally consist of one straight line, representing the trunk,
crossed by two straight lines at right angles to the body
line: one, at about a third of the distance from the top, represents the two arms as far as the elbows, where upward
lines represent the lower part of the arms; the other, which
is at the lower end, represents the two legs as far as the
knees, from which point downward lines represent the lower
part of the legs. A round dot, or a small circle, at the
top of the trunk-line forms the head; and there are a few
radiating lines where the fingers, a few more where the toes,
should be. Occasionally the trunk-line is produced down-

wards as if to represent a long tail. Perhaps the tail-less
figures represent men, the tailed monkeys. In a few cases
the trunk, instead of being indicated by one straight line, is
formed by two curved lines, representing the rounded outlines of the body ; and the body, thus formed, is bisected by
a row of dots, almost invariably nine in number, which seem
to represent vertebræ.

Most of the other figures at Warrapoota are very simple
combinations of two, three, or four straight lines, similar to
the so-called ' Greek meander pattern,' which is of such wide-
spread occurrence. Combinations of curved lines and simple
spiral lines also frequently occur. Many of these combinations closely resemble the figures which the Indians of the
present day paint on their faces and naked bodies. The resemblance is, however, not so great but that it may be
merely due to the fact that the figures are just such simple
combinations of lines which would occur independently to the
rock-engravers and to the body-painters, as to all other untaught designers.

At Warrapoota there are only two instances of figures
occurring in only a single representation : one of these is a
rayed sun, the other is the top of a rounded arch. The
former, at least, of these figures occurs frequently in other
places. Not at Warrapoota, but in many places on the rivers
of the Essequibo system, and also probably on the Berbice,
in addition to the drawings mentioned above, figures of
lizards, alligators, birds, or other animals occur.

Two rock-engravings, mentioned and figured by Sir
Robert Schomburgk in his ' Views in the Interior of British
Guiana,' are peculiar, in that, as far as can be judged from
Schomburgk's figures, they can hardly be classed as ordinary
deep engravings, still less as shallow. One, which is said to
occur near the Camoodi rock on the Essequibo, is a most elaborately intricate combination of lines (Fig. 38, p. 400). It
seems that the figure as given by Schomburgk, which is here
copied, represents only part of the engraving as it really
appears. The second occurs at the Ilha de Pedra on the

Rio Negro ; and, therefore, not in British Guiana. But as it throws some light on the subject of rock-engravings, some

FIG. 38.

ROCK ENGRAVING. CAMOODI ROCK, ESSEQUIBO.

FIG. 39.

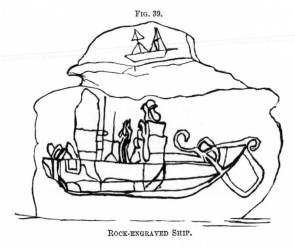

ROCK-ENGRAVED SHIP.

mention must here be made of it. It represents a large and a small ship, one above the other, and evidently of European build (Fig. 39). The upper figure is small and comparatively unimportant. The other figure, on the other hand, is very elaborate and curious. Comparing it with the figure of any Spanish galley of about the date of the early explorers of America, it is, I think, evident that the Rio Negro rock-drawing represents, roughly enough, such a galley (Fig. 40). It is a well-known fact that Francisco Orellana, who was the first white man who penetrated beyond the mouth of the Amazons, in his journey from the Napo, *past the Rio Negro* to the Amazon, and so to the Atlantic, once found himself in difficulties and, with surprising energy, set to work, in the heart of unknown South America, to build himself a ship.

Fig. 40.

SPANISH GALLEY (FROM TOMB OF COLUMBUS).

The building of this vessel, A.D. 1540, must most strongly have impressed the minds of the Indian companions of Orellana. It is by no means impossible, therefore, that these Indians, on their return home, may have recorded the appearance of this most strange canoe on the rock in the Rio Negro. However this may be, it is at least certain that this particular rock-engraving must date from about that time.

One characteristic which these shallow and deep engravings seem to have in common is that they always—or nearly always, for there is said to be an exception in the Pacaraima mountains—occur near water, and, as I believe, near a waterfall or cataract. There is indeed another possible exception, mentioned by Mr. Brown, in the district of the

Cotinga, where he observed figures of suns, curved snakes, spirals, and circles on a jasperous rock exposed on a savannah ; but even this was not very far from the river. By far the larger part in Guiana are situated not many feet above the surface of the water, or even, in times of flood, below the surface. There are, however, examples, as, for instance, on the upper part of the Corentyn, which are high up on the face of some cliff, and are not to be reached unless by difficult climbing. On the Orinoco Humboldt saw such engravings high up on apparently inaccessible cliffs ; and similar cases have been reported from almost all parts of the world.

The many differences seem sufficient to show that the two kinds are the work of different people, and have different intentions.

No satisfactory theory as to the origin of these rock-pictures has ever been formed. The Indians of the present day know nothing about them; and if they ever speak of them, tell some such story as that 'women made them,' or that they are the work of *Makenaima Moo-moo* (God's Son), who when he wandered about on earth, drew them with the point of his finger on the rock. It is hardly necessary to point out that the latter quasi-tradition has not even the merit of antiquity ; for it must have originated after white missionaries came into South America and there first told the story of Christ. On the Orinoco Humboldt was told by the Indians that their fathers made them long ago, when the water was higher and they could reach these now inaccessible places in canoes. These and similar explanations have been given in other parts of South America and elsewhere. Every one of such state-ments may, however, be disregarded as merely due to the inveterate Indian habit of having an answer, indifferently true or invented, for every question.

The chances of finding an answer to the question, with which we now have to deal, as to the intention of these rock-pictures, would obviously be increased by bringing to-

gether for comparison a large number of examples, not only
from Guiana, but from wherever they occur. An elaborate
attempt to do this has been made by Richard Andrèe,[1] who
has described and figured a very large number of examples
of 'petroglyphs,' as he calls rock-drawings, apparently
identical in many points, from America, Europe, Africa,
Asia, and Australia. And having, with some show of reason,
indicated something in common in all these, he then proceeds to identify them with all the figures which, under
conditions of civilisation such as those under which we live,
boys cut with their pocket-knives on the desks and walls
of their schoolrooms, and also with those which adults of
brutal mind scrawl on the walls of lanes and retired places
Thus he thinks that one and the same purpose is to be
attributed to the rock-drawings of uncivilised folk, to the
names and figures which Eton boys write, or cause to be
written, on the walls of their sixth-form room, to the drawings with which roughs deface the walls of public places, and
even to the names, verses, or designs which the witless
tourist puts in visitors' books or scratches in places the
beauty or interest of which attracts such folk. All these
are said to be but the work of idle hands, and are due to the
insignificant instinct which impels the human animal to make
his mark.

While accepting with gratitude this author's collection
of facts and, above all, of figures, we may I think unhesitatingly reject his final conclusion. It is sufficient to
remember the enormous amount of time and labour which
these rock-engravings must have cost, necessarily executed
as they were, in Guiana at least, without the aid of any but
stone implements, or by friction. Making all allowance for
the patience with which an Indian works for any object that
pleases him, even if the practical result appears but little—as
when he spends weeks in ornamenting a war-club which, as
soon as it is finished, he exchanges, perhaps, for some arrow or

[1] *Ethnographische Parallelen und Vergleiche*, by Richard Andrèe (Stutt-
gart, 1878), pp. 258-299.

ornament representing hardly an hour's work—it is yet impossible to suppose that Indians ever undertook the enormous labour involved in producing an extensive series of rock-engravings for actually no purpose except to occupy his idle time. Indeed, though, as in the instance above cited of the club and arrow, the Indian will labour for apparently small results, yet a still more surprising feature in his character is the contrast with which, when he sees nothing to be done, he spends day after day, for weeks, doing literally nothing, without *ennui*. It would, therefore, be absolutely contrary to Indian habit to make rock-engravings from mere idleness. But there is other evidence to show that these engravings had some meaning no longer apparent. The similarity of some of the figures, such as those of men and other animals, of circles and waving lines, is evident throughout the rock-drawings of the world : these things are either more or less rude representations of such animal forms as are indigenous to the country in which the representations are, or are very simple combinations of lines; in either case these figures are such as would most naturally occur to the untaught artist. It by no means follows from this that these figures mean nothing more than they express to an eye ignorant of their intention. This is well shown by such instances as that given by Schoolcraft, of some picture-writing from a rock near Lake Superior, in which are rudely represented five canoes, containing in all fifty-one men, a kingfisher, a man on horseback, a land-tortoise, and a figure made up of three concentric semicircles arched over three small circles. This drawing appears rude enough, but it has a meaning. It records an expedition consisting of fifty-one men in five canoes, which was led by a chief on horseback, who had an ally of the name of Kingfisher, which expedition before it reached land—signified by the land-tortoise—was three days, signified by the accepted sign of the heavens arched over three suns.

But if these simple figures have an intention, much more must this be the case with the more intricate examples. For instance, in the rock-engravings of North-umberland, a peculiar, much coiled line occurs in great abundance and almost exclusively. This cannot have been the mere representation of anything visible to the maker ; and the abundance of its occurrence necessarily suggests that it must have had a use or intention. Andrèe himself admits this : " Jedenfalls ist aber sicher, dass gegenüber dem stil-losen Charakter der meisten übrigen Felsritzungen, diese von Northumberland, etc., die nach einem ganz bestimmten System ausgeführt sind und durch die regelmässige Wiederholung einer und derselben Form . . . . sich auszeichnen und daher wohl eine Bedeutung haben müs-sen.'[1]   And not only in this case, but wherever a peculiar, complex, and not very obvious figure occurs in many examples, it is legitimate to assume that this had some ulterior object and meaning.   Now the figure which I have described as occurring in the shallow engravings of Guiana is of such kind.   It is not a figure which an Indian would be likely to invent in an idle moment even once ; for such a man very seldom, probably never, except in these parti-cular figures, has been known to draw straight lines.   More-over, even if it were a figure that one Indian might idly invent, it is certainly highly improbable that this would be copied by many other Indians in various places.   And lastly, a figure strikingly like the one in question, if indeed it is not identical, occurs in certain Mexican picture-writings. For example, in the Bodleian library is a Mexican MS. in which occur several figures so like that of the shallow en-gravings of Guiana that there can be but little doubt of their connection (Fig. 41, p. 406).[2]   The recurrence of this peculiar figure in these writings is surely sufficient evidence of the fact that they are not without intention.   If it were possible to obtain a clue to the meaning of the Mexican

---

[1] Andrèe, p. 267.

[2] These Mexican figures are reproduced in Lord Kingsborough's *Anti-quities of Mexico*, vol. i. ; from Sir Thomas Bodley's MSS., pp. 22, 23, and from the Selden MSS., also in the Bodleian, p. 3.

figures, it might serve as a key to decipher the hieroglyphic writings of Guiana.

But rejecting, for these reasons, Andrèe's conclusion as to the identity in intention, or no intention, of rock-engravings and schoolboy scribblings, we may yet get much good from his book. He well shows that, beside the similarity, to which we have already alluded, of some of the figures, there are several other striking features common to the rock-engravings of Guiana and those of the rest of the world. These are worth examination.

First, two facts are noticeable as to the position of these engravings : that they occur generally, especially in Guiana,

FIG. 41.

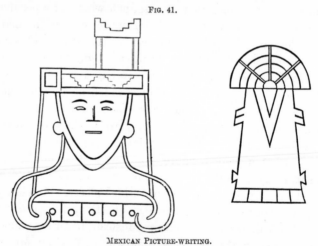

MEXICAN PICTURE-WRITING.

in places the natural features of which have some striking peculiarity, as, for instance, at the side of a cataract; and that in many cases and in various regions, for instance in Guiana as in Siberia,[1] they occur far up on apparently inaccessible faces of rock. For the first of these facts Andrèe accounts in this way: Assuming the truth of his theory, that rock-engraving was a mere idle diversion, he truly enough says that such drawings were naturally made

---

[1] Andrèe, *loc. cit.*, p. 297.

in places where the imagination of the artist was roused by
the beauty or interest of the scene, just as the modern
tourist defaces with his name the most beautiful rock, or the
building with the noblest traditions. But those who reject
his fundamental theory are bound to find some different
explanation. This is readily found. Man in a primitive
condition would naturally draw his figures, whether these
had religious significance, or whether, as is more probable,
they were commemorative, in places where the most striking
events of his life occurred. For example, there is hardly a
fall or rapid in Guiana which is not associated in the mind
of the Indian with some canoe accident, in which men of his
race have been drowned; and it is therefore not surprising
that it is generally on the rocks over or through which the
water falls that these engravings generally appear. Moreover, there is yet another fact connected with the same
circumstance which is worthy of notice. In an earlier
chapter it has been told, that at certain seasons of the year
large parties of Indians gather at the falls to procure certain
fish which then frequent such places. These expeditions
into dangerous places, and possibly into an enemy's country,
must often have been occasions of stirring events; so that
this fact also may afford some explanation of the frequent
occurrence of rock-engravings near waterfalls. On the
second of the two facts which we are now considering—the
occurrence of rock-engravings on apparently inaccessible
rocks—Andrèe possibly throws some light in this way: He
points out that Strahlenberg [1] suggested that these elevated
drawings were made by means of stone wedges, driven
into the rock, and used as steps; and that the same
traveller actually saw such stone wedges in position (solche
eingetriebene Steinkeile) on the Yenissei.

Another set of facts reported by Andrèe of rock-engravings in general—especial mention being made in this respect
of the Guiana examples—is that the art of making them has

---

[1] Strahlenberg's *Der Nord- und Oestliche Theil von Europa und Asien,*
&c. (Stockholm, 1730), p. 337. Quoted by Andrèe, p. 297.

been lost ; that their origin has been quite forgotten ; and that they are rarely, if ever, regarded with superstition. Where they occur in countries long civilised, as in England, this fact is only part of the wider fact that the habits of the primitive inhabitants of that country have been forgotten. That the art has been lost and the origin forgotten in countries first visited by civilised men in recent times, and then found to be still in the stone age, is easily explained. They can, wherever they occur, only have been made while the savage art of working stone, which is not lineally connected with the stone-cutting of civilised communities, was practised. This art would naturally be used principally for the production of necessary stone implements, and only secondarily for the production of rock-engravings, which cannot have been absolutely necessary to life. On the arrival of civilised men in any savage community, implements of metal rapidly spread in the latter, and the necessity, and consequently the art, of making stone implements dies out ; and this same art, being no longer used for the production of necessaries, is naturally not retained for the mere purpose of producing rock-engravings, since the savage soon finds that he can live without these. Again, this art is thus destroyed by the indirect influence of the civilised new-comers long before these new-comers so blend with the natives that the latter acquire from the former the habit of history ; so that by the time the natives, if they survive, are able to communicate intelligibly with the strangers, they have naturally entirely forgotten the very existence and reason of any art, whether of rock-engraving or of anything else, which their ancestors, though perhaps not many generations back, relinquished. Stone implements are still made in some countries, and it is possible that in these the art of rock-engraving, and the knowledge of its purpose, may survive. The fact that rock-engravings are found in many scattered parts of the world by no means proves that such must occur in all ; so that if in countries in which the stone age still prevails the practice of rock-engraving has not been observed, this fact in no

way disproves the above theory as to the interdependence of
the arts of rock-engraving and stone-implement making. And,
moreover, it is impossible for civilised men so thoroughly to
know any country in which the stone age still prevails as to
be able to say with certainty that rock-engraving is not practised
in that country; for long before such men have penetrated
every nook and corner, the stone age must necessarily die
out. The statement that rock-engravings are not regarded (as
might be expected if they had any intention and were not
mere idle diversions) with superstition, even in countries
where, if they were made up to the time at which the stone-
age there ceased, they must still have been comparatively
recently made, is to be met in two ways. In the first place
the statement is not true of Guiana, for almost the only
superstitious rite practised by the Indians—the rubbing of
red-pepper juice into the eyes[1]—is practised especially in the
presence of engraved rocks. And secondly, even if these
rocks are not regarded with superstition, as may be the case
in places, this is no proof that the drawings had no commemorative significance, for in that case no superstition
would necessarily be connected with them, nor even that
they had no religious significance, but is only evidence
that the cause of their making has been entirely forgotten.

Last of all, the facts that we may here gather from
Andrée's pages and notice is that, as in Guiana, so in
various other parts of the world—for example in Siberia,
instances are found in which figures of the character of
those engraved are painted on rocks; generally, it may be
observed, with red pigment. Of any possible significance of
this special colour nothing need be said. The occurrence of
these painted rocks at all—since, in that the duration of the
figures must be much less than when engraved, they are
probably of more recent, certainly of recent, origin—may be
due to the fact that after the art of rock-engraving had been
lost, a habit was substituted, and retained for a short time, of

[1] See *ante*, p. 368.

painting, since it was no longer possible to engrave, the customary figures.

It may be as well briefly to sum up the few facts that can be said, with any probability, of these rock-pictures in Guiana. The engravings are of two kinds, which may or may not have had different authors and different intention. They were still produced after the first arrival of Europeans, as is shown by the sculptured ship. They were, therefore, probably made by the ancestors of the Indians now in the country; for, from the writings of Raleigh and other early explorers, as well as from the statements of early colonists, it is to be gathered that the present tribes were already in Guiana at the time of the first arrival of Europeans, though not perhaps in the same relative positions as at present. The art of stone working being destroyed by the arrival of Europeans, the practice of rock-engraving ceased. Possibly the customary figures were for a time painted instead of engraved; but this degenerated habit was also soon relinquished. As to the intention of the figures, that they had some seems certain, but of what kind this was is not clear. Finally, these figures really seem to indicate some very slight connection with Mexican civilisation.

SHELL-MOUNDS.

After the rock-drawings the shell-mounds claim attention. These are very similar in structure and contents to the well-known kitchen-middens of Europe; but those of Guiana were made at a much later time than were those in Europe. The earlier stages of civilisation through which a people passes are much the same in all parts of the world and at all periods of the world's history; and so, just as the primitive European made kitchen-middens in the far-off so-called ' prehistoric ages,' certain Indians made them a very few centuries ago in South America, and possibly—in very remote parts of the continent—still make them even now.

A kitchen-midden—for it is convenient to use this

generally accepted semi-Scandinavian word—is simply the heap made by people who throw the refuse of that which they eat—shells of ' shell-fish,' on which people in the stage in which were those who made the best-known middens chiefly live, bones of animals, and other such matter. Often the fragments of the rude implements or weapons of the midden-makers, when any of these are broken, are thrown or fall neglected on to this general refuse heap: sometimes even whole tools fall on to the heap by accident, and are soon covered and lost. The deserted middens remain, and by searching into these it is possible to discover something of the food of those who made them, how they ate it, often what tools they used, and, generally, not a little of their way of life.

The Indians of Guiana still throw fish-bones and all other such sharp-edged or pointed fragments as might wound their uncovered feet into some definite place; but, except among the Warraus, no special place is long used for the refuse of a whole settlement, and so no large collections of refuse, such as might in after times be recognised as kitchen-middens, are formed. That their ancestors, or predecessors in the same country, were not in the habit, at least in the ordinary course of their lives, of accumulating large kitchen-middens is evident from the fact that all such heaps found in Guiana occur within a certain small and comparatively little-known district, north of the Pomeroon, while throughout the rest of the country, even in the thoroughly explored coast-region, no traces of such heaps have been found. It is true that it was reported, some years ago, that a shell-mound had been found at Skeldon, at the other extremity of the colony, on the borders of Dutch Guiana. Having after some difficulty traced the history of this report, I found that the so-called shell-mound was in reality only a natural sand-reef, on which, as is remembered by people still alive, the Indians who came annually from the interior to town, to receive the presents then allowed them by the government, used to encamp on the journey. The statement that all the known kitchen-middens are in the district

between the Pomeroon and the Orinoco is therefore absolutely true.   The fact that the Indians, though there is no
reason to suppose that their habits have changed, do not, as
a rule, accumulate these heaps, and that those which occur
are all within a special district, seems to indicate that some
special circumstance at one time induced a group of the
Indians to make these large heaps.   What this special
circumstance was, I think, we shall be able to read by
careful observation of the known facts.

First, as to the number of these mounds.   At least eight
are at present known[1]—five in the neighbourhood of the
Pomeroon; two on the Waini; and one on the Moraybo, a
river north of the Pomeroon, between the Waini and the
Barima.   In the latter district the Indians say that there
are many more, and as that country is almost unknown,
it may be so.   Nearest to the coast is the mound at Warramoori on the Morooca, a river which runs into the sea side
by side with the Pomeroon.   Further from the sea, and some
distance up the Pomeroon, two mounds lie close together
at Sireeki and Warrapana;   the fourth is at the mission
house at Cabacaboori;   and the fifth, first discovered during
a visit which I paid to the Pomeroon in December 1878,
is a mile or two further up, on a small side-stream called
Piracca.   Two of these, those at Warramoori and Cabacaboori,
are placed on high hills close to and overlooking the river.
The others are in secluded places, on islands of firm ground in
the midst of swamps overgrown by troolie palms (*Manicaria
saccifera*).   All, therefore, are in strong defensive positions,
and near running water.   Of the two mounds on the Waini,
for knowledge of which I am indebted to my friend the
Rev. Walter Heard, one is near a small side-stream called
Pawaiēykĕmoo, on the right bank of the main river; the
second is on another side-stream, called Quiaro, nearer the
mouth of the main river.

The mound at Warramoori was first opened in 1865, under
the direction of the Rev. W. H. Brett, and was again opened

---

[1] Since the above was written several more have been discovered.

in February 1866, in the presence of the governor of the colony. Samples of the material of this mound, and a large number of stone implements, procured on this occasion, were forwarded to Sir Joseph Hooker, by whom they were given to Sir John Lubbock, who deposited some of the implements in the Christy collection.

Early in the following year the mound at Sireeki was measured and opened, though, I believe, not under the personal superintendence of an educated man. The mound at Cabacaboori was searched at various times by Mr. Brett; and in the autumn of 1877 I devoted two days to excavating this mound in a new place. About the same time I was present at the opening of the newly discovered mound up the Piracca creek. In 1877 Mr. Heard roughly examined and measured the mound on the Pawaiēykĕmoo. This is, I believe, a full list of all attempts that have yet been made to search these shell-mounds of Guiana.

The mounds vary considerably in size. That at Warramoori is about 20 ⅃o 25 feet in height with a diameter of about 130 feet.

The mound at Sireeki, which must be far the largest known, is said to be oblong, 250 feet long by 90 feet wide, and between 20 and 25 feet high; and that at Piracca, which I measured myself, and which is almost completely circular, has a diameter of 38 feet, and a height, in the centre, of only 4 feet. As, however, it stands on an island of high ground, it rises considerably above the surrounding swamp. It is the smallest of the mounds, but is exactly similar in structure and contents to the others. The mound on the Pawaiēykĕmoo is, according to Mr. Heard, ' oblong in shape, across the narrowest part about 60 feet, the longest 90 feet, and round the base 220 feet.

All the mounds—so far as they have been examined—are alike in character and contents. They consist chiefly of great accumulations of a small snail-like black and white shell (*Neritina lineolata*). In some the more decayed state of the shells and other refuse, even in the uppermost strata, seems to indicate a somewhat greater age. The mass evidently lies in more or less distinct layers, between each two of which is a thin stratum of a hard, apparently burned, substance.

Perhaps the most remarkable feature in all the mounds is the presence of these burnt-clay-like slabs between the layers of refuse. It has been suggested that these were used as baking-slabs, like the stone slabs used by some of the Arecunas, and other remote tribes, at the present day. But the suggestion is absurd. In the first place, these hard slabs do not occur in small pieces, unless when broken by the pickaxes and shovels of excavators, but extend in parallel strata over the whole mound; and in the second place, they are so irregular in thickness, that bread could only be baked on them very unevenly. Nor are they in the least like the baking-slabs of the Indians of the interior, which are very regularly shaped, oblong, and of sandstone. A very much more probable explanation is that fires were made at intervals on the mounds, and that these ' slabs ' are merely the burnt surface of shell and earth on which the fires rested.

Among the shells which constitute the bulk of the mounds, have been found various objects deserving attention. In the Cabacaboori mound, among the vast accumulation of one species of shells, but in far less abundance, were some bivalve shells (*Lucina*), a few oyster-shells and fragments of a freshwater shell, common in the river at the present day, and called by the Indians *Kee-way*, together with pieces of crab-shells, bones of fish and of mammals, and lastly—and most important—human bones. These bones are invariably found scattered, and not as entire skeletons, and have been split, so as to allow of the extraction of the marrow. There were also some broken, and a few entire, stone implements, hammers probably and axe-heads, pieces of charcoal, and lumps of the red pigment called faroah, with which the Indians paint their bodies. Great quantities of sharp-edged fragments of white semi-transparent quartz were also present.

The shape of these and the fact that they do not occur naturally in the immediate neighbourhood, seems to suggest
that they were used as implements, probably as knives, for
which purpose they must have been brought from a distance.
These objects occur in more or less abundance in all the
mounds. It must, however, be noticed that the oyster-shell
occurs very sparingly in the Pomeroon mounds, but more
abundantly in those nearer the Orinoco. But besides these
objects which occur in all the mounds, a few peculiar examples
were found, and peculiar features noticed in some. For
instance, at Cabacaboori, Mr. Brett found two small silver
ornaments very similar to ear-
rings, and still more to the
nose-pieces worn by some of
the Savannah Indians at the
present day ; and in the same
mound I myself found two
implements delicately carved in
bone, and some rod-like bodies
of very puzzling nature. The
only possible explanation of the
latter which has occurred to me

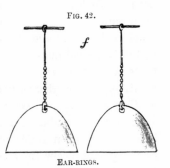

FIG. 42.

EAR-RINGS.

is that they are the calcined fore-teeth of deer or some
such animal ; but this seems hardly satisfactory. One new
species of shell (*Purpura coronata*)—in a single example—
I also found in this mound. In one place there were a few
fragments of pottery, evidently all belonging to one vessel ;
these are noticeable as the only examples of pottery ever
recorded as discovered in a Guiana shell-mound. In the
Sireeki mound it is worth notice that among other human
bones was found one skull, in twenty-seven pieces, which
was afterwards fitted together, and proved to be perfect but
for a hole in the top apparently made by some such implement as a stone hatchet. In the Piracca mound, at a depth
of three feet from the surface, I found the stem of a tobacco-
pipe of European manufacture, which is conclusive evidence
that this mound at least was added to after Europeans first

reached America. The only specially noticeable peculiarity of the Warramoori mound seems to have been that it seemed to contain an unusually large proportion of stone implements. This circumstance may, however, be due merely to the fact that it has been more extensively, if not thoroughly, searched than any of the other mounds.

The chief results of such examination as has been made of these mounds is, therefore, that they all occur about the Pomeroon, and northward from that to the Orinoco; that they were still made after the discovery of America; that they consist mainly of shells of one species (*Neritina lineolata*), arranged in layers, the upper surface of each of which has been hardened, apparently by the action of fire; that a few other shells are included, and especially of an oyster, which occurs more and more abundantly in the mounds the nearer these are to the Orinoco; that stone implements occur comparatively in abundance, but that domestic implements, including pottery, and body ornaments, are almost entirely absent; that remains of mammals occur, but in strikingly less quantity than relics of molluscs and fish; and that human bones occur in a condition which clearly indicates cannibalism.

Such are the facts concerning these mounds, and an attempt must now be made to infer from these something of their history. It may be as well to state at once that the natural conclusions are (1) that they were made not by the resident inhabitants of the country, but by strangers; (2) that these strangers came from the sea and not from further inland; and (3) that these strangers were certain Island Caribs, who afterwards took tribal form in Guiana as the so-called Caribisi, or, as I have called them, True Caribs.

I have already shown, that the habit of making these large kitchen-middens was not general among the Indians of Guiana, and that those which occur must be due to some special circumstance which for a time affected the makers. This special circumstance was, I think, that the makers were strangers and marauders in a hostile country.

That the mound-makers were strangers is shown in this way. The stratification of these mounds, which has been described, points to the likelihood that the places were not continuously, but repeatedly, occupied. Each layer probably consists of the refuse thrown away during one single visit. The fires made for cooking on each occasion on the surface of the layer deposited on the previous occasion would, together with the action of the weather on that surface in the interval, harden the top of the layer and produce such strata as actually occur. The scarcity of the bones of mammals is further evidence of the same fact. Indians invariably prefer flesh as food, and are only driven to live upon molluscs by inability to procure meat. Now game is still abundant in the mound district, and was, presumably, yet more abundant formerly. But, as I have often experienced with discomfort, Indians, capital hunters as they are at home, cannot hunt in a strange country; even only fifty miles from their homes I have known them declare their ignorance of the country as an excuse for their failure to obtain game. The natural inference from these facts is that the mound-makers were strangers who were driven by their ignorance of the country to feed upon what they could most readily procure—that is, upon molluscs and fish.

The almost entire absence of pottery is yet further evidence. Indians, when at home, almost invariably boil their meat, and keep their supply of water, in clay vessels; but when travelling, they carry no pottery with them, but cook their meat by roasting it on split sticks; and, if it is absolutely necessary to carry any supply of water with them, keep it in hollow gourds. If, therefore, the mound-makers had been at home, fragments of pottery would certainly have occurred; but if, as I suppose, they were travellers, this at once explains the absence of such fragments. Moreover, most of the mounds are in swamps, on islands far too small to serve as permanent settlements. It may, therefore, be taken for granted that the mound-makers were not permanent residents.

They were not only strangers, but strangers in a hostile country. This is indicated by the positions of the mounds; for, with the exception of those at Warramoori and Cabaca-boori, which are in strong positions on two of the very few hills in the district, they all stand in swamps, on islands of firm ground which might easily be temporarily defended. The need of defence against the people of the country, and of fresh water for their meals, seem to have been the chief points which regulated the choice of sites for these temporary camps. The same circumstance is also indicated by the large quantities of human bones which occur mingled with the refuse of countless meals. These were not placed there in the ordinary course of burial, for not whole skeletons, but only separate scattered bones, are found. The skull, already mentioned, on which was the mark of a murderous blow from some instrument, confirms this. Moreover, these bones are found at a greater depth than would be the case if they had been placed there in burial; and they have been broken, as is the case with the bones in the kitchen-middens of Europe, evidently to allow the marrow, of which all Indians are very fond, to be extracted. But as each Indian tribe lives in a separate district, within which come no interlopers of any other tribe, and as the tribal feeling is always very strong among Indians, so that they cannot be suspected of feeding on individuals of their own tribe, the mound-makers could only have obtained human flesh for food in or from a foreign country. That they obtained their supply from a foreign country—that they brought prisoners, that is to say, captured elsewhere, to these mounds and there eat them is very improbable, seeing that these mounds were not their homes. It is nearly certain, therefore, that they were marauders in a hostile country.

That these stranger mound-makers came from the sea seems probable from the fact that they lived, at least during their stay in those parts, largely on the sea-fish, of the remnants of which the mounds are in great part formed. Of all the mounds, that at Warramoori, which is only two or three hours' pull from the mouth of the Morooca, is the only one near the sea ; the others are at a considerable distance, more or less great, up the rivers. From the occurrence of the sea-shells it is evident that the mound-makers made frequent long journeys between the sea and the sites of their camps. Now it is far more likely that strangers making raids into the interior carried with them large stores of sea-fish as food, than that strangers making a raid toward the sea from inland penetrated further than was necessary through a hostile country merely to get a supply of sea-fish when they had plenty of animal food nearer at hand ; and even if they had done so, they would have devoured the sea-fish near the shore rather than have dragged it back with them for so many miles. But to this probable evidence may be added the certain evidence that the oyster, the shells of which are found in the mounds, does not occur on the coast of Guiana.

For all these reasons, therefore, it seems probable that the mounds were made by a people hostile to the natives of the district, and coming from the sea. It now remains to be shown that there were in all probability parties of Caribs from the islands.

That the True Caribs came from the islands is a tradition of the Indians, and is shown by the close similarity in their manners, language, and appearance to those of the Caribs of the island ; and also by the hostility towards the True Caribs which to this day is the only feeling common to all the other tribes of Guiana. Moreover, the records of the earlier voyages in the Caribbean seas tell of the migration. In passing to the mainland in their somewhat unseaworthy canoes they would naturally land at the first point reached. This would be the district in which the shell-mounds occur, and the mounds apparently date from a time just about that at which the Carib immigration took place, which was about the time of the discovery of Guiana, between three and four centuries ago. The state of the materials of the mounds certainly does not indicate an earlier date, but rather that the mounds, though perhaps begun some four centuries ago, were possibly not finished till considerably later. The occurrence, to which I have already alluded, of a piece of tobacco-pipe of European manufacture in the Pirocca mounds, also makes it certain that parts of the mounds, at least, are not older than this; and if they had been much more recent some record of their origin must have remained.

That the Caribs were cannibals at the time indicated there is little doubt. Travellers of those days were all agreed as to this. Moreover, all the other tribes yet retain a tradition and dread of the man-eating habits of this, and of no other tribe. The Caribs all deny the fact when charged with it; but they do this with a superfluity of indignation which is in itself suspicious. On the other hand, there is not the least evidence to suggest that any of the other tribes then and now inhabiting the coast region of Guiana retained that custom up to so recent a date.

Some slight evidence is also afforded by the fact that the True Caribs are in the habit of eating certain animals which most Indians hold unclean and will not touch, and that the remains of these unclean animals—for example, those of the sting-ray—are amongst the commonest constituents of the mounds. In short, there can be little doubt that the mounds were made by the Caribs at the time when they were passing from the islands, but had not yet permanently settled on the mainland.

Lastly, it is almost an historic fact that the True Caribs did not come, once for all, in a body to the mainland and there remain; but that they were in the habit of passing to and from the mainland in their raids from the islands, and only gradually settled in Guiana. This satisfactorily accounts both for the stratification of the mounds—each layer representing one visit—and for the fact that the mounds are most abundant near the Orinoco—that is, at the point at which the marauders first landed; and are less and less common further away from this point—that is, in proportion as each part of the country was less and less easily reached by these Caribs.

It may be as well to meet a possible suggestion that the shell-mounds were made by Warraus, who are known to have long inhabited the swamps in which these heaps occur, to have lived very largely upon fish, and who, alone of all Indians of Guiana, still make small kitchen-middens. The suggestion, despite these facts, must be rejected for these among other reasons: the oyster-shells certainly were brought from the islands, and there is nothing to show that Warraus crossed the sea at the time when the mounds were made. Moreover, they were at that time, even more than now, a miserable and weak tribe who had not the power, even had they the will, to be cannibals; and, as I have already shown, these mounds must have been made by strangers in the Warrau country.

STONE IMPLEMENTS.

Mention has already been made of the stone implements which occur within the shell-mounds; but, besides these, many others are found elsewhere in the country. Though, with a few trifling exceptions which will presently be described, they are no longer used, they occur in three different ways—in the shell-mounds, or scattered like natural stones on the surface of the ground, or, lastly, stored and carefully preserved in the houses of the modern Indians.

The shell-mounds are, we have found reason to believe, made by Caribs from the West Indian islands. If so, it might à priori be supposed that the implements occurring in the shell-mounds would be identical in form with those of Carib origin from the islands. But if an equal number from each of the two sources is compared in some European museums, it appears that those from the islands are far more elaborately finished and far more ornamental in shape. The explanation of this fact is, I think, simple, and will throw some light on a habit of the Caribs, and probably of other users of stone implements. The Indians of Guiana still often spend their leisure time in making comparatively highly ornamental weapons (though these are no longer of stone) and utensils; but they do not actually use these, but keep them at home, and are proud of them, while when they travel they take with them implements the production of which cost less labour. It has already been explained that Indians when travelling do not risk their pottery by carrying it with them; and it has been shown that this modern habit of the Indians almost certainly prevailed among the old mound-makers. This points to the likelihood that the Caribs, on their predatory raids from the islands to the mainland, carried with them only their less elaborate implements. It is these, therefore, that occur in the shell-mounds. But if this is so, it is evident that among the elaborate implements from the islands ought to be found others of simpler form, corresponding to those from the shell-mounds. That these simpler forms do not appear in museum series as abundantly as, according to this theory, would seem natural, is probably due simply to the fact that the finer forms have been more diligently collected and brought to Europe than the simpler.

As regards the implements which are found scattered on the surface of the ground, they occur singly throughout the country, except in the eastern district about the Corentyn river. They are, however, most numerous nearer the Orinoco; this may be due to the fact that that district was the gate through which the most warlike tribes—those of the Carib branch—first entered Guiana, and was the place where they had to fight for footing among the hostile natives. These implements are also remarkably abundant about a small spot in the interior called by the Indians Toocano, on the Brazilian side of the Takootoo river. A possible explanation of this latter fact may be that at Toocano was once a manufactory of such things. It has already been stated that each tribe in Guiana does not make for itself all that it requires, but has some special object which it manufactures for exchange with other tribes. It therefore seems not improbable that the making of stone implements may have been chiefly carried on by special tribes, or even, as is still the case with the far-famed ourali-poison, by special families, one of which may have had its home at Toocano.[1]

The third set of stone implements is composed of those which are found at the present time stored among the odds and ends in the possession of Indians.   These are now never used for their original purpose, though I have seen stone-pointed arrows in use, but only as toys.   There are probably two reasons for the retention of these implements now that their original use has disappeared.   In the first place, stone axe-heads are now chiefly valued and kept by the Indians as being the best instruments for smoothing and polishing the clay in pottery-making; though, if one of these is not at hand, any smooth, water-worn pebble is used instead.[2]   In the second place, some superstitious value seems to be attributed to these stones.   They are sometimes to be found among the separately kept personal properties of men; in which cases they cannot be potters' implements, as that art is practised only by the women.   Moreover, a considerable number of these implements are found more or less ornamented with colouring matter—sometimes merely a coating of the red pigments (faroah or caraweera) ordinarily used by the Indians, but sometimes, as in an example in the Christy collection, with a somewhat elaborate pattern, of indubitable Indian execution.   The useless preservation of these stones by men, and their occasional ornamentation, seem to indicate that some special value, not dependent on their usefulness, is

[1] In this connection, readers of 'Hiawatha' will probably remember the special 'arrow-maker' mentioned in North American Indian traditions.

[2] In passing, I may repeat that the so-called 'charm-stones' from Guiana, of which there are two examples in the Christy collection, and which have been supposed to be pebbles worn into their present shape artificially, merely by being perpetually carried in the hands of young children, as a means of divining, by the shape finally assumed by the stone, the character of the individual, are probably merely naturally water-worn porphyry pebbles, such as occur in large numbers in the beds of certain rivers in the interior of Guiana, and, because of their smoothness, are collected by the Indians and used as polishing implements for clay; at least, that is the use to which they are now put, and such is the explanation given me by the Indians themselves.

attached to them ; and this value can hardly but be superstitious.

Though these implements have thus been roughly classified according to their present mode of occurrence, it must
not be supposed that any real difference in character, either
as regards form or degree of finish, marks the three classes.
At one time I thought that those from the shell-mounds
were less finely finished than those from elsewhere ; but
after seeing a larger number of examples from all sources I
was obliged to conclude that no such distinction can be
drawn.

I now turn from the general subject of stone implements
in British Guiana to consider certain actual examples, seven
in number, from which one or two isolated facts may be
learned.

The two types that occur most commonly are shown in
Figs. 1 and 3, Plate 10. No. 3 is the most abundant of all. Its
shape, though slightly variable, has been well compared to
that of the section of a ' button mushroom,' cut from the apex
of the cap down through the stem. Further allusion will
presently be made to the groove or notch on each side of the
stone. Implements of this form, though they occur elsewhere, are especially abundant in the shell-mounds, from
which circumstance, as from the fact that they can hardly
have been very formidable as weapons, it seems not unlikely
that they were domestic implements such as would be used
for pounding, etc., for cracking shells of molluscs and bones
of animals.[1] No. 1 is only less abundant in Guiana, but is a
far commoner type elsewhere. This, too, occurs in the shell-
mounds, as a surface implement, and in the possession of
Indians.

No. 2 is somewhat similar in shape to the last type, but
differs from this in being flatter, more like the blade of a
knife, and in all the examples, not few in number, that I
have seen of this type, the narrow end—that which was un-

[1] This form seems to correspond closely with the 'hammer' represented on the left in fig. 11 of Wilson's *Prehistoric Man* (London, 1865).

Plate X

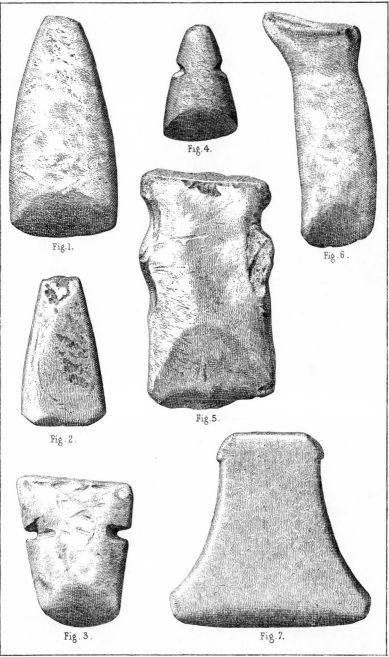

Fig.1.

Fig.4.

Fig.6.

Fig.2.

Fig.5.

Fig.3.

Fig.7.

J.P.EMSLIE, DEL.

J.P. & W.R.EMSLIE, LITH.

STONE IMPLEMENTS.
Half real size.

From the Journal of the Anthropological Institute.

doubtedly attached to the handle—is peculiarly fractured. The chief interest of this latter fact is that, I think, it indicates the exact use of these blades and an unusual mode of attachment to the handle. The chief weapons of war of the Indians are the clubs (*tiki*) of heavy wood, which have already been described. The habit of inter-tribal war having practically disappeared, though only within a few years, such clubs are rarely made. The few that are still to be found in the possession of Indians are wholly of wood. But there is an Indian tradition that these used to be made more formidable by the addition of a stone blade ; and in the Christy collection there is an example with a small stone blade, identical in shape with that now under notice, inserted in one side, as an axe-blade is in its handle.[1] The curious fracture at the narrow end of blades of this type is not only exactly such as would be made if a blade of this kind were broken, by some sudden shock, from a club of heavy wood into a pit in which it had been fastened, but is also, as far as I am aware, not seen in blades of any other shape. It is therefore very probable that these blades formed part of war-clubs ; and, if so, the mode of attachment to the handle, by socketing into the wood, is very unusual. There is one other circumstance which, though by itself of little significance, may be mentioned in connection with this hypothesis. Having on one occasion asked some Indians to show me how they thought such implements ought to be fastened into handles, they procured examples and fitted them. The nature of the result is shown in this figure—

FIG. 43.

WAR-CLUB WITH STONE BLADE.

The handle is of light wood, which would certainly split at the first blow, and the whole weapon appear absurd. But

[1] Since this was written, I have procured an example of one of these stones stuck in its handle. See p. 300, *ante*.

closer attention shows that the blade is fastened into the handle just as appears to have been the case in the war-clubs.

No. 4 is a small, but beautifully finished, grooved blade. These grooves, or, to use a more expressive word, notches, are just such as would be favourable to fastening the stone on to one side of a stick. They are very like the notches which the Indian still makes on the cross-beams of his house, at the point at which, with flexible plant stems, he lashes these beams on to the upright corner posts. Yet this actual example, even if thus lashed to a wooden handle, is so small that its use is hardly realisable.

No. 5 is again a grooved form, but with the difference that just below each groove is a projecting shoulder, which may have had some definite use, but which is certainly ornamental, and makes this implement approach more nearly than any other I know from Guiana to the elaborate stone implements of the island Caribs.

No. 6 is a very peculiar example. In shape it much resembles a human foot, with the leg as far as the knee. The cutting edge is where the knee would be in a leg; and the sole of the foot is so hollowed as exactly to fit the thumb when the stone is grasped in the hand. There can be little doubt that this implement was never intended to be fitted with a handle, but to be grasped; and under these circumstances it would admirably answer the purpose of a chisel or adze, or would make a formidable offensive weapon when the holder was at close quarters with his antagonist. Mr. Tylor has pointed out to me that some Indians, I believe in British Columbia, have been seen to fight with stones thus grasped in the hand, and that this is done with such agility and dexterity that the Indian with but a stone in his hand can be formidable to an opponent armed with a revolver. My implement was possibly used in this way.

No. 7 is in shape so strikingly like an ordinary European hatchet-blade that it is undoubtedly a copy in stone of such a metal blade. Its beautiful finish indicates that it was made while the art of stone-working was still well understood. It may, therefore, be assumed that it was made after the arrival of Europeans, but before these new comers had destroyed the stone age—or probably in the sixteenth century. It probably corresponds in date with the rock-engraved figure of a European galley, of which mention has been made.

One kind of stone utensil which sometimes occurs, and is still in use in very remote parts of the country, deserves mention. This is the cooking slab on which their flat oat-cake-like cassava bread is cooked. At the present time Indians generally use a circular iron griddle of European manufacture for this purpose; but before they were able to procure this, they chose the flattest slabs of stone, generally sandstone, and baked their bread on these. Even now the Arecunas near Roraima—as probably also the yet more remote tribes—who seldom or never visit town, and who live in a sandstone region, use these stone slabs. These are so highly valued that it is difficult to persuade an Indian to part with one. The only example I was able to procure was a flat piece of sandstone about three-quarters of an inch in thickness, oblong in shape, and with the corners neatly cut off. It requires, as I have seen, a considerably longer time to bake bread on these stones than on the iron griddles.

STANDING STONES.

The two traces of old Indian life which yet remain to be mentioned are both given on the authority of Mr. C. Barrington Brown. One is a circle of standing stones. Of this Mr. Brown says, ' In the Pacaraima mountains, between the villages of Mora and Itabay, the path passes through a circle of square stones placed on one end, one of which has a carving on it.' In a note he adds that ' this circle of stones is very like that on Stanton Moor, shown in Ferguson's ' Rude Stone Monuments.'

SITES OF ANCIENT VILLAGES.

Many examples of ancient village sites are also mentioned by this same traveller. These are said to be only distinguishable from the surrounding country by the rich black colour of the soil, and by the abundance of broken fragments of pottery. Of course it is possible that these sites are those of deserted villages of comparatively, or even very, modern date. But, on the other hand, as all the reported examples occur far inland, and as the inland tribes make but very little pottery, it is more likely that such places were the homes of tribes other than those which now inhabit the surrounding country. Only a very careful search in such places can settle this question. And such a search would probably be rewarded by results of extreme ethnological and archæological value.

INDEX.

PART I.—GENERAL.

PART II.—ANTHROPOLOGY.

PART III.—FAUNA.

Elephant beetle (see *Dynaster her-cules*)
Emys amazonica, 135
E. tracaja, 135
Erythrinus macrodon, 137
Eunectes murina, 71, 133
Euphonia minuta, 118
E. violacea, 118
Eurypyga helias, 123

Felis concolor, 111
F. jaguarundi, 111
F. macrura, 111
F. nigra, 111
F. sp. (see Warracaba tiger, 111
Fishes, 137
Frogs, 12, 136

Galictis barbara, 111
Greenheart bird (see *Lipangus cine-raceus*)
Guana (see *Iguana tuberculata*)
Gymnocephalus calvus, 119
Gymnotus electricus, 137, 138

HACKA (see *Galictis barbara*)
Hacka-tiger (see *Felis jaguarundi*)
Haimara (see *Erythrinus macrodon*)
'Hard-backs,' 142
Heron (see also *Ardea*), 16, 122
Honuré (see Heron), 16
Houma (see *Serasalmo niger*)
Howling Monkey (see *Mycetes seni-culus*)
Humming-birds (see also *Topaza pella* and *Trochilus bicolor*), 117, 121, 124
Hunting-ants (see *Eciton*)
Hydrochærus capybara, 108, 218

Ibis rubra, 13, 116
Ibis, scarlet (see *Ibis rubra*)
Icterus jamacaii, 122
I. xanthornus, 121
Iguana tuberculata, 18, 40, 130, 241
Insects, 140
Ixodes, sp. var., 154

JACOMBI (see *Psophia crepitans*)
Jagdmann ant (see *Eciton*)
Jaguar (see also under *Felis*), 23, 132
Jigger (see *Pulex penetrans*)

KABOORI fly (see *Simulium*)
Kairooni (see *Dicotyles labiatus*)
Keskedie (see *Lanius sulphuratus*)
Kibihee (see *Nasua*)
Kingfisher (see also *Alcedo*), 121
King Humming-bird (see *Topaza pella*)
King Vulture (see *Sarcoramphus papa*)

Labaria (see *Trigonocephalus atrox*)
Labba (·e *Cælogenys paca*)
Lanius sulphuratus, 120
Leistes americana, 121, 179
Lipangus cineraceus, 15, 118
'Louis d'or' (see *Euphonia minuta* and *E. violacea*)
Low-low (see *Silurus*)

MAAM (see *Tinamus*)
Macaws, 117
Maipuri (see *Tapirus americanus*)
Maipuri-tiger (see *Felis nigra*)
Manatee (see *Manatus australis*)
Manatus australis, 40, 114
Manoorie-ant (see *Ponera clavata*)
Maroodie (see *Penelope*)
Mata-mata turtle (see *Chelys mata-mata*)
'Mocking-bird' (see *Cassicus persi-cus*)
Monkeys (see also *Mycetes, Chryso-thrix*), 110
Mora moroota (see *Icterus jamacaii*)
Mosquitoes, 141, 151
Mosquito-worm, 152
'Mother-in-law of Scorpions' (see *Phrynus reniformis*)
Moths, 145
Muscovy duck (see Musk duck)
Musk duck (see *Anas moschatus*)
Mycetes seniculus, 13, 111, 244
Mycteria americana, 31, 129
Mygale avicularia, 154
Myrmecophaga didactyla, 112
M. jubata, 111, 266
M. tamandua, 111

Nasua socialis, 114
N. solitaris, 114
'Negrocop' (see *Mycteria americana*)
Nightjar (see *Caprimulgus*)

OCELOTS, 112
Odontophorus guianensis, 120
'Old witch bird' (see *Crotophagus ani*)

PART IV.—FLORA.

CATALOGUE OF DOVER BOOKS

Philosophy, Religion

GUIDE TO PHILOSOPHY, C. E. M. Joad. A modern classic which examines many crucial problems which man has pondered through the ages: Does free will exist? Is there plan in the universe? How do we know and validate our knowledge? Such opposed solutions as subjective idealism and realism, chance and teleology, vitalism and logical positivism, are evaluated and the contributions of the great philosophers from the Greeks to moderns like Russell, Whitehead, and others, are considered in the context of each problem. "The finest introduction," BOSTON TRANSCRIPT. Index. Classified bibliography. 592pp. 5⅜ x 8.
T297 Paperbound **$2.00**

HISTORY OF ANCIENT PHILOSOPHY, W. Windelband. One of the clearest, most accurate comprehensive surveys of Greek and Roman philosophy. Discusses ancient philosophy in general, intellectual life in Greece in the 7th and 6th centuries B.C., Thales, Anaximander, Anaximenes, Heraclitus, the Eleatics, Empedocles, Anaxagoras, Leucippus, the Pythagoreans, the Sophists, Socrates, Democritus (20 pages), Plato (50 pages), Aristotle (70 pages), the Peripatetics, Stoics, Epicureans, Sceptics, Neo-platonists, Christian Apologists, etc. 2nd German edition translated by H. E. Cushman. xv + 393pp. 5⅜ x 8.
T357 Paperbound **$1.85**

ILLUSTRATIONS OF THE HISTORY OF MEDIEVAL THOUGHT AND LEARNING, R. L. Poole. Basic analysis of the thought and lives of the leading philosophers and ecclesiastics from the 8th to the 14th century—Abailard, Ockham, Wycliffe, Marsiglio of Padua, and many other great thinkers who carried the torch of Western culture and learning through the "Dark Ages": political, religious, and metaphysical views. Long a standard work for scholars and one of the best introductions to medieval thought for beginners. Index. 10 Appendices. xiii + 327pp. 5⅜ x 8.
T674 Paperbound **$2.00**

PHILOSOPHY AND CIVILIZATION IN THE MIDDLE AGES, M. de Wulf. This semi-popular survey covers aspects of medieval intellectual life such as religion, philosophy, science, the arts, etc. It also covers feudalism vs. Catholicism, rise of the universities, mendicant orders, monastic centers, and similar topics. Unabridged. Bibliography. Index. viii + 320pp. 5⅜ x 8.
T284 Paperbound **$1.85**

AN INTRODUCTION TO SCHOLASTIC PHILOSOPHY, Prof. M. de Wulf. Formerly entitled SCHOLASTICISM OLD AND NEW, this volume examines the central scholastic tradition from St. Anselm, Albertus Magnus, Thomas Aquinas, up to Suarez in the 17th century. The relation of scholasticism to ancient and medieval philosophy and science in general is clear and easily followed. The second part of the book considers the modern revival of scholasticism, the Louvain position, relations with Kantianism and Positivism. Unabridged. xvi + 271pp. 5⅜ x 8.
T296 Clothbound **$3.50**
T283 Paperbound **$1.75**

A HISTORY OF MODERN PHILOSOPHY, H. Höffding. An exceptionally clear and detailed coverage of western philosophy from the Renaissance to the end of the 19th century. Major and minor men such as Pomponazzi, Bodin, Boehme, Telesius, Bruno, Copernicus, da Vinci, Kepler, Galileo, Bacon, Descartes, Hobbes, Spinoza, Leibniz, Wolff, Locke, Newton, Berkeley, Hume, Erasmus, Montesquieu, Voltaire, Diderot, Rousseau, Lessing, Kant, Herder, Fichte, Schelling, Hegel, Schopenhauer, Comte, Mill, Darwin, Spencer, Hartmann, Lange, and many others, are discussed in terms of theory of knowledge, logic, cosmology, and psychology. Index. 2 volumes, total of 1159pp. 5⅜ x 8.
T117 Vol. 1, Paperbound **$2.25**
T118 Vol. 2, Paperbound **$2.25**

ARISTOTLE, A. E. Taylor. A brilliant, searching non-technical account of Aristotle and his thought written by a foremost Platonist. It covers the life and works of Aristotle; classification of the sciences; logic; first philosophy; matter and form; causes; motion and eternity; God; physics; metaphysics; and similar topics. Bibliography. New Index compiled for this edition. 128pp. 5⅜ x 8.
T280 Paperbound **$1.00**

THE SYSTEM OF THOMAS AQUINAS, M. de Wulf. Leading Neo-Thomist, one of founders of University of Louvain, gives concise exposition to central doctrines of Aquinas, as a means toward determining his value to modern philosophy, religion. Formerly "Medieval Philosophy Illustrated from the System of Thomas Aquinas." Trans. by E. Messenger. Introduction. 151pp. 5⅜ x 8.
T568 Paperbound **$1.25**

LEIBNIZ, H. W. Carr. Most stimulating middle-level coverage of basic philosophical thought of Leibniz. Easily understood discussion, analysis of major works: "Theodicy," "Principles of Nature and Grace," "Monadology"; Leibniz's influence; intellectual growth; correspondence; disputes with Bayle, Malebranche, Newton; importance of his thought today, with reinterpretation in modern terminology. "Power and mastery," London Times. Bibliography. Index. 226pp. 5⅜ x 8.
T624 Paperbound **$1.35**

CATALOGUE OF DOVER BOOKS

THE SENSE OF BEAUTY, G. Santayana. A revelation of the beauty of language as well as an important philosophic treatise, this work studies the "why, when, and how beauty appears, what conditions an object must fulfill to be beautiful, what elements of our nature make us sensible of beauty, and what the relation is between the constitution of the object and the excitement of our susceptibility." "It is doubtful if a better treatment of the subject has since been published," PEABODY JOURNAL. Index. ix + 275pp. 5⅜ x 8.
T238 Paperbound **$1.00**

PROBLEMS OF ETHICS, Moritz Schlick. The renowned leader of the "Vienna Circle" applies the logical positivist approach to a wide variety of ethical problems: the source and means of attaining knowledge, the formal and material characteristics of the good, moral norms and principles, absolute vs. relative values, free will and responsibility, comparative importance of pleasure and suffering as ethical values, etc. Disarmingly simple and straightforward despite complexity of subject. First English translation, authorized by author before his death, of a thirty-year old classic. Translated and with an introduction by David Rynin. Index. Foreword by Prof. George P. Adams. xxi + 209pp. 5⅜ x 8.   T946 Paperbound **$1.60**

AN INTRODUCTION TO EXISTENTIALISM, Robert G. Olson. A new and indispensable guide to one of the major thought systems of our century, the movement that is central to the thinking of some of the most creative figures of the past hundred years. Stresses Heidegger and Sartre, with careful and objective examination of the existentialist position, values—freedom of choice, individual dignity, personal love, creative effort—and answers to the eternal questions of the human condition. Scholarly, unbiased, analytic, unlike most studies of this difficult subject, Prof. Olson's book is aimed at the student of philosophy as well as at the reader with no formal training who is looking for an absorbing, accessible, and thorough introduction to the basic texts. Index. xv + 221pp. 5⅜ x 8½.   T55 Paperbound **$1.65**

SYMBOLIC LOGIC, C. I. Lewis and C. H. Langford. Since first publication in 1932, this has been among most frequently cited works on symbolic logic. Still one of the best introductions both for beginners and for mathematicians, philosophers. First part covers basic topics which easily lend themselves to beginning study. Second part is rigorous, thorough development of logistic method, examination of some of most difficult and abstract aspects of symbolic logic, including modal logic, logical paradoxes, many-valued logic, with Prof. Lewis' own contributions. 2nd revised (corrected) edition. 3 appendixes, one new to this edition. 524pp. 5⅜ x 8.   S170 Paperbound **$2.00**

WHITEHEAD'S PHILOSOPHY OF CIVILIZATION, A. H. Johnson. A leading authority on Alfred North Whitehead synthesizes the great philosopher's thought on civilization, scattered throughout various writings, into unified whole. Analysis of Whitehead's general definition of civilization, his reflections on history and influences on its development, his religion, including his analysis of Christianity, concept of solitariness as first requirement of personal religion, and so on. Other chapters cover views on minority groups, society, civil liberties, education. Also critical comments on Whitehead's philosophy. Written with general reader in mind. A perceptive introduction to important area of the thought of a leading philosopher of our century. Revised index and bibliography. xii + 211pp. 5⅜ x 8½.
T996 Paperbound **$1.50**

WHITEHEAD'S THEORY OF REALITY, A. H. Johnson. Introductory outline of Whitehead's theory of actual entities, the heart of his philosophy of reality, followed by his views on nature of God, philosophy of mind, theory of value (truth, beauty, goodness and their opposites), analyses of other philosophers, attitude toward science. A perspicacious lucid introduction by author of dissertation on Whitehead, written under the subject's supervision at Harvard. Good basic view for beginning students of philosophy and for those who are simply interested in important contemporary ideas. Revised index and bibliography. xiii + 267pp. 5⅜ x 8½.
T989 Paperbound **$2.00**

MIND AND THE WORLD-ORDER, C. I. Lewis. Building upon the work of Peirce, James, and Dewey, Professor Lewis outlines a theory of knowledge in terms of "conceptual pragmatism." Dividing truth into abstract mathematical certainty and empirical truth, the author demonstrates that the traditional understanding of the a priori must be abandoned. Detailed analyses of philosophy, metaphysics, method, the "given" in experience, knowledge of objects, nature of the a priori, experience and order, and many others. Appendices. xiv + 446pp. 5⅜ x 8.   T359 Paperbound **$2.25**

SCEPTICISM AND ANIMAL FAITH, G. Santayana. To eliminate difficulties in the traditional theory of knowledge, Santayana distinguishes between the independent existence of objects and the essence our mind attributes to them. Scepticism is thereby established as a form of belief, and animal faith is shown to be a necessary condition of knowledge. Belief, classical idealism, intuition, memory, symbols, literary psychology, and much more, discussed with unusual clarity and depth. Index. xii + 314pp. 5⅜ x 8.   T235 Clothbound **$3.50**
T236 Paperbound **$1.75**

LANGUAGE AND MYTH, E. Cassirer. Analyzing the non-rational thought processes which go to make up culture, Cassirer demonstrates that beneath both language and myth there lies a dominant unconscious "grammar" of experience whose categories and canons are not those of logical thought. His analyses of seemingly diverse phenomena such as Indian metaphysics, the Melanesian "mana," the Naturphilosophie of Schelling, modern poetry, etc., are profound without being pedantic. Introduction and translation by Susanne Langer. Index. x + 103pp. 5⅜ x 8.   T51 Paperbound **$1.25**

CATALOGUE OF DOVER BOOKS

AN ESSAY CONCERNING HUMAN UNDERSTANDING, John Locke. Edited by A. C. Fraser. Unabridged reprinting of definitive edition; only complete edition of "Essay" in print. Marginal analyses of almost every paragraph; hundreds of footnotes; authoritative 140-page biographical, critical, historical prolegomena. Indexes. 1170pp. 5⅜ x 8.

T530 Vol. 1 (Books 1, 2) Paperbound **$2.50**
T531 Vol. 2 (Books 3, 4) Paperbound **$2.50**
2 volume set **$5.00**

THE PHILOSOPHY OF HISTORY, G. W. F. Hegel. One of the great classics of western thought which reveals Hegel's basic principle: that history is not chance but a rational process, the realization of the Spirit of Freedom. Ranges from the oriental cultures of subjective thought to the classical subjective cultures, to the modern absolute synthesis where spiritual and secular may be reconciled. Translation and introduction by J. Sibree. Introduction by C. Hegel. Special introduction for this edition by Prof. Carl Friedrich. xxxix + 447pp. 5⅜ x 8.

T112 Paperbound **$2.25**

THE PHILOSOPHY OF HEGEL, W. T. Stace. The first detailed analysis of Hegel's thought in English, this is especially valuable since so many of Hegel's works are out of print. Dr. Stace examines Hegel's debt to Greek idealists and the 18th century and then proceeds to a careful description and analysis of Hegel's first principles, categories, reason, dialectic method, his logic, philosophy of nature and spirit, etc. Index. Special 14 x 20 chart of Hegelian system. x + 526pp. 5⅜ x 8.

T254 Paperbound **$2.45**

THE WILL TO BELIEVE and HUMAN IMMORTALITY, W. James. Two complete books bound as one. THE WILL TO BELIEVE discusses the interrelations of belief, will, and intellect in man; chance vs. determinism, free will vs. determinism, free will vs. fate, pluralism vs. monism; the philosophies of Hegel and Spencer, and more. HUMAN IMMORTALITY examines the question of survival after death and develops an unusual and powerful argument for immortality. Two prefaces. Index. Total of 429pp. 5⅜ x 8.

T291 Paperbound **$2.00**

THE WORLD AND THE INDIVIDUAL, Josiah Royce. Only major effort by an American philosopher to interpret nature of things in systematic, comprehensive manner. Royce's formulation of an absolute voluntarism remains one of the original and profound solutions to the problems involved. Part One, Four Historical Conceptions of Being, inquires into first principles, true meaning and place of individuality. Part Two, Nature, Man, and the Moral Order, is application of first principles to problems concerning religion, evil, moral order. Introduction by J. E. Smith, Yale Univ. Index. 1070pp. 5⅜ x 8.

T561 Vol. 1 Paperbound **$2.75**
T562 Vol. 2 Paperbound **$2.75**
Two volume set **$5.50**

THE PHILOSOPHICAL WRITINGS OF PEIRCE, edited by J. Buchler. This book (formerly THE PHILOSOPHY OF PEIRCE) is a carefully integrated exposition of Peirce's complete system composed of selections from his own work. Symbolic logic, scientific method, theory of signs, pragmatism, epistemology, chance, cosmology, ethics, and many other topics are treated by one of the greatest philosophers of modern times. This is the only inexpensive compilation of his key ideas. xvi + 386pp. 5⅜ x 8.

T217 Paperbound **$2.00**

EXPERIENCE AND NATURE, John Dewey. An enlarged, revised edition of the Paul Carus lectures which Dewey delivered in 1925. It covers Dewey's basic formulation of the problem of knowledge, with a full discussion of other systems, and a detailing of his own concepts of the relationship of external world, mind, and knowledge. Starts with a thorough examination of the philosophical method; examines the interrelationship of experience and nature; analyzes experience on basis of empirical naturalism, the formulation of law, role of language and social factors in knowledge; etc. Dewey's treatment of central problems in philosophy is profound but extremely easy to follow. ix + 448pp. 5⅜ x 8.

T471 Paperbound **$2.00**

THE PHILOSOPHICAL WORKS OF DESCARTES. The definitive English edition of all the major philosophical works and letters of René Descartes. All of his revolutionary insights, from his famous "Cogito ergo sum" to his detailed account of contemporary science and his astonishingly fruitful concept that all phenomena of the universe (except mind) could be reduced to clear laws by the use of mathematics. An excellent source for the thought of men like Hobbes, Arnauld, Gassendi, etc., who were Descarte's contemporaries. Translated by E. S. Haldane and G. Ross. Introductory notes. Index. Total of 842pp. 5⅜ x 8.

T71 Vol. 1, Paperbound **$2.00**
T72 Vol. 2, Paperbound **$2.00**

THE CHIEF WORKS OF SPINOZA. An unabridged reprint of the famous Bohn edition containing all of Spinoza's most important works: Vol. I: The Theologico-Political Treatise and the Political Treatise. Vol. II: On The Improvement Of Understanding, The Ethics, Selected Letters. Profound and enduring ideas on God, the universe, pantheism, society, religion, the state, democracy, the mind, emotions, freedom and the nature of man, which influenced Goethe, Hegel, Schelling, Coleridge, Whitehead, and many others. Introduction. 2 volumes. 826pp. 5⅜ x 8.

T249 Vol. I, Paperbound **$1.50**
T250 Vol. II, Paperbound **$1.50**

CATALOGUE OF DOVER BOOKS

THE ANALYSIS OF MATTER, Bertrand Russell. A classic which has retained its importance in understanding the relation between modern physical theory and human perception. Logical analysis of physics, prerelativity physics, causality, scientific inference, Weyl's theory, tensors, invariants and physical interpretations, periodicity, and much more is treated with Russell's usual brilliance. "Masterly piece of clear thinking and clear writing," NATION AND ATHENAEUM. "Most thorough treatment of the subject," THE NATION. Introduction. Index. 8 figures. viii + 408pp. 5⅜ x 8. S231 Paperbound **$1.95**

CONCEPTUAL THINKING (A ˙LOGICAL INQUIRY), S. Körner. Discusses origin, use of general concepts on which language is based, and the light they shed on basic philosophical questions. Rigorously examines how different concepts are related; how they are linked to experience; problems in the field of contact between exact logical, mathematical, and scientific concepts, and the inexactness of everyday experience (studied at length). This work elaborates many new approaches to the traditional problems of philosophy—epistemology, value theories, metaphysics, aesthetics, morality. "Rare originality . . . brings a new rigour into philosophical argument," Philosophical Quarterly. New corrected second edition. Index. vii + 301pp. 5⅜ x 8 T516 Paperbound **$1.75**

INTRODUCTION TO SYMBOLIC LOGIC, S. Langer. No special knowledge of math required — probably the clearest book ever written on symbolic logic, suitable for the layman, general scientist, and philosopher. You start with simple symbols and advance to a knowledge of the Boole-Schroeder and Russell-Whitehead systems. Forms, logical structure, classes, the calculus of propositions, logic of the syllogism, etc., are all covered. "One of the clearest and simplest introductions," MATHEMATICS GAZETTE. Second enlarged, revised edition. 368pp. 5⅜ x 8. S164 Paperbound **$1.85**

LANGUAGE, TRUTH AND LOGIC, A. J. Ayer. A clear, careful analysis of the basic ideas of Logical Positivism. Building on the work of Schlick, Russell, Carnap, and the Viennese School, Mr. Ayer develops a detailed exposition of the nature of philosophy, science, and metaphysics; the Self and the World; logic and common sense, and other philosophic concepts. An aid to clarity of thought as well as the first full-length development of Logical Positivism in English. Introduction by Bertrand Russell. Index. 160pp. 5⅜ x 8. T10 Paperbound **$1.25**

ESSAYS IN EXPERIMENTAL LOGIC, J. Dewey. Based upon the theory that knowledge implies a judgment which in turn implies an inquiry, these papers consider the inquiry stage in terms of: the relationship of thought and subject matter, antecedents of thought, data and meanings. 3 papers examine Bertrand Russell's thought, while 2 others discuss pragmatism and a final essay presents a new theory of the logic of values. Index. viii + 444pp. 5⅜ x 8. T73 Paperbound **$2.25**

TRAGIC SENSE OF LIFE, M. de Unamuno. The acknowledged masterpiece of one of Spain's most influential thinkers. Between the despair at the inevitable death of man and all his works and the desire for something better, Unamuno finds that "saving incertitude" that alone can console us. This dynamic appraisal of man's faith in God and in himself has been called "a masterpiece" by the ENCYCLOPAEDIA BRITANNICA. xxx + 332pp. 5⅜ x 8. T257 Paperbound **$2.00**

HISTORY OF DOGMA, A. Harnack. Adolph Harnack, who died in 1930, was perhaps the greatest Church historian of all time. In this epoch-making history, which has never been surpassed in comprehensiveness and wealth of learning, he traces the development of the authoritative Christian doctrinal system from its first crystallization in the 4th century down through the Reformation, including also a brief survey of the later developments through the Infallibility decree of 1870. He reveals the enormous influence of Greek thought on the early Fathers, and discusses such topics as the Apologists, the great councils, Manichaeism, the historical position of Augustine, the medieval opposition to indulgences, the rise of Protestantism, the relations of Luther's doctrines with modern tendencies of thought, and much more. "Monumental work; still the most valuable history of dogma . . . luminous analysis of the problems . . . abounds in suggestion and stimulus and can be neglected by no one who desires to understand the history of thought in this most important field," Dutcher's Guide to Historical Literature. Translated by Neil Buchanan. Index. Unabridged reprint in 4 volumes. Vol I: Beginnings to the Gnostics and Marcion. Vol II & III: 2nd century to the 4th century Fathers. Vol IV & V: 4th century Councils to the Carlovingian Renaissance. Vol VI & VII: Period of Clugny (c. 1000) to the Reformation, and after. Total of cii + 2407pp. 5⅜ x 8.

T904 Vol I	Paperbound	**$2.50**
T905 Vol II & III	Paperbound	**$2.75**
T906 Vol IV & V	Paperbound	**$2.75**
T907 Vol VI & VII	Paperbound	**$2.75**
	The set	**$10.75**

THE GUIDE FOR THE PERPLEXED, Maimonides. One of the great philosophical works of all time and a necessity for everyone interested in the philosophy of the Middle Ages in the Jewish, Christian, and Moslem traditions. Maimonides develops a common meeting-point for the Old Testament and the Aristotelian thought which pervaded the medieval world. His ideas and methods predate such scholastics as Aquinas and Scotus and throw light on the entire problem of philosophy or science vs. religion. 2nd revised edition. Complete unabridged Friedländer translation. 55 page introduction to Maimonides's life, period, etc., with an important summary of the GUIDE. Index. lix + 414pp. 5⅜ x 8. T351 Paperbound **$2.00**

Americana

THE EYES OF DISCOVERY, J. Bakeless. A vivid reconstruction of how unspoiled America appeared to the first white men. Authentic and enlightening accounts of Hudson's landing in New York, Coronado's trek through the Southwest; scores of explorers, settlers, trappers, soldiers. America's pristine flora, fauna, and Indians in every region and state in fresh and unusual new aspects. "A fascinating view of what the land was like before the first highway went through," Time. 68 contemporary illustrations, 39 newly added in this edition. Index. Bibliography. x + 500pp. 5⅜ x 8.
T761 Paperbound $2.00

AUDUBON AND HIS JOURNALS, J. J. Audubon. A collection of fascinating accounts of Europe and America in the early 1800's through Audubon's own eyes. Includes the Missouri River Journals —an eventful trip through America's untouched heartland, the Labrador Journals, the European Journals, the famous "Episodes," and other rare Audubon material, including the descriptive chapters from the original letterpress edition of the "Ornithological Studies", omitted in all later editions. Indispensable for ornithologists, naturalists, and all lovers of Americana and adventure. 70-page biography by Audubon's granddaughter. 38 illustrations. Index. Total of 1106pp. 5⅜ x 8.
T675 Vol I Paperbound $2.25
T676 Vol II Paperbound $2.25
The set $4.50

TRAVELS OF WILLIAM BARTRAM, edited by Mark Van Doren. The first inexpensive illustrated edition of one of the 18th century's most delightful books is an excellent source of first-hand material on American geography, anthropology, and natural history. Many descriptions of early Indian tribes are our only source of information on them prior to the infiltration of the white man. "The mind of a scientist with the soul of a poet," John Livingston Lowes. 13 original illustrations and maps. Edited with an introduction by Mark Van Doren. 448pp. 5⅜ x 8.
T13 Paperbound $2.00

GARRETS AND PRETENDERS: A HISTORY OF BOHEMIANISM IN AMERICA, A. Parry. The colorful and fantastic history of American Bohemianism from Poe to Kerouac. This is the only complete record of hoboes, cranks, starving poets, and suicides. Here are Pfaff, Whitman, Crane, Bierce, Pound, and many others. New chapters by the author and by H. T. Moore bring this thorough and well-documented history down to the Beatniks. "An excellent account," N. Y. Times. Scores of cartoons, drawings, and caricatures. Bibliography. Index. xxviii + 421pp. 5⅝ x 8⅜.
T708 Paperbound $1.95

THE EXPLORATION OF THE COLORADO RIVER AND ITS CANYONS, J. W. Powell. The thrilling first-hand account of the expedition that filled in the last white space on the map of the United States. Rapids, famine, hostile Indians, and mutiny are among the perils encountered as the unknown Colorado Valley reveals its secrets. This is the only uncut version of Major Powell's classic of exploration that has been printed in the last 60 years. Includes later reflections and subsequent expedition. 250 illustrations, new map. 400pp. 5⅝ x 8⅜.
T94 Paperbound $2.25

THE JOURNAL OF HENRY D. THOREAU, Edited by Bradford Torrey and Francis H. Allen. Henry Thoreau is not only one of the most important figures in American literature and social thought; his voluminous journals (from which his books emerged as selections and crystallizations) constitute both the longest, most sensitive record of personal internal development and a most penetrating description of a historical moment in American culture. This present set, which was first issued in fourteen volumes, contains Thoreau's entire journals from 1837 to 1862, with the exception of the lost years which were found only recently. We are reissuing it, complete and unabridged, with a new introduction by Walter Harding, Secretary of the Thoreau Society. Fourteen volumes reissued in two volumes. Foreword by Henry Seidel Canby. Total of 1888pp. 8⅜ x 12¼.
T312-3 Two volume set, Clothbound $20.00

GAMES AND SONGS OF AMERICAN CHILDREN, collected by William Wells Newell. A remarkable collection of 190 games with songs that accompany many of them; cross references to show similarities, differences among them; variations; musical notation for 38 songs. Textual discussions show relations with folk-drama and other aspects of folk tradition. Grouped into categories for ready comparative study: Love-games, histories, playing at work, human life, bird and beast, mythology, guessing-games, etc. New introduction covers relations of songs and dances to timeless heritage of folklore, biographical sketch of Newell, other pertinent data. A good source of inspiration for those in charge of groups of children and a valuable reference for anthropologists, sociologists, psychiatrists. Introduction by Carl Withers. New indexes of first lines, games. 5⅜ x 8½. xii + 242pp.
T354 Paperbound $1.75

GARDNER'S PHOTOGRAPHIC SKETCH BOOK OF THE CIVIL WAR, Alexander Gardner. The first published collection of Civil War photographs, by one of the two or three most famous photographers of the era, outstandingly reproduced from the original positives. Scenes of crucial battles: Appomattox, Manassas, Mechanicsville, Bull Run, Yorktown, Fredericksburg, etc. Gettysburg immediately after retirement of forces. Battle ruins at Richmond, Petersburg, Gaines'Mill. Prisons, arsenals, a slave pen, fortifications, headquarters, pontoon bridges, soldiers, a field hospital. A unique glimpse into the realities of one of the bloodiest wars in history, with an introductory text to each picture by Gardner himself. Until this edition, there were only five known copies in libraries, and fewer in private hands, one of which sold at auction in 1952 for $425. Introduction by E. F. Bleiler. 100 full page 7 x 10 photographs (original size). 224pp. 8½ x 10¾. T476 Clothbound **$6.00**

A BIBLIOGRAPHY OF NORTH AMERICAN FOLKLORE AND FOLKSONG, Charles Haywood, Ph.D. The only book that brings together bibliographic information on so wide a range of folklore material. Lists practically everything published about American folksongs, ballads, dances, folk beliefs and practices, popular music, tales, similar material—more than 35,000 titles of books, articles, periodicals, monographs, music publications, phonograph records. Each entry complete with author, title, date and place of publication, arranger and performer of particular examples of folk music, many with Dr. Haywood's valuable criticism, evaluation. Volume I, "The American People," is complete listing of general and regional studies, titles of tales and songs of Negro and non-English speaking groups and where to find them, Occupational Bibliography including sections listing sources of information, folk material on cowboys, riverboat men, 49ers, American characters like Mike Fink, Frankie and Johnnie, John Henry, many more. Volume II, "The American Indian," tells where to find information on dances, myths, songs, ritual of more than 250 tribes in U.S., Canada. A monumental product of 10 years' labor, carefully classified for easy use. "All students of this subject . . . will find themselves in debt to Professor Haywood," Stith Thompson, in American Anthropologist. ". . . a most useful and excellent work," Duncan Emrich, Chief Folklore Section, Library of Congress, in "Notes." Corrected, enlarged republication of 1951 edition. New Preface. New index of composers, arrangers, performers. General index of more than 15,000 items. Two volumes. Total of 1301pp. 6⅛ x 9¼. T797-798 Clothbound **$12.50**

INCIDENTS OF TRAVEL IN YUCATAN, John L. Stephens. One of first white men to penetrate interior of Yucatan tells the thrilling story of his discoveries of 44 cities, remains of once-powerful Maya civilization. Compelling text combines narrative power with historical significance as it takes you through heat, dust, storms of Yucatan; native festivals with brutal bull fights; great ruined temples atop man-made mounds. Countless idols, sculptures, tombs, examples of Mayan taste for rich ornamentation, from gateways to personal trinkets, accurately illustrated, discussed in text. Will appeal to those interested in ancient civilizations, and those who like stories of exploration, discovery, adventure. Republication of last (1843) edition. 124 illustrations by English artist, F. Catherwood. Appendix on Mayan architecture, chronology. Two volume set. Total of xxviii + 927pp.
Vol I T926 Paperbound **$2.00**
Vol II T927 Paperbound **$2.00**
The set **$4.00**

A GENIUS IN THE FAMILY, Hiram Percy Maxim. Sir Hiram Stevens Maxim was known to the public as the inventive genius who created the Maxim gun, automatic sprinkler, and a heavier-than-air plane that got off the ground in 1894. Here, his son reminisces—this is by no means a formal biography—about the exciting and often downright scandalous private life of his brilliant, eccentric father. A warm and winning portrait of a prankish, mischievous, impious personality, a genuine character. The style is fresh and direct, the effect is unadulterated pleasure. "A book of charm and lasting humor . . . belongs on the 'must read' list of all fathers," New York Times. "A truly gorgeous affair," New Statesman and Nation. 17 illustrations, 16 specially for this edition. viii + 108pp. 5⅜ x 8½. T948 Paperbound **$1.00**

HORSELESS CARRIAGE DAYS, Hiram P. Maxim. The best account of an important technological revolution by one of its leading figures. The delightful and rewarding story of the author's experiments with the exact combustibility of gasoline, stopping and starting mechanisms, carriage design, and engines. Captures remarkably well the flavor of an age of scoffers and rival inventors not above sabotage; of noisy, uncontrollable gasoline vehicles and incredible mobile steam kettles. ". . . historic information and light humor are combined to furnish highly entertaining reading," New York Times. 56 photographs, 12 specially for this edition. xi + 175pp. 5⅜ x 8½. T964 Paperbound **$1.35**

BODY, BOOTS AND BRITCHES: FOLKTALES, BALLADS AND SPEECH FROM COUNTRY NEW YORK, Harold W. Thompson. A unique collection, discussion of songs, stories, anecdotes, proverbs handed down orally from Scotch-Irish grandfathers, German nurse-maids, Negro workmen, gathered from all over Upper New York State. Tall tales by and about lumbermen and pirates, canalers and injun-fighters, tragic and comic ballads, scores of sayings and proverbs all tied together by an informative, delightful narrative by former president of New York Historical Society. ". . . a sparkling homespun tapestry that every lover of Americana will want to have around the house," Carl Carmer, New York Times. Republication of 1939 edition. 20 line-drawings. Index. Appendix (Sources of material, bibliography). 530pp. 5⅜ x 8½. T411 Paperbound **$2.25**

Literature, History of Literature

ARISTOTLE'S THEORY OF POETRY AND THE FINE ARTS, edited by S. H. Butcher. The celebrated Butcher translation of this great classic faced, page by page, with the complete Greek text. A 300 page introduction discussing Aristotle's ideas and their influence in the history of thought and literature, and covering art and nature, imitation as an aesthetic form, poetic truth, art and morality, tragedy, comedy, and similar topics. Modern Aristotelian criticism discussed by John Gassner. lxxvi + 421pp. 5⅜ x 8. **T42 Paperbound $2.00**

INTRODUCTIONS TO ENGLISH LITERATURE, edited by B. Dobrée. Goes far beyond ordinary histories, ranging from the 7th century up to 1914 (to the 1940's in some cases.) The first half of each volume is a specific detailed study of historical and economic background of the period and a general survey of poetry and prose, including trends of thought, influences, etc. The second and larger half is devoted to a detailed study of more than 5000 poets, novelists, dramatists; also economists, historians, biographers, religious writers, philosophers, travellers, and scientists of literary stature, with dates, lists of major works and their dates, keypoint critical bibliography, and evaluating comments. The most compendious bibliographic and literary aid within its price range.

Vol. I. THE BEGINNINGS OF ENGLISH LITERATURE TO SKELTON, (1509), W. L. Renwick, H. Orton. 450pp. 5⅛ x 7⅞. **T75 Clothbound $4.50**

Vol. II. THE ENGLISH RENAISSANCE, 1510-1688, V. de Sola Pinto. 381pp. 5⅛ x 7⅞. **T76 Clothbound $4.50**

Vol. III. AUGUSTANS AND ROMANTICS, 1689-1830, H. Dyson, J. Butt. 320pp. 5⅛ x 7⅞. **T77 Clothbound $4.50**

Vol. IV. THE VICTORIANS AND AFTER, 1830-1940's, E. Batho, B. Dobrée. 360pp. 5⅛ x 7⅞. **T78 Clothbound $4.50**

EPIC AND ROMANCE, W. P. Ker. Written by one of the foremost authorities on medieval literature, this is the standard survey of medieval epic and romance. It covers Teutonic epics, Icelandic sagas, Beowulf, French chansons de geste, the Roman de Troie, and many other important works of literature. It is an excellent account for a body of literature whose beauty and value has only recently come to be recognized. Index. xxiv + 398pp. 5⅜ x 8. **T355 Paperbound $2.25**

THE POPULAR BALLAD, F. B. Gummere. Most useful factual introduction; fund of descriptive material; quotes, cites over 260 ballads. Examines, from folkloristic view, structure; choral, ritual elements; meter, diction, fusion; effects of tradition, editors; almost every other aspect of border, riddle, kinship, sea, ribald, supernatural, etc., ballads. Bibliography. 2 indexes. 374pp. 5⅜ x 8. **T548 Paperbound $1.85**

MASTERS OF THE DRAMA, John Gassner. The most comprehensive history of the drama in print, covering drama in every important tradition from the Greeks to the Near East, China, Japan, Medieval Europe, England, Russia, Italy, Spain, Germany, and dozens of other drama producing nations. This unsurpassed reading and reference work encompasses more than 800 dramatists and over 2000 plays, with biographical material, plot summaries, theatre history, etc. "Has no competitors in its field," THEATRE ARTS. "Best of its kind in English," NEW REPUBLIC. Exhaustive 35 page bibliography. 77 photographs and drawings. Deluxe edition with reinforced cloth binding, headbands, stained top. xxii + 890pp. 5⅜ x 8. **T100 Clothbound $6.95**

THE DEVELOPMENT OF DRAMATIC ART, D. C. Stuart. The basic work on the growth of Western drama from primitive beginnings to Eugene O'Neill, covering over 2500 years. Not a mere listing or survey, but a thorough analysis of changes, origins of style, and influences in each period; dramatic conventions, social pressures, choice of material, plot devices, stock situations, etc.; secular and religious works of all nations and epochs. "Generous and thoroughly documented researches," Outlook. "Solid studies of influences and playwrights and periods," London Times. Index. Bibliography. xi + 679pp. 5⅜ x 8. **T693 Paperbound $2.75**

A SOURCE BOOK IN THEATRICAL HISTORY (SOURCES OF THEATRICAL HISTORY), A. M. Nagler. Over 2000 years of actors, directors, designers, critics, and spectators speak for themselves in this potpourri of writings selected from the great and formative periods of western drama. On-the-spot descriptions of masks, costumes, makeup, rehearsals, special effects, acting methods, backstage squabbles, theatres, etc. Contemporary glimpses of Molière rehearsing his company, an exhortation to a Roman audience to buy refreshments and keep quiet, Goethe's rules for actors, Belasco telling of $6500 he spent building a river, Restoration actors being told to avoid "lewd, obscene, or indecent postures," and much more. Each selection has an introduction by Prof. Nagler. This extraordinary, lively collection is ideal as a source of otherwise difficult to obtain material, as well as a fine book for browsing. Over 80 illustrations. 10 diagrams. xxiii + 611pp. 5⅜ x 8. **T515 Paperbound $3.00**

CATALOGUE OF DOVER BOOKS

WORLD DRAMA, B. H. Clark. The dramatic creativity of a score of ages and eras — all in two handy compact volumes. Over ⅓ of this material is unavailable in any other current edition! 46 plays from Ancient Greece, Rome, Medieval Europe, France, Germany, Italy, England, Russia, Scandinavia, India, China, Japan, etc. — including classic authors like Aeschylus, Sophocles, Euripides, Aristophanes, Plautus, Marlowe, Jonson, Farquhar, Goldsmith, Cervantes, Molière, Dumas, Goethe, Schiller, Ibsen, and many others. This creative collection avoids hackneyed material and includes only completely first-rate works which are relatively little known or difficult to obtain. "The most comprehensive collection of important plays from all literature available in English," SAT. REV. OF LITERATURE. Introduction. Reading lists. 2 volumes. 1364pp. 5⅜ x 8.

Vol. 1, T57 Paperbound **$2.50**
Vol. 2, T59 Paperbound **$2.50**

MASTERPIECES OF THE RUSSIAN DRAMA, edited with introduction by G. R. Noyes. This only comprehensive anthology of Russian drama ever published in English offers complete texts, in 1st-rate modern translations, of 12 plays covering 200 years. Vol. 1: "The Young Hopeful," Fonvisin; "Wit Works Woe," Griboyedov; "The Inspector General," Gogol; "A Month in the Country," Turgenev; "The Poor Bride," Ostrovsky; "A Bitter Fate," Pisemsky. Vol. 2: "The Death of Ivan the Terrible," Alexey Tolstoy "The Power of Darkness," Lev Tolstoy; "The Lower Depths," Gorky; "The Cherry Orchard," Chekhov; "Professor Storitsyn," Andreyev; "Mystery Bouffe," Mayakovsky. Bibliography. Total of 902pp. 5⅜ x 8.

Vol. 1 T647 Paperbound **$2.25**
Vol. 2 T648 Paperbound **$2.00**

EUGENE O'NEILL: THE MAN AND HIS PLAYS, B. H. Clark. Introduction to O'Neill's life and work. Clark analyzes each play from the early THE WEB to the recently produced MOON FOR THE MISBEGOTTEN and THE ICEMAN COMETH revealing the environmental and dramatic influences necessary for a complete understanding of these important works. Bibliography. Appendices. Index. ix + 182pp. 5⅜ x 8. T379 Paperbound **$1.35**

THE HEART OF THOREAU'S JOURNALS, edited by O. Shepard. The best general selection from Thoreau's voluminous (and rare) journals. This intimate record of thoughts and observations reveals the full Thoreau and his intellectual development more accurately than any of his published works: self-conflict between the scientific observer and the poet, reflections on transcendental philosophy, involvement in the tragedies of neighbors and national causes, etc. New preface, notes, introductions. xii + 228pp. 5⅜ x 8. T741 Paperbound **$1.50**

H. D. THOREAU: A WRITER'S JOURNAL, edited by L. Stapleton. A unique new selection from the Journals concentrating on Thoreau's growth as a conscious literary artist, the ideals and purposes of his art. Most of the material has never before appeared outside of the complete 14-volume edition. Contains vital insights on Thoreau's projected book on Concord, thoughts on the nature of men and government, indignation with slavery, sources of inspiration, goals in life. Index. xxxiii + 234pp. 5⅜ x 8. T678 Paperbound **$1.65**

THE HEART OF EMERSON'S JOURNALS, edited by Bliss Perry. Best of these revealing Journals, originally 10 volumes, presented in a one volume edition. Talks with Channing, Hawthorne, Thoreau, and Bronson Alcott; impressions of Webster, Everett, John Brown, and Lincoln; records of moments of sudden understanding, vision, and solitary ecstasy. "The essays do not reveal the power of Emerson's mind . . . as do these hasty and informal writings," N.Y. Times. Preface by Bliss Perry. Index. xiii + 357pp. 5⅜ x 8. T477 Paperbound **$1.85**

FOUNDERS OF THE MIDDLE AGES, E. K. Rand. This is the best non-technical discussion of the transformation of Latin pagan culture into medieval civilization. Covering such figures as Tertullian, Gregory, Jerome, Boethius, Augustine, the Neoplatonists, and many other literary men, educators, classicists, and humanists, this book is a storehouse of information presented clearly and simply for the intelligent non-specialist. "Thoughtful, beautifully written," AMERICAN HISTORICAL REVIEW. "Extraordinarily accurate," Richard McKeon, THE NATION. ix + 365pp. 5⅜ x 8. T369 Paperbound **$2.00**

PLAY-MAKING: A MANUAL OF CRAFTSMANSHIP, William Archer. With an extensive, new introduction by John Gassner, Yale Univ. The permanently essential requirements of solid play construction are set down in clear, practical language: theme, exposition, foreshadowing, tension, obligatory scene, peripety, dialogue, character, psychology, other topics. This book has been one of the most influential elements in the modern theatre, and almost everything said on the subject since is contained explicitly or implicitly within its covers. Bibliography. Index. xlii + 277pp. 5⅜ x 8. T651 Paperbound **$1.75**

HAMBURG DRAMATURGY, G. E. Lessing. One of the most brilliant of German playwrights of the eighteenth-century age of criticism analyzes the complex of theory and tradition that constitutes the world of theater. These 104 essays on aesthetic theory helped demolish the regime of French classicism, opening the door to psychological and social realism, romanticism. Subjects include the original functions of tragedy; drama as the rational world; the meaning of pity and fear, pity and fear as means for purgation and other Aristotelian concepts; genius and creative force; interdependence of poet's language and actor's interpretation; truth and authenticity; etc. A basic and enlightening study for anyone interested in aesthetics and ideas, from the philosopher to the theatergoer. Introduction by Prof. Victor Lange. xxii + 265pp. 4½ x 6⅜. T32 Paperbound **$1.45**

Language Books and Records

GERMAN: HOW TO SPEAK AND WRITE IT. AN INFORMAL CONVERSATIONAL METHOD FOR SELF STUDY, Joseph Rosenberg. Eminently useful for self study because of concentration on elementary stages of learning. Also provides teachers with remarkable variety of aids: 28 full- and double-page sketches with pertinent items numbered and identified in German and English; German proverbs, jokes; grammar, idiom studies; extensive practice exercises. The most interesting introduction to German available, full of amusing illustrations, photographs of cities and landmarks in German-speaking cities, cultural information subtly woven into conversational material. Includes summary of grammar, guide to letter writing, study guide to German literature by Dr. Richard Friedenthal. Index. 400 illustrations. 384pp. 5⅜ x 8½.
T271 Paperbound **$2.00**

FRENCH: HOW TO SPEAK AND WRITE IT. AN INFORMAL CONVERSATIONAL METHOD FOR SELF STUDY, Joseph Lemaitre. Even the absolute beginner can acquire a solid foundation for further study from this delightful elementary course. Photographs, sketches and drawings, sparkling colloquial conversations on a wide variety of topics (including French culture and custom), French sayings and quips, are some of aids used to demonstrate rather than merely describe the language. Thorough yet surprisingly entertaining approach, excellent for teaching and for self study. Comprehensive analysis of pronunciation, practice exercises and appendices of verb tables, additional vocabulary, other useful material. Index. Appendix. 400 illustrations. 416pp. 5⅜ x 8½.
T268 Paperbound **$2.00**

DICTIONARY OF SPOKEN SPANISH, Spanish-English, English-Spanish. Compiled from spoken Spanish, emphasizing idiom and colloquial usage in both Castilian and Latin-American. More than 16,000 entries containing over 25,000 idioms—the largest list of idiomatic constructions ever published. Complete sentences given, indexed under single words—language in immediately useable form, for travellers, businessmen, students, etc. 25 page introduction provides rapid survey of sounds, grammar, syntax, with full consideration of irregular verbs. Especially apt in modern treatment of phrases and structure. 17 page glossary gives translations of geographical names, money values, numbers, national holidays, important street signs, useful expressions of high frequency, plus unique 7 page glossary of Spanish and Spanish-American foods and dishes. Originally published as War Department Technical Manual TM 30-900. iv + 513pp. 5⅜ x 8.
T495 Paperbound **$1.75**

SPEAK MY LANGUAGE: SPANISH FOR YOUNG BEGINNERS, M. Ahlman, Z. Gilbert. Records provide one of the best, and most entertaining, methods of introducing a foreign language to children. Within the framework of a train trip from Portugal to Spain, an English-speaking child is introduced to Spanish by a native companion. (Adapted from a successful radio program of the N. Y. State Educational Department.) Though a continuous story, there are a dozen specific categories of expressions, including greetings, numbers, time, weather, food, clothes, family members, etc. Drill is combined with poetry and contextual use. Authentic background music is heard. An accompanying book enables a reader to follow the records, and includes a vocabulary of over 350 recorded expressions. Two 10" 33⅓ records, total of 40 minutes. Book. 40 illustrations. 69pp. 5¼ x 10½.
T890 The set **$4.95**

AN ENGLISH-FRENCH-GERMAN-SPANISH WORD FREQUENCY DICTIONARY, H. S. Eaton. An indispensable language study aid, this is a semantic frequency list of the 6000 most frequently used words in 4 languages—24,000 words in all. The lists, based on concepts rather than words alone, and containing all modern, exact, and idiomatic vocabulary, are arranged side by side to form a unique 4-language dictionary. A simple key indicates the importance of the individual words within each language. Over 200 pages of separate indexes for each language enable you to locate individual words at a glance. Will help language teachers and students, authors of textbooks, grammars, and language tests to compare concepts in the various languages and to concentrate on basic vocabulary, avoiding uncommon and obsolete words. 2 Appendixes. xxi + 441pp. 6½ x 9¼.
T738 Paperbound **$2.45**

NEW RUSSIAN-ENGLISH AND ENGLISH-RUSSIAN DICTIONARY, M. A. O'Brien. Over 70,000 entries in the new orthography! Many idiomatic uses and colloquialisms which form the basis of actual speech. Irregular verbs, perfective and imperfective aspects, regular and irregular sound changes, and other features. One of the few dictionaries where accent changes within the conjugation of verbs and the declension of nouns are fully indicated. "One of the best," Prof. E. J. Simmons, Cornell. First names, geographical terms, bibliography, etc. 738pp. 4½ x 6¼.
T208 Paperbound **$2.00**

96 MOST USEFUL PHRASES FOR TOURISTS AND STUDENTS in English, French, Spanish, German, Italian. A handy folder you'll want to carry with you. How to say "Excuse me," "How much is it?", "Write it down, please," etc., in four foreign languages. Copies limited, no more than 1 to a customer.
FREE

CATALOGUE OF DOVER BOOKS

Say It language phrase books

These handy phrase books (128 to 196 pages each) make grammatical drills unnecessary for an elementary knowledge of a spoken foreign language. Covering most matters of travel and everyday life each volume contains:

Over 1000 phrases and sentences in immediately useful forms — foreign language plus English.

Modern usage designed for Americans. Specific phrases like, "Give me small change," and "Please call a taxi."

Simplified phonetic transcription you will be able to read at sight.

The only completely indexed phrase books on the market.

Covers scores of important situations: — Greetings, restaurants, sightseeing, useful expressions, etc.

These books are prepared by native linguists who are professors at Columbia, N.Y.U., Fordham and other great universities. Use them independently or with any other book or record course. They provide a supplementary living element that most other courses lack. Individual volumes in:

Russian 75¢	Italian 75¢	Spanish 75¢	German 75¢
Hebrew 75¢	Danish 75¢	Japanese 75¢	Swedish 75¢
Dutch 75¢	Esperanto 75¢	Modern Greek 75¢	Portuguese 75¢
Norwegian 75¢	Polish 75¢	French 75¢	Yiddish 75¢
Turkish 75¢		English for German-speaking people 75¢	
English for Italian-speaking people 75¢		English for Spanish-speaking people 75¢	

Large clear type. 128-196 pages each. 3½ x 5¼. Sturdy paper binding.

Listen and Learn language records

LISTEN & LEARN is the only language record course designed especially to meet your travel and everyday needs. It is available in separate sets for FRENCH, SPANISH, GERMAN, JAPANESE, RUSSIAN, MODERN GREEK, PORTUGUESE, ITALIAN and HEBREW, and each set contains three 33⅓ rpm long-playing records—1½ hours of recorded speech by eminent native speakers who are professors at Columbia, New York University, Queens College.

Check the following special features found only in LISTEN & LEARN:

- **Dual-language recording.** 812 selected phrases and sentences, over 3200 words, spoken first in English, then in their foreign language equivalents. A suitable pause follows each foreign phrase, allowing you time to repeat the expression. You learn by unconscious assimilation.
- **128 to 206-page manual** contains everything on the records, plus a simple phonetic pronunciation guide.
- **Indexed for convenience. The only set on the market** that is completely indexed. No more puzzling over where to find the phrase you need. Just look in the rear of the manual.
- **Practical.** No time wasted on material you can find in any grammar. LISTEN & LEARN covers central core material with phrase approach. Ideal for the person with limited learning time.
- **Living, modern expressions,** not found in other courses. Hygienic products, modern equipment, shopping—expressions used every day, like "nylon" and "air-conditioned."
- **Limited objective.** Everything you learn, no matter where you stop, is immediately useful. You have to finish other courses, wade through grammar and vocabulary drill, before they help you.
- **High-fidelity recording.** LISTEN & LEARN records equal in clarity and surface-silence any record on the market costing up to $6.

"Excellent . . . the spoken records . . . impress me as being among the very best on the market," **Prof. Mario Pei,** Dept. of Romance Languages, Columbia University. "Inexpensive and well-done . . . it would make an ideal present," CHICAGO SUNDAY TRIBUNE. "More genuinely helpful than anything of its kind which I have previously encountered," **Sidney Clark,** well-known author of "ALL THE BEST" travel books.

UNCONDITIONAL GUARANTEE. Try LISTEN & LEARN, then return it within 10 days for full refund if you are not satisfied.

Each set contains three twelve-inch 33⅓ records, manual, and album.

SPANISH	the set $5.95	GERMAN	the set $5.95
FRENCH	the set $5.95	ITALIAN	the set $5.95
RUSSIAN	the set $5.95	JAPANESE	the set $5.95
PORTUGUESE	the set $5.95	MODERN GREEK	the set $5.95
MODERN HEBREW	the set $5.95		

Trubner Colloquial Manuals

These unusual books are members of the famous Trubner series of colloquial manuals. They have been written to provide adults with a sound colloquial knowledge of a foreign language, and are suited for either class use or self-study. Each book is a complete course in itself, with progressive, easy to follow lessons. Phonetics, grammar, and syntax are covered, while hundreds of phrases and idioms, reading texts, exercises, and vocabulary are included. These books are unusual in being neither skimpy nor overdetailed in grammatical matters, and in presenting up-to-date, colloquial, and practical phrase material. Bilingual presentation is stressed, to make thorough self-study easier for the reader.

COLLOQUIAL HINDUSTANI, A. H. Harley, formerly Nizam's Reader in Urdu, U. of London. 30 pages on phonetics and scripts (devanagari & Arabic-Persian) are followed by 29 lessons, including material on English and Arabic-Persian influences. Key to all exercises. Vocabulary. 5 x 7½. 147pp.   Clothbound $1.75

COLLOQUIAL PERSIAN, L. P. Elwell-Sutton. Best introduction to modern Persian, with 90 page grammatical section followed by conversations, 35-page vocabulary. 139pp.
Clothbound $1.75

COLLOQUIAL ARABIC, DeLacy O'Leary. Foremost Islamic scholar covers language of Egypt, Syria, Palestine, & Northern Arabia. Extremely clear coverage of complex Arabic verbs & noun plurals; also cultural aspects of language. Vocabulary. xviii + 192pp. 5 x 7½.
Clothbound $2.50

COLLOQUIAL GERMAN, P. F. Doring. Intensive thorough coverage of grammar in easily-followed form. Excellent for brush-up, with hundreds of colloquial phrases. 34 pages of bilingual texts. 224pp. 5 x 7½.   Clothbound $1.75

COLLOQUIAL SPANISH, W. R. Patterson. Castilian grammar and colloquial language, loaded with bilingual phrases and colloquialisms. Excellent for review or self-study. 164pp. 5 x 7½.
Clothbound $1.75

COLLOQUIAL FRENCH, W. R. Patterson. 16th revision of this extremely popular manual. Grammar explained with model clarity, and hundreds of useful expressions and phrases; exercises, reading texts, etc. Appendixes of new and useful words and phrases. 223pp. 5 x 7½.
Clothbound $1.75

COLLOQUIAL CZECH, J. Schwarz, former headmaster of Lingua Institute, Prague. Full easily followed coverage of grammar, hundreds of immediately useable phrases, texts. Perhaps the best Czech grammar in print. "An absolutely successful textbook," JOURNAL OF CZECHO-SLOVAK FORCES IN GREAT BRITAIN. 252pp. 5 x 7½.   Clothbound $3.00

COLLOQUIAL RUMANIAN, G. Nandris, Professor of University of London. Extremely thorough coverage of phonetics, grammar, syntax; also included 70-page reader, and 70-page vocabulary. Probably the best grammar for this increasingly important language. 340pp. 5 x 7½.
Clothbound $2.50

COLLOQUIAL ITALIAN, A. L. Hayward. Excellent self-study course in grammar, vocabulary, idioms, and reading. Easy progressive lessons will give a good working knowledge of Italian in the shortest possible time. 5 x 7½.   Clothbound $1.75

COLLOQUIAL TURKISH, Yusuf Mardin. Very clear, thorough introduction to leading cultural and economic language of Near East. Begins with pronunciation and statement of vowel harmony, then 36 lessons present grammar, graded vocabulary, useful phrases, dialogues, reading, exercises. Key to exercises at rear. Turkish-English vocabulary. All in Roman alphabet. x + 288pp. 4¾ x 7¼.   Clothbound $4.00

DUTCH-ENGLISH AND ENGLISH-DUTCH DICTIONARY, F. G. Renier. For travel, literary, scientific or business Dutch, you will find this the most convenient, practical and comprehensive dictionary on the market. More than 60,000 entries, shades of meaning, colloquialisms, idioms, compounds and technical terms. Dutch and English strong and irregular verbs. This is the only dictionary in its size and price range that indicates the gender of nouns. New orthography. xvii + 571pp. 5½ x 6¼.   T224 Clothbound $2.75

LEARN DUTCH, F. G. Renier. This book is the most satisfactory and most easily used grammar of modern Dutch. The student is gradually led from simple lessons in pronunciation, through translation from and into Dutch, and finally to a mastery of spoken and written Dutch. Grammatical principles are clearly explained while a useful, practical vocabulary is introduced in easy exercises and readings. It is used and recommended by the Fulbright Committee in the Netherlands. Phonetic appendices. Over 1200 exercises; Dutch-English, English-Dutch vocabularies. 181pp. 4¼ x 7¼.   T441 Clothbound $2.25

Social Sciences

SOCIAL THOUGHT FROM LORE TO SCIENCE, H. E. Barnes and H. Becker. An immense survey of sociological thought and ways of viewing, studying, planning, and reforming society from earliest times to the present. Includes thought on society of preliterate peoples, ancient non-Western cultures, and every great movement in Europe, America, and modern Japan. Analyzes hundreds of great thinkers: Plato, Augustine, Bodin, Vico, Montesquieu, Herder, Comte, Marx, etc. Weighs the contributions of utopians, sophists, fascists and communists; economists, jurists, philosophers, ecclesiastics, and every 19th and 20th century school of scientific sociology, anthropology, and social psychology throughout the world. Combines topical, chronological, and regional approaches, treating the evolution of social thought as a process rather than as a series of mere topics. "Impressive accuracy, competence, and discrimination . . . easily the best single survey," Nation. Thoroughly revised, with new material up to 1960. 2 indexes. Over 2200 bibliographical notes. Three volume set. Total of 1586pp. 5⅜ x 8.

T901 Vol I   Paperbound **$2.50**
T902 Vol II Paperbound **$2.50**
T903 Vol III Paperbound **$2.50**
The set **$7.50**

FOLKWAYS, William Graham Sumner. A classic of sociology, a searching and thorough examination of patterns of behaviour from primitive, ancient Greek and Judaic, Medieval Christian, African, Oriental, Melanesian, Australian, Islamic, to modern Western societies. Thousands of illustrations of social, sexual, and religious customs, mores, laws, and institutions. Hundreds of categories: Labor, Wealth, Abortion, Primitive Justice, Life Policy, Slavery, Cannibalism, Uncleanness and the Evil Eye, etc. Will extend the horizon of every reader by showing the relativism of his own culture. Prefatory note by A. G. Keller. Introduction by William Lyon Phelps. Bibliography. Index. xiii + 692pp. 5⅜ x 8.   T508 Paperbound **$2.49**

PRIMITIVE RELIGION, P. Radin. A thorough treatment by a noted anthropologist of the nature and origin of man's belief in the supernatural and the influences that have shaped religious expression in primitive societies. Ranging from the Arunta, Ashanti, Aztec, Bushman, Crow, Fijian, etc., of Africa, Australia, Pacific Islands, the Arctic, North and South America, Prof. Radin integrates modern psychology, comparative religion, and economic thought with first-hand accounts gathered by himself and other scholars of primitive initiations, training of the shaman, and other fascinating topics. "Excellent," NATURE (London). Unabridged reissue of 1st edition. New author's preface. Bibliographic notes. Index. x + 322pp. 5⅜ x 8.
T393 Paperbound **$2.00**

PRIMITIVE MAN AS PHILOSOPHER, P. Radin. A standard anthropological work covering primitive thought on such topics as the purpose of life, marital relations, freedom of thought, symbolism, death, resignation, the nature of reality, personality, gods, and many others. Drawn from factual material gathered from the Winnebago, Oglala Sioux, Maori, Baganda, Batak, Zuni, among others, it does not distort ideas by removing them from context but interprets strictly within the original framework. Extensive selections of original primitive documents. Bibliography. Index. xviii + 402pp. 5⅜ x 8.   T392 Paperbound **$2.25**

A TREATISE ON SOCIOLOGY, THE MIND AND SOCIETY, Vilfredo Pareto. This treatise on human society is one of the great classics of modern sociology. First published in 1916, its careful catalogue of the innumerable manifestations of non-logical human conduct (Book One); the theory of "residues," leading to the premise that sentiment not logic determines human behavior (Book Two), and of "derivations," beliefs derived from desires (Book Three); and the general description of society made up of non-elite and elite, consisting of "foxes" who live by cunning and "lions" who live by force, stirred great controversy. But Pareto's passion for isolation and classification of elements and factors, and his allegiance to scientific method as the key tool for scrutinizing the human situation made his a truly twentieth-century mind and his work a catalytic influence on certain later social commentators. These four volumes (bound as two) require no special training to be appreciated and any reader who wishes to gain a complete understanding of modern sociological theory, regardless of special field of interest, will find them a must. Reprint of revised (corrected) printing of original edition. Translated by Andrew Bongiorno and Arthur Livingston. Index. Bibliography. Appendix containing index-summary of theorems. 48 diagrams. Four volumes bound as two. Total of 2063pp. 5⅜ x 8½.   The set Clothbound **$15.00**

THE POLISH PEASANT IN EUROPE AND AMERICA, William I. Thomas, Florian Znaniecki. A seminal sociological study of peasant primary groups (family and community) and the disruptions produced by a new industrial system and immigration to America. The peasant's family, class system, religious and aesthetic attitudes, and economic life are minutely examined and analyzed in hundreds of pages of primary documentation, particularly letters between family members. The disorientation caused by new environments is scrutinized in detail (a 312-page autobiography of an immigrant is especially valuable and revealing) in an attempt to find common experiences and reactions. The famous "Methodological Note" sets forth the principles which guided the authors. When out of print this set has sold for as much as $50. 2nd revised edition. 2 vols. Vol. 1: xv + 1115pp. Vol. 2: 1135pp. Index. 6 x 9.
T478 Clothbound 2 vol. set **$12.50**

Art, History of Art, Antiques, Graphic Arts, Handcrafts

ART STUDENTS' ANATOMY, E. J. Farris. Outstanding art anatomy that uses chiefly living objects for its illustrations. 71 photos of undraped men, women, children are accompanied by carefully labeled matching sketches to illustrate the skeletal system, articulations and movements, bony landmarks, the muscular system, skin, fasciae, fat, etc. 9 x-ray photos show movement of joints. Undraped models are shown in such actions as serving in tennis, drawing a bow in archery, playing football, dancing, preparing to spring and to dive. Also discussed and illustrated are proportions, age and sex differences, the anatomy of the smile, etc. 8 plates by the great early 18th century anatomic illustrator Siegfried Albinus are also included. Glossary. 158 figures, 7 in color. x + 159pp. 5⅝ x 8⅜.　　　　　　T744 Paperbound **$1.50**

AN ATLAS OF ANATOMY FOR ARTISTS, F Schider. A new 3rd edition of this standard text enlarged by 52 new illustrations of hands, anatomical studies by Cloquet, and expressive life studies of the body by Barcsay. 189 clear, detailed plates offer you precise information of impeccable accuracy. 29 plates show all aspects of the skeleton, with closeups of special areas, while 54 full-page plates, mostly in two colors, give human musculature as seen from four different points of view, with cutaways for important portions of the body. 14 full-page plates provide photographs of hand forms, eyelids, female breasts, and indicate the location of muscles upon models. 59 additional plates show how great artists of the past utilized human anatomy. They reproduce sketches and finished work by such artists as Michelangelo, Leonardo da Vinci, Goya, and 15 others. This is a lifetime reference work which will be one of the most important books in any artist's library. "The standard reference tool," AMERICAN LIBRARY ASSOCIATION. "Excellent," AMERICAN ARTIST. Third enlarged edition. 189 plates, 647 illustrations. xxvi + 192pp. 7⅞ x 10⅝.　　　T241 Clothbound **$6.00**

AN ATLAS OF ANIMAL ANATOMY FOR ARTISTS, W. Ellenberger, H. Baum, H. Dittrich. The largest, richest animal anatomy for artists available in English. 99 detailed anatomical plates of such animals as the horse, dog, cat, lion, deer, seal, kangaroo, flying squirrel, cow, bull, goat, monkey, hare, and bat. Surface features are clearly indicated, while progressive beneath-the-skin pictures show musculature, tendons, and bone structure. Rest and action are exhibited in terms of musculature and skeletal structure and detailed cross-sections are given for heads and important features. The animals chosen are representative of specific families so that a study of these anatomies will provide knowledge of hundreds of related species. "Highly recommended as one of the very few books on the subject worthy of being used as an authoritative guide," DESIGN. "Gives a fundamental knowledge," AMERICAN ARTIST. Second revised, enlarged edition with new plates from Cuvier, Stubbs, etc. 288 illustrations. 153pp. 11⅜ x 9.　　　　　　　　　　　　　　T82 Clothbound **$6.00**

THE HUMAN FIGURE IN MOTION, Eadweard Muybridge. The largest selection in print of Muybridge's famous high-speed action photos of the human figure in motion. 4789 photographs illustrate 162 different actions: men, women, children—mostly undraped—are shown walking, running, carrying various objects, sitting, lying down, climbing, throwing, arising, and performing over 150 other actions. Some actions are shown in as many as 150 photographs each. All in all there are more than 500 action strips in this enormous volume, series shots taken at shutter speeds of as high as 1/6000th of a second! These are not posed shots, but true stopped motion. They show bone and muscle in situations that the human eye is not fast enough to capture. Earlier, smaller editions of these prints have brought $40 and more on the out-of-print market. "A must for artists," ART IN FOCUS. "An unparalleled dictionary of action for all artists," AMERICAN ARTIST. 390 full-page plates, with 4789 photographs. Printed on heavy glossy stock. Reinforced binding with headbands. xxi + 390pp. 7⅞ x 10⅝.
　　　　　　　　　　　　　　　　　　　　　　　　　T204 Clothbound **$10.00**

ANIMALS IN MOTION, Eadweard Muybridge. This is the largest collection of animal action photos in print. 34 different animals (horses, mules, oxen, goats, camels, pigs, cats, guanacos, lions, gnus, deer, monkeys, eagles—and 21 others) in 132 characteristic actions. The horse alone is shown in more than 40 different actions. All 3919 photographs are taken in series at speeds up to 1/6000th of a second. The secrets of leg motion, spinal patterns, head movements, strains and contortions shown nowhere else are captured. You will see exactly how a lion sets his foot down; how an elephant's knees are like a human's—and how they differ; the position of a kangaroo's legs in mid-leap; how an ostrich's head bobs; details of the flight of birds—and thousands of facets of motion only the fastest cameras can catch. Photographed from domestic animals and animals in the Philadelphia zoo, it contains neither semiposed artificial shots nor distorted telephoto shots taken under adverse conditions. Artists, biologists, decorators, cartoonists, will find this book indispensable for understanding animals in motion. "A really marvelous series of plates," NATURE (London). "The dry plate's most spectacular early use was by Eadweard Muybridge," LIFE. 3919 photographs; 380 full pages of plates. 440pp. Printed on heavy glossy paper. Deluxe binding with headbands. 7⅞ x 10⅝.　　　　　　　　　　　　　　　　　　T203 Clothbound **$10.00**

ART ANATOMY, William Rimmer, M.D. Often called one of America's foremost contributions to art instruction, a work of art in its own right. More than 700 line drawings by the author, first-rate anatomist and dissector as well as artist, with a non-technical anatomical text. Impeccably accurate drawings of muscles, skeletal structure, surface features, other aspects of males and females, children, adults and aged persons show not only form, size, insertion and articulation but personality and emotion as reflected by physical features usually ignored in modern anatomical works. Complete unabridged reproduction of 1876 edition slightly rearranged. Introduction by Robert Hutchinson. 722 illustrations. xiii + 153pp. 7¾ x 10¾.
T908 Paperbound **$2.00**

ANIMAL DRAWING: ANATOMY AND ACTION FOR ARTISTS, C. R. Knight. The author and illustrator of this work was "the most distinguished painter of animal life." This extensive course in animal drawing discusses musculature, bone structure, animal psychology, movements, habits, habitats. Innumerable tips on proportions, light and shadow play, coloring, hair formation, feather arrangement, scales, how animals lie down, animal expressions, etc., from great apes to birds. Pointers on avoiding gracelessness in horses, deer; on introducing proper power and bulk to heavier animals; on giving proper grace and subtle expression to members of the cat family. Originally titled "Animal Anatomy and Psychology for the Artist and Layman." Over 123 illustrations. 149pp. 8¼ x 10½.
T426 Paperbound **$2.00**

DESIGN FOR ARTISTS AND CRAFTSMEN, L. Wolchonok. The most thorough course ever prepared on the creation of art motifs and designs. It teaches you to create your own designs out of things around you — from geometric patterns, plants, birds, animals, humans, landscapes, and man-made objects. It leads you step by step through the creation of more than 1300 designs, and shows you how to create design that is fresh, well-founded, and original. Mr. Wolchonok, whose text is used by scores of art schools, shows you how the same idea can be developed into many different forms, ranging from near representationalism to the most advanced forms of abstraction. The material in this book is entirely new, and combines full awareness of traditional design with the work of such men as Miro, Léger, Picasso, Moore, and others. 113 detailed exercises, with instruction hints, diagrams, and details to enable you to apply Wolchonok's methods to your own work. "A great contribution to the field of design and crafts," N. Y. SOCIETY OF CRAFTSMEN. More than 1300 illustrations. xv + 207pp. 7⅞ x 10¾.
T274 Clothbound **$4.95**

HAWTHORNE ON PAINTING. A vivid recreation, from students' notes, of instruction by Charles W. Hawthorne, given for over 31 years at his famous Cape Cod School of Art. Divided into sections on the outdoor model, still life, landscape, the indoor model, and water color, each section begins with a concise essay, followed by epigrammatic comments on color, form, seeing, etc. Not a formal course, but comments of a great teacher-painter on specific student works, which will solve problems in your own painting and understanding of art. "An excellent introduction for laymen and students alike," Time. Introduction. 100pp. 5⅜ x 8.
T653 Paperbound **$1.00**

THE ENJOYMENT AND USE OF COLOR, Walter Sargent. This book explains fascinating relations among colors, between colors in nature and art; describes experiments that you can perform to understand these relations more thoroughly; points out hundreds of little known facts about color values, intensities, effects of high and low illumination, complementary colors, color harmonies. Practical hints for painters, references to techniques of masters, questions at chapter ends for self-testing all make this a valuable book for artists, professional and amateur, and for general readers interested in world of color. Republication of 1923 edition. 35 illustrations, 6 full-page plates. New color frontispiece. Index. xii + 274pp. 5⅜ x 8.
T944 Paperbound **$2.25**

DECORATIVE ALPHABETS AND INITIALS, ed. by Alexander Nesbitt. No payment, no permission needed to reproduce any one of these 3924 different letters, covering 1000 years. Crisp, clear letters all in line, from Anglo-Saxon mss., Luebeck Cathedral, 15th century Augsburg; the work of Dürer, Holbein, Cresci, Beardsley, Rossing Wadsworth, John Moylin, etc. Every imaginable style. 91 complete alphabets. 123 full-page plates. 192pp. 7¾ x 10¾.
T544 Paperbound **$2.25**

THREE CLASSICS OF ITALIAN CALLIGRAPHY, edited by Oscar Ogg. Here, combined in a single volume, are complete reproductions of three famous calligraphic works written by the greatest writing masters of the Renaissance: Arrighi's OPERINA and IL MODO, Tagliente's LO PRESENTE LIBRO, and Palatino's LIBRO NUOVO. These books present more than 200 complete alphabets and thousands of lettered specimens. The basic hand is Papal Chancery, but scores of other alphabets are also given: European and Asiatic local alphabets, foliated and art alphabets, scrolls, cartouches, borders, etc. Text is in Italian. Introduction. 245 plates. x + 272pp. 6⅛ x 9¼.
T212 Paperbound **$2.25**

CALLIGRAPHY, J. G. Schwandner. One of the legendary books in the graphic arts, copies of which brought $500 each on the rare book market, now reprinted for the first time in over 200 years. A beautiful plate book of graceful calligraphy, and an inexhaustible source of first-rate material copyright-free, for artists, and directors, craftsmen, commercial artists, etc. More than 300 ornamental initials forming 12 complete alphabets, over 150 ornate frames and panels, over 200 flourishes, over 75 calligraphic pictures including a temple, cherubs, cocks, dodos, stags, chamois, foliated lions, greyhounds, etc. Thousand of calligraphic elements to be used for suggestions of quality, sophistication, antiquity, and sheer beauty. Historical introduction. 158 full-page plates. 368pp. 9 x 13.
T475 Clothbound **$10.00**

CATALOGUE OF DOVER BOOKS

THE HISTORY AND TECHNIQUE OF LETTERING, A. Nesbitt. The only thorough inexpensive history of letter forms from the point of view of the artist. Mr. Nesbitt covers every major development in lettering from the ancient Egyptians to the present and illustrates each development with a complete alphabet. Such masters as Baskerville, Bell, Bodoni, Caslon, Koch, Kilian, Morris, Garamont, Jenson, and dozens of others are analyzed in terms of artistry and historical development. The author also presents a 65-page practical course in lettering, besides the full historical text. 89 complete alphabets; 165 additional lettered specimens. xvii + 300pp. 5⅜ x 8.   T427 Paperbound **$2.00**

FOOT-HIGH LETTERS: A GUIDE TO LETTERING (A PRACTICAL SYLLABUS FOR TEACHERS), M. Price. A complete alphabet of Classic Roman letters, each a foot high, each on a separate 16 x 22 plate—perfect for use in lettering classes. In addition to an accompanying description, each plate also contains 9 two-inch-high forms of letter in various type faces, such as "Caslon," "Empire," "Onyx," and "Neuland," illustrating the many possible derivations from the standard classical forms. One plate contains 21 additional forms of the letter A. The fully illustrated 16-page syllabus by Mr. Price, formerly of the Pratt Institute and the Rhode Island School of Design, contains dozens of useful suggestions for student and teacher alike. An indispensable teaching aid. Extensively revised. 16-page syllabus and 30 plates in slip cover, 16 x 22.   T239 Clothbound **$6.00**

THE STYLES OF ORNAMENT, Alexander Speltz. Largest collection of ornaments in print— 3765 illustrations of prehistoric, Lombard, Gothic, Frank, Romanesque, Mohammedan, Renaissance, Polish, Swiss, Rococo, Sheraton, Empire, U. S. Colonial, etc., ornament. Gargoyles, dragons, columns, necklaces, urns, friezes, furniture, buildings, keyholes, tapestries, fantastic animals, armor, religious objects, much more, all in line. Reproduce any one free. Index. Bibliography. 400 plates. 656pp. 5⅝ x 8⅜.   T557 Paperbound **$2.50**

HANDBOOK OF DESIGNS AND DEVICES, C. P. Hornung. This unique book is indispensable to the designer, commercial artist, and hobbyist. It is not a textbook but a working collection of 1836 basic designs and variations, carefully reproduced, which may be used without permission. Variations of circle, line, band, triangle, square, cross, diamond, swastika, pentagon, octagon, hexagon, star, scroll, interlacement, shields, etc. Supplementary notes on the background and symbolism of the figures. "A necessity to every designer who would be original without having to labor heavily," ARTIST AND ADVERTISER. 204 plates. 240pp. 5⅜ x 8.
                                                        T125 Paperbound **$2.00**

THE UNIVERSAL PENMAN, George Bickham. This beautiful book, which first appeared in 1743, is the largest collection of calligraphic specimens, flourishes, alphabets, and calligraphic illustrations ever published. 212 full-page plates are drawn from the work of such 18th century masters of English roundhand as Dove, Champion, Bland, and 20 others. They contain 22 complete alphabets, over 2,000 flourishes, and 122 illustrations, each drawn with a stylistic grace impossible to describe. This book is invaluable to anyone interested in the beauties of calligraphy, or to any artist, hobbyist, or craftsman who wishes to use the very best ornamental handwriting and flourishes for decorative purposes. Commercial artists, advertising artists, have found it unexcelled as a source of material suggesting quality. "An essential part of any art library, and a book of permanent value," AMERICAN ARTIST. 212 plates. 224pp. 9 x 13¾.   T20 Clothbound **$10.00**

1800 WOODCUTS BY THOMAS BEWICK AND HIS SCHOOL. Prepared by Dover's editorial staff, this is the largest collection of woodcuts by Bewick and his school ever compiled. Contains the complete engravings from all his major works and a wide range of illustrations from lesser-known collections, all photographed from clear copies of the original books and reproduced in line. Carefully and conveniently organized into sections on Nature (animals and birds, scenery and landscapes, plants, insects, etc.), People (love and courtship, social life, school and domestic scenes, misfortunes, costumes, etc.), Business and Trade, and illustrations from primers, fairytales, spelling books, frontispieces, borders, fables and allegories, etc. In addition to technical proficiency and simple beauty, Bewick's work is remarkable as a mode of pictorial symbolism, reflecting rustic tranquility, an atmosphere of rest, simplicity, idyllic contentment. A delight for the eye, an inexhaustible source of illustrative material for art studios, commercial artists, advertising agencies. Individual illustrations (up to 10 for any one use) are copyright free. Classified index. Bibliography and sources. Introduction by Robert Hutchinson. 1800 woodcuts. xiv + 247pp. 9 x 12.
                                                        T766 Clothbound **$10.00**

A HANDBOOK OF EARLY ADVERTISING ART, C. P. Hornung. The largest collection of copyright-free early advertising art ever compiled. Vol. I contains some 2,000 illustrations of agricultural devices, animals, old automobiles, birds, buildings, Christmas decorations (with 7 Santa Clauses by Nast), allegorical figures, fire engines, horses and vehicles, Indians, portraits, sailing ships, trains, sports, trade cuts — and 30 other categories! Vol. II, devoted to typography, has over 4000 specimens: 600 different Roman, Gothic, Barnum, Old English faces; 630 ornamental type faces; 1115 initials, hundreds of scrolls, flourishes, etc. This third edition is enlarged by 78 additional plates containing all new material. "A remarkable collection," PRINTERS' INK. "A rich contribution to the history of American design," GRAPHIS. Volume I, Pictorial. Over 2000 illustrations. xiv + 242pp. 9 x 12.   T122 Clothbound **$10.00**
Volume II, Typographical. Over 4000 specimens. vii + 312pp. 9 x 12. T123 Clothbound **$10.00**
Two volume set, T121 Clothbound, only **$18.50**

THE 100 GREATEST ADVERTISEMENTS, WHO WROTE THEM AND WHAT THEY DID, J. L. Watkins. 100 (plus 13 added for this edition) of most successful ads ever to appear. "Do You Make These Mistakes in English," "They laughed when I sat down," "A Hog Can Cross the Country," "The Man in the Hathaway Shirt," over 100 more ads that changed habits of a nation, gave new expressions to the language, built reputations. Also salient facts behind ads, often in words of their creators. "Useful . . . valuable . . . enlightening," Printers' Ink. 2nd revised edition. Introduction. Foreword by Raymond Rubicam. Index. 130 illustrations. 252pp. 7¾ x 10¾. T540 Paperbound **$2.50**

THE DIDEROT PICTORIAL ENCYCLOPEDIA OF TRADES AND INDUSTRY, MANUFACTURING AND THE TECHNICAL ARTS IN PLATES SELECTED FROM "L'ENCYCLOPEDIE OU DICTIONNAIRE RAISONNE DES SCIENCES, DES ARTS, ET DES METIERS" OF DENIS DIDEROT, edited with text by C. Gillispie. The first modern selection of plates from the high point of 18th century French engraving, Diderot's famous Encyclopedia. Over 2000 illustrations on 485 full-page plates, most of them original size, illustrating the trades and industries of one of the most fascinating periods of modern history, 18th century France. These magnificent engravings provide an invaluable source of fresh, copyright-free material to artists and illustrators, a lively and accurate social document to students of cultures, an outstanding find to the lover of fine engravings. The plates teem with life, with men, women, and children performing all of the thousands of operations necessary to the trades before and during the early stages of the industrial revolution. Plates are in sequence, and show general operations, closeups of difficult operations, and details of complex machinery. Such important and interesting trades and industries are illustrated as sowing, harvesting, beekeeping, cheesemaking, operating windmills, milling flour, charcoal burning, tobacco processing, indigo, fishing, arts of war, salt extraction, mining, smelting iron, casting iron steel, extracting mercury, zinc, sulphur, copper, etc., slating, tinning, silverplating, gilding, making gunpowder, cannons, bells, shoeing horses, tanning, papermaking, printing, dying, and more than 40 other categories. Besides being a work of remarkable beauty and skill, this is also one of the largest collections of working figures in print. 920pp. 9 x 12. Heavy library cloth. T421 Two volume set **$18.50**

THE HANDBOOK OF PLANT AND FLORAL ORNAMENT, R. G. Hatton. One of the truly great collections of plant drawings for reproduction: 1200 different figures of flowering or fruiting plants—line drawings that will reproduce excellently. Selected from superb woodcuts and copperplate engravings appearing mostly in 16th and 17th century herbals including the fabulously rare "Kreuter Büch" (Bock) "Cruijde Boeck" (Dodoens), etc. Plants classified according to botanical groups. Also excellent reading for anyone interested in home gardening or any phase of horticulture. Formerly "The Craftsman's Plant-Book: or Figures of Plants." Introductions. Over 1200 illustrations. Index. 548pp. 6⅛ x 9¼. T649 Paperbound **$3.00**

HANDBOOK OF ORNAMENT, F. S. Meyer. One of the largest collections of copyright-free traditional art in print. It contains over 3300 line cuts from Greek, Roman, Medieval, Islamic, Renaissance, Baroque, 18th and 19th century sources. 180 plates illustrate elements of design with networks, Gothic tracery, geometric elements, flower and animal motifs, etc., while 100 plates illustrate decorative objects: chairs, thrones, daises, cabinets, crowns, weapons, utensils, vases, jewelry, armor, heraldry, bottles, altars, and scores of other objects. Indispensable for artists, illustrators, designers, handicrafters, etc. Full text. 3300 illustrations. xiv + 548pp. 5⅜ x 8. T302 Paperbound **$2.50**

COSTUMES OF THE GREEKS AND ROMANS, Thomas Hope. Authentic costumes from all walks of life in Roman, Greek civilizations, including Phrygia, Egypt, Persia, Parthia, Etruria, in finely drawn, detailed engravings by Thomas Hope (1770-1831). Scores of additional engravings of ancient musical instruments, furniture, jewelry, sarcophagi, other adjuncts to ancient life. All carefully copied from ancient vases and statuary. Textual introduction by author. Art and advertising personnel, costume and stage designers, students of fashion design will find these copyright-free engravings a source of ideas and inspiration and a valuable reference. Republication df 1st (1812) edition. 300 full-page plates, over 700 illustrations. xliv + 300pp. 5⅝ x 8⅜. T21 Paperbound **$2.00**

PRINCIPLES OF ART HISTORY, H. Wölfflin. Analyzing such terms as "baroque," "classic," "neoclassic," "primitive," "picturesque," and 164 different works by artists like Botticelli, van Cleve, Dürer, Hobbema, Holbein, Hals, Rembrandt, Titian, Brueghel, Vermeer, and many others, the author establishes the classifications of art history and style on a firm, concrete basis. This classic of art criticism shows what really occurred between the 14th century primitives and the sophistication of the 18th century in terms of basic attitudes and philosophies. "A remarkable lesson in the art of seeing," SAT. REV. OF LITERATURE. Translated from the 7th German edition. 150 illustrations. 254pp. 6⅛ x 9¼. T276 Paperbound **$2.00**

AFRICAN SCULPTURE, Ladislas Segy. First publication of a new book by the author of critically acclaimed AFRICAN SCULPTURE SPEAKS. It contains 163 full-page plates illustrating masks, fertility figures, ceremonial objects, etc., representing the culture of 50 tribes of West and Central Africa. Over 85% of these works of art have never been illustrated before, and each is an authentic and fascinating tribal artifact. A 34-page introduction explains the anthropological, psychological, and artistic values of African sculpture. "Mr. Segy is one of its top authorities," NEW YORKER. 164 full-page photographic plates. Bibliography. 244pp. 6 x 9. T396 Paperbound **$2.00**

DESIGN MOTIFS OF ANCIENT MEXICO, J. Enciso. This unique collection of pre-Columbian stamps for textiles and pottery contains 766 superb designs from Aztec, Olmec, Totonac, Maya, and Toltec origins. Plumed serpents, calendrical elements, wind gods, animals, flowers, demons, dancers, monsters, abstract ornament, and other designs. More than 90% of these illustrations are completely unobtainable elsewhere. Use this work to bring new barbaric beauty into your crafts or drawing. Originally $17.50. Printed in three colors. 766 illustrations, thousands of motifs. 192pp. 7⅞ x 10¾. **T84 Paperbound $1.85**

DECORATIVE ART OF THE SOUTHWEST INDIANS, D. S. Sides. A magnificent album of authentic designs (both pre- and post-Conquest) from the pottery, textiles, and basketry of the Navaho, Hopi, Mohave, Santo Domingo, and over 20 other Southwestern groups. Designs include birds, clouds, butterflies, quadrupeds, geometric forms, etc. A valuable book for folklorists, and a treasury for artists, designers, advertisers, and craftsmen, who may use without payment or permission any of the vigorous, colorful, and strongly rhythmic designs. Aesthetic and archeological notes. 50 plates. Bibliography of over 50 items. xviii + 101pp. 5⅝ x 8⅜. **T139 Paperbound $1.00**

PAINTING IN THE FAR EAST, Laurence Binyon. Excellent introduction by one of greatest authorities on subject studies 1500 years of oriental art (China, Japan; also Tibet, Persia), over 250 painters. Examines works, schools, influence of Wu Tao-tzu, Kanaoka, Toba Sojo, Masanobu, Okio, etc.; early traditions; Kamakura epoch; the Great Decorators; T'ang Dynasty; Matabei, beginnings of genre; Japanese woodcut, color print; much more, all chronological, in cultural context. 42 photos. Bibliography. 317pp. 6 x 9¼. **T520 Paperbound $2.25**

ON THE LAWS OF JAPANESE PAINTING, H. Bowie. This unusual book, based on 9 years of profound study-experience in the Late Kano art of Japan, remains the most authentic guide in English to the spirit and technique of Japanese painting. A wealth of interesting and useful data on control of the brush; practise exercises; manufacture of ink, brushes, colors; the use of various lines and dots to express moods. It is the best possible substitute for a series of lessons from a great oriental master. 66 plates with 220 illustrations. Index. xv + 177pp. 6⅛ x 9¼. **T30 Paperbound $2.00**

THE MATERIALS AND TECHNIQUES OF MEDIEVAL PAINTING, D. V. Thompson. Based on years of study of medieval manuscripts and laboratory analysis of medieval paintings, this book discusses carriers and grounds, binding media, pigments, metals used in painting, etc. Considers relative merits of painting al fresco and al secco, the procession of coloring materials, burnishing, and many other matters. Preface by Bernard Berenson. Index. 239pp. 5⅜ x 8. **T327 Paperbound $1.85**

THE CRAFTSMAN'S HANDBOOK, Cennino Cennini. This is considered the finest English translation of IL LIBRO DELL' ARTE, a 15th century Florentine introduction to art technique. It is both fascinating reading and a wonderful mirror of another culture for artists, art students, historians, social scientists, or anyone interested in details of life some 500 years ago. While it is not an exact recipe book, it gives directions for such matters as tinting papers, gilding stone, preparation of various hues of black, and many other useful but nearly forgotten facets of the painter's art. As a human document reflecting the ideas of a practising medieval artist it is particularly important. 4 illustrations. xxvii + 142pp. D. V. Thompson translator. 6⅛ x 9¼. **T54 Paperbound $1.35**

VASARI ON TECHNIQUE, G. Vasari. Pupil of Michelangelo and outstanding biographer of the Renaissance artists, Vasari also wrote this priceless treatise on the technical methods of the painters, architects, and sculptors of his day. This is the only English translation of this practical, informative, and highly readable work. Scholars, artists, and general readers will welcome these authentic discussions of marble statues, bronze casting, fresco painting, oil painting, engraving, stained glass, rustic fountains and grottoes, etc. Introduction and notes by G. B. Brown. Index. 18 plates, 11 figures. xxiv + 328pp. 5⅜ x 8. **T717 Paperbound $2.25**

METHODS AND MATERIALS OF PAINTING OF THE GREAT SCHOOLS AND MASTERS, C. L. Eastlake. A vast, complete, and authentic reconstruction of the secret techniques of the masters of painting, collected from hundreds of forgotten manuscripts by the eminent President of the British Royal Academy: Greek, Roman, and medieval techniques; fresco and tempera; varnishes and encaustics; the secrets of Leonardo, Van Eyck, Raphael, and many others. Art historians, students, teachers, critics, and laymen will gain new insights into the creation of the great masterpieces; while artists and craftsmen will have a treasury of valuable techniques. Index. Two volume set. Total of 1025pp. 5⅜ x 8. **T718 Paperbound $2.25**
T719 Paperbound $2.25
The set $4.50

BYZANTINE ART AND ARCHAEOLOGY, O. M. Dalton. Still the most thorough work in English—both in breadth and in depth—on the astounding multiplicity of Byzantine art forms throughout Europe, North Africa, and Western Asia from the 4th to the 15th century. Analyzes hundreds of individual pieces from over 160 public and private museums, libraries, and collections all over the world. Full treatment of Byzantine sculpture, painting, mosaic, jewelry, textiles, etc., including historical development, symbolism, and aesthetics. Chapters on iconography and ornament. Indispensable for study of Christian symbolism and medieval art. 457 illustrations, many full-page. Bibliography of over 2500 references. 4 Indexes. xx + 727pp. 6⅛ x 9¼. **T776 Clothbound $8.50**

METALWORK AND ENAMELLING, H. Maryon. This is probably the best book ever written on the subject. Prepared by Herbert Maryon, F.S.A., of the British Museum, it tells everything necessary for home manufacture of jewelry, rings, ear pendants, bowls, and dozens of other objects. Clearly written chapters provide precise information on such topics as materials, tools, soldering, filigree, setting stones, raising patterns, spinning metal, repoussé work, hinges and joints, metal inlaying, damascening, overlaying, niello, Japanese alloys, enamelling, cloisonné, painted enamels, casting, polishing, coloring, assaying, and dozens of other techniques. This is the next best thing to apprenticeship to a master metalworker. 363 photographs and figures. 374pp. 5½ x 8½. T183 Clothbound **$8.50**

SILK SCREEN TECHNIQUES, J. I. Biegeleisen, Max A. Cohn. A complete-to-the-last-detail copiously illustrated home course in this fast growing modern art form. Full directions for building silk screen out of inexpensive materials; explanations of five basic methods of stencil preparation—paper, blockout, tusche, film, photographic—and effects possible: light and shade, washes, dry brush, oil paint type impastos, gouaches, pastels. Detailed coverage of multicolor printing, illustrated by proofs showing the stages of a 4 color print. Special section on common difficulties. 149 illustrations, 8 in color. Sources of supply. xiv + 187pp. 6⅛ x 9¼. T433 Paperbound **$1.75**

A HANDBOOK OF WEAVES, G. H. Oelsner. Now back in print! Probably the most complete book of weaves ever printed, fully explained, differentiated, and illustrated. Includes plain weaves; irregular, double-stitched, and filling satins; derivative, basket, and rib weaves; steep, undulating, broken, offset, corkscrew, interlocking, herringbone, and fancy twills; honeycomb, lace, and crepe weaves; tricot, matelassé, and montagnac weaves; and much more. Translated and revised by S. S. Dale, with supplement on the analysis of weaves and fabrics. 1875 illustrations. vii + 402pp. 6 x 9¼. T209 Clothbound **$5.00**

BASIC BOOKBINDING, A. W. Lewis. Enables the beginner and the expert to apply the latest and most simplified techniques to rebinding old favorites and binding new paperback books. Complete lists of all necessary materials and guides to the selection of proper tools, paper, glue, boards, cloth, leather, or sheepskin covering fabrics, lettering inks and pigments, etc. You are shown how to collate a book, sew it, back it, trim it, make boards and attach them in easy step-by-step stages. Author's preface. 261 illustrations with appendix. Index. xi + 144pp. 5⅜ x 8. T169 Paperbound **$1.45**

BASKETRY, F. J. Christopher. Basic introductions cover selection of materials, use and care of tools, equipment. Easy-to-follow instructions for preparation of oval, oblong trays, lidded baskets, rush mats, tumbler holders, bicycle baskets, waste paper baskets, many other useful, beautiful articles made of coiled and woven reed, willow, rushes, raffia. Special sections present in clear, simple language and numerous illustrations all the how-to information you could need: linings, skein wire, varieties of stitching, simplified construction of handles, dying processes. For beginner and skilled craftsman alike. Edited by Majorie O'Shaugnessy. Bibliography. Sources of supply. Index. 112 illustrations. 108pp. 5 x 7¼. T903 Paperbound $1.00

THE ART OF ETCHING, E. S. Lumsden. Everything you need to know to do etching yourself. First two sections devoted to technique of etching and engraving, covering such essentials as relative merits of zinc and copper, cleaning and grounding plates, gravers, acids, arrangement of etching-room, methods of biting, types of inks and oils, mounting, stretching and framing, preserving and restoring plates, size and color of printing papers, much more. A review of the history of the art includes separate chapters on Dürer and Lucas van Leyden, Rembrandt and Van Dyck, Goya, Meryon, Haden and Whistler, British masters of nineteenth century, modern etchers. Final section is a collection of prints by contemporary etchers with comments by the artists. Professional etchers and engravers will find this a highly useful source of examples. Beginners and teachers, students of art and printing will find it a valuable tool. Index. 208 illustrations. 384pp. 5⅜ x 8. T49 Paperbound **$2.50**

WHITTLING AND WOODCARVING, E. J. Tangerman. What to make and how to make it for even a moderately handy beginner. One of the few works that bridge gap between whittling and serious carving. History of the art, background information on selection and use of woods, grips, types of strokes and cuts, handling of tools and chapters on rustic work, flat toys and windmills, puzzles, chains, ships in bottle, nested spheres, fans, more than 100 useful, entertaining objects. Second half covers carving proper: woodcuts, low relief, sculpture in the round, lettering, inlay and marquetry, indoor and outdoor decorations, pierced designs, much more. Final chapter describes finishing, care of tools. Sixth edition. Index. 464 illustrations. x + 239pp. 5½ x 8⅛. T965 Paperbound **$1.75**

THE PRACTICE OF TEMPERA PAINTING, Daniel V. Thompson, Jr. A careful exposition of all aspects of tempera painting, including sections on many possible modern uses, propensities of various woods, choice of material for panel, making and applying the gesso, pigments and brushes, technique of the actual painting, gilding and so on—everything one need know to try a hand at this proven but neglected art. The author is unquestionably the world's leading authority on tempera methods and processes and his treatment is based on exhaustive study of manuscript material. Drawings and diagrams increase clarity of text. No one interested in tempera painting can afford to be without this book. Appendix, "Tempera Practice in Yale Art School," by Lewis E. York. 85 illustrations by York; 4 full-page plates. ix x 149pp. 5⅜ x 8½. T343 Paperbound **$1.50**

SHAKER FURNITURE, E. D. Andrews and F. Andrews. The most illuminating study on what many scholars consider the best examples of functional furniture ever made. Includes the history of the sect and the development of Shaker style. The 48 magnificent plates show tables, chairs, cupboards, chests, boxes, desks, beds, woodenware, and much more, and are accompanied by detailed commentary. For all antique collectors and dealers, designers and decorators, historians and folklorists. "Distinguished in scholarship, in pictorial illumination, and in all the essentials of fine book making," Antiques. 3 Appendixes. Bibliography. Index. 192pp. 7⅞ x 10¾.   T679 Paperbound **$2.00**

JAPANESE HOMES AND THEIR SURROUNDINGS, E. S. Morse. Every aspect of the purely traditional Japanese home, from general plan and major structural features to ceremonial and traditional appointments—tatami, hibachi, shoji, tokonoma, etc. The most exhaustive discussion in English, this book is equally honored for its strikingly modern conception of architecture. First published in 1886, before the contamination of the Japanese traditions, it preserves the authentic features of an ideal of construction that is steadily gaining devotees in the Western world. 307 illustrations by the author. Index. Glossary. xxxvi + 372pp. 5⅝ x 8⅜.   T746 Paperbound **$2.25**

COLONIAL LIGHTING, Arthur H. Hayward. The largest selection of antique lamps ever illustrated anywhere, from rush light-holders of earliest settlers to 1880's—with main emphasis on Colonial era. Primitive attempts at illumination ("Betty" lamps, variations of open wick design, candle molds, reflectors, etc.), whale oil lamps, painted and japanned hand lamps, Sandwich glass candlesticks, astral lamps, Bennington ware and chandeliers of wood, iron, pewter, brass, crystal, bronze and silver. Hundreds of illustrations, loads of information on colonial life, customs, habits, place of acquisition of lamps illustrated. A unique, thoroughgoing survey of an interesting aspect of Americana. Enlarged (1962) edition. New Introduction by James R. Marsh. Supplement "Colonial Chandeliers," photographs with descriptive notes. 169 illustrations, 647 lamps. xxxi + 312pp. 5⅝ x 8¼.   T975 Paperbound **$2.00**

CHINESE HOUSEHOLD FURNITURE, George N. Kates. The first book-length study of authentic Chinese domestic furniture in Western language. Summarises practically everything known about Chinese furniture in pure state, uninfluenced by West. History of style, unusual woods used, craftsmanship, principles of design, specific forms like wardrobes, chests and boxes, beds, chairs, tables, stools, cupboards and other pieces. Based on author's own investigation into scanty Chinese historical sources and surviving pieces in private collections and museums. Will reveal a new dimension of simple, beautiful work to all interior decorators, furniture designers, craftsmen. 123 illustrations; 112 photographs. Bibliography. xiii + 205pp. 5¼ x 7¾.   T958 Paperbound **$1.50**

ART AND THE SOCIAL ORDER, Professor D. W. Gotshalk, University of Illinois. One of the most profound and most influential studies of aesthetics written in our generation, this work is unusual in considering art from the relational point of view, as a transaction consisting of creation-object-apprehension. Discussing material from the fine arts, literature, music, and related disciplines, it analyzes the aesthetic experience, fine art, the creative process, art materials, form, expression, function, art criticism, art and social life and living. Graceful and fluent in expression, it requires no previous background in aesthetics and will be read with considerable enjoyment by anyone interested in the theory of art. "Clear, interesting, the soundest and most penetrating work in recent years," C. J. Ducasse, Brown University. New preface by Professor Gotshalk. xvi + 248pp. 5⅝ x 8½.
                              T294 Paperbound **$1.65**

FOUNDATIONS OF MODERN ART, A. Ozenfant. An illuminating discussion by a great artist of the interrelationship of all forms of human creativity, from painting to science, writing to religion. The creative process is explored in all facets of art, from paleolithic cave painting to modern French painting and architecture, and the great universals of art are isolated. Expressing its countless insights in aphorisms accompanied by carefully selected illustrations, this book is itself an embodiment in prose of the creative process. Enlarged by 4 new chapters. 226 illustrations. 368pp. 6⅛ x 9¼.   T215 Paperbound **$2.00**

VITRUVIUS: TEN BOOKS ON ARCHITECTURE. Book by 1st century Roman architect, engineer, is oldest, most influential work on architecture in existence; for hundreds of years his specific instructions were followed all over the world, by such men as Bramante, Michelangelo, Palladio, etc., and are reflected in major buildings. He describes classic principles of symmetry, harmony; design of treasury, prison, etc.; methods of durability; much more. He wrote in a fascinating manner, and often digressed to give interesting sidelights, making this volume appealing reading even to the non-professional. Standard English translation, by Prof. M. H. Morgan, Harvard U. Index. 6 illus. 334pp. 5⅜ x 8.   T645 Paperbound **$2.00**

THE BROWN DECADES, Lewis Mumford. In this now classic study of the arts in America, Lewis Mumford resurrects the "buried renaissance" of the post-Civil War period. He demonstrates that it contained the seeds of a new integrity and power and documents his study with detailed accounts of the founding of modern architecture in the work of Sullivan, Richardson, Root, Roebling; landscape development of Marsh, Olmstead, and Eliot; the graphic arts of Homer, Eakins, and Ryder. 2nd revised enlarged edition. Bibliography. 12 illustrations. Index. xiv + 266pp. 5⅜ x 8.   T200 Paperbound **$1.75**

THE AUTOBIOGRAPHY OF AN IDEA, Louis Sullivan. The pioneer architect whom Frank Lloyd Wright called "the master" reveals an acute sensitivity to social forces and values in this passionately honest account. He records the crystallization of his opinions and theories, the growth of his organic theory of architecture that still influences American designers and architects, contemporary ideas, etc. This volume contains the first appearance of 34 full-page plates of his finest architecture. Unabridged reissue of 1924 edition. New introduction by R. M. Line. Index. xiv + 335pp. 5⅜ x 8.   **T281 Paperbound $2.00**

THE DRAWINGS OF HEINRICH KLEY. The first uncut republication of both of Kley's devastating sketchbooks, which first appeared in pre-World War I Germany. One of the greatest cartoonists and social satirists of modern times, his exuberant and iconoclastic fantasy and his extraordinary technique place him in the great tradition of Bosch, Breughel, and Goya, while his subject matter has all the immediacy and tension of our century. 200 drawings. viii + 128pp. 7¾ x 10¾.   **T24 Paperbound $1.85**

MORE DRAWINGS BY HEINRICH KLEY. All the sketches from Leut' Und Viecher (1912) and Sammel-Album (1923) not included in the previous Dover edition of Drawings. More of the bizarre, mercilessly iconoclastic sketches that shocked and amused on their original publication. Nothing was too sacred, no one too eminent for satirization by this imaginative, individual and accomplished master cartoonist. A total of 158 illustrations. lv + 104pp. 7¾ x 10¾.   **T41 Paperbound $1.85**

PINE FURNITURE OF EARLY NEW ENGLAND, R. H. Kettell. A rich understanding of one of America's most original folk arts that collectors of antiques, interior decorators, craftsmen, woodworkers, and everyone interested in American history and art will find fascinating and immensely useful. 413 illustrations of more than 300 chairs, benches, racks, beds, cupboards, mirrors, shelves, tables, and other furniture will show all the simple beauty and character of early New England furniture. 55 detailed drawings carefully analyze outstanding pieces. "With its rich store of illustrations, this book emphasizes the individuality and varied design of early American pine furniture. It should be welcomed," ANTIQUES. 413 illustrations and 55 working drawings. 475. 8 x 10¾.   **T145 Clothbound $10.00**

THE HUMAN FIGURE, J. H. Vanderpoel. Every important artistic element of the human figure is pointed out in minutely detailed word descriptions in this classic text and illustrated as well in 430 pencil and charcoal drawings. Thus the text of this book directs your attention to all the characteristic features and subtle differences of the male and female (adults, children, and aged persons), as though a master artist were telling you what to look for at each stage. 2nd edition, revised and enlarged by George Bridgman. Foreword. 430 illustrations. 143pp. 6⅛ x 9¼.   **T432 Paperbound $1.50**

LETTERING AND ALPHABETS, J. A. Cavanagh. This unabridged reissue of LETTERING offers a full discussion, analysis, illustration of 89 basic hand lettering styles — styles derived from Caslons, Bodonis, Garamonds, Gothic, Black Letter, Oriental, and many others. Upper and lower cases, numerals and common signs pictured. Hundreds of technical hints on make-up, construction, artistic validity, strokes, pens, brushes, white areas, etc. May be reproduced without permission! 89 complete alphabets; 72 lettered specimens. 121pp. 9¾ x 8.   **T53 Paperbound $1.35**

STICKS AND STONES, Lewis Mumford. A survey of the forces that have conditioned American architecture and altered its forms. The author discusses the medieval tradition in early New England villages; the Renaissance influence which developed with the rise of the merchant class; the classical influence of Jefferson's time; the "Mechanicsvilles" of Poe's generation; the Brown Decades; the philosophy of the Imperial facade; and finally the modern machine age. "A truly remarkable book," SAT. REV. OF LITERATURE. 2nd revised edition. 21 illustrations. xvii + 228pp. 5⅜ x 8.   **T202 Paperbound $1.65**

THE STANDARD BOOK OF QUILT MAKING AND COLLECTING, Marguerite Ickis. A complete easy-to-follow guide with all the information you need to make beautiful, useful quilts. How to plan, design, cut, sew, appliqué, avoid sewing problems, use rag bag, make borders, tuft, every other aspect. Over 100 traditional quilts shown, including over 40 full-size patterns. At-home hobby for fun, profit. Index. 483 illus. 1 color plate. 287pp. 6¾ x 9½.   **T582 Paperbound $2.00**

THE BOOK OF SIGNS, Rudolf Koch. Formerly $20 to $25 on the out-of-print market, now only $1.00 in this unabridged new edition! 493 symbols from ancient manuscripts, medieval cathedrals, coins, catacombs, pottery, etc. Crosses, monograms of Roman emperors, astrological, chemical, botanical, runes, housemarks, and 7 other categories. Invaluable for handicraft workers, illustrators, scholars, etc., this material may be reproduced without permission. 493 illustrations by Fritz Kredel. 104pp. 6½ x 9¼.   **T162 Paperbound $1.00**

PRIMITIVE ART, Franz Boas. This authoritative and exhaustive work by a great American anthropologist covers the entire gamut of primitive art. Pottery, leatherwork, metal work, stone work, wood, basketry, are treated in detail. Theories of primitive art, historical depth in art history, technical virtuosity, unconscious levels of patterning, symbolism, styles, literature, music, dance, etc. A must book for the interested layman, the anthropologist, artist, handicrafter (hundreds of unusual motifs), and the historian. Over 900 illustrations (50 ceramic vessels, 12 totem poles, etc.). 376pp. 5⅜ x 8.   **T25 Paperbound $2.00**

Orientalia

ORIENTAL RELIGIONS IN ROMAN PAGANISM, F. Cumont. A study of the cultural meeting of east and west in the Early Roman Empire. It covers the most important eastern religions of the time from their first appearance in Rome, 204 B.C., when the Great Mother of the Gods was first brought over from Syria. The ecstatic cults of Syria and Phrygia — Cybele, Attis, Adonis, their orgies and mutilatory rites; the mysteries of Egypt — Serapis, Isis, Osiris, the dualism of Persia, the elevation of cosmic evil to equal stature with the deity, Mithra; worship of Hermes Trismegistus; Ishtar, Astarte; the magic of the ancient Near East, etc. Introduction. 55pp. of notes; extensive bibliography. Index. xxiv + 298pp. 5⅜ x 8.
T321 Paperbound **$2.00**

THE MYSTERIES OF MITHRA, F. Cumont. The definitive coverage of a great ideological struggle between the west and the orient in the first centuries of the Christian era. The origin of Mithraism, a Persian mystery religion, and its association with the Roman army is discussed in detail. Then utilizing fragmentary monuments and texts, in one of the greatest feats of scholarly detection, Dr. Cumont reconstructs the mystery teachings and secret doctrines, the hidden organization and cult of Mithra. Mithraic art is discussed, analyzed, and depicted in 70 illustrations. 239pp. 5⅜ x 8.
T323 Paperbound **$2.00**

CHRISTIAN AND ORIENTAL PHILOSOPHY OF ART, A. K. Coomaraswamy. A unique fusion of philosopher, orientalist, art historian, and linguist, the author discusses such matters as: the true function of aesthetics in art, the importance of symbolism, intellectual and philosophic backgrounds, the role of traditional culture in enriching art, common factors in all great art, the nature of medieval art, the nature of folklore, the beauty of mathematics, and similar topics. 2 illustrations. Bibliography. 148pp. 5⅜ x 8.
T378 Paperbound **$1.50**

TRANSFORMATION OF NATURE IN ART, A. K. Coomaraswamy. Unabridged reissue of a basic work upon Asiatic religious art and philosophy of religion. The theory of religious art in Asia and Medieval Europe (exemplified by Meister Eckhart) is analyzed and developed. Detailed consideration is given to Indian medieval aesthetic manuals, symbolic language in philosophy, the origin and use of images in India, and many other fascinating and little known topics. Glossaries of Sanskrit and Chinese terms. Bibliography. 41pp. of notes. 245pp. 5⅜ x 8.
T368 Paperbound **$1.75**

BUDDHIST LOGIC, F.Th. Stcherbatsky. A study of an important part of Buddhism usually ignored by other books on the subject: the Mahayana buddhistic logic of the school of Dignaga and his followers. First vol. devoted to history of Indian logic with Central Asian continuations, detailed exposition of Dignaga system, including theory of knowledge, the sensible world (causation, perception, ultimate reality) and mental world (judgment, inference, logical fallacies, the syllogism), reality of external world, and negation (law of contradiction, universals, dialectic). Vol. II contains translation of Dharmakirti's Nyayabindu with Dharmamottara's commentary. Appendices cover translations of Tibetan treatises on logic, Hindu attacks on Buddhist logic, etc. The basic work, one of the products of the great St. Petersburg school of Indian studies. Written clearly and with an awareness of Western philosophy and logic; meant for the Asian specialist and for the general reader with only a minimum of background. Vol. I, xii + 559pp. Vol. II, viii + 468pp. 5⅜ x 8½.
T955 Vol. I Paperbound **$2.50**
T956 Vol. II Paperbound **$2.50**
The set **$5.00**

THE TEXTS OF TAOISM. The first inexpensive edition of the complete James Legge translations of the Tao Te King and the writings of Chinese mystic Chuang Tse. Also contains several shorter treatises: the T'ai Shang Tractate of Actions and Their Retributions; the King Kang King, or Classic of Purity; the Yin Fu King, or Classic of the Harmony of the Seen and Unseen; the Yu Shu King, or Classic of the Pivot of Jade; and the Hsia Yung King, or Classic of the Directory for a Day. While there are other translations of the Tao Te King, this is the only translation of Chuang Tse and much of other material. Extensive introduction discusses differences between Taoism, Buddhism, Confucianism; authenticity and arrangement of Tao Te King and writings of Chuang Tse; the meaning of the Tao and basic tenets of Taoism; historical accounts of Lao-tse and followers; other pertinent matters. Clarifying notes incorporated into text. Originally published as Volumes 39, 40 of SACRED BOOKS OF THE EAST series, this has long been recognized as an indispensable collection. Sinologists, philosophers, historians of religion will of course be interested and anyone with an elementary course in Oriental religion or philosophy will understand and profit from these writings. Index. Appendix analyzing thought of Chuang Tse. Vol. I, xxiii + 396pp. Vol. II, viii + 340pp. 5⅜ x 8½.
T990 Vol. I Paperbound **$2.25**
T991 Vol. II Paperbound **$2.25**

CATALOGUE OF DOVER BOOKS

EPOCHS OF CHINESE AND JAPANESE ART, Ernest T. Fenollosa. Although this classic of art history was written before the archeological discovery of Shang and Chou civilizations, it is still in many respects the finest detailed study of Chinese and Japanese art available in English. It is very wide in range, covering sculpture, carving, painting, metal work, ceramics, textiles, graphic arts and other areas, and it considers both religious and secular art, including the Japanese woodcut. Its greatest strength, however, lies in its extremely full, detailed, insight-laden discussion of historical and cultural background, and in its analysis of the religious and philosophical implications of art works. It is also a brilliant stylistic achievement, written with enthusiasm and verve, which can be enjoyed and read with profit by both the Orientalist and the general reader who is interested in art. Index. Glossary of proper names. 242 illustrations. Total of 704 pages. 5⅜ x 8½.
T364-5 Two vol. set, paperbound **$5.00**

THE VEDANTA SUTRAS OF BADARAYANA WITH COMMENTARY BY SANKARACHARYA. The definitive translation of the consummation, foremost interpretation of Upanishads. Originally part of SACRED BOOKS OF THE EAST, this two-volume translation includes exhaustive commentary and exegesis by Sankara; 128-page introduction by translator, Prof. Thibaut, that discusses background, scope and purpose of the sutras, value and importance of Sankara's interpretation; copious footnotes providing further explanations. Every serious student of Indian religion or thought, philosophers, historians of religion should read these clear, accurate translations of documents central to development of important thought systems in the East. Unabridged republication of Volumes 34, 38 of the Sacred Books of the East. Translated by George Thibault. General index, index of quotations and of Sanskrit. Vol. I, cxxv + 448pp. Vol. II, iv + 506pp. 5⅜ x 8½.
T994 Vol. I Paperbound **$2.00**
T995 Vol. II Paperbound **$2.00**

THE UPANISHADS. The Max Müller translation of the twelve classical Upanishads available for the first time in an inexpensive format: Chandogya, Kena, Aitareya aranyaka and upanishad, Kaushitaki, Isa, Katha, Mundaka, Taittiriyaka Brhadaranyaka, Svetarasvatara. Prasna — all of the classical Upanishads of the Vedanta school—and the Maitriyana Upanishad. Originally volumes 1, 15 of SACRED BOOKS OF THE EAST series, this is still the most scholarly translation. Prof. Müller, probably most important Sanskritologist of nineteenth century, provided invaluable introduction that acquaints readers with history of Upanishad translations, age and chronology of texts, etc. and a preface that discusses their value to Western readers. Heavily annotated. Stimulating reading for anyone with even only a basic course background in Oriental philosophy, religion, necessary to all Indologists, philosophers, religious historians. Transliteration and pronunciation guide. Vol. I, ciii + 320pp. Vol. II, liii + 350pp.
T992 Vol. I Paperbound **$2.25**
T993 Vol. II Paperbound **$2.25**
The set **$4.50**

Prices subject to change without notice.

Dover publishes books on art, music, philosophy, literature, languages, history, social sciences, psychology, handcrafts, orientalia, puzzles and entertainments, chess, pets and gardens, books explaining science, intermediate and higher mathematics, mathematical physics, engineering, biological sciences, earth sciences, classics of science, etc. Write to:

Dept. catrr.
Dover Publications, Inc.
180 Varick Street, N. Y. 14, N. Y.

Date Due
